TWENTIETH-CENTURY YUGOSLAVIA

By the same author

YUGOSLAVIA (*with M. Heppell*)
WORKERS' CONTROL IN YUGOSLAVIA (*with A. J. Topham*)
BACKGROUND TO EASTERN EUROPE
YUGOSLAVIA: THE COUNTRY AND ITS PEOPLE

TWENTIETH-CENTURY YUGOSLAVIA

Fred Singleton

Columbia University Press
NEW YORK 1976

Fred Singleton is Chairman of the Postgraduate School of Yugoslav Studies at the University of Bradford.

Published in Great Britain in 1976 by The Macmillan Press Ltd.

Printed in Great Britain

Library of Congress Cataloging in Publication Data

Singleton, Frederick Bernard.
Twentieth-century Yugoslavia.

Bibliography: p. 315–34
Includes index.
1. Yugoslavia—Politics and government—1945–
2. Yugoslavia—Economic conditions—1945–
I. Title.
DR370.S49 1976 949.7'02 75-16322
ISBN 0-231-04016-4
ISBN 0-231-08341-6 pbk.

for Elizabeth

Contents

Figures

Maps

Tables

Preface

Although the problems which beset socialist Yugoslavia today are in many respects unique to that society and are matters primarily for the Yugoslavs themselves, there are important aspects in which the Yugoslav experience is of more general relevance. The interested outsider may hope to trace the path which the Yugoslavs have followed in their efforts to industrialise an economically underdeveloped country, and to grapple with the problems of cultural diversity within a multinational federation, but he must be wary of offering ready made solutions to problems for which the Yugoslav peoples have not yet found the answers.

When, at the end of the Second World War, the Communists first set out on the road to a socialist Yugoslavia, they consciously trod in the footsteps of Stalin. Later, largely under the pressure of external forces, they abandoned the Soviet model and began to feel their way towards a distinctively Yugoslav path. The system of workers' self-management which evolved during the 1950s has endured now for a generation. It can no longer be called an experiment. Yet there is no agreement either inside Yugoslavia or amongst socialists outside, as to its success. It has been condemned as a revisionist heresy, derided as a sham and praised as an ideal middle road between the evils of authoritarian state capitalism and unbridled private capitalism. Although it has provoked violent reactions, it has found few imitators. Only the Algerians admit to borrowing and adopting ideas from the Yugoslavs.

Yugoslavia's independent road to socialism has, however, given a small, economically weak country a place in world affairs out of all proportion to its size and material power. President Tito's position as the elder statesman of the non-aligned nations is the symbol of this international role. Even here there is controversy as to whether the reality is as solid as outward appearances suggest.

Whatever one's view of these matters, there is no doubt that Yugoslavia's development is of great and continuing interest to the outside world. This in itself provides a justification for the author to write and the publisher to issue yet another book on Yugoslavia.

My own interest in Yugoslavia goes back to my late teens, when at the end of the Second World War I spent a short time with the Royal Navy in the Adriatic. A few years later, as a student, I joined a work brigade and spent a long, hot summer helping to build the Zagreb–Belgrade highway. Since 1948 I have been in Yugoslavia almost every year. During the 1950s I led parties of walkers and climbers to the Julian Alps and to the mountains of Bosnia. As a tutor for the WEA I helped to organise summer schools for adult students in Split and Ljubljana, and also to participate in a study tour sponsored by UNESCO to report on Workers' and People's Universities. Since the mid-1960s I have been occupied with the development of Yugoslav studies in Bradford University, and my visits have been primarily of an academic character. In 1964, however, I was able to compare my experience on the work brigade in 1948 with that of a younger generation of students, when I participated in the reconstruction of earthquake stricken Skopje with a party of 150 students from Bradford. In the course of these many visits over a period of more than twenty years I have made many friends at all levels of Yugoslav society. I have watched Yugoslavia grow and change, and I feel not unduly alien, although I hope I am aware of the dangers of responding uncritically to the hospitality which I have received, and of assuming an understanding of the current situation which an outsider cannot presume to have. In particular I am aware – thanks to the brutal frankness of some of my students – that the aspirations of young Yugoslavs today are greatly different from those of their parents. The generation gap between partisan veterans and their children is probably wider in Yugoslavia than it is between the survivors of Dad's Army and their offspring in Britain. My view of Yugoslavia's problems is obviously coloured by my own experiences there during the early days of the revolution. However, to be aware of one's limitations does not necessarily imply that one can overcome them. At least the reader is now aware of them and can judge accordingly the value of what follows.

The book could not have been written without the help of others. It is impossible to acknowledge them all, and many may be unaware of the help they have given because it came as the result of my recollection of discussions amongst friends over a period of several years. In a more formal sense I am indebted to Miss Phyllis Auty for reading and commenting on the chapter dealing with the Second World War, and to Mrs Stella Alexander for her comments on the chapter on religion. Several colleagues in the Postgraduate School of Yugoslav Studies, Bradford University, have also been helpful in reading and commenting on parts of the book, and in giving me the benefit of their knowledge and experience. These include Messrs Allcock, Mirčev, Mančevski, Dr Copperthwaite and Mr J. J. Horton, Social Sciences Librarian. Mr Michael Lear drew the excellent maps and diagrams. Mr J. Waller has not only made comments on some of the economics sections, but he has written a great deal of the material on banking and investment in chapter 12. The responsibility for any errors or shortcomings in what appears in print is, however, entirely mine.

Finally, I wish to record my deepest gratitude to my wife, who has typed the manuscript and assisted in the compilation of the index and the bibliography. Without her help the book would never have arrived on the desk of my patient publishers.

F.S.

Hebden Ghyll
March 1975

Abbreviations

AVNOJ	(Anti-Fascist Council for the National Liberation of Yugoslavia)
COMECON	Council for Mutual Economic Aid
CPY	(Yugoslav Communist Party)
EEC	European Economic Community
FEC	Federal Executive Council
FNRJ	*Federativna Narodna Republika Jugoslavije* (Federative People's Republic of Yugoslavia)
GDR	German Democratic Republic (East Germany)
GNP	Gross National Product
HSS	*Hrvatska Seljačka Stranka* (Croat Peasant Party)
ILO	International Labour Organisation
IVZ	(Moslem Religious Community)
JRZ	(Yugoslav Radical Union)
LCY	League of Communists of Yugoslavia
NATO	North Atlantic Treaty Organisation
NDH	*Nezavisna Država Hrvatska* (Independent State of Croatia)
OF	*Osvobodilna Fronta* (Slovene Liberation Front)
SAWPY	Socialist Alliance of the Working People of Yugoslavia
SFRY	Socialist Federal Republic of Yugoslavia (*Socialistička Federativna Republika Jugoslavija*)
SS	(Nazi Secret Service)
UNCTAD	United Nation Conference on Trade and Development
UNRRA	United Nations Relief and Rehabilitation Administration
VMRO	(International Macedonian Revolutionary Organisation)

PART I

1 Introduction

The South Slav peoples have lived in the Balkans for over a thousand years, but during the whole of this time there have been only two short periods when a Yugoslav state has existed. The first survived for twenty-three years, from the declaration of the Kingdom of the Serbs, Croats and Slovenes on 4 December 1918 to the German invasion of April 1941. The second has existed since the end of the Second World War and, although it has appeared during most of its life to have been a more durable state than its predecessor, it has inherited some of the divisive elements which bedevilled the life of the pre-war kingdom.

One of the main causes of internal weakness in pre-war Yugoslavia was the inability of the Serbian-dominated government to persuade the Croats to accept wholeheartedly the constitutional basis of the kingdom. Both Serbs and Croats refused to recognise the national aspirations of any of the other Yugoslav groups save the Slovenes. Preoccupation with the national question prevented any serious attempt to tackle the equally serious threat to the stability of the kingdom that arose from the unresolved social problems of a predominantly peasant society. When the German invasion came Yugoslavia broke up into its component parts. The disintegration of the state was, of course, instigated by the occupying forces, but their task was made easy by the divisions already existing amongst the Yugoslavs. During the four years between 1941 and 1945, more people in Yugoslavia were killed by their fellow countrymen than by the German, Italian, Hungarian and Bulgarian occupying forces.

The revolutionary regime, which came to power at the end of the Second World War, proclaimed the brotherhood and unity (*bratsvo–jedinstvo*) of all the Yugoslav peoples and has made valiant efforts to turn this slogan into reality. The problems of relations between the national groups, which in pre-war days was a source of weakness to the Kingdom of Yugoslavia, and which took on the characteristics of an open civil conflict during the Second World War, has re-emerged in a new form. The disharmony between the national groups now expresses itself primarily in economic terms. Yugoslavia is caught in the dilemma of all industrialising countries. Development is uneven between different regions within the country. Areas that had an initial advantage have maintained their lead over those regions that were historically backward and underdeveloped. It is openly admitted that the full realisation of the socialist ideal cannot be achieved in a state where, for example, Slovenes have an average per capita income five times greater than that of the Albanians of Kosovo. Yet so far all the efforts of the regime to narrow the gap have failed. The level of the poorest has certainly risen, but that of the richest has risen faster. In the developed republics – notably in Slovenia and Croatia – there is a strongly expressed sentiment among people at all levels of society that their progress would have been even more rapid if they had not been compelled to divert resources into the less developed areas. The divisive power of economic inequality is made sharper by the cultural and linguistic differences between the six republics and two autonomous provinces of the federation, and these differences are rooted in the historical experiences of the Yugoslav peoples. Yet in essence the Yugoslav problem presents in microcosm the world problem of relations between the rich and the poor nations. As no one has found an answer to this problem, it is not to be wondered at that a solution has eluded the Yugoslavs.

In the long view of history it is surprising that the new regime has survived for so long, but despite its many problems, I do not believe that it is in imminent danger of dissolution. The crisis over Croatia's position following the passing of the new constitution in 1971 assumed ugly features during the winter of that year, and led even President Tito to hint at the appalling prospect of civil war and foreign intervention.* I believe, how-

* Speech to the Praesidium of the TU Federation, reported by *Tanjug*, 18 December 1971.

ever, that the forces which make for the survival of Yugoslavia are stronger than those which appear to be pulling it apart.

One factor which has helped to preserve the integrity of the new society has been the personality of its leader, President Tito, who has been in a position of undisputed authority throughout the whole of the post-war period. His death will, no doubt, create various problems for Yugoslavia, but only the most pessimistic observers would suggest that socialist Yugoslavia now depends for its existence on one man.

The new social order which has evolved during the last quarter of a century is based on avowedly Marxist socialist principles, but the interpretation of these principles has varied from time to time. The dogmas proclaimed by the Communist Party in the first post-war years became heresies during the period following Yugoslavia's expulsion from the Cominform in 1948. The League of Communists no longer exercises direct administrative control over the state machine, but, as the events since 1972 have shown, it still retains the keys to political power. Decision making is a complex process, involving the interaction of a multitude of social groups and organisations. In the 1950s the system of workers self-management was introduced into the factories, and was later extended to all social, cultural and economic activities in the public domain. In the 1960s the concept of market socialism was introduced. The ideal is to develop autonomous, self-managed enterprises, competing with each other, their viability being measured by the yardstick of profitability and commercial success. In the transitional stage, however, may vestiges of the old centralist system remain. In the sphere of international trade the frontiers have been opened to the West. Yugoslav workers are free to migrate to West Germany, Italy and Austria, and Western capital, both private and public, is encouraged to be invested in Yugoslavia. Despite the rapid shift of emphasis toward the West in foreign trade, Yugoslavia still retains special trading relations with the countries of COMECON, and has an unique position within that organisation: 32 per cent of her exports and 24 per cent of her imports are with COMECON countries.

Complementary to these economic relationships, the foreign policy of Yugoslavia is firmly grounded in the concept of non-alignment. This policy, which evolved during the 1950s in the aftermath of the expulsion of the Yugoslav Communist Party from the Cominform in 1948, may not have been consciously conceived in economic terms. Nevertheless Yugoslavia's viability has depended to a great extent on her ability to trade with all the major economic groups, and, even more important, the posture of non-alignment has enabled her to attract massive quantities of foreign aid during the 1950s and early 1960s, at a crucial period in her struggle for survival.

The role that this small, developing nation of 20 million people, with all its internal divisions and weaknesses, has been able to play on the world stage is out of all proportion to its size and its economic and military strength. One has only to compare Yugoslavia's role in the post-war world with that of Romania (20 million), Poland (33 million), Spain (32 million) or Argentina (23 million) to realise the truth of this. Yugoslavia's special importance in world affairs began with the Cominform dispute in 1948. Since that time she has occupied a unique place in the constellation of world political groupings. The 'two camps' concept, shared by Stalin and Mr Dulles and still a dominant theme in the political philosophy of the major powers, was rejected by Yugoslavia in her determination to survive as an independent socialist state. The evolution of a new type of socialist order, based on the idea of workers' self-management, threw down a challenge to socialist theorists in both East and West. The pragmatism and flexibility of the Yugoslavs in both domestic and foreign relations called into question many of the deeply held convictions of the Left. The question, however, still remains open as to whether the Yugoslavs can really square the circle. Can they reconcile the apparent contradictions in their political and economic systems? Is 'market socialism' a new political concept, or is it a first step in the peaceful transition from socialism to capitalism? Can socialism in any recognisable form survive in a country that is becoming increasingly dependent economically on the bastions of capitalism in western Europe – notably on West Germany? Can a one-party system continue to operate in the face of the increasing liberalisation of economic and political relations? Can a state survive as a credible political entity with the wide – and possibly widening – cultural and economic differences between its component parts?

These questions are not new. They have been expressed in various forms ever since Yugoslavia began to tread her independent path after 1948. Since the reforms of 1965, however, they have been posed ever more sharply. As one examines the development of 'market socialism' it may be possible to suggest tentative answers to them, based on the experience of the last few years. It is not the purpose of this book – nor is it possible – to provide dogmatic answers to these questions, but merely to ask them and to offer an explanation of the background from which they have emerged.

As a vital basis for understanding this background, it will first be necessary to examine briefly the geographical framework within which the Yugoslavs operate and to sketch the main themes in the historical experience of the Yugoslav peoples. The geographical framework, in the widest meaning of the term, will help to explain the potentialities and limitations of the environment, and the historical outline will trace the origins of the patterns of cultural differentiation which underlie so many of Yugoslavia's contemporary problems.

2 Geography

THE GEOGRAPHICAL FRAMEWORK

Few countries of similar size display the diversity of terrain that is to be found in Yugoslavia. Within its borders several major physiographic regions meet. Fifty per cent of the Yugoslav people live in the lowlands of the Sava and Danube, in the northern and north-eastern parts of the country. These lowland areas – an extension of the Pannonian Plains of Central Europe – occupy only 25 per cent of the land area. Most of Yugoslavia is mountainous, but the nature of the mountains varies enormously from place to place. In the north-west the Alps of Slovenia form part of the western Alpine system of North Italy and Austria. The Dinaric Alps, which lie behind the coasts of Dalmatia, present a totally different aspect. Here huge masses of limestone, folded into ridges that run parallel to the coast, enclose long valleys (*polja*) drained by intermittent streams. The few rivers that succeed in crossing the grain of the Dinaric ranges – for example the Cetina, near Split, and the Neretva, which reaches the sea at Metković – flow either through narrow defiles trenched deep into the bare limestone mountains or across the flat, ill-drained floors of the *polja*. The Dinaric system seals off the Mediterranean fringe of the Dalmatian coastal plain and the offshore islands from the plateaux and lowlands of the interior. At its greatest width the karstic[1] terrain extends inland for over 100 miles, and it forms a continuous rampart behind the coast from Istria to the Albanian border, a distance of over 400 miles.

East of the main Dinaric system, in Bosnia and Montenegro, the massive limestones, characteristic of the coastal region, are still a major feature of the surface geology but are intermixed with a series of newer sedimentary rocks – sandstones, marls and clays – which modify the gaunt severity of the karstic landscape. The relief is generally lower, and the sedimentary cover has in many places been eroded from the surface to expose masses of ancient crystalline rocks such as serpentines and granites.

These crystalline rocks are outliers of the Rodopi (Rhodope) massif, the primeval core of the Balkan Peninsula, against which the Tertiary ranges of the Balkan and Dinaric mountains have folded. The crystalline rocks are exposed in two main areas of Macedonia, one in the west, surrounding the alluvial lowlands of the Pelagonia and extending from Pelister on the Greek border to the Skopska Crna Gora, west of Skopje, and the other along the Bulgarian border in the east. Between these two crystalline blocks is an area of Tertiary sediments and recent alluvial deposits, which is drained by the Vardar and its tributaries. North-east of Skopje these deposits have been buried beneath more recent lava flows.

A similar pattern to that of Macedonia is also found in southern Serbia and Kosovo. The Južna Morava flows northward to the Danube along a valley cut in Tertiary sediments and floored by recent alluvium. On either side are the ancient crystalline rocks of the Rodopi system. In contrast to the Vardar basin, however, that of the Južna Morava is narrower, and the area of crystalline rocks in this part of Serbia is more extensive than in Macedonia. Further west, in Kosovo, the Rodopi massif is represented by the wild Kopaonik mountains, rising to a height of 6560 feet (2000 metres), which contain great masses of serpentine rocks.

The north-east corner of Serbia Proper,[2] adjoining the Romanian and Bulgarian borders, is crossed by an arc of the Carpathian mountain system known locally as the Stara Planina. This is an area of varied relief and geology. The mountains rise in places to over 6000 feet (1830 metres) but the general level of the summits is nearer to 3000 feet (915 metres). Intense fracturing and a complicated pattern of folding has resulted in a medley of rock types and physiographic phenomena. There are karstic plateaux and bare limestone peaks reminiscent of the Dinaric Alps; large areas of post-Tertiary volcanic rocks; and exposures of the core masses of crystalline

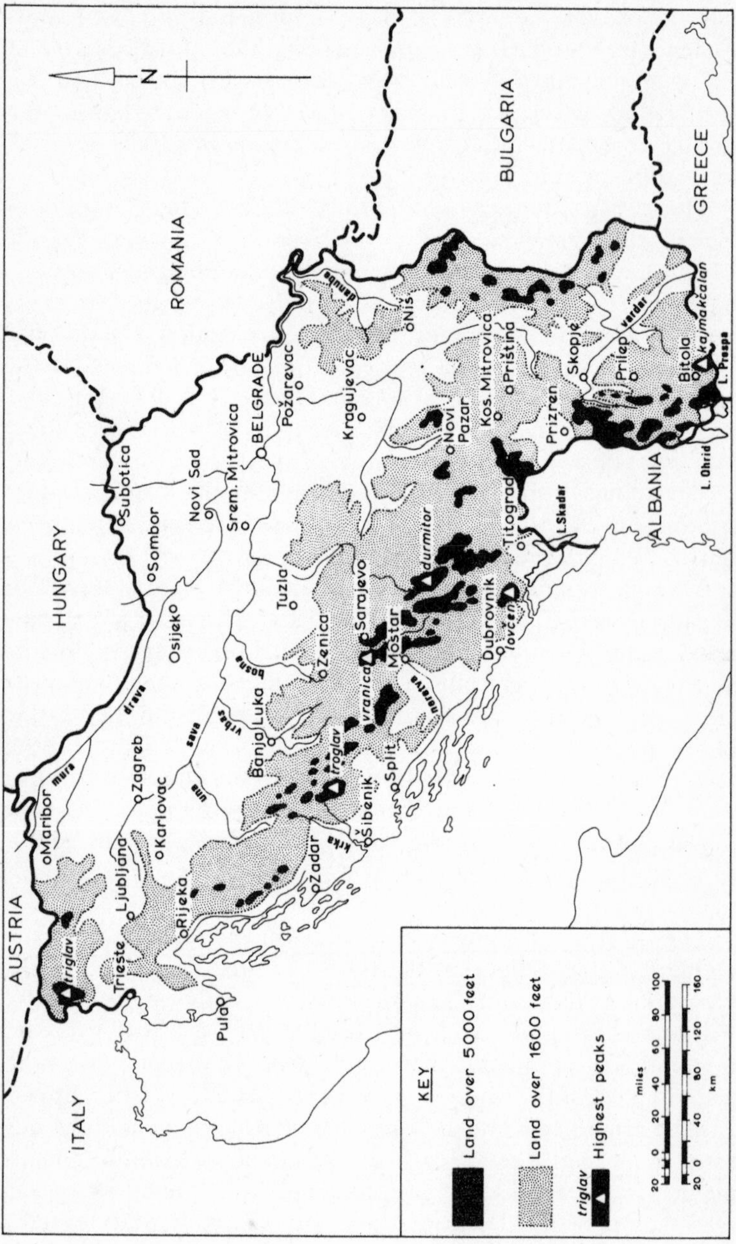

MAP 1 Physical geography

schists and granites, rich in non-ferrous metal ores. The most spectacular feature of the scenery is the Iron Gate,[3] on the Romanian–Yugoslav border, where the Danube cuts through the Carpathians in a series of gorges.

Two other river systems cut into the Stara Planina, the westward-flowing Nišava and the northward-flowing Timok. The Nišava, which joins the Južna Morava a few miles below Niš, has cut its valley through the limestones of the Suva Planina. Although there are several narrow gorges like that at Sićevo, the river valley provides a valuable line of communication, linking the Pirot, Bela Palanka and Niš basins, and in a wider context forming a passage between Niš and Sofia. The Timok river, which flows directly to join the main system of the Danube near Negotin, also links a series of flat-floored basins, but the surrounding relief is lower than that of the Nišava, and crystalline rocks predominate over limestones.

West of the lower Morava lies a region known as the Šumadija,[4] which extends southward from the Danube at Belgrade to the Zapadna Morava, where the southern limits of the Šumadija overlook Čačak and Kraljevo. The wooded, deeply dissected plateaux of Šumadija formed the heart of old Serbia. They contain the last crystalline outliers of the Rodopi massif, but more commonly the surface is composed of Tertiary and Cretaceous sandstones and limestones. One spur of the Šumadija hills projects northward to Belgrade. At its extremity the fortress of Kalemegdan now stands, overlooking the meeting of the Danube and the Sava.

Kalemegdan marks the northernmost point of Balkan Yugoslavia. Beyond its ramparts, across the rivers, the plains of Central Europe extend across the loess-covered lowlands of the Vojvodina and on into Hungary. Vojvodina is the name of an autonomous province within the Republic of Serbia, although in a broader geographical sense the term is used to refer to the areas of the Pannonian lowlands which were for centuries part of Hungary – Bačka, Baranja and the Banat. The largest, Bačka, is a rectangular area bounded by the Danube on the west and south, the Tisa on the east, and the Hungarian frontier to the north. Baranja is a triangular lowland in the angle of the Drava and the Danube. The Banat lies between the Tisa and the Romanian border. Across the Danube from Novi Sad, the capital of the autonomous province, is a wooded upland region, the Fruška Gora, the crystalline core of which is partly overlain by Tertiary sediments. Between the Fruška Gora and the valley of the Sava are the lowlands of Srem, which were part of Croatia until 1945. Thus the modern province of Vojvodina has lost Baranja to Croatia and acquired Srem.

The whole area was once part of the floor of a huge Tertiary inland sea, the Pannonian Sea. The sands, clays and gravels that underly the Vojvodina are derived from the sediments that were deposited during this period. The sea was drained in late Tertiary times, and during the subsequent Quaternary period the older deposits were covered by thick layers of wind-blown materials known as loess. These fine-grained yellow-brown sands and loams, which reach depths of over 100 feet (30 metres), weather to form very fertile soils. Although the Vojvodina is of low relief, seldom attaining heights of over 400 feet above sea level, its surface is far from even. The soft loess is easily eroded by even the smallest and most transient of surface streams, so that beyond the deeply cut water-courses of the main rivers the plains are furrowed by hundreds of minor channels, many of them no longer carrying streams. The interfluves between these valleys are pockmarked by shallow hollows. The porous loess is interleaved in places with bands of impervious clay, creating local watertables at various levels, but it is often necessary for farmers on the Vojvodina to sink wells of up to 100 feet down in order to tap the main subterranean reservoirs. A traditional feature of the landscape of the Pannonian lowlands is the tall pole, to which the well buckets are attached.

The Vojvodina straddles the lower courses of the Sava, Drava and Tisa rivers around their confluences with the mainstream of the Danube. To the west lies the historic province of Slavonia, drained by the middle Sava and Drava. The region between Srem and Zagreb is known as Posavina, and that along the Drava between Osijek and Varaždin as Podravina. These two elongated lowlands, which in Tertiary times were gulfs of the Pannonian Sea, are separated by the low, wooded ranges of the Slavonian mountains, which seldom rise above 3000 feet (915 metres). Zagreb, the Croatian capital, is built on the foothills of one of these ranges, the Medvednica (3400 feet–1000 metres). The Medvednica is typical in its structure of the other Slavonian ranges. A central crystalline core, which stood out as an island above the Tertiary sea, is flanked by newer, softer deposits, originating from the old sea floor.

The upper Sava, in Slovenia, flows across a belt of limestone plateaus, between Ljubljana and Zagreb. It has cut deep gorges through the limestone, so that its usefulness as a line of communication between the Ljubljana Basin and the lowlands of Posavina is considerably reduced.

Ljubljana lies in a wide basin some 400 square miles in area, the city itself lying a little to the south of the Sava, on its tributary, the Ljubljanica. Part of this lowland was inundated until Neolithic times. Its southern section, Ljubljansko Barje (the Ljubljana marsh), is still badly drained and is liable to flood in winter. The Ljubljana basin is dotted with low hills, which once were islands rising above the waters of the old lake. On one of these stands the castle around which the old city of Ljubljana was built.

The Ljubljana basin is encircled by mountains and plateaux. To the north are the Kamnik Alps (Kamniška Planina), which rise steeply from the plain, reaching heights of over 8000 feet (2420 metres)[5] within twenty miles of the city centre. To the west the plateaux of the Idrija–Sora region lie between Ljubljana and the soaring peaks of the Julian Alps. In this area the east–west trend lines of the main Alpine system, to which the Julian, Karawanken and Kamnik Alps belong, give way to the north-west-to-south-east grain of the Dinaric system.

The route south-westward from the Ljubljansko Barje crosses the limestone plateaux of the northern fringes of the Dinaric system. The main Ljubljana–Trieste road and railway routes crossing the Postojna Gate climb on to these karstic plateaux before descending steeply to the narrow coastal area around the head of the Adriatic. The Postojna Gate is one of the few comparatively easy routes by which the peoples of central Europe have been able to break through the mountain rim encircling the Mediterranean basin, to reach the inland sea. It has carried traders, soldiers and migrants in both directions since the dawn of history.[6]

GEOGRAPHICAL OBSTACLES TO UNITY

Yugoslavia's physical geography, with its varied terrain, has created many problems for those who have sought to unite the Yugoslav peoples within a single economic and political unit. The northern lowlands were for centuries part of the Habsburg Empire. The nature of the relief made communications northward into the lands of their Austro-Hungarian masters easier than those southward into the Balkan Peninsula. The lowlands of Podravina, Baranja and the Vojvodina are similar in relief, climate and agricultural potential to those which lie across the Hungarian frontier, and the Alpine ranges of northern Slovenia resemble those of Carinthia and Styria. In both cases there has been a long history of intermixing between the peoples on either side of the present frontiers. Magyars are found throughout the northern lowlands, from Prekmurje in Slovenia to the Tisa valley in Vojvodina, and there are still Slovenes in the villages around Klagenfurt (Slovene: Celovec) and Villach (Beljak) in Carinthia. The Austro-German or Volksdeutsche settlers who formed an important element in towns such as Maribor (Marburg), Subotica (Maria Theresiopol), Novi Sad or Osijek have been reduced in number as a result of expulsions and emigration since the end of the Second World War, but their influence remains.

The ease with which the Slovenes and Croats can communicate with their former masters contrasts sharply with the difficulties experienced not only in linking the northerners with their Slav cousins in Bosnia, Montenegro and Dalmatia, but also in providing facilities for contact across the 'grain of the land', between the various groups that inhabit the mountain-girt *polja* of the interior. Montenegro's isolation saved her from the Turks, but it presents serious problems to modern Yugoslav economic planners. The value of the mineral resources of Bosnia, Kosovo and Macedonia is reduced by the enormous cost of transportation. The greatest handicap of all is the isolation of the Adriatic coastal strip from the inland centres of population.

Climatic diversity

The different ways of life of the Yugoslav peoples have been greatly influenced by the variety of natural environments. In an area slightly larger than that of the United Kingdom, several distinct natural regions are to be found. The thin coastal strip and the Adriatic islands belong climatically and culturally to the Mediterranean world, but although in the Mediterranean zone, the climate of Dalmatia is modified in winter by the occurrence of a fierce, cold wind, the Bura. It sets in when cold air from the interior is drawn across the mountains towards a depression over the Mediterranean or Adriatic. The configuration of the local relief creates in some areas a funnelling effect, which concentrates the full fury of the wind into certain breaks in the mountain wall behind the coast. Many of the offshore islands present a bleak and treeless face towards the mainland from which the Bura blows, but their lee-shores smile upon the open waters of the Adriatic where, sheltered by their mountain pines, they can support a rich vegetation of Mediterranean shrubs and trees.

The vine and the olive, the typical fruits of the Mediterranean, are grown throughout Dalmatia, wherever the Bura permits. The traditions of urban life go back to Roman times. Maritime trade has always been an integral part of the life of cities like Ragusa (Dubrovnik), which gave its name to the argosy, or to Zadar (Zara), where the carved stone lion of St Mark remains as a relic of the centuries when Venetian governors ruled Dalmatia.

The Pannonian lowlands experience a continental climatic regime. In winter dry cold air from the heart of Eurasia brings freezing conditions. The average monthly temperature is two or three degrees below freezing in January, but it is up in the seventies in July. Belgrade has a range of 40°F (22°C) between its coldest and warmest months. The characteristic feature of continental climates, the tendency to a rainfall maximum in spring and early summer, is in sharp contrast to the long dry summer of the Mediterranean. Belgrade has twice as much rain as Split in July, but in January the position is reversed, with Belgrade receiving only 1·3in and Split 2·9in.

The life of the peasant on the rich loess earth of the Vojvodina belongs to a tradition which embraces the steppelands of the Ukraine and the *pusztas* of Hungary. It is a world away from that of the farmer–fisherman and trader of the Dalmatian littoral. Between these two extremes there are several intermediate zones. Relief exercises a strong influence on climate in the high mountain ranges and plateaux that shut off the Adriatic fringe from the heart of Balkan Yugoslavia. Rainfall and snowfall are heavy, and there are great local variations between the enclosed *polja* of the Dinaric ranges. For example Titograd, the Montenegrin capital, has average monthly temperatures 10°F (6°C) hotter than Cetinje, which lies 25 miles to the east. Titograd's annual rainfall, 61in, is less than half that of Cetinje. Crkvice, 20 miles north of Cetinje, has an annual rainfall of 182in. The key to these enormous variations in climatic conditions within so small an area is the difference in relief and aspect between these three places. Titograd is in a broad valley which drains towards Lake Skadar, and it stands only 131 feet (40 metres) above sea level. Cetinje lies on a plateaux, 2200 feet (670 metres) above sea level, and Crkvice is on a pass 3600 feet (1100 metres) high (see table 1).

Table 1 Temperature and rainfall, Montenegro

		Mean monthly temperatures (°F)		
	Altitude (ft)	*Jan.*	*July*	*Annual range*
Crkvice	3609	32	65	33
Cetinje	2205	31	70	39
Titograd	131	39	80	41

		Rainfall (in)	
	Wettest month	*Driest month*	*Annual total*
Crkvice	26·6 (Dec.)	2·8 (July)	182·2
Cetinje	19·8 (Nov.)	2·6 (July)	139·7
Titograd	8·6 (Oct., Nov.)	1·9 (Aug.)	61·6

Source: Admiralty Handbook, I (*London*), *Appendix* VI

One can find similar contrasts in the Balkan region, which covers eastern Bosnia and southern Serbia. In this area the range of temperature between summer and winter is even greater than in the Pannonian lowlands, but rainfall is lower.

For example, the town of Prijepolje in the Lim valley of western Serbia lies fifteen miles east of Pljevlja in Montenegro. Pljevlja is 1000 feet higher than Prijepolje (see table 2).

Table 2 Temperature and rainfall, central Yugoslavia

		Mean monthly temperature (°F)		
	Altitude (ft)	*Jan.*	*July*	*Annual range*
Prijepolje	1450	29	68	39
Pljevlja	2523	25	63	38

	Rainfall (in)		
	Wettest month	*Driest month*	*Annual total*
Prijepolje	4·3 (June)	1·7 (Feb.)	29·8
Pljevlja	4·7 (June, Oct.)	2·5 (Aug.) 2·6 (Jan., Feb.)	40·0

Source: Admiralty Handbook, I (London), Appendix VI

A tongue of Mediterranean warmth extends along the Vardar valley into southern Macedonia, bringing to the plains of Pelagonia the possibilities of subtropical agriculture. With irrigation, cotton, groundnuts and rice may be grown. Although enjoying Mediterranean summers, the Vardar is open in winter to cold winds from central Europe, which sweep down the Vardar–Morava corridor bringing a taste of Belgrade's winter to places that are less than a hundred miles from the Aegean coast at Thessaloniki (Solun). As elsewhere in Yugoslavia, Macedonia experiences wide variations in climatic conditions. Much depends on height and aspect. A place open to the full force of the Vardarac winds will endure a more severe winter than one that is sheltered on the north and faces southward to the Aegean.

NOTES

1 The term karst is used by geomorphologists throughout the world. It is the German form of the Slovene word *kras*, the original name of the

limestone plateaux of the Julian Region, behind Trieste. Karstic landscapes display the characteristic erosion features of limestone areas.

2 The Socialist Republic of Serbia is divided into three administrative regions – Vojvodina, occupying the lowlands between the Sava and the Hungarian border; Kosovo, in the south-east near the Albanian border, occupying the upper valleys of the Ibar and Drim; and Serbia Proper (Uža Srbija) in the centre, which is based on the basin of the Morava river.

3 Strictly speaking, the Iron Gate refers to the last of the gorges, at Sip, where the Prigrada reef almost completely obstructs the river, but in practice it covers the whole seventy-mile stretch from Golubac to Kladovo. The Iron Gate Dam, built between 1964 and 1972, has completely changed the navigational possibilities.

4 Šumadija comes from the Serbian word *šuma*, meaning woods. The wooded hills of Šumadija were the base from which Serbia emerged in the early nineteenth century, after 400 years of Turkish rule.

5 Grintavec, the highest point, is 2550 metres.

6 The route has varied in detail from time to time. The present-day main line railway (the Süd Bahn, built by the Austrians between 1846 and 1850) and the Ljubljana–Trieste road cross the saddle between Planina and Postojna. The old Roman road lay a few kilometres to the north, crossing the Pear Tree Pass (Hrušica) and entering Italy by way of the Vipava valley. A new motorway was built over the Postojna route between 1969 and 1974.

3 The economic framework

MINERAL WEALTH

The geological history of Yugoslavia explains the distribution of economically workable mineral deposits. The areas where the ancient crystalline core of the Rodopi massif is exposed, and those where the predominant influence came from the volcanic activity in late Tertiary times, are rich in mineral ores. In the former, rocks of the serpentine group contain large deposits of non-ferrous metals – chromite, magnesite, asbestos.

The Kopaonik mountains, north of Kosovska Mitrovica, where the great Trepča mine is situated, contain some of the largest deposits of lead–zinc ores in Europe. The Bor and Majdanpek areas in eastern Serbia are rich in copper ores.

The chief iron ore producing areas are in Bosnia, at Ljubija near the Croatian border, and at Vareš in the upper Bosna Basin, between Sarajevo and Tuzla. Poorer iron ores than those of Bosnia are found in western Macedonia and are now being used in the recently established iron and steel industry of Skopje. Macedonia also produces chrome, manganese and uranium.

The only significant area for the production of metal ores outside Bosnia, Kosovo, Serbia and Macedonia is in the mountains of Slovenia. At Idrija in the Julian Region there is one of the most important mercury mines in Europe, with a production rate of over 500 tons per annum. This mine, formerly in Italy, passed into Yugoslav hands as a result of the post-1945 frontier changes. The old established iron mine at Jesenice, which produced ore in Roman times, and the lead–zinc mine at Mežica in the Karavanke (Karawanken) mountains, are of minor importance.

In the limestones of the Dinaric region rich deposits of bauxite occur. They stretch in a broken chain from Istria to

Montenegro, the main centres of production being near Rovinj and Umag in Istria, in the *polja* behind Split and Šibenik, in central Dalmatia, and in the Nikšić and Cetinje areas of Montenegro.

Almost all the mineral exploitation that occurred in Yugoslavia before 1945 was in foreign hands. The Trepča mines of Kosovo were operated by an Anglo-American company, the French owned the Bor copper mines, the Slovene lead mines at Mežica were British owned,[1] and after 1938 the Germans dominated the bauxite industry of Dalmatia. British and German capital controlled the exploitation of the chrome resources of Macedonia.

There has been considerable expansion of metal mining under Yugoslav control since the Second World War but the main centres are still those which were opened up by foreign capital in the inter-war period. There are signs that the Yugoslavs are again turning to foreign capital to assist them in the modernisation and expansion of the metal mining industry, and there has been a great deal of prospecting under the control of a federal agency. There is still a great untapped potential, which can be realised only when there is an improvement in the infra-structure of communications and a massive expenditure of capital.

POWER RESOURCES

Nowhere are there any significant deposits of high-grade bituminous coals, and the few localities where they do occur are difficult of access. The Istrian field, around Raša (Arsa), was under Italian control between 1918 and 1945. The Timok deposits, which lie close to the Bulgarian border, and the Ibar field in central Serbia are both remote from the main industrial centres of the northern lowlands. Brown coal and lignite of Pliocene and Oligocene geological age constitute the largest coal reserves. Most of these are in the interior of Bosnia and Serbia, the largest of all being the lignite basin of Kosovo. These lower-grade coals are of poor calorific value, are useless for the manufacture of metallurgical coke and, apart from the Velenje field in Slovenia, are hidden away in remote regions where lack of good communications has until recently restricted their availability for any but purely local use. Production of hard coal has been falling steadily during the last twenty years and is now only three-quarters of a million tons per year.[2] Brown coal and lignite production has been steady at around 25 million tons per year, compared with the pre-war figure of 5·5 million tons.

The inadequacy of the coal reserves is not compensated for by other realised sources of energy, although there are potentialities for the development of oil, natural gas and hydroelectric power. The oil and natural gas reserves of the Pannonian lowlands, which have been developed in the last twenty years, constitute the only important fuel resources in the area north of the Sava and the Danube. Although new discoveries in the Sisak area, east of Zagreb, and in the Banat have made possible an annual output of 2·5 million tons of crude petroleum and 320 million cubic metres of gas, production is still inadequate to meet the country's growing needs, and 4·25 million tons of petroleum products were imported in 1970.

Yugoslavia's hydroelectricity potential is far greater than that of the fossil fuels. Most of this is found in the mountainous regions of the Dinaric and Slovene Alps and in central Bosnia. Since 1956 the production of electricity from water power has outstripped that from all other sources, but despite a heavy investment programme only about 20 per cent of the known hydroelectric potential has yet been realised. Nevertheless Yugoslavia's progress in this field has been spectacular. In 1939 566 million kWh was produced by water power, compared with 607 million kWh from thermal stations. In 1970 hydroelectricity production was over 12,000 million kWh, while thermal stations produced only 9000 million kWh.

The major problem that inhibits the full development of the water power resources is that the rivers that are capable of being utilised are mainly in the remote heartland of the Balkan region or in the wild Dinaric Alps. The costs of building power stations in difficult terrain, and of transmitting the energy produced across hundreds of miles of rough mountain country to the main industrial users, are serious limiting factors.[3] The absence as yet of a complete electricity transmission grid covering the whole country limits the possibilities of seasonal transfers of power, which could be of great importance in a country that covers several climatic zones. The sources of water for the Yugoslav rivers extend from the Austrian Alps to the Dinaric karst, and when conditions are favourable for electricity generation along the Drava, for example, there may be a drought in the gathering grounds of the Drina. Thus, the performance of Yugoslav industry is regularly affected by power shortages that are caused as much by weaknesses in the transmission system as by a lack of generating capacity. A great contribution to the solution of the power problem will be made when the joint Yugoslav–Romanian Iron Gate scheme on the Danube comes fully into operation.[4] For details of hydroelectric power stations see tables 3–7.

Table 3 Hydroelectric stations in Yugoslavia built up to 1948

*Name of station**	*River*	*Megawatts*	*Date*
Kraljevac	Cetina	68	1913–28
Fala	Drava	35	1918–31
Doblar	Isonzo (Soča)	34	1939
Plave	Isonzo	15	1945
Dravograd	Drava	14	1945
Other		45	
Total		211	

Source: Siegfried Gehrecke, 'Die Elektrizatäts wirtschaft Jugoslaviens', *Osteuropa wirtschaft*, 4 (1971)

When examining the geographical basis for industrial development in Yugoslavia one is constantly brought up against an apparent paradox. The areas where the raw material and power supply potential are greatest are those that are least developed industrially, and those with the poorest endowment of natural resources show the highest level of industrialisation. This pattern has not always existed. In medieval times Kosovo, Macedonia, Southern Serbia and Bosnia were relatively as well developed as the northern regions. German miners – the 'Saxons' – opened up the lead, zinc and silver mines of the

* All except Kraljevac were in Slovenia.

Trepča area in Kosovo during the period of the Nemanjić dynasty (twelfth to fifteenth centuries), when medieval Serbia was at the peak of its prosperity. Novo Brdo, near Priština, was described in the late fourteenth century as 'the largest and finest city in all the Balkans', and Peć in Metohija was compared to Paris by one enthusiastic traveller of the fifteenth

Table 4 Hydroelectric stations built 1948–55

Republic	*Name of station*	*River*	*Megawatts*	*Date*
Sl.	Maribor	Drava	51	1948
Cr.	Vinodol (N. Dalmatia)	Ličanka	84	1952
Sl.	Moste (near Jesenice)	Sava	16	1952
Sl.	Medvode (near Skofja Loka)	Sora	17	1953
Sl.	Vuzenica (Dravograd)	Drava	53	1953
Sb.	Vrla I (S.E. Serbia)	Vrla	22	1954
B–H	Jajce II	Vrbas	30	1954
Sb.	Vrla II	Vrla	11	1955
B–H	Zvornik	Drina	90	1955
B–H	Jablanica	Neretva	144	1955
Total			518	

381 megawatts (73 per cent) in Bosnia–Hercegovina and the less developed parts of Serbia and Croatia

Source: Siegfried Gehrecke, 'Die Elektrizatäts wirtschaft Jugoslaviens', *Osteuropa wirtschaft*, 4 (1971)

century. Despite the difficulties of travel from the interior of the Balkans to the coast, merchants from Ragusa (Dubrovnik) regularly traded with the cities of Raška, Bosnia and Macedonia. Some of the mines had a history of operation from Roman times, especially the argentiferous galena deposits of Zletovo (Macedonia) and the silver ores of Srebrenica in eastern Bosnia.

This early metalworking in the Balkans ceased to have more than local significance after the Turkish invasions of the fourteenth and fifteenth centuries. There were signs of a revival in the late nineteenth century but large-scale mining operations did not recommence until after the establishment of the Yugoslav kingdom in 1918, when British and French companies moved in.[5]

Table 5 Hydroelectric stations built 1956–65

Republic	*Name of station*	*River*	*Megawatts*	*Date*
Sl.	Vuhred	Drava	59	1956
B–H	Jajce I	Vrbas	48	1957
Sb.	Vrla III	Vrla	13	1957
Sb.	Vrla IV	Vrla	10	1957
Mac.	Vrutok I	Mavrovo	75	1957
B–H	Gojak	Dobra/Kupa	48	1958
Cr.	Peruča	Cetina	42	1959
Mac.	Vrben	Mavrovo	14	1959
Mac.	Raven I	Mavrovo	13	1959
Mg.	Peručica	Zeta	72	1960
Sl.	Ozbalt	Drava	60	1960
Sb.	Bistrica	Uvac/Drina	104	1960
Cr.	Split I	Cetina	216	1961
Mg.	Peručica II	Zeta	108	1962
Sb.	Kokin Brod	Uvac/Drina	23	1962
Cr.	Dubrovnik I	Trebišnica	216	1965
Mac.	Globočica	Crni Drim	42	1965
Cr.	Senj	Lika/Gočka	216	1965
Total			1399	

1200 megawatts (90 per cent) in Macedonia, Montenegro, Bosnia–Hercegovina and the less developed areas of Serbia and Croatia

Source: Siegfried Gehrecke, 'Die Elektrizatäts wirtschaft Jugoslaviens', *Osteuropa wirtschaft*, 4 (1971)

The efforts of the Yugoslav regime since 1945 to develop still further the industrial resources of the area south of the Sava–Danube axis are dealt with in later chapters. At this point one can merely indicate the main geographical and historical factors that help to explain the low level of development in the Balkan region and, in contrast, the much higher degree of industrialisation in the Pannonian area.

Table 6 Hydroelectric stations built 1966–8

Republic	*Station*	*River*	*Megawatts*	*Date*
Sb.	Bajina Basta	Drina	348	1967
B–H	Potpeć	Lim/Drina	36	1967
B–H	Rama I	Neretva	160	1968
Sl.	Middle Drava	Drava	133	1968
Cr.	Trebinje	Trebišnica	108	1968
Cr.	Rijeka	Riječnica	36	1968
Mac.	Tikveš	Vardar	48	1968
Total			869	

700 megawatts (80 per cent) in the less developed areas

Source: Siegfried Gehrecke, 'Die Elektrizatäts wirtschaft Jugoslaviens', *Osteuropa wirtschaft*, 4 (1971)

Table 7 Hydroelectric projects begun since 1971

Republic	*Station*	*River*	*Megawatts*	*Date*
Sb.	Iron Gate	Danube	1025	1971
Cr.	Varaždin	Drava	75	1971
Mg.	Mratinje	Piva/Drina	336	1971
Cr.	Orlova	Cetina	237	1971
Mac.	Špilje	Drim	66	1971
Mac.	Kalimanci	Vardar	13	1971
Cr.	Sklope	Lika	23	1972
Total			1775	

Source: Siegfried Gehrecke, 'Die Elektrizatäts wirtschaft Jugoslaviens', *Osteuropa wirtschaft*, 4 (1971)

GEOGRAPHICAL FACTORS INHIBITING DEVELOPMENT IN THE SOUTH

Mention has already been made of the inaccessibility of many of the natural resources of southern Yugoslavia. Many of the richest ores occur in the crystalline rocks of the Rodopi system, particularly in a belt extending from Kosovo, through southern and central Serbia to the Vareš region of Bosnia. In this belt occur the iron ores of Vareš, the lead–zinc deposits of Kopaonik, which include the Trepča mines, and of the Drina bend, as well as a whole range of copper, chrome and silver ores. Two important mineral areas outside this central belt are the copper of eastern Serbia (Bor and Majdanpek) and the rich iron ore field of north-west Bosnia (Ljubija). Only the last of these is within reach of the Sava lowlands. Adequate means of transport is a prerequisite of industrial development. Britain, Germany and the United States were all well endowed with navigable waterways, which were soon supplemented by easily constructed canals when they began their industrialisation. The only rivers with more than 100 kilometres of navigable waterway in Yugoslavia are the Danube (588km), the Sava (583km), the Tisa (164km) and the Drava (105km), all of which lie hundreds of miles from the main sources of industrial raw materials. Only in the Sava–Danube lowlands are conditions suitable for canal construction.

If the courses of the 'heartland' rivers are unsuitable for navigation, their valleys are frequently inadequate as routeways for roads or railways. Their upper courses wind through wild mountain country, often cutting spectacular gorges through the limestone ribs of the Dinaric ranges. Between the deeply entrenched valleys the interfluves rise steeply to high, desolate plateaux and towering peaks. Movement from east to west across the grain of the country is restricted to a few natural gateways, like the one providing access from Sarajevo to the coast by way of the Ivan Pass and the Neretva valley.

Despite the long coastline, with its excellent deepwater anchorages, coastal shipping can play little part in the economic development of the country. The barrier of the Dinaric Alps stands as a formidable obstacle between the coast and the mineral wealth of the interior. Between Rijeka and Bar, a distance of 400 miles, only two main railway lines cross from the interior to the coast, and both are single track for most of their length. These are the old Zagreb–Split–Šibenik line, which follows a tortuous path through the karstic *polja* of Lika and Knin, and the Sarajevo–Ploče line, completed in 1966.[6]

In recent years the stimulus of tourism has led to the opening of a number of new highways, the most important of which being the Adriatic *magistrala*, which runs along the coast from Rijeka to the Albanian border. Several link roads from the *magistrala* lead into the interior, e.g. from Senj, via the Plitvice lakes to Zagreb, and from Metković to Sarajevo. Eventually it is hoped to link the Adriatic highway by several roads to the main artery of the autoput Bratsvo–Jedinstvo, which follows the Sava from Ljubljana to Belgrade and then turns south by the Vardar–Morava route to the Greek border. This highway, planned immediately after the war, and built largely by youth brigades, was not finally completed until the 1960s. It is already below standard for the traffic it bears, as also is the *magistrala*. Over much of the interior, between the coast and the Sava–Danube–Vardar axis, road and rail communications are woefully inadequate.

Hundreds of square miles in the mineral-rich mountain areas of Kosovo, eastern Bosnia and south Serbia are without modern rail or road communications. Even with the most up-to-date techniques of civil engineering, the problems of providing this core area with an adequate infra-structure are almost insuperable. Yet until this task is completed Yugoslavia will be unable to exploit fully her mineral resources.

The northern lowlands and their southerly extension along the Vardar–Morava corridor are not only well endowed for the construction of an internal communications network, linking the republican capitals of Ljubljana, Zagreb, Belgrade and Skopje and the score of subsidiary centres that lie along the riverine axis, but they are also open to international traffic. At Ljubljana routes from Italy and Austria converge. Between Zagreb and Belgrade there are several important road and rail links northward into the Hungarian plain. Niš is the junction from which the Orient Express turns eastward into Bulgaria, by way of the Dragoman Pass, and from Skopje the road and rail routes down the Vardar lead to Salonika. The accessibility of the northern lowlands to Hungary, Austria and beyond to western and central Europe contrasts sharply with the isolation of the Balkan interior. This geographical factor has had a powerful influence on the history of the Yugoslav peoples. The experience of the inhabitants of Slovenia, Croatia–

Slavonia and the Vojvodina during their long history of association with the Habsburg monarchy has imprinted on them a completely different set of cultural attitudes from those which distinguish their brother Slavs in Bosnia, Montenegro, Serbia and Macedonia.

NOTES

1 Central European Mines Ltd.

2 Compared with 1·4 million tons in 1939.

3 The investment required to produce 1 kWh of electricity in 1956 was 36·3 dinars in Slovenia, and 541·9 dinars in Montenegro (figures from J. T. Bombelles).

4 The first phase came into operation in 1971 and was officially inaugurated by Presidents Tito and Ceauşcscu in May 1972. The scheme is due to be completed in 1975.

5 The Bor copper mines were under the French Société des Mines de Bor, and the lead–zinc ores of Trepča were worked by the British-owned Trepča Mines Ltd, founded in 1927, and later by the Anglo-American Selection Trust Ltd.

6 A branch from the Zagreb–Split line was opened to Zadar in 1967 and a through route from Belgrade to Bar across Montenegro is now under construction. There is also an old narrow-gauge line to Dubrovnik.

4 Historical survey

The origins of many of the tensions which strain the unity of the Yugoslav peoples today are deeply rooted in the early history of the Balkans. Yugoslavs themselves have a strong sense of history, and frequently draw analogies from their colourful past in order to buttress their current attitudes to social and political problems. Each of the national groups can discover a time when its ancestors commanded a much larger territory than that of its present republic. Croatia looks back to the tenth century, when the Dalmatian chieftan Tomislav received papal blessing when he assumed the title of King of Croatia. Under his successors the state he founded extended its borders to include most of Bosnia as well as the territory of the present-day Croatian Republic. Bosnia's short-lived days of glory were under the Kotromanić dynasty in the fourteenth century, when Tvrtko I (1353–91) declared himself to be 'King of Serbia, Bosnia, Dalmatia, Croatia and Primorje'. The Macedonians claim Samuilo, tsar of a Bulgaro–Macedonian state during the early eleventh century, as their own, although the Bulgarians dispute this. Montenegrins cannot forget that they maintained their independence from the Turk from the time of the Serbian defeat at Kosovo in 1389 until they deposed Nikola, the last of the Njegoš dynasty, in 1918. Before 1389 Montenegro had been part of a Serbian state which emerged in the ninth century and which survived in some form for five hundred years. At its zenith, under Tsar Dušan, it included all Macedonia, Albania, Kosovo, Montenegro, most of Serbia Proper and the southern parts of Bosnia and Dalmatia, as well as central and northern Greece. Even the Slovenes, who were linked to the Frankish empire during the time of Charlemagne and who, from the fourteenth century, came under Habsburg rule, can claim that under the legendary Samo (627–58) they formed part of a great Slavonic empire, stretching from Leipzig to Ljubljana.

The real or imaginary medieval glories of these various South Slav states may seem to bear little significance to the modern realities of socialist Yugoslavia. However, historical memories and historical myths form important strands in the complex psychological pattern which contribute to the feeling of national consciousness, and they cannot be ignored. It may be, as a detached English observer once wrote, that the peoples of this part of the world are united by a common error as to their origins and a common dislike of their neighbours,[1] but knowledge of what they themselves feel about their past is essential to an understanding of contemporary problems. Furthermore, there are tangible cultural legacies from the formative years which constantly remind us of the immanence of the historical past. The line that divided the western Roman Empire from Byzantium, first sketched by Diocletian in AD 285 and made more permanent a century later by Theodosius, roughly corresponds to the present division between the Cyrillic and Latin alphabets and between the Roman and Orthodox Churches. Croatia–Slavonia, Dalmatia, Slovenia and part of Bosnia lie to the west of this great cultural divide; to the east are Serbia, Kosovo, Montenegro, Macedonia and the rest of Bosnia.

When the Slavs first entered the Balkans during the fifth century they were one of the many groups of tribes which had operated in the twilight lands beyond the eastern limits of the Roman Empire. As the Empire began to crumble, wave upon wave of invaders from the steppelands to the east moved in to plunder and later to colonise the territories that the Romans could no longer hold. The South Slavs appear to have broken off from a parent group settled in the area between the Vistula and the Dnieper. They were at first associated with the Avars, but later freed themselves from this attachment.

SETTLEMENT OF YUGOSLAVIA BY THE SLAVS

The Slovenes

The first group to settle were the Slovenes, who travelled further west than the others and established themselves in the late sixth century in the area between the northern shore of the Adriatic and the Alpine valleys of the Upper Sava. They even penetrated a short distance into the Friulian lowlands of northern Italy. The Slovenes were an important element in the Slavonic empire established by Samo, which extended from the Sava between Zagreb and Ljubljana to the Upper Elbe, embracing most of modern Austria, Czechoslovakia and Saxony. The links between the Slovenes and their Germanic neighbours to the north were further strengthened a century after the death of Samo when they fell under Frankish control. Under Charlemagne the majority were converted to Christianity, and ever since the Slovenes have adhered to the western Church. With German bishops and German feudal overlords they became fully integrated into the Holy Roman Empire, firstly as part of the Duchy of Carantania, and later were divided between Carniola, Carinthia and Styria.

For a few years in the late thirteenth century they were wrested from German control as part of the empire of Ottakar, who attempted to form a Slav state similar in extent to that of Samo, although with a centre of gravity further to the east. Ottakar's ambitions were thwarted by the counter-attack of the Holy Roman Empire at the Battle of the Marchfeld, in 1278. The Habsburgs acquired Styria then, and fifty years later Carinthia and Carniola also. Thus, from 1335 until 1918 the fortunes of the Slovenes were tied to those of the Habsburgs. The six centuries of incorporation into a German-speaking, Roman Catholic cultural entity moulded the character of the Slovenes and marked them off as a distinct group from their Croat and Serb brothers. Despite periods of strong Germanisation – including the colonisation of many areas by Germans – the Slovene language remained the vernacular of the mass of the peasantry, and in the nineteenth century there was a cultural renaissance which produced a rich Slovene national literature. Nevertheless, the Slovenes absorbed many influences from their German masters, including their Roman Catholic faith.

The Croats

The Croats moved in to their present homeland between the seventh and tenth centuries. Their territories extended from the plains of the middle Sava, across the Dinaric ranges to the Adriatic. The northern groups were at first under Frankish rule, and those in Dalmatia came under the Byzantine Empire. The first Croatian kingdom was established in the coastal area by Tomislav in 924. Tomislav repudiated Byzantine suzerainty and also declared his allegiance to the Roman Church, which brought him recognition from Pope John x. After a struggle with his bishops, led by the majestic Gregory of Nin (Grgur Ninski), the Croatian Church was forced to abandon the old Slavonic liturgy in favour of Latin.[2]

Tomislav's capital was at Biograd-na-Moru, between Zadar and Šibenik, and the Croat state was originally confined to Dalmatia. During the next century its territory was enlarged, and at its greatest extent it covered most of Slavonia. Bosnia and Dalmatia.[3] In the north it bordered the vigorous, expansionist Magyar state which, under German influence, had become a Christian kingdom in AD 1000.[4] Croatia lay across land-locked Hungary's route to the sea. In 1089, after the death of the Croatian king, Zvonimir, the Hungarian Ladislas I was asked to intervene to settle the problem of the succession to the Croatian crown. In 1102[5] Kálmán, the successor of Ladislas, was crowned King of Croatia at Biograd. Henceforward, Croatia's fortunes were to be linked with those of Hungary, although Croatian historians stress that the association was that of a personal union of the two crowns, and not an incorporation of Croatia into the Hungarian realm.[6]

The Hungarians governed Croatia through a *ban*, or governor, appointed by the king. The degree of Croatian autonomy varied from time to time: sometimes the *ban* was chosen from the Croatian nobility, whose privileges were respected by the Hungarians. A Croatian *sabor*, or diet, was recognised, and at times acted as the spokesman of Croatian national interests.[7]

Although Kálmán was crowned in Tomislav's old capital of Biograd, the centre of gravity of Croatia shifted to Slavonia during the early years of Hungarian rule. Zagreb became the main ecclesiastical centre even before Kálmán was crowned, for Ladislas established a diocese there in 1094.

Dalmatia was never for long under undisputed Hungarian rule. After the defeat of Byzantium the Venetians struggled with Hungary for the control of the coastlands and islands for three hundred years. After 1420 the Turks replaced the Hungarians as the adversaries of Venice in Dalmatia, and for the greater part of the period from 1420 to 1797 the Venetians held the whole area except for Ragusa (Dubrovnik).[8] Although the coastal cities were under Venetian overlordship there was a steady infiltration of Croats into Dalmatia. It became a 'Slavonic land with an Italian fringe', and a unique culture grew during the Renaissance from a blending of the traditions of the two peoples.

In 1805 Dalmatia was ceded to France and became part of Napoleon's Illyrian Provinces. After the Congress of Vienna it was given to Austria and was not reunited to Croatia until 1918, despite repeated demands from the Dalmatian Diet, established under the Austrian 'October Diploma' of 1861.

The original homeland of the first Croatian kingdom, Dalmatia, therefore underwent a different historical experience from that of Slavonia, which remained in close contact with Hungary and shared with her a common struggle against the Turk in the period from the fall of Bosnia in 1463 to the cession by the Turks of Croatia–Slavonia and Hungary to the Habsburgs in 1699. The eighteenth century saw the two nations struggling together against Austrian centralist pressures, but after the Napoleonic episode they began to draw apart. Croat nationalism, stimulated by the romantic movement, found itself increasingly in conflict with Hungarian nationalism. In 1848 Croat troops under *Ban* Jelačić assisted the Habsburgs in the suppression of the Hungarian national revolt. Twenty years later a Croatian Diet was pressured and bribed into accepting a form of home rule within the Hungarian half of the monarchy. The *Nagoda* accepted the existence of a Croat nation 'possessing a special territory of its own', and a Croatian assembly (the *sabor*) was given a limited authority over internal administration. This partial recognition of Croatian national aspirations served merely to whet the appetites of the nationalists and to encourage them to demand more than Hungary was prepared to concede. As the First World War approached more and more Croats turned towards the South Slav solution to their national problem – i.e. towards a complete break with the Hungarians, and the formation of a Serbo–Croat state.

The Serbs

The Serbs established themselves in the mountainous heartland of the Balkans at about the time the Croats were settling in Slavonia and Dalmatia. In the ninth century a group of Serbian tribes living in the remote valleys where Montenegro, Kosovo and Bosnia meet formed a union under one of their *župani*, named Vlastimir. They were brought together by a common danger that threatened from the east – the Bulgars. Vlastimir acknowledged Byzantine suzerainty as a means of enlisting the support of the emperor. Just as Tomislav ensured his success by embracing western Christendom, so Vlastimir and his successors brought the Serbs into the orbit of the eastern Church. Byzantine missionaries, of whom Kiril and Metodije (Constantine-Cyril and Methodius) were the most famous,[9] worked to spread their faith amongst both the Serbs and the Macedonians. With the faith came also the glagolitic alphabet, from which modern Cyrillic developed.

There were three main areas of Serbian activity between Vlastimir's time and the coronation of the first king of the Nemanjić dynasty, Stephen,[10] in 1217. One centre was in the west, around present-day Montenegro, and appears at different times under the names Zeta and Duklija.[11] The second was known as Raška, from the river of that name which joins the Ibar north of Novi Pazar. A third group of Serbs occupied central Bosnia.

In 1196 Stephen retired to Studenica, the monastery he had founded. His sons, Sava and Stephen, both achieved honourable places in the roll of Serbian national history. Sava became the first archbishop of the independent Serbian Orthodox Church, and Stephen was crowned, with papal approval, as the first Serbian king.

The Nemanjić dynasty ruled Serbia until 1371. At its greatest extent, under Tsar Stephen Dušan (1331–55), the Serbian Empire covered the whole of the southern Balkans from the Neretva and the Drina south-eastwards to Thessaly. His title was 'Emperor and Autocrat of the Serbs, the Greeks, the Bulgarians and the Albanians'. His Code of Laws (*Zakonik*), promulgated at Skopje in 1349, earned him the title of 'Dušan the Lawgiver'. His empire was a great centre of learning and its military power, equal to that of Byzantium, rested on a strong and well-organised economic basis.

However, it did not survive long after his death. Internal dissensions weakened it, and Dušan's successors were unable to withstand the onslaught of the Ottoman Turks. In 1371 Dušan's son, Tsar Stephen Uroš, was defeated by a Turkish army, and the last Nemanjić emperor died a few months later. When the Turks reached Kosovo Polje in 1389 the Slav army that faced them was led by Lazar, a Serbian *knez*[12] who did not even aspire to the title of king. Serbia survived for fifty years after the defeat at Kosovo. Its capital during this period was at Smederovo, on the Danube, east of Belgrade, and its rulers were given the Byzantine title of Despot. Smederovo fell to the Turks in 1459, and Belgrade in 1521. Hundreds of thousands of Serbian refugees crossed the Danube into the Vojvodina, where their descendants still form a major part of the population. In 1526 the Turks crossed the Danube and advanced into Hungary, defeating the young King Lájos at Mohács. Hungary remained under Turkish rule until the end of the seventeenth century.

The arrival of the Turks not only broke the unified Serbian Empire, but it also created the conditions for the emergence of two new Slav national groups – the Montenegrins and the Bosnians. Until the fourteenth century these groups were indistinguishable from the main body of Serbs. Zeta, which covered most of modern Montenegro, was in fact one of the original nuclei of the Serbian Empire. Bosnia was inhabited by Serb-speaking tribes who retained a degree of local autonomy under their own *župani* before the Nemanjić period.

Montenegro

Montenegro's inaccessibility saved it from Turkish occupation, and during the early fifteenth century it emerged as a distinct political unit, based on the old Serbian territory of Zeta. The Crnojević dynasty ruled for less than a century before 1516. Its first and greatest ruler, Ivan, founded the capital city of Cetinje and built many Orthodox monasteries. In 1493 he imported a printing press from Venice and published the first printed Cyrillic texts to be seen in the Balkans.

After the death of the last Crnojević ruler in 1516 the Bishop of Cetinje assumed power. A custom developed under which the new ruler, or *vladika*, was always a bishop, and after 1696 the title was held continuously by a member of the Petrović–Njegoš family.[13] In 1851 Danilo II broke the tradition of celibacy and founded a hereditary royal house. The functions of king and bishop were separated. During the rule of the last two *vladikas*, Peter I, 'the holy Vladika' (1782–1830) and Peter II, the soldier-poet (1830–51), the country was stabilised and given the rudiments of a modern administration, after a century of internal feuding and dissension. The gradual weakening of Turkish rule during the second half of the nineteenth century gave opportunities for expansion, and these were seized by Nikola I.

In 1878 the European powers at Berlin recognised some of the gains made with Russian help at the Treaty of San Stefano, four months earlier. Most important was the granting of the Adriatic port of Bar. In 1880 this tiny maritime frontage was extended as far as the Albanian border near Ulcinj. The Balkan Wars of 1912–13 resulted in further territorial gains inland, which brought Serbia and Montenegro into direct contact as a result of the partitioning of the Sandžak of Novi Pazar. Thus, on the eve of the First World War, the two small Slav states shared a common frontier, and the question of their ultimate union was being discussed.

The Bosnians

Bosnia is a land-locked region in the heart of the Balkan peninsula. Its population in the early Middle Ages was partly Serb and partly Croat. Croatia governed most of it during the eleventh century, but later there were periods during which Serbs, Byzantines and Hungarians held large parts of the country. The schism which split Christendom between Rome and Byzantium, and which divides the Yugoslavs into two main linguistic and cultural groups, ran through the centre of Bosnia. To complicate matters the Bosnians developed a heretical church of their own during the eleventh century. The Bogomils ('the Beloved of God') were so persecuted by their Christian brothers from Hungary that many of them embraced Islam when the Turks overran the country in 1463. Shortly before this period there had been a brief period of Bosnian independence under the Kotromanić dynasty, whose greatest king, Tvrtko (1353–91), styled himself 'King of the Serbs, of Bosnia and of the Coast'. This was a fair description, for Tvrtko's domain included central Dalmatia, from Biograd-na-Moru to Kotor, and extended inland to the Drina. The majority of his subjects were Serbs, and their numbers were greatly increased after Lazar's defeat at Kosovo in 1389. After Tvrtko's death in 1391 the Bosnian state gradually disintegrated and the Turks finally took over in 1463. A small enclave held out until 1483 under the *Herceg* (Duke) of St Sava. This is the region known today as Hercegovina.

The significant distinguishing characteristic of Bosnia during the four centuries of Turkish rule was that it had a native Slav-speaking Moslem aristocracy, based on the former Bogomil heretics who voluntarily accepted Islam.[14] The Turkish period is not, therefore, spoken of in Bosnia as 'the long Turkish night', as it is in Serbia and Macedonia. It is this historical background which forms the starting point for a consideration of the Bosnian Moslems as a distinct national entity within Yugoslavia.

The Macedonians

The Macedonians' claims to national identity are clouded by a bitter dispute as to whether they are, in fact, Bulgarians. The first Slav settlers in the area between the Black Sea and Albania were probably an undifferentiated group of tribes speaking a common language. Those in the east fell under the domination of the Bulgars, Finno-Ugrian-speaking invaders from the Eurasian steppelands. The Bulgars arrived towards the end of the seventh century and intermixed with the Slavs in the territories they overran, ultimately adopting their speech and culture. In the ninth century a Macedo-Bulgarian Empire was established by Simeon the Great (893–927) at the expense of the Byzantine Empire. Simeon's realm broke up into two provinces. The eastern half – roughly corresponding to modern Bulgaria – was soon recovered by the Byzantines, but the west remained independent for another half-century. Under Samuilo (976–1014), who ruled from Ohrid, Macedonia flourished. Ohrid was a centre of ecclesiastical art, which manifested itself in architecture, painting and sculpture and in the translation of

Greek texts into old Slavonic. Modern Macedonian nationalist historians claim that this was the first evidence of an indigenous Macedonian culture,[15] but other scholars see it as part of a wider Slavonic culture associated with Bulgaria.[16]

Samuilo's empire fell to the Byzantines after the Battle of Kleidon (1014). For the next three centuries most of Macedonia was controlled by the Byzantines, although there were several revolts by the Slavs, and for a short time after 1086 some areas were incorporated into the Second Bulgarian Empire. Although Basil II[17] (976–1025) acted with savage cruelty against Samuilo's defeated army[18] and reduced the patriarchate of Ohrid to an archbishopric, neither he nor his successors attempted to destroy the Slav culture of Macedonia, which was, of course, derived from the Church.[19]

During the fourteenth century Macedonia was brought into the Serbian Empire of Dušan, who was able to take advantage of the weakness of Byzantium in face of the Turkish invasions of Asia Minor. The Serbian victory was short-lived, however – by the mid-fourteenth century all Macedonia lay under Turkish rule, and remained so until 1913. Thus, Macedonia was the first Yugoslav territory to bear the weight of the Turkish occupation and the last to be liberated from it. During these six centuries Macedonians were not recognised as a separate nation, and there is little evidence that they had a concept of themselves as members of a distinct national group.

The long Turkish occupation had an important influence on the ethnic composition of Macedonia. Turkish landowners and peasants settled in the Vardar valley and Pelagonia, bringing with them their Moslem faith and their system of feudal land tenure. Turkish officials moved into the towns, especially those, like Bitola and Skopje, which were administrative centres. Some Slavs and many Albanians accepted Islam. Over the centuries, the Albanian population in the rural areas of western Macedonia increased, partly by migration encouraged by the Turks, and in the later years of the occupation the numbers of Albanians in the towns began to grow. Although the Orthodox Christian Slavs on the whole fared worse than the Moslems, they were not prevented from exercising their religion. Under the 'millet' system the Turks regarded the Christian Church leaders as having the responsibility for the civil discipline of their flocks, as well as of ministering to their religious needs. In certain circumstances they became the spokesman of the national aspirations of their people. This was only possible, of course, where the Church leaders were of the same national origin as their congregations. The Macedonians and the Bulgarians, however, were placed under the rule of Phanariot Greek bishops, and it was not until foreign influence was overthrown that the identification of Church and nation could be fully realised. The Bulgarians achieved this in 1870 with the creation of the Bulgarian Exarchate; the Macedonians had to wait until 1967 for the creation of an autocephalous Macedonian Church. In the intervening century they exchanged Greek for Bulgarian bishops in 1874[20] and Bulgarians for Serbs in 1918.

The education of Christians in Macedonia during the Turkish period was left to the churches. Until the late nineteenth century the services were usually conducted in Greek, and many of the clergy spoke only Greek. After the creation of the Bulgarian Exarchate Slav-speaking priests and Slav schools became more common, although the Greek influence was not entirely eliminated until 1913. An account of the linguistic situation in Gevgelija describes how a Slav school[21] was opened in 1860, financed by voluntary parental contributions. The teacher 'used Slav church books and taught arithmetic and folk-songs. The Greek bishop started a school, but with no great success, and although it went on until 1913, it was patronised by fewer and fewer children'.[22] Under the Exarchate a Bulgarian school was established, and in 1882 a Serbian school was opened. By the end of the century Gevgelija had acquired a Turkish, a Romanian and a Catholic school, the last supported by Austrian and French donations.

The problem of linguistic identification for the Macedonians is well illustrated by the unhappy struggle of the poet Grigor Prličev to decide in which language he should express himself. Prličev has been described as 'the outstanding creative personality of nineteenth century Macedonian literature'.[23] Born at Ohrid in 1830 and educated in a Greek school, Prličev was a medical student in Athens in 1860 when he won a prize for the best poem of the year. His winning entry, 'Serdarot', derived its inspiration from a Macedonian folk epic, *Kuzman Kariman*, but it was written in Greek. Prličev later rejected hellenism, and returned home to Ohrid to lead the fight against the Phanariot influence in the Church. After the success of this campaign he went to Bulgaria, where he became a teacher, and then a librarian in the national library in Sofia. During this period he unsuccessfully attempted to translate the *Iliad* into Bulgarian, and then turned to writing in 'a general Slavonic language based on old Slavonic and Macedonian. However, this attempt naturally failed as well'.[24]

Earlier, Bishop Zografski had attempted to develop a Macedo-Bulgarian literary language. 'He produced many text books for Macedonian schools in . . . a language based on Macedonian, in particular the speech of Galičnik, his native place, with traces of other Macedonian variants, of Bulgarian . . . and important elements from Church Slavonic and Russian'.[25]

The strivings of poets and scholars to find a true Macedonian voice – not Greek, nor Bulgarian, nor Serbian – in which the people could express their distinct national identity were reflected also in the political sphere. The rivalry between Belgrade and Sofia to establish schools in their own languages was part of a political power struggle in which the Macedonian people were the pawns. There was a third tendency, however, which promoted the idea of 'Macedonia for the Macedonians.'[26] In 1893 at Resen, near Lake Prespa, the Internal Macedonian Revolutionary Organisation (VMRO) was founded. VMRO operated both in Macedonia and in Bulgaria – in fact, through all the territory of the Exarchate. There was a large Macedonian population in Bulgaria, and after the unification of Bulgaria and Eastern Rumelia in 1886 the enlarged Bulgarian state became a centre for agitation in Macedonia.

The new state was not, however, interested in Macedonian autonomy, but in the annexation of Macedonia to create the 'Big Bulgaria' of the abortive San Stefano Treaty. The fears of King Milan of Serbia that a newly unified Bulgaria would undermine Serbia's position in Macedonia led to his disastrous attack on the Bulgarians at Slivnica in 1886.

In these circumstances it is not surprising that VMRO, formed only seven years after Bulgaria's triumph, should be seen as an instrument of Bulgarian expansionism. A significant group of Macedonians rejected this role and worked for Macedonian autonomy. They could agree with the Bulgarians on the need for expelling the Turks, but they were not disposed to exchange Turkish for Bulgarian – or Serbian – domination. One of the most remarkable of the Macedonian revolutionaries of this period was Goce Delčev (1872–1903). He was only twenty-one when VMRO was formed, and he was killed in 1903 at the age of thirty-one. During these ten years he was the spokesman of a generous, humanist nationalism, which, whilst proclaiming the rights to liberation for his own people, denied the necessity to hate others.

> I do not hate the Osmanlis as a people; I fight against Osmanli tyranny as a ruling system. . . .
> Macedonia . . . belongs to all Macedonians; whoever hankers after, and works for unification with Bulgaria and Greece may consider himself a good Bulgar or Greek, but not a good Macedonian.[27]

Delčev was more than a nationalist, he was also a socialist in the tradition of Svetozar Marković, the father of Balkan socialism. In his own words, 'I have the soul of an anarchist, the convictions of a social democrat, and I act like a revolutionary'.[28]

In 1896 Delčev and his fellow Macedonian, Gjorče Petrov, were elected to the supreme committee of VMRO in Sofia as border representatives. They served in this capacity until 1901. The last few years of the nineteenth century was a period of intense guerilla activity against the Turks and of equally intense repression by the Turks of their Slav subjects. It was also a period during which the pro-Bulgarian and autonomist groups within VMRO drew further apart. Amongst the latter, the group headed by Delčev, Petrov, Gruev and Sandanski began to prepare a Macedonian national uprising. On 2 August 1903 (St Elijah's Day, or Ilinden)[29] the revolutionaries raised the banner of an independent Macedonia in the little town of Kruševo, near Prilep, and appealed to all inhabitants of Macedonia – 'Turks, Albanians and Moslems', as well as Christian Slavs – to overthrow the Sultan's rule.[30]

The 'Kruševo Republic' was ruthlessly suppressed by the Turks after a life of only eleven days. Delčev was already dead before the rising occurred, having been shot during a skirmish at Banica in May. Damion Gruev continued a guerilla campaign until he too was killed, in December 1906.

The savage repression by the Turks that followed the defeat of the Ilinden Rising led to yet another attempt by the European powers to persuade the Sultan to behave in a more civilised way towards the Christians under Ottoman rule. The Sultan accepted the 'Murzsteg Programme', which involved the appointment of British, French, Italian, Russian and Austrian observers in Macedonia to supervise the implementation of the reforms. The Bulgarians for their part agreed to curb the activities of VMRO. The Turks, as so often had happened before, failed to carry out their reforms. The Bulgarians were more concerned with Bulgarianising VMRO, and the various other groups of insurgents – Greeks, Albanians and Serbs – took no notice of the powers.

In the short-lived euphoria following the success of the Young Turk revolt in 1908, when Enver Bey proclaimed the equality of all Ottoman subjects, the system of international control was abandoned. Within a year further anti-Turkish outbreaks occurred and Turkish repression was resumed. Meanwhile, Macedonia's neighbours were preparing for war with Turkey. Serbia and Bulgaria agreed to partition Macedonia between them when they had overthrown the Turks. The Macedonians themselves were divided in their allegiance, and these divisions continued for another generation. After the Balkan Wars central and western Macedonia came under Serbian rule, and in the 1920s became the Vardar province of South Serbia.

The existence of a Macedonian nation was denied by the royalist regime of Yugoslavia. Many thousands of Macedonians in the Salonika (Solun) region were subjected to hellenisation under the Kingdom of Greece, and others in the Pirin region came under Bulgarian rule. Between 1915 and 1918 most of central Macedonia (the Vardar region) was occupied by Bulgarian troops. Those under Serbian rule, denied the right to national existence, turned to Bulgaria for the hope of salvation. The relations of the various factions of VMRO to the Bulgarians, and later to the Balkan Communist organisations, are far from easy to disentangle. The issues raised are still so sensitive as to be matters of burning political controversy today, and the facts are clouded by propagandist falsification.

It would appear that many who have later been claimed as Macedonian nationalists were in fact anti-Serb protagonists of the Bulgarian cause. When Bulgarian troops marched into Macedonia during the Second World War, with German support – as they had done in 1915 – many Macedonians welcomed them as liberators from the Serbian yoke. However, they were soon disillusioned. Towards the end of the war the Macedonian partisan movement joined with Tito's partisans, and by so doing ensured that under the flag of socialist Yugoslavia there would be a Federal Macedonian People's Republic.[31] Although most of historic Macedonia is now included within Yugoslavia, there are still Macedonian minorities in Bulgaria and Greece, and the former does not appear to have abandoned its territorial claims in Macedonia.

Whatever may be said of the history of the Macedonian movement, it is clear today that a Macedonian nation exists. It has a strong sense of its own unique identity, and its national consciousness has been encouraged by the post-war Yugoslav regime. It has now its own language and literature, its own republican institutions, its national university and even its own autonomous Macedonian Orthodox Church.[32] Because it has gained so much both economically and culturally from socialist Yugoslavia, Macedonia is deeply committed to the preservation of Yugoslavia in its present form.

SERBS, CROATS AND SLOVENES IN THE NINETEENTH CENTURY

As we have seen in the brief account given above, the different Slav-speaking national groups[33] which together constitute the peoples of Yugoslavia have undergone different historical experiences. At various periods in their history they have been conscious of the common interests that all of them share, but at other periods they have emphasised their differences. Usually it is a common external danger which makes them feel that they are first and foremost Yugoslavs, and only secondarily Croats, Serbs or Slovenes. In periods when the external danger is absent their historically rooted cultural differences come to the surface.

The Yugoslav movement, which developed during the nineteenth century and came to fruition in the twentieth, had two main strands. The first affected the lands to the north of the Sava–Danube line and also Dalmatia. These were the territories which were attached to the Habsburg monarchy. The Croats and Slovenes were deeply affected by the ideals of the French Revolution, which were brought directly to them

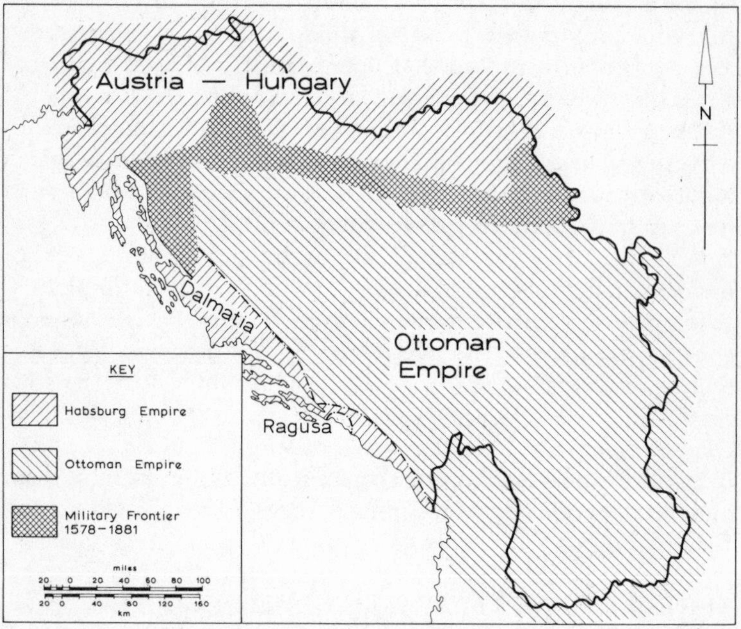

Map 2 The Yugoslav lands under Turkish and Habsburg rule, 1578–1881

by Napoleon's troops. The Illyrian Provinces established by the French in 1809 lasted only four years. They covered Slovenia and most of historic Croatia and Dalmatia. Twenty years after the defeat of Napoleon a nationalist movement developed which acknowledged its debt to France by adopting the title of the Illyrian Movement. It was primarily a linguistic and literary movement, led by men like Ljudevit Gaj, the Croat philologist. It helped to create a feeling of common interest between Slovenes and Croats in opposing the Germanising and

Magyarising tendencies of the Austrians and Hungarians in their respective zones of occupation. It even looked beyond these two groups to the Serbs, and envisaged a South Slav union. When it moved from cultural to political objectives it concentrated on the creation of an autonomous Slav unit within the Habsburg Monarchy, rather than a separate South Slav state.

In the Turkish-held lands south of the Sava and the Danube the Serbs in particular were always in favour of complete separation from the Ottoman Empire. In contrast to the middle-class, constitutionally minded leaders of the Illyrian Movement, the Serbs looked to their salvation through armed revolt. Throughout the Turkish occupation Serbian outlaw bands, known as *hajduks*, had operated against the Sultan's representatives. The tradition of outlawry was strong, and the *hajduks* were a popular element amongst the Serbs, their deeds being celebrated in innumerable legends and popular folk epics. It only needed a strong leader to weld these 'Robin Hood' bands together to make them the spearhead of a national uprising. In the early nineteenth century the opportunity came.

Serbian independence

George Petrović (Karadjordje) raised a revolt in 1804 against the tyranny of the Janissaries,[34] who ruled Serbia in the name of the Sultan. Sultan Selim III had no reason to love the Janissaries. For some time he had been trying to discipline them, but the conservative forces within the Ottoman Empire were too strong for a reforming Sultan. Although he promised the Serbs some relief from their oppression he was unable to honour his pledge, for in 1806 he was overthrown by the Janissaries.[35] The Serbs then turned to open revolt, and by December had captured Belgrade, Russia and Austria both interfered, hoping to benefit from the possible retreat of Turkey in Europe, and Karadjordje intrigued with both. In the long run the Serbs were left to face the Turks alone.

Russia, on the eve of Napoleon's attack on her, was too concerned with her own safety, and Austria was not anxious to challenge the Turks when they counter-attacked and drove Karadjordje into exile. Turkish troops entered Belgrade in

1813, and the first Serbian rising was at an end. With Karadjordje living as a refugee in Austrian territory, the leadership of the Serbs passed to Miloš Obrenović. Miloš probably arranged the murder of Karadjordje, and under their new leader, who was now in undisputed control, the Serbs gradually won a position of autonomy within the Ottoman Empire. After fifteen years, during which diplomatic negotiation was combined with sporadic outbursts of armed revolt, Miloš was recognised by the Hatisherif of December 1830 as Prince of Serbia.[36]

Throughout the nineteenth century the Obrenović and Karadjordjević dynasties struggled for the throne. Gradually the Serbs won territory from the Turks, and extended their principality from its original base in the Šumadija. In 1833 six disputed districts in the south were added to Serbia. Despite his successes in winning autonomy for his country and extending its frontiers, Miloš became unpopular with influential sections of the population because of his despotic manner of governing, and in 1834 he was faced with an armed revolt.[37]

In order to quieten his liberal-minded opponents he agreed in 1835 to a constitution which gave wide powers to an elected parliament.[38] A month after its promulgation this constitution was withdrawn, to be replaced three years later by another one worked out in Constantinople in an atmosphere of diplomatic intrigue. The 'Turkish' Constitution of 1838 provided for an advisory senate, nominated by the Prince, whose members could only be removed by the Sultan. The struggle between Miloš and the opposition politicians produced a deadlock which Miloš attempted to break by encouraging a rising in his favour. Eventually the Russians intervened and forced Miloš to abdicate in 1839 in favour of his ailing elder son Milan. A month later, on Milan's death, the sixteen-year-old second son, Mihailo, became the nominal ruler, under the guidance of advisors appointed by the Sultan. Three years later one of the advisers, Vučić, supported by a group known as the Defenders of the constitution,[39] organised a *coup d'état* which replaced Mihailo by Alexander Karadjordjević, the second son of the man who had led the Serbian Revolt of 1804. Throughout the sixteen years of his reign Alexander was subjected to rival pressures from Austria and Russia, as well as having to face internal unrest fomented by the supporters of the Obrenović family.

The Austrians, fearful of an increase in Russian influence, saw the maintenance of the Ottoman Empire as a bulwark against Pan-Slavism – an ironical situation in view of the former role of the Habsburgs as defenders of Christendom against the Turk. The Habsburgs also feared the possibility of Serbia becoming a rallying point for Slav nationalism within the Monarchy, and their interest was in a weak Serbia under Austrian influence. Their success was apparent in 1848, when Alexander, despite a great loss of popularity at home, refused to aid the Slavs who revolted against Hungarian rule. In 1848 the Russians urged caution on the Serbs because they feared that any intervention by Alexander on behalf of the Serbs of the Vojvodina would provide an excuse for a Habsburg attack on Serbia.

Under similar pressures, Serbia remained neutral during the Crimean War, despite strong Pan-Slav sentiments amongst the people, which were encouraged by the Obrenović party. The Treaty of Paris (1856), which ended the Crimean War, included clauses guaranteeing the integrity of Serbia under the protection of all the major powers.[40] Serbia, as a riparian power, also gained a seat on the Danube Commission. The country remained, however, under Turkish suzerainty, and the Turks were allowed to maintain their garrison in the Kalemegdan fortress at Belgrade.

Alexander's apparent subservience to Austria[41] provoked a reaction among his subjects and led in 1859 to his overthrow by the Skupština (parliament). Miloš Obrenović, then in his eightieth year, was recalled from exile. The steps that he took during his brief resumption of power prepared the way for his son Mihailo, who was restored to the throne in 1860.

During his second reign (1860–8) Mihailo achieved the withdrawal of all the Turkish garrisons in 1867.[42] He also encouraged his prime minister, Ilija Garašanin, to establish links with Slav groups within the Ottoman and Habsburg Empires, and to promote the idea of Yugoslav brotherhood.

Mihailo displayed many of the autocratic tendencies of his father. Nevertheless, his reign saw great advances in the development of political and juridical institutions in Serbia, in addition to considerable economic progress. Mihailo was also responsible for founding a modern conscript army of 100,000 men, trained by French officers. He has been described as a man who did 'much for his country and was one of the ablest rulers it ever had',[43] but despite his achievements he made many enemies. In June 1868 he was assassinated by an unknown assailant whilst walking in a park near Belgrade. The allegation that the crime was inspired by Alexander Karadjordjević, from his exile in Austria, was rejected by an Austrian court but was upheld by the Serbian court which tried him *in absentia*. Whatever the truth, there was no Karadjordjević restoration.

Mihailo was succeeded by his thirteen-year-old cousin Milan, who was elected by the Skupština. Until 1872 a three-man regency council, headed by Jovan Ristić, exercised the prerogatives of the ruler. The regency introduced constitutional reforms which provided for a Skupština of 120 members, 90 of whom were elected on a broad franchise and 30 of whom were nominated by the ruler. Although elected on a liberal franchise, the Skupština had limited powers and was unable to restrain the autocracy first of the regents and later of Milan.

In 1875 a revolt against Turkish rule broke out in Hercegovina, and soon spread to Bosnia, Macedonia and Bulgaria. The savage Turkish reprisals shocked liberal opinion throughout Europe[44] and, for example, prevented the usual British support which the Sultan had previously obtained when faced with a crisis in his relations with the Slavs.[45] Although strongly under Austrian pressure not to intervene, Milan was forced by public opinion to join with Montenegro in an attack on the Turks in July 1876.

The Montenegrin army, directed by Peter Karadjordjević (later King Peter of Serbia), was successful, but Milan's forces were driven back and saved from total defeat only by the diplomatic intervention of the Russians, who forced the Turks to agree to an armistice. In May 1877 Russia, Romania, Montenegro and Serbia together successfully attacked Turkey. An armistice was signed in January 1878 and in March the Turks were forced to accept the Treaty of San Stefano, which provided, *inter alia*, for the creation of a 'Big Bulgaria' covering most of Macedonia, for the recognition of Serbian independence and for the accession of territory to both Serbia and Montenegro.

The other great powers were unwilling to see the spread of Russian influence in the Balkans which this settlement implied, and at the Congress of Berlin in July 1878 they forced Russia to withdraw the San Stefano Treaty. In its place they imposed their own settlement of the 'Eastern Question'.[46] This restored Turkish rule to Macedonia, permitted Austria to occupy Bosnia and Hercegovina[47] and the Sandžak of Novi Pazar,[48] gave the Pirot, Niš and Vranje districts to Serbia, and allowed some extension of Montenegro's frontiers. Serbian independence within her enlarged territories was recognised by the powers. Serbia was disappointed in her failure to obtain an outlet to the sea either through a friendly Montenegro[49] or through a Serbian-administered Macedonia.[50]

In 1882 Milan Obrenović was proclaimed king of the newly independent Serbia, but in reality Turkish legal suzerainty had been exchanged for *de facto* Austrian domination. Milan hoped that, by promising to discipline Serbian irredentists in Bosnia, the Habsburgs would support his claims to Macedonia. The policy failed on both counts, and the Obrenović dynasty was discredited in the eyes of the Serbian nationalists. Milan was forced to abdicate in 1889 and was succeeded by his son Alexander, whose personal behaviour, as well as his policies, alienated all support for the dynasty. When Alexander and his Queen Draga were brutally murdered in 1903 the event was celebrated in Belgrade in an atmosphere reminiscent of a carnival. The Skupština (parliament) then invited Peter Karadjordjević to the throne, and in the eleven years of his reign Serbia became the rallying point for the disaffected Slavs within the Habsburg Monarchy. Serbian prestige grew with her victories in the Balkan Wars (1912–13), when most of Macedonia and half the Sandžak were annexed.

THE YUGOSLAV MOVEMENT

The development of Serbian national consciousness

The struggles of the Serbs to free themselves from Turkish rule were more than a mere protest against an alien tyranny: they were also an assertion of Serbian nationhood. The idea that Serbia should also become the focal point for South Slav unification – a kind of Yugoslav Piedmont – came later, and was less deeply rooted than that of Serb nationalism. Although some of the Serbian leaders did encourage the Yugoslav idea – notably Prince Mihailo, Ilija Garašanin and the socialist Svetozar Marković[51] – it was far from being a widely held concept until the twentieth century. In the first half of the nineteenth century the main current was that of Serbianism. Even when, as in 1848 and 1875, the sympathies of the Serbs were directed towards the plight of their brothers still under foreign rule, the chief concern was for the Serbs of the Vojvodina and Bosnia, rather than for the Croats and Slovenes.

Nationalism in modern Europe is based on the realisation by a group of people that they share a common cultural heritage, with its own language and literature. Where there is no great literary tradition, the oral traditions of the people provide the inspiration for national self-assertion. The oral tradition is by its nature democratic, and is expressed in the language of the ordinary people. The educated classes, even if they are of the same stock as the masses, often express themselves in an alien tongue. In the early nineteenth century, stimulated by the Romantic movement in literature and by the political ideals of the French Revolution, many of the smaller nations of Europe awoke to the riches of their oral folk traditions, and gained from this discovery the self-confidence needed to assert their distinct national identities. Thus, the awakening of Finnish nationalism owed much to the rediscovery of the oral traditions of *Kalevala*, at a time when Swedish and Russian were the languages of the establishment. In Slovenia German, and in Croatia German and Magyar, were the languages of the establishment, although Dalmatia had a Slavonic literary tradition going back to the fifteenth century,[52] and in Slovenia the *New Testament* had been translated into the vernacular by Primož Trubar in 1555.

The Serbs inherited one of the richest oral traditions in Europe. The great epic poems (*narodne pesme*) were of particular importance to the national movement, as they sang of the heroes of medieval Serbia – Stefan Nemanja, Tsar Dušan, Prince Lazar and Kraljević Marko. The Kosovo cycle and the ballads of Kraljević Marko told of the epic battles against the Turks in the fourteenth century, and in later cycles the heroes were the Serbian guerillas (the *hajduks*) who continued the struggle under the Turkish occupation.

The language of the ordinary people who kept alive and added to these oral traditions was quite different from the form of Church Slavonic that was the literary language of the educated minority.[53]

During the period when the Serbs were struggling to establish their national independence two scholars made invaluable contributions to the creation of a new Serbian literary language, based on the speech of the ordinary people. The pioneer was Dimitrije Obradović (1742–1811), known to history as Dositej, the name he took in 1757 when he became a monk in the monastery of Hopovo in the Fruška Gora.[54] Dositej rebelled against the obscurantism of his brother monks, and in 1760 he left to embark on travels that took him to many parts of the Balkans, to France, England, Russia and Germany. For several years in the 1770s he taught languages in Vienna and later settled for a time in Germany, where he studied philosophy at Halle. His first books were published in Leipzig in 1783. Dositej was greatly influenced by the writings of the French encyclopedists and the German Romantics, and he translated many of their works into a form of Serbian that was closer to the vernacular than to the literary language of the Church. The leaders of the Orthodox Church in the Habsburg lands bitterly attacked Dositej's work. They saw him as an instrument of Austrian secularism and as a threat to their church's monopoly over the education of young Serbs. In a sense they were right, for Joseph II's policy towards the Serbs in the Empire, which his successor Leopold II continued, did undermine the position of the Church in education. The Serbs themselves were divided in their attitude to the Austrian reforms. Dositej was one of the leaders of the pro-reform group, and Metropolitan Stratimirović was, understandably, the defender of the privileges of the Church. The struggle between them was at its most intense in the border town of Sremski Karlovci, which lies on the right bank of the Danube, sixty miles upstream from Belgrade and almost opposite Novi Sad. Karlovci, the seat of the Orthodox Metropolitan, had been visited in 1727 by an educational mission, sent by the Synod of Moscow, which stayed for ten years and set the pattern for

Orthodox education amongst the Serbs of Srem and the Vojvodina. Karlovci was also the home of the first Serbian secondary school, founded in 1791 by Leopold II.

One of the pupils at this school between 1805 and 1806 was Vuk Stefanović Karadžić, a peasant's son from a Serbian village near to the Bosnian border. Vuk had acquired a rudimentary education in Serbia before he crossed the Sava into Austrian territory, and unlike most of his contemporaries he could read and write. Although he stayed for only a year in Karlovci,[55] Vuk was greatly influenced by the ideas of Dositej and his liberal-minded followers among the Serbian community in Srem. When he returned to Serbia his ability to read and write enabled him to obtain a minor clerical post in the administration of Karadjordje. In Belgrade he continued his education for a short time in a high school opened in 1808. In 1809 he went abroad for medical treatment[56] and after a period in Novi Sad and Budapest he returned to Belgrade and served the Karadjordje administration until the collapse of the revolt in 1813, when, like his leader, he crossed into Austrian territory. For the remaining fifty years of his life Vienna was the main centre of his activities.[57] Here he began his two great works – the reform of the Serbian language and the publication of his collections of Serbian folk literature. One of the great influences on him during the early years in Vienna was the Slovene scholar Jernej Kopitar (1780–1844), who was the imperial censor for Slavonic languages.

> It was in fact principally Kopitar's literary programme that Vuk carried out from 1814 until his death fifty years later . . . The literary programme, as expounded in one of Kopitar's letters to Vuk, comprised a grammar and dictionary of the 'popular' Serb language – the former to illustrate the rules of popular speech, the latter to illustrate popular usage by copious examples; also the collection and publication of 'popular songs' which were to bring Vuk much fame abroad even during his lifetime, and of folk tales and proverbs . . . By 1864 Vuk had completed the tasks laid down for him by Kopitar.[58]

Vuk's first published works appeared in Vienna in 1814 – a

song book and a grammar. The first edition of his dictionary appeared in 1818, and a greatly enlarged and revised edition of it in 1852.

Much of Vuk's work had a hostile reception in his native Serbia, especially from the leaders of the Orthodox Church, and the 1852 edition of his dictionary was banned by Prince Alexander Karadjordjević. Despite the opposition, however, he came to be regarded as the father of modern Serbian. He described his grammar as being that 'of the Serbian language as spoken by the common people', and in his dictionary 'he included only words which he himself had heard, or which his main sources guaranteed to be part of current speech in their various districts'.[59] In laying the foundations for a standard Serbian language he favoured 'the dialect of central Hercegovina, where, in his view, the purest popular language had been spoken, and as being the dialect in which he heard the best popular songs collected by him'.[60]

The alphabet that Vuk devised is the form of Cyrillic still in use in Yugoslavia.[61] It is entirely phonetic and contains thirty letters, compared with the forty used in the modified form of the Old Slavonic orthography used by the Church. Kopitar had earlier produced a phonetic Latin alphabet for Slovene.

The Yugoslav movement in the Habsburg Empire

Vuk's work in standardising Cyrillic orthography also encouraged Ljudevit Gaj (1809–72) in Zagreb to produce a phonetic alphabet for Croatian. Gaj was a protagonist of the Illyrian Movement and believed in an 'Illyrian' language group comprising the main Yugoslav languages. By the middle of the nineteenth century it was possible for Serbian and Croatian writers to acknowledge the existence of a common literary language, with two main variants, each using its own phonetic alphabet which reflected the speech forms of the ordinary people.[62] Vuk, however, was sceptical of the so-called 'Illyrian' language. In 1836 he wrote: 'The name, too, is one of the big difficulties. It is hard to induce them to acknowledge that they are Serbs, and we would be crazy if we agreed to abandon our famous name and to adopt another one which is dead and to-day has no meaning in itself'.[63]

Although Vuk's work contributed to the creation among

educated people of the notion of a common Yugoslav cultural community, the mass of the people were not deeply affected by this concept. Vague feelings of South Slav solidarity were less potent than the more sharply defined Serbian nationalism, focused on the emerging Serbian independent state and buttressed by loyalty to the Orthodox Church.

Croatia

The point of departure for the Yugoslav movement which developed in the Habsburg lands of Croatia–Slavonia, Slovenia and Dalmatia during the nineteenth century was the Napoleonic occupation of 1809. For a brief period of four years western Croatia, Dalmatia and the Slovene provinces of Austria were joined under one authority in the Illyrian Provinces. The population included Serbs,[64] Croats and Slovenes, and the experience of sharing a common political unit stimulated the dreamers to think of a more permanent form of union that would embrace at least all the South Slavs in the Monarchy. After the defeat of Napoleon Austria was allowed to occupy Dalmatia,[65] thus bringing all the territories of the Illyrian Provinces under the Habsburg sceptre.

The Illyrian Movement, which grew up during the first half of the nineteenth century, was at first primarily a linguistic and cultural manifestation of a handful of educated Slavs. In Slovenia it was led by poets like Kopitar and Prešeren.[66] In Croatia it was Ljudevit Gaj who promoted the idea of an 'Illyrian' language, and who advocated the union of south Slavs in his journal *Illyrian News*.

The crisis of 1848 within the Monarchy ultimately strengthened the South Slav movement and gave it a more political character. Three weeks after Lájos Kossuth's defiant address to the Hungarian Diet in March 1848 the Croats summoned an assembly in Zagreb and submitted a series of demands to the Emperor which included the establishment of a Croat national unit within the Monarchy, under the governorship of the Croat Josip Jelačić, which would comprise Croatia–Slavonia, the Military Frontier and Dalmatia. The Emperor appointed Jelačić as governor (*ban*) although he did not concede the demand for an autonomous Slav unit within the Empire. The Croats responded by supporting the emperor when, with

Russian help, he crushed the Magyar rebellion in 1849.[67] For a brief period after 1849 it seemed as if the Croats might receive from the Emperor a just reward for their assistance, when Croatia–Slavonia was detached from Hungary and given an outlet to the sea at Fiume (Rijeka).[68]

Croat illusions were soon dispelled. The Croats were first denied any effective self-rule by the Austrians, and later, in 1867, when Austria made its peace with Hungary by establishing the Dual Monarchy, the Croats were returned to Hungarian rule. The *Nagoda* or Agreement of 1868 between Hungary and Croatia, which was accepted by a managed Croatian *sabor*, paid lip service to the existence of a Croatian national entity, and recognised that eventually the Military Frontier[69] and Dalmatia would belong to Croatia. The Croats felt betrayed by the Austrians and bitterly resented the oppressive rule of the Hungarians. It was natural that they should look again at the possibilities of an autonomous Slav unit – at first within the Monarchy, later outside it.

The great figure in this new movement was Bishop Strossmayer (1815–1905). His vision was far wider than merely the creation of a Croat national unit: he saw the possibility of making Zagreb a focus for Yugoslav culture, bridging the gaps between Serb and Croat, Orthodox and Catholic. In 1867 he founded the South Slav Academy of Arts and Sciences in Zagreb, and in 1874 the University of Zagreb. After 1881 the Serb element in Croatia was increased by the incorporation of the Military Frontier,[70] and Strossmayer believed that reconciliation between Serbs and Croats was vital to the future of the Slav peoples. His Yugoslav policy was opposed by the extreme Croat nationalists – including many Catholic priests – who dreamed of a Greater Croatia.

The Yugoslav solution gradually won adherents, despite the efforts of the Hungarian governor, Khuen-Hédervåry[71] to set the two communities against each other. In 1905, shortly after Strossmayer's death, the Serb and Croat deputies in Croatia, Istria and Dalmatia began to talk of formulating a joint programme that included the demand for a union of Dalmatia and Croatia.[72] The fragile solidarity of the Serbs and Croats was strengthened in 1908 by the crude attempt of the Hungarians to arraign some fifty prominent Serbs on charges of 'treason'.

Slovenia

Whilst the Croats were struggling to find a way to gain greater national freedom either within or outside the Monarchy, the Slovenes showed little inclination to support them until the Zagreb trials of 1908 and the Austrian annexation of Bosnia in the same year. Under Austrian rule the Slovenes, despite periods of Germanisation, had gradually established cultural and political rights for themselves within the Province of Carniola, which was overwhelmingly Slovene in its national composition. They were less successful in Styria, where the 400,000 Slovenes formed less than a third of the population, or in Görz-Gradisca, where the 150,000 Slovenes comprised two-thirds of the inhabitants. Until the eve of the collapse of the Monarchy most Slovene leaders demanded no more than political and cultural autonomy under the Habsburgs. Although they might feel some sympathy for the Catholic Croats, they had no interest in a union with the Orthodox Serbs.

During the late nineteenth and early twentieth centuries Slovene particularism had replaced the earlier Illyrian ideals as the objective of the rising Slovene middle classes. They had already made headway in local government and in education. There were adequate Slovene-language elementary schools, although higher education was still dominated by Germans. In 1882 Slovene representatives gained a majority of the seats on the Laibach (Ljubljana) Municipal Council, and a year later they captured the Landtag of Carniola. The majority of priests, schoolmasters and local officials were Slovene speakers by the end of the century, and Slovenes were beginning to make inroads into the previously German-dominated commercial and professional life of the towns. Many educated Slovenes felt that they had more to gain by pressing for Slovene autonomy within the Monarchy than by chasing the chimeras of Illyrianism, and still less by exchanging Austro-German for Serbian domination.

The shift of opinion came in two stages. First there was a move towards a union of the South Slavs under Habsburg rule, and then to an acceptance of a South Slav state formed by a union of the Kingdoms of Serbia and Montenegro with the Slavs of the Monarchy. In the spring of 1917 their spokesman in the Reichsrat in Vienna, Mgr Korošec, demanded 'the unification of all districts of the Monarchy inhabited by Slovenes, Croats and Serbs in an autonomous State, free from any national domination, resting on a democratic basis, under the sceptre of the House of Habsburg–Lorraine'. This was the furthest that the Slovene leaders were prepared to go in public at this stage, and it probably represented the private view also at this time, although there had been contacts between Korošec and the Yugoslav leaders in exile.

The Serbs, Croats and Slovenes were finally brought together in a South Slav State because the circumstances surrounding the collapse of the Habsburg Monarchy in 1918 excluded any other solution that would enable the Yugoslav peoples to enjoy the self-determination to which they aspired. Serbia had gained great prestige by her successes in the Balkan Wars. The events leading up to the assassination in Sarajevo and Austria–Hungary's subsequent declaration of war had further enhanced Serbia's role as the champion of the South Slavs against their foreign rulers. Left to themselves the Slovenes and the Dalmatians would have been the prey of Italian designs. The Montenegrins, deserted by their king in the hour of their defeat in 1916, were also vulnerable to foreign pressure, and looked to their Serbian brothers for salvation.

Bosnia

There was undoubtedly genuine enthusiasm for the Yugoslav idea, and during the decade before the outbreak of the First World War this enthusiasm had permeated from the liberal intelligentsia to the masses. The romantic Illyrianism of the nineteenth century was translated into practical politics in a remarkably short time. Its development was greatly encouraged by the behaviour of the Austro–Hungarians, especially in Bosnia and Hercegovina. This area, which had been placed under Austrian military occupation in 1878, contained a mixture of South Slav peoples. The largest single group comprised those of Serbian origin, who formed over 40 per cent of the population. Another 32 per cent were Moslems, most of whom were Slav descendants of the Bogomil heretics who had accepted Islam after the Turkish occupation of the fifteenth century. The third important group were the Catholics – many of Croatian origin – who constituted over a fifth of the inhabitants.[73] Austrian policy was to foster the inherent divisions amongst the Bosnians and to discourage any growth of Pan-Slav feeling.[74]

The unilateral decision of the Austrian government in October 1908 that Bosnia–Hercegovina was to be annexed, may have made little practical difference to the Bosnians,[75] but the psychological impact was of crucial importance. It was seen by the Serbs both in Bosnia and Serbia as a hostile act, directed against the Kingdom of Serbia, and it offended the Moslems by repudiating Turkish claims to sovereignty. Even the Croats were displeased, as the annexation raised the possibility of an intensification of Germanising influence from Vienna.

After 1908 the activities of Slav dissidents in Bosnia were intensified and were covertly supported by the Serbian government. Many Bosnians crossed into Serbia and Montenegro to join the armies of the two South Slav kingdoms during the Balkan Wars of 1912–13. The aspirations of young Bosnians turned increasingly to the idea of a Yugoslav state under Serbian leadership.

In June 1914 the Austrians decided to make a provocative military display in Sarajevo, culminating in an official visit of the heir to the throne, Gavrilo Princip, one of a group of young Bosnian Serbs, succeeded in assassinating Franz Ferdinand and his wife during their drive from a civic reception at the town hall. Austria–Hungary seized on this incident as an excuse for war with Serbia, and within a few weeks all Europe was aflame. By initiating the events that led to the First World War, the young Bosnian sealed the fate of the Monarchy and prepared the way for the emergence of the first Yugoslav state.

THE FIRST WORLD WAR

The Serbian army at first held out against the Austrians. Their losses during the winter of 1914–15 were more from a typhus outbreak, which carried off 150,000 people, than from the enemy. In the autumn of 1915 however Von Mackenson led a German force across the Danube, and simultaneously the Bulgarians invaded Macedonia. The ineffectual efforts of the British and French to establish a bridgehead at Salonika for an advance along the Vardar–Morava route into Serbia brought no relief to the Serbs and their Montenegrin allies. The tattered remnants of the Serbian army struggled across Kosovo and Montenegro to reach the Adriatic in Albania. After delays occasioned by the unfeeling malice of the Italians in command at Valona, the survivors were taken to Corfu. By July a force of 100,000 was moving into Salonika to support the Anglo-French forces. After establishing a foothold around Bitola in southern Macedonia, at a cost of 27,000 casualties, they remained stationary until the end of 1918, when they were able to advance in company with their allies and to take Belgrade a few days before the German surrender on 11 November.

In 1915 the King and his government retreated with the army and established themselves in Corfu. A number of prominent Slavs from the Habsburg lands also fled abroad, where they formed a Yugoslav Committee in exile. During the war the Slovene and Croat delegates continued to participate in the Habsburg parliaments in Vienna and Budapest. Although they pressed for a union of the South Slavs within the Monarchy, to form an autonomous state under the Habsburg crown, they also maintained contact with the Yugoslav Committee, which believed in an independent South Slav state under Serbian leadership. The news that the secret Treaty of London (April 1915) promised the cession to Italy of Habsburg lands in Dalmatia and the Julian region, a majority of whose inhabitants were Slavs, was received with dismay by the Yugoslavs. Italy entered the war as a result of the London Treaty, and moved her troops into the areas that had been promised to her. The fierce resistance of the Slovene troops on the Isonzo front, which contributed to the Italian debacle at Caporetto, showed what the Slavs felt about the Allied intention to give away pieces of their homeland. In 1917 the Serbian government in exile and the Yugoslav Committee joined to sign the Pact of Corfu, which called for a Serb–Croat–Slovene state under the Karadjordjević dynasty.

The Croats within the Monarchy, led by the newly appointed *ban*, Anton Mihailović, responded to the call of their exiled brothers in Corfu and declared their support for the Yugoslav idea. Even the peasant leader Stjepan Radić and the nationalist Pavelić (later leader of the *ustaše*) were Yugoslavs in 1917. The Slovene leader Korošec called for 'liberation from the Germans' and for an 'independent Yugoslav state within the

Monarchy'. A few months later he dropped the phrase 'within the Monarchy' and organised a Yugoslav National Council (*Narodno Vijeće*) which openly supported the Corfu agreement.

In September 1918, the Council moved its headquarters from Ljubljana to Zagreb and, with growing support from all political parties, soon developed into a *de facto* government for the South Slav provinces of the Monarchy. In October the Croatian Diet dissolved the union with Hungary and accepted the authority of the National Council. The Council in its turn declared in favour of a union of the territories under its control with the Kingdom of Serbia to form a democratic Yugoslav state 'from the Isonzo to Salonika'. When the Habsburg Emperor Charles sued for peace he handed over his Yugoslav territories to the National Council, and much to the annoyance of the Italians he allowed his fleet in the Adriatic – many of whose sailors were Dalmatians – to surrender to the Yugoslavs rather than to the Italians.

Whilst developments within the Monarchy moved rapidly towards a successful Yugoslav conclusion, all was not well in the camp of the exiles. The Yugoslav Committee, led by Trumbić, Supilo and Meštrović,[76] represented the Dalmatian Croats. The other party to the Pact of Corfu was the Serbian government in exile, led by its premier, Nikola Pašić. Although both groups had agreed to a Yugoslav state under the Serbian monarchy, the Pact of Corfu left open many questions concerning the form of the state. It proposed a parliamentary monarchy in which the three main religions – Roman Catholic, Orthodox and Moslem – and the three national groups – Slovenes, Croats and Serbs – would have equal status. It did not however decide whether the new state was to have a federal or a centralist constitution.

Another issue between the Yugoslavs and the Allied Powers that was unsettled even after 1918 concerned the frontiers of the new state. The Yugoslav Committee participated in the 'Congress of Oppressed Nationalities', held in Rome in April 1918, and appeared to have gained recognition for the idea of a Yugoslav state even from the Italians. The Italians, however, had territorial designs on Dalmatia which conflicted with the aspirations of the Yugoslavs, and these had been given Allied sanction by the Treaty of London in 1915. If the Yugoslav

Committee and the Serbian government had stood together in 1918, as they appeared to have done at Corfu in 1917, they would have had a better chance of persuading the Italians to moderate their demands. It was well known, however, that the Pan-Serb ambitions of Pašić were creating disunity amongst the Yugoslavs, and the Italians were able at the end of the war to go back on the understanding reached at Rome in April, and to demand the full implementation of the terms of the Treaty of London.

Thus, the rift between the Serbs and Croats, which has caused so much distress to the Yugoslavs since 1918, was already appearing as a source of weakness even before the creation of the new state.

NOTES

1 J. S. Huxley and A. C. Haddon, *We Europeans* (London 1939), p. 19.

2 Although when Pope Alexander III visited Zadar in 1177 and attended Mass at the church of Sv. Stošija, he wrote of 'Immensis laudibus et canticis in eorum sclavica lingua' – quoted by Zvane Črnja in *Kulturna Historija Hrvatske* (Zagreb 1965), p. 128.

3 Croat historians claim that it reached from Istria to the mouth of the Neretva along the coast, and inland to the Drava in the north and the upper Drina in the south. 'Granice Kraljevine Hrvatske i Dalmacije dopirale su tada do Raše, Neretve, Drine, Bosne, Drave, Mure i Kupe . . .' Črnja in *Kulturna Historija Hrvatske*, p. 124.

4 The crowning of St Stephen (István) on Christmas Day, AD 1000, symbolised Hungary's adherence to the western Church.

5 C. A. Macartney gives 1106 in *Hungary: A Short History* (Edinburgh 1962), p. 22.

6 E.g. when the Croatian *sabor* assented to the Pragmatic Sanction in 1712, it declared: 'Neither force nor conquest united us to the Hungarians, but by our spontaneous and free desire we submitted ourselves not to the Kingdom but to their King'.

7 In 1527, after the Hungarian defeat at Mohács, the Sabor voted the crown to Ferdinand of Austria.

8 Dubrovnik was an independent city-state until Napoleonic times.

9 Kiril died in Rome in 869 and Metodije in 885 in Vojvodina.

10 Known as *Prvovenčani* ('the first crowned').

11 The Zeta is a Montenegrin river which joins the Morača near Titograd, five miles north of the mouth of the Morača, which flows into Lake Skadar. Duklija is the Slav name for the Roman town of Doclea, near the site of modern Titograd.

12 *Knez* – prince.

13 Orthodox bishops take a vow of celibacy, although other priests may

marry. Between 1696 and 1851 the *vladikas* were usually succeeded by their nephews.

14 The acceptance of Islam in preference to Rome was noticed also amongst the Greek Orthodox clergy elsewhere in the Balkans. In Voltaire's phrase, they 'preferred the turban of a Turkish priest[sic] to the red hat of a Roman cardinal'.

15 Dr S. Dimevski, 'The Archbishopric of Ohrid', in *From the Past of the Macedonian People* (Skopje 1969), pp. 55–72.

16 E.g. the great historian of the Byzantines, G. Ostrogorsky (see his *History of the Byzantine State* [Oxford 1956], pp. 267–75).

17 Known as 'Bulgaroktonos', the Bulgar-slayer.

18 He blinded all the prisoners save one in every hundred, and the sighted were forced to lead their blind comrades back to Prilep, where Samuilo awaited them. He is reputed to have died of shock on seeing his stricken army.

19 Examples of the work of the 'Macedonian School' can be seen today at Nerezi, near Skopje, and in the monasteries around Ohrid.

20 The Ohrid Archbishopric came under the Bulgarian Exarchate in 1874.

21 It is not clear whether this 'Slav' school was Serbian or Bulgarian.

22 H. Baerlein, *The Birth of Yugoslavia* (London 1922), p. 169.

23 Tome Sazdov, 'The Macedonian revival and Grigor Prličev', in *Macedonian Review*, 1 (1970), p. 63.

24 Blagoja Korubin, 'The formation of the Macedonian literary language', in *Macedonian Review*, 1 (1970), p. 56.

25 Korubin, in *MR*, 1, p. 57.

26 The phrase was used by Gladstone in his Midlothian campaign of 1879–80, and is still gratefully remembered by Macedonian nationalists as the first sign of international recognition of their cause.

27 Hristo Andonov-Poljanski, 'Goče Delčev and his views', in *Macedonian Review*, 1, (1971), p. 23.

28 Andonov-Poljanski, *MR*, 1, p. 20.

29 Now celebrated as Macedonia's national day.

30 An English text of the Kruševo Declaration appears in G. Nurigiani, *Macedonia Yesterday and To-day* (Rome 1967), pp. 44–6.

31 The name was changed under the 1963 constitution to that of the Socialist Republic of Macedonia, in keeping with the change of Yugoslavia's title from that of Federal People's Republic to Federal Socialist Republc.

32 With encouragement from the government, the Macedonian Church achieved *de facto* independence of the Serbian Patriarchate in 1958. It formally declared its autocephalus status in July 1967, despite the rejection of its claims by the Serbian Church. See Chapter 8.

33 The non-Slav groups will be treated separately.

34 The Janissaries (*Yeniçeri* – new troops) were originally a *corps d'élite* of the Sultan's army, raised from the sons of Christian subjects who were abducted from their parents and brought up as Moslems.

35 The Seyhu'l-Islam (the Chief Mufti) pronounced it lawful to depose Selim because of his reforms, and the Janissaries carried out his wishes.

36 The Hatisherif confirmed Turkish promises made under Russian pressure in the Treaty of Bucharest (1812), the Convention of Ackerman (1826) and the Treaty of Adrianople (1829). Serbia became a self-governing principality within the Ottoman Empire, under the hereditary rule of the Obrenović dynasty. The Turkish garrison in Belgrade remained, and the status of the Russians as guarantors of Serbian independence was recognised.

37 Known as the Miletin Rising, after its leader Mileta Radojković.

38 The 'Sretenje' Constitution.

39 *Ustavobranitelji.*

40 Formerly Russia had the sole right to 'protect' the Serbs.

41 'Patriotic Serbs complained that the Austrian Consul-General might as well have been a minister without portfolio in the Serbian Cabinet.' H. L. Lorimer, in *Yugoslavia*, ed. John Buchan (London 1923), p. 51.

42 Mihailo went to Constantinople to receive the keys to the Turkish forts, although he had to acknowledge the nominal suzerainty of the Sultan, symbolised by the flying of the Turkish colours alongside those of Serbia above the citadel of Kalemegdan.

43 Admiralty Handbook, *Jugoslavia*, (London, 1944), I., p. 106.

44 Gladstone was moved to a fierce attack on Beaconsfield's pro-Turkish policy in his pamphlet *The Bulgarian Horrors and the Eastern Auestion.*

45 'The events in Bulgaria had "completely destroyed sympathy with Turkey" and rendered British intervention against a Russian declaration of war "practically impossible".' Reference to a letter from Lord Beaconsfield to Sir Henry Elliott, British Ambassador in Constantinople, quoted by R. C. K. Ensor in *England 1870–1914* (Oxford 1952), p. 44.

46 Salisbury, the British Foreign Secretary, wrote afterwards: 'We shall set up a rickety sort of Turkish rule again, south of the Balkans. But it is a mere respite. There is no vitality left in them'. Minute of 29 December 1878, quoted by B. H. Sumner, *Russia and the Balkans 1870–80* (London 1967).

47 The San Stefano settlement had provided for an autonomous Christian province of Bosnia.

48 Austrian military occupation of the Sandžak drove a wedge between Montenegro and Serbia.

49 The Austrian control of the Sandžak provided another step on the all-German route to the east which the protagonists of the *drang nach osten* dreamed, but it killed Serbian hopes of a Belgrade to Bar route. The Belgrade–Bar railway is now (1975) under construction in socialits Yugoslavia.

50 The Serbian claim to 'South Serbia' (i.e. Macedonia) was rejected at Berlin.

51 Marković, who died in 1875, was one of the early advocates of a Balkan Federation.

52 One of the earliest writers of the Dalmatian Renaissance, Marko Marulić, from Split (1450–1524), wrote in both Latin and Croatian, and the last significant figures were the great Ragusan dramatists Ivan Gundulić (1588–1638) and Dzivo Bunić (1591–1658). 'The

Dalmatian literary movement did not radiate to other parts of the country . . . and literature did not grow into a national movement until the nineteenth century.' *Admiralty Handbook*, (London 1944), I., p. 313.

53 The literary language was a Russianised form of Church Slavonic, which was kept alive by the Orthodox monasteries both in the Vojvodina and in Serbia Proper.

54 Hopovo was in the Austrian province of Srem. In both Srem and in the Hungarian-occupied Vojvodina, Serbian culture flourished during the long period of Turkish occupation of Serbia Proper.

55 He also spent six months in a German language school before returning to Serbia in 1807.

56 He suffered from arthritis.

57 He did not live continuously in Vienna, but he always returned there from his visits – often lengthy – to Buda, Belgrade, Russia, Germany and Montenegro. He died in Vienna in 1864.

58 Sir Duncan Wilson, *The Life and Times of Vuk Stefanović Karadžić* (Oxford 1970), p. 3. I am also indebted to Sir Duncan Wilson's book for much of the foregoing material on Vuk.

59 Wilson, *The Life and Times of Karadžić*, p. 331.

60 Wilson, *Life and Times of Karadžić*, p. 389. The dialect of Hercegovina was in the *ijekavski* form of *štokavski*.

61 Macedonian Cyrillic contains some letters not used in Serbian.

62 Serbian and Croatian writers reaffirmed this standpoint in the Novi Sad agreement of 1954, but this was later repudiated by the Croats in the *Deklaracija* of 1967.

63 Quoted by Wilson, *Life and Times of Karadžić*, p. 301.

64 The numbers of Serbs in the area at the time of the Illyrian Provinces is difficult to estimate. In 1910 there were over 100,000 Serbs in Dalmatia, and there were also Serbian colonies in the Military Frontier areas of Croatia.

65 From the fifteenth century until the extinction of the Venetian Republic by Napoleon in 1797, the coastal cities of Dalmatia were under Venetian rule, and parts of the interior were under the Turks. Ragusa (Dubrovnik) remained independent until seized by the French in 1805. Ragusa was included in the Illyrian Provinces and was handed over to Austria with the rest of Dalmatia.

66 Kopitar's relations with Vuk Karadžic are referred to on p. 52 above. France Prešeren (1800–49) was perhaps the greatest of the poets to write in Slovene, but he was not the first. Valentin Vodnik (1758–1819) laid the foundations for the Slovene literary revival.

67 Jelačić led 40,000 Croat troops against the Hungarians.

68 Fiume was first given to Hungary by Maria Theresa in 1779. Between 1809 and 1814 it was in the Illyrian Provinces. From 1814 it was under Austrian rule until 1822, when it was handed over to Hungary again. In 1868, as part of the *Nagoda*, it was restored to Hungary.

69 The Military Frontier was relinquished by Austria in 1881, but Dalmatia remained Austrian until the collapse of the Monarchy in 1918.

70 Even today there is a Serbian majority in many of the communes within

the former Military Frontier zone: e.g. Dvor, 88·4 per cent Serb; Vrgin Most, 75·9 per cent Serb; Kostajnica, 63·5 per cent Serb; Obrovac, 60 per cent Serb; Glina, 59·8 per cent Serb (census returns for 1971).

71 Khuen-Hedérváry was *ban* of Croatia from 1883 to 1903.

72 The Croat deputies declared their intentions in 'The Resolution of Fiume', and the Serbs indicated their support in a separate 'Resolution of Zara', ten days later.

73 The 1879 and 1910 censuses gave the following figures of population, according to religious persuasion, for Bosnia and Hercegovina:

	1879	*1910*	*Percentage of total 1910 population*
Orthodox	496,485	825,418	43·5
Moslem	448,613	612,137	32·4
Catholic	209,391	434,061	22·8
Others		26,346	1·3

74 Baron von Kállay, the governor of Bosnia between 1882 and 1903, even banned the circulation of his own work, *The History of the Serbs*, because in it he had stated that the Bosnians formed part of the Serb race.

75 It led to the grant of a constitution in 1910 which created a legislature elected by adult male suffrage, but without power, thereby opening the door to political activity without satisfying the demand for responsible government.

76 Dr Ante Trumbić was mayor of Split before the war, and had been a member of the Austrian Reichsrat. He became foreign minister of the new state in 1919–20. Dr Franjo Supilo was a journalist from Rijeka (Fiume) and a former member of the Croatian and Habsburg Diets. He died in 1917. Ivan Meštrović, who came of Dalmatian peasant stock, became a world famous sculptor and died in the United States in 1962.

5 The Kingdom of Yugoslavia

The Kingdom of Serbs, Croats and Slovenes was proclaimed on 1 December 1918 by Alexander Karadjordjević, acting as regent for his father, King Peter of Serbia. The proclamation was supported by the National Council in Zagreb. A week earlier, on 26 November, the Montenegrins had deposed King Nikola and voted to join Serbia.

The frontiers of the new state were not finally agreed upon until 1924, when the Yugoslavs dropped their claims to Fiume (Rijeka), but the main lines were settled by 1920. The result of the actions of the Yugoslavs and the work of the Allied peacemakers of Versailles was to produce a state composed of disparate elements, brought together by force of circumstances into a shotgun marriage. The realities of the situation left the Serbs, Croats and Slovenes with no viable alternative but to unite, and although their leaders genuinely wanted the union to succeed, there were strong underlying tensions between them, which soon came to the surface. The new state was composed of the following elements:

(1) the Kingdom of Serbia, with a population of 3,350,000, of whom 550,000 were Macedonians who had been under Serbian rule only since the end of the Balkan Wars in 1913;

(2) the Kingdom of Montenegro, with a population of 250,000, most of whom were Serbian in speech but who had a long tradition of independence. Montenegro had enlarged its territory in 1913 and had acquired 80,000 Moslem Albanians from the Sandžak of Novi Pazar, which was partitioned between Serbia and Montenegro at the end of the Balkan Wars;

(3) Croatia–Slavonia, a former province of Hungary, which had acquired a measure of autonomy during the late nineteenth century. Croatia–Slavonia covered the Sava valley, from Srem to Zagreb, and included a frontage on the Adriatic between Fiume (Rijeka) and Zara (Zadar). It contained 1,638,000 Croats and 645,000 Serbs;

(4) the former Austrian province of Dalmatia, which stretched for over two hundred miles along the Adriatic coast from Zadar to Kotor, and included many of the offshore islands and the cities of Šibenik, Split and Dubrovnik. Dalmatia had a mixed population of Serbs and Croats amounting to 611,000 in all;

(5) the former Austrian province of Carniola (Krain) and parts of Styria (Steiermark), Carinthia (Kärnten) and Istria. In these areas Slovenes made up the overwhelming majority of the one million inhabitants, but there were significant German-speaking minorities in the Styrian towns of Marburg (Maribor) and Cilli (Celje) and in Gottschee (Kočevje) in South Carniola. On the other hand there were some 300,000 Slovenes left in the Julian Region and Istria, which went to Italy, and in the Klagenfurt (Celovec) area of Carinthia, which remained in Austria;

(6) the former Hungarian districts of Baranja and Bačka, part of the Banat (which was divided between Romania and Yugoslavia), and two small areas near the confluence of the Mur (Mura) and Drava rivers, Prekomurje and Medjumurje. The last two had a mixed Slovene, Croat and Magyar population, and the others a complicated ethnic structure, in which Magyars formed the largest single group, but by no means an overall majority;[1]

(7) Bosnia–Hercegovina, a former Habsburg province, occupied by the Monarchy in 1878 and formally annexed in 1908. The 1910 Austrian census records 823,000 Serbs, 400,000 Croats and 610,000 Moslems of Slav speech. This last group is composed of the descendants of Slavs who embraced Islam during the 400 years of Turkish rule before the Austrian occupation of 1878.

In 1919, by the Treaty of Neuilly, Bulgaria ceded four small areas along the Macedonian and Serbian borders, the largest of which was the Strumica salient near the meeting place of the Greek, Bulgarian and Yugoslav frontiers. These accessions gave Yugoslavia an extra few thousand citizens of Bulgarian origin.

The first Yugoslav census of 1921 records twelve linguistic groups with over 10,000 representatives. Serbs, Croats and Slovenes comprised almost 10 million of the 12 million inhabitants. Five other non-Slav groups each had 150,000 or more members. The largest were the Germans (505,000), of whom 316,000 were in the Vojvodina and the majority of the others in Slovenia. The Magyars with 467,000, also mainly in the Vojvodina, were the second largest non-Slav group, followed by the Albanians (439,000), the Romanians (231,000) and the Turks (150,000). It should have been noted that the kingdom did not recognise the separate existence of the Macedonians, either as a linguistic or national group, and that as the classification was based on linguistic criteria, it does not distinguish between such Slav-speaking groups as the Bosnian Moslems or the Montenegrins. The census figures for religious groups give a slightly different picture. Five and a half million are recorded as being of Orthodox faith – this will have included most Serbs, Montenegrins and Macedonians – and 4,700,000 as Roman Catholic – Slovenes, Croats and Magyars. The only other group with over a million adherents were the Moslems, with 1,345,000. This included most Albanians and Turks, and the Bosnian Moslems.

FRONTIER PROBLEMS

For the first two years of its life the new state was deeply involved with two vital matters – its territorial limits and its form of government. The frontier problems were not capable of being solved by the Yugoslavs alone. The Allied Powers had made various agreements between themselves during the course of the First World War which assumed the continued existence of the Habsburg Monarchy in some form, even after the defeat of the Central Powers. The creation of a Yugoslav state by the union of Serbia and Montenegro with the Slav territories of the Monarchy did not appear on the agenda until the Corfu Declaration of 1917. The new state was to be a 'constitutional, democratic and parliamentary monarchy', uniting Serbs, Croats and Slovenes under the Karadjordjevć dynasty. Equality was to be accorded to the Latin and Cyrillic alphabets, and the three main religious groups – Orthodox, Catholic and Moslem – were to enjoy equal rights. The Italians reeling from their defeat on the Isonzo front at the hands of Marshal Boroević, came to an agreement with the Yugoslav Committee, and Woodrow Wilson incorporated the Yugoslav idea into his Fourteen Points.

Despite these favourable developments the Yugoslavs were by no means united on a number of essential questions when the war ended. The three main groups were the Serbian government in exile under Pašić; the Yugoslav Committee under Trumbić; and the National Council (*Narodno Vijeće*), composed of Slav deputies to the Vienna parliament, led by Mgr Korošec.

In the circumstances it is understandable that the Allies in 1915 should have ignored the possibility of a South Slav state when they signed the Secret Treaty of London, which assigned to Italy some 750,000 Yugoslavs as an inducement to persuade her to break the Triple Alliance and to enter the war on the Allied side. The Treaty gave Italy the Austrian province of Küstenland, which included Istria, Trieste, and Gorizia, part of western Carniola, the Zara region of Dalmatia, and most of the Dalmatian islands. These territories all belonged to the Habsburg domain at the beginning of the war, and it was considered fair dealing to take them from the enemy as a reward to an ally, regardless of the wishes of the inhabitants of the areas to be transferred. When the war came to an end there was a new claimant, the infant Yugoslav state, whose case was at least based on the principle of national self-determination,[2] rather than that of *sacro egiosmo*, which the Italians embraced. At Versailles the Adriatic question provoked a serious disagreement amongst the Allies, and the Italian delegates withdrew for a time from the Peace Conferance in protest against Woodrow Wilson's pro-Yugoslav attitude. Eventually Italy and Yugoslavia negotiated directly and reached an agreement,[3] which assigned Istria and the Julian Region to Italy but reduced the Italian claims in Dalmatia to Zara and the island of Lagosta (Lastovo). The Fiume problem was also settled by direct negotiation, after the Allies had failed to enforce their solution – a Free City – against the Italian adventurer D'Annunzio, who seized the port in the name of Italy. In 1924 the Yugoslavs recognised the *fait accompli* of Italian occupation and abandoned their claims to Fiume.

The Slovenes were forced to accept not only the loss of the Julian Region to Italy, but also of the Slovene-speaking areas of Carinthia to Austria. In this case the Allies conducted a plebiscite in October 1920 in the Klagenfurt region, where there was a mixed Slovene and Austrian population. The vote favoured Austria, and the frontier was fixed along the watershed of the Karavanke, leaving many Slovene-speaking villages in Austria.

The frontiers with Hungary were determined by the Treaty of Trianon (June 1920), which gave the Yugoslavs many Magyar-speaking areas in Bačka, Baranja, Prekomurje and Medjumurje. The extreme Yugoslav claim to the mining town of Pecs (Funfkirchen) was not allowed, and the Yugoslav army withdrew under protest in August 1921.

The secret Treaty of London was not the only such pact made between the Allies to hand over parts of the Habsburg Empire to their friends. Romania had also, like Italy, received a promise of territory – the Banat – as a reward for entering the war on the Allied side. Romania was less troublesome than Italy, however, and agreed to give up her claim to the whole of the Banat. Yugoslavia acquired the greater part of the area, and with it 75,000 Romanians, by an award of the Peace Conference in June 1919, a year which also saw the final settlement of Yugoslav claims against Bulgaria by the terms of the Treaty of Neuilly (November 1919).

The Albanian frontier dispute was also a legacy from the Balkan Wars. In November 1912 Albanian independence was proclaimed at Valona, and this was recognised by the European powers at a conference of ambassadors held in London in 1913 under the chairmanship of the British foreign secretary, Earl Grey. The frontiers of the new state corresponded roughly to those of today,[4] thus leaving over 400,000 Albanians in Serbia's newly acquired territories. Serbia had long hoped for an outlet on the Adriatic, through territory awarded to Albania, but largely under Austrian pressure the ambassadors agreed to recognise an independent Albania. During the First World War Albania was occupied first by the Central Powers and later by the Allies. The Secret Treaty of London (1915) assigned to Montenegro or Serbia[5] the northern Albanian zone. Italy was to receive 'full sovereignty over Valona, the Island of Saseno and surrounding territory sufficient to ensure the defence of these points' (Article 6).[6] Italy was also given a virtual protectorate over 'the independent Moslem state of Albania' which would remain when the Slavs and the Italians had received their shares. The Italians, who were in occupation of large areas of Albanian territory at the end of the war, could not wait until the Allies at Versailles had determined whether or not fully to implement the London treaty. Their occupation was, however, resisted by the Albanians, and fighting broke out in 1920. At the same time the Yugoslavs and Greeks took advantage of the situation to press their claims, and in 1921 Yugoslav troops occupied some areas in the north.[7]

In September 1921 a conference of ambassadors in Paris reaffirmed both Albanian independence and 'Italy's right to intervene there in the name of the Allied Powers, in the event of the League of Nations being unable to ensure Albania's independence'.[8] Britain, whilst accepting Albanian independence, entered a reservation in favour of Yugoslavia's claims in the Prizren and Debar (Dibra) regions, but Italy abandoned her claims to Valona and to a protectorate and reverted to 'the text agreed on in 1913'.[9]

However, all was not settled, for the Yugoslavs and Greeks continued to interfere in Albanian affairs. In 1923 the League received the report of a commission of inquiry that Albania's foreign relations with her neighbour were satisfactory.[10] It was not, however, until 1926 that final agreement was reached concerning the Yugoslav–Albanian border. The final delimitations scarcely satisfied the principle of self-determination for the Albanians, especially as the 400,000 Albanians left under Yugoslav rule were subjected to a Serbianisation campaign. In 1939 Italy occupied Albania, and in 1941 the Albanians of Kosovo and western Macedonia were temporarily united with those under Italian rule, but after the Second World War the pre-war boundary was restored.

THE CONSTITUTION

Whilst the negotiations concerning the limits of the new state were in progress the Yugoslavs were also occupied with the form of constitution they were to adopt within their new boundaries. The provisional government formed in December 1918 was chosen from the representatives of the various groups that supported the Yugoslav idea, with Nikola Pašić, leader of the Serbian Radicals, as its premier. A provisional parliament met in Belgrade in March 1919, in the building formerly used by the Serbian Skupština. Like the government, it was composed of members of the Slovene and Croat national councils and of the provincial assemblies of Bosnia and Dalmatia. Once the main frontier questions had been settled it was possible to consider elections to a constituent Assembly. These were held in November 1920. Fifteen political parties were represented amongst the 419 deputies who sat in the Constituent Assembly. The largest, with 92 seats, was the newly formed Democrat Party, led by Stojan Pribičević. This party included some dissident members of Pašić's Serbian Radical Party, and a number of Serbs in Croatia, Dalmatia and Bosnia, together with a few Slovene and Croat liberals. Its social composition was strongly biased towards the intellectual middle classes and its programme was for a constitutional monarchy responsible to a democratic parliament, operating within the framework of a unitary Yugoslav state.

One seat behind the Democrats was the Serbian Radical Party, with 91 members. This party, formed by Nikola Pašić in 1881, had dominated Serbian politics since the Karadjordjević restoration in 1903. The enjoyment of power had blunted its early radicalism, and it had come to represent the Serbian middle classes and the wealthier peasants. It also, like the Democrat Party, attracted some support from the '*prečani*' Serbs[11] of the Habsburg lands. The Radicals shared the centralist views of the Democrats, although the two parties differed on matters of social policy. The Democrats voted for a centralist constitution, but when it appeared that it was not working a group broke away from Pribičević's leadership and demanded a revision of its constitution.

Next in order of size were the Communists, with 59 seats. This newly formed party had strong links with the trade unions and youth organisations and was a member of the Soviet-led Third Communist International. The programme agreed at its second Congress in 1920 declared that its aim was 'to gain power and establish a Soviet Republic'.[12] The party's greatest strength at this time was in Macedonia, Bosnia and Montenegro. It now had a Yugoslav platform, and might have been expected to support a centralist constitution, but the Communists did not, in fact, participate in the final vote in the Assembly. On 29 December 1920, following Communist-led strikes in Bosnia and Slovenia, the government issued a proclamation (*obznana*) outlawing all Communist activity. It was not until August 1921 that the deputies were deprived of their mandates, following the passing of a law on the Protection of the State, but the Communists withdrew from the Assembly early in 1921.

Another group that withdrew from the Assembly before the constitution was approved was the Croat Peasant Party (Hrvatska Seljačka Stranka), led by Stjepan Radić. They had received fifty seats in the elections of 1920. As the name suggests, the appeal of HSS was mainly to the Croat peasants, although it did have some support among Croat workers and intellectuals. It advocated the establishment of an independent Croat peasant republic. For a time Radić flirted with the Communists, and in 1924 he affiliated the HSS to the International Peasants Union, the 'Green International', which was sponsored by the Soviet Union. According to Franjo Tudjman, the poor performance of the Communist Party in Croatia was because of the appeal of the progressive nationalism of Radić to the Croat workers. He also claims that the Communists and HSS worked closely together to resist the 'fascist tendencies' of the Serbian centralists.[13] Certainly after the banning of the Communist Party the two found a common cause in opposing the Vidovdan Constitution. The Comintern resolution of July 1924, which demanded a federation of worker–peasant republics within the Balkans, including Croatia,[14] provided a basis for common ground with Radić only if the Communists were prepared to ignore Radić's assertions at the Green International that 'Croats are not part of the Balkans either geographically, politically or culturally', and that 'A Balkan federation might include Bulgaria, Serbia and Macedonia, but not Croatia'.[15]

The HSS was the focus of opposition to the centralist concept, and although the party did not participate in the deliberations of the Constituent Assembly it published proposals for a loose confederation of the Yugoslav peoples.[16]

Another peasant party that opposed centralism was the Serb Agrarian Party, which, with some smaller peasant groups, won thirty-nine seats in the Assembly. The Agrarians drew their support from Serb-speaking peasants in Bosnia, as well as from the poorer peasants in Serbia.

The majority of the deputies from Slovenia were representatives of the Slovene Popular Party, a Catholic party led by a priest, Mgr Korošec. This party had been formed by a union of the Austrian and Slovene Catholics in 1905 and had participated in the work of the Vienna parliament.[17] In the elections of the Assembly they obtained twenty-seven seats. Although in favour of Slovene autonomy, Korošec was able to achieve a great deal for Slovenia by his skilled bargaining with the Radicals, after the passing of the Vidovdan Constitution. The Slovenes withdrew from the Assembly when they realised that a centralist solution was likely to be adopted, but after their initial protest they collaborated with the Democrats and Moslems in the formation of a coalition government in 1924, and with the Radicals in 1926.

The Moslems of Bosnia followed a similar line to that of the Slovenes, although they did go a little further in collaborating with the Radicals. Pašić bargained with them, and won the support of the twenty-four representatives of the Moslem organisation for the centralist constitution. The Albanian and Turkish Moslems of Macedonia and Kosovo also supported the centralist position, and later joined a Radical-led government. Their party, the Džemijet, had five seats in the elections of 1923.

The Vidovdan Constitution

The Constituent Assembly adopted the constitution on the Serbian national day, the feast of St Vitus (Vidovdan), 28 June 1921. The Vidovdan Constitution provided for a Kingdom of Serbs, Croats and Slovenes under the hereditary, constitutional monarchy of the Karadjordjević dynasty. There was a single legislative chamber, the Skupština, elected by proportional representation. The Council of Ministers was responsible both to the king and to parliament, and the king had much wider powers than is customary in the practice of the constitutional monarchies of western Europe. The usual rights of free speech, freedom of religion and equality before the law, which are enshrined in all the written constitutions from the American in 1777 to Stalin's 1936 constitution, were guaranteed.

Local government was under the control of prefects (*župani*), professional civil servants appointed by the king on the nomination of the minister of the interior. The *župan's* chief function was to see that the central government's orders were carried out in his province (*oblast*) and to supervise the work of the sub-prefects (*načelniki*), who administered the smaller districts (*srezovi*) within his *oblast*. The smallest unit of local government was the commune (*opština*), headed by a mayor, whose election could be vetoed by the central government. Although there were elected councils at all levels, their powers were limited, and vital questions of finance were controlled by the central government. Clearly, such a highly centralised constitution, headed by a strong Serbian king, was completely contrary to the wishes of the federalists in Croatia and Slovenia.

The Vidovdan Constitution was passed by 223 votes to 35, with over 160 deputies – including the Croats, Slovenes and Communists – absent in protest against the centralist character of the constitution. Pašić and Pribičević had won a paper majority for the concept of a greater Serbia, but, as later events showed, it was a Pyrrhic victory.

THE POLITICS OF THE 1920s

The Kingdom thus started out with a fundamental flaw in its construction. Constitutions based on the concepts of Western parliamentary liberalism work only if the basic constitutional order is accepted by the overwhelming majority of the people. The parliamentary game can only be played by opponents who accept the rules under which it is conducted. There was no such consensus in the first Yugoslav state. A significant minority – the Croats – rejected the assumptions of the Constitution and refused to participate fully in the political life of the country and between 1921 and 1925 the HSS deputies boycotted the Skupština. After the elections of February 1923 Radić was imprisoned and his party was dissolved. By a strange twist of the political game he was released a few months later, to join a coalition government in which the two arch enemies – Serbian Radicals under Pašić and Croat Peasants under Radić – attempted to work together. This experiment failed after eighteen months, and Radić then turned another somersault and joined with the old centralist, Stojan Pribičević, to form a Peasant–Democrat opposition group. Pribičević had come to realise that the centralist solution was not working, not only for the Croats, but also for the *prečani* Serbs whom he represented. In 1928 there was a complete breakdown of the parliamentary system. After several months, during which parliamentary sessions were disrupted by fights, on 20 June a Montenegrin deputy drew a gun and shot dead two Croat members and wounded Radić. Seven weeks later Radić died of his wounds. The Peasant–Democrat group withdrew their 83 deputies. The King asked Mgr Korošec to form a government, but after a few months he gave up the attempt. The Vidovdan Contitution had come to the end of the road. There was no alternative but to scrap it.

King Alexander took the initiative in January 1929 by appointing an administration of his own choice, headed by General Živković, commander of the Royal Guard. By adopting a royal dictatorship, Yugoslavs set up a pattern that was to be followed in the next few years by her neighbours Bulgaria and Romania. Poland in 1926 and Hungary in 1920 had both abandoned the attempt to operate their political life within the framework of liberal parliamentary constitutions inspired by western Europe.

Alexander attempted to reorganise the state – renamed the Kingdom of Yugoslavia in October – by royal decree. The old local government units – *oblasti* and *srezovi* – were abolished, and nine *banovine* were established.[18] Their boundaries were drawn so as to cut across the old historic provinces (see map 3). The press was controlled and political activities against dissidents of all shades was intensified. Many trade unionists and Communists were imprisoned, and there were allegations of torture and police brutality. There was repression also of extreme nationalist views, and a group of militant Croats led

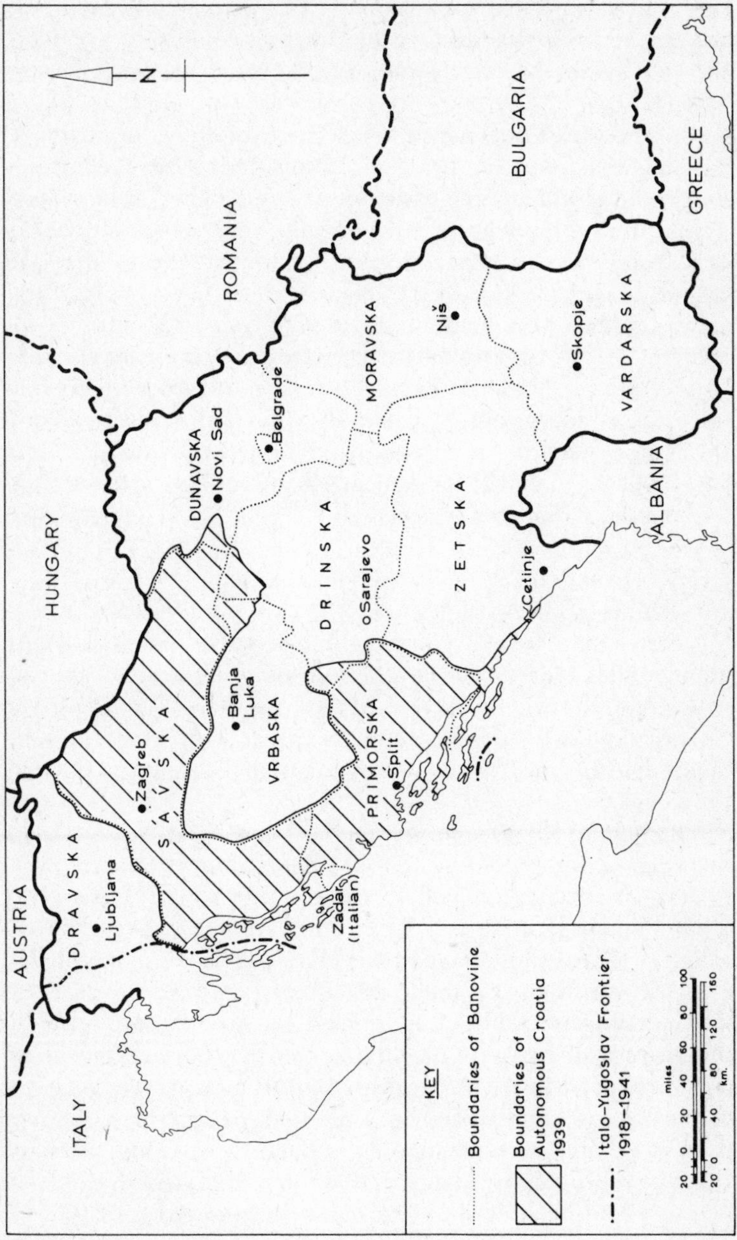

Map 3 The administrative boundaries of the Kingdom of Yugoslavia, 1929–41

by Ante Pavelić fled into exile. These members of the *ustaša* movement were given refuge in Hungary and Italy and were allowed by their hosts to plot the downfall of the Yugoslav state.

Alexander did not intend to rule indefinitely without constitutional sanction. In 1931 he introduced a new centralist constitution, which gave wide powers to the king. A bicameral legislature, subservient to the royal will, was created, and one of its first acts was to give retrospective approval to all that had passed during the two years of open royal dictatorship. Elections of a kind were held, in which votes were cast publicly for a single list of government candidates. A government party – the Yugoslav National Party – was then formed, and civilian rule was restored. But the Croats were not impressed, and Dr Maček, who had succeeded Radić in 1928 as leader of the Croat Peasants, called for a fresh start. The king's answer was to have the Croat leader arrested.

THE REGENCY OF PRINCE PAUL

In October 1934 Alexander set off on a state visit to France. On arrival at Marseilles he was murdered by *ustaša* assassins, acting under orders from Pavelić. The news of the king's murder was received with shock and horror, even by Yugoslavs who disagreed with his policies, and there was widespread popular anger against the Italians and Hungarians for giving refuge to the *ustaša*.

The heir to the throne, Alexander's son Peter, was a boy of ten years at the time of his father's death, and it was necessary to form a regency council to exercise the royal prerogatives. The senior regent, Prince Paul, Peter's uncle, was in fact the inheritor of Alexander's mantle.[19] He continued to operate the 1931 constitution, but made conciliatory gestures towards the Croats, Slovenes and other opposition groups and turned a blind eye to the strictly illegal emergence of moderate opposition groups. Maček was released from prison,[20] and in the elections of 1935 he headed an opposition coalition that obtained 67 seats to the government's 300. There was strong suspicion that the voting figures had been manipulated and that official pressure had been used to ensure a government majority.[21]

The Croat deputies boycotted the Skupština and met in

Zagreb as an anti-parliament. The Slovenes and the Moslems, however, were persuaded to join a government headed by Dr Stojadinović, a young Serbian Radical. Stojadinović made little headway on the vital issue of reconciliation with the Croats, and he alienated many Serbs by his authoritarianism and his handling of the proposed Concordat with the Vatican.[22] Elections in 1938 gave the opposition headed by Maček 44.9 per cent of the votes but only 67 of the 373 seats in the Skupština. Although the curious electoral arithmetic which made such a distribution of seats possible ensured a working majority for Stojadinovic's Radical Union, the premier suffered a moral defeat. Two months later, in February 1939, Prince Paul called on Dragiša Cvetković, one of Stojadinović's cabinet colleagues, to form a government. By this time the international situation made it imperative that the Croats should be brought back into the political life of the country.

The *Anschluss* of 1938 brought German troops to the Yugoslav borders, and the loss of Czechoslovak independence brought German control over one of Yugoslavia's main trading partners (see table 8). If the country was to have any hope of

Table 8 Trading partners, 1938 (percentages)

Country	*Imports*	*Exports*
Germany	32·52	35·94
Czechoslovakia	10·65	7·89
UK	8·67	9·61
Italy	8·94	6·42
Austria	6·88	6·06
USA	6·02	5·07

Source: Admiralty Handbook, III (London 1945), pp. 237–41

maintaining its independence, it must present a united front to the outside world. Prince Paul took the initiative by starting secret talks with Dr Maček, which led to a reconciliation in August 1939. The *Sporazum* (Understanding) provided for the union of the *banovine* of Savska and Primorska to form Croatia.

The Croatian parliament (*sabor*) was to be revised and given considerable powers over internal matters. Dr Maček joined the government as vice-premier, and his close associate, Dr Šubašić, became *ban* of Croatia. Political prisoners were released and restriction on the press was removed. The reconciliation was far from complete, however. Many Croats felt that their leaders should have held out for a greater degree of autonomy, and the more extreme ones began to look to Italy and Germany as possible allies of Croatian nationalism. The onset of the Second World War left the Yugoslavs no time to digest the implications of the '*Sporazum*', and the fragility of the compromise was tragically demonstrated when Yugoslavia herself was drawn in to the war in 1941. Serb and Croat fell upon each other with a savagery that shocked even the Germans.

Prince Paul was the prime mover in foreign policy during the period of the regency. He inherited from Alexander a series of treaties which linked Yugoslavia to two groups of countries. The first group consisted of France, Czechoslovakia and Romania. The three smaller states, all of them beneficiaries of the Versailles settlement at the expense of Hungary, first came together in 1921. Czechoslovakia and Yugoslavia had signed a treaty in August 1920, which included a clause providing for mutual assistance 'in the case of an unprovoked attack on the part of Hungary' against either of the signatories.

After the attempted restoration of the last Habsburg emperor, Charles, in March 1921 Yugoslavia and Czechoslovakia each signed treaties with Romania on similar lines to those of 1920. This was the basis of the Little Entente, which was formally inaugurated by a pact of organisation signed by all three in Geneva in 1933.

The Little Entente powers wanted to preserve the *status quo* established by the Versailles settlement. The Bulgarians and Hungarians, and later the Germans, aimed at revising the Versailles agreements in order to recoup their losses. The only major European power on which the Little Entente could hope to rely for support against the 'revisionists' was France. In 1924 France signed treaties with Czechoslovakia and Romania and in 1927, after some hesitation, with Yugoslavia. France's hesitation was because of her fear that a close alliance with Yugoslavia might jeopardise her relations with Italy.

Italo-Yugoslav relations had not recovered from the disputes over the Dalmatian and Julian frontiers, and were made worse by Italian support for Croat separatists and ill-treatment of her (Italy's) Slovene minority. However, as Mussolini told Prince Paul in 1929, the real conflict was between Italy and France, over the Mediterranean and North Africa, rather than between Italy and Yugoslavia.[23] France eventually accepted her role as protector of the Little Entente, although she disappointed her protégés when the revisionists, led by Germany, began to press their demands.

In addition to the Little Entente, Alexander involved Yugoslavia in a Balkan Entente, including Greece, Romania and Turkey, which was concluded in Athens in February 1934, a few months before the King's assassination. Although the Balkan Entente was an attempt to organise Balkan resistance to Italian pressure, Alexander also made overtures to Italy but was rebuffed by Mussolini. As long as there was no agreement with Italy, the support of France was essential both to the Balkan Entente and to the Little Entente. The French, for their part, supported the idea of a Yugoslav–Italian reconciliation as part of a general policy of lining up all powers – great or small – who might act to restrain German expansionist aims. Such a grand design did not suit the Yugoslavs, whose objectives were more narrowly confined. They even resented France's attempt to persuade them to settle their differences with Italy, although this was precisely what Alexander had attempted to do between 1932 and 1934. In the summer of 1934 Alexander had begun to look to the possibility of German assistance if agreement with Italy was impossible. As Hoptner writes, 'The Yugoslavs undoubtedly realised they were playing a dangerous game in inviting the bear to drive out the wolf'.[24] Nevertheless, when Alexander went to France in October 1934 he sent a message to Von Papen, the German minister in Vienna, saying 'I am travelling to Paris because I have an alliance with the French and because we have a number of interests in common, but irrespective of all that might be said in Paris, I shall never take part in a coalition to settle Central European affairs if it does not include Germany'.[25] Alexander never reached Paris. On arrival in Marseilles he and his French host M Barthou were assassinated.

Paul gradually edged away from the Little Entente, which became less and less credible as Nazi Germany grew in power and influence and France did nothing. As Hitler emerged, always stronger, from each of the crises which he manufactured – the Rhineland, Austria, Czechoslovakia, Memel, Danzig – the Yugoslav 'realists' gained in influence. They believed, with some justification, that France and Britain would be unable to help them, and that the sensible thing for a small Balkan nation to do was to establish friendly relations with Germany and its allies.

In January 1937 Stojadinović signed a 'Pact of Eternal Friendship' with Bulgaria, and in March of the same year an Italo-Yugoslav agreement was concluded, despite the protests of the Little Entente. With the signing of a 'Pact of Lasting Peace and Eternal Friendship' with Hungary in 1940, it only remained to come to an accord with the arch-revisionists, Germany, to complete Yugoslavia's total reversal of her system of alliances. The Munich crisis and its aftermath effectively killed the Little Entente. The fall of Czechoslovakia also cut off the main source of military supplies to the Yugoslav army. For a time Paul attempted to pursue a policy of strict neutrality, but in 1941 he was pushed into opening talks with the Germans, which led to Yugoslavia's adherence to the Tripartite Pact on 25 March.

The Coup d'etat of 1941

Prime Minister Cvetković and his foreign minister Cincar-Marković returned from Vienna on 26 March after signing the pact. Already there were signs that the pact was rejected by many Yugoslavs.[26] During the night they were arrested on the orders of a group of officers who had organised a *coup d'etat* in the name of the young King Peter. The leader of the *coup* was General Dušan Simović, the commander of the Air Force, although one of the driving forces behind it was his assistant, General Borivoje Mirković, who had been convinced of the need to overthrow the regime as early as 1937, after Stojadinović had signed the pact with Italy.[27] Prince Paul, who was *en route* for Slovenia when the *coup* occurred, returned immediately to Belgrade and resigned his office. He left the next day, with his family, for exile in Greece.

King Peter was sworn in by Patriarch Gavrilo on 28 March, and a broadly based government was formed, under the premiership of General Simović. It included all the Croat and Slovene ministers in the Cvetković government except Maček. The Bosnian Moslem leader, Džafer Kulenović, also remained a member. Of the new members, the most important were General Simović, Professor Slobodan Jovanović, who became a vice-premier, and General Ilić, who replaced General Pešić as minister of war. Maček, after some hesitation and long consultations with the Germans, agreed on 3 April to resume his post as a vice-premier.

The *coup d'état* was received with acclaim by crowds in Belgrade, Kragujevac and other towns throughout Serbia. Crowds in Belgrade shouted the now famous slogan, '*Bolje rat nego pakt*!' ('Better war than the Pact') and '*Bolje grob nego rob*' ('Better the grave than slavery'). Elsewhere, and especially in Croatia, spontaneous popular demonstrations were less in evidence, but the Communist Party organised mass demonstrations against the Tripartite Pact in other cities between 25 and 27 March. Nevertheless, there is evidence of widespread opposition to Paul's foreign policy, from all parts of the country and from all political groups. Simović, in his unpublished memoirs, quoted by Ristić,[28] writes of a flood of petitions, telegrams and letters that reached him when rumours of the impending Pact were circulating in mid-March.

Winston Churchill later told the House of Commons that by the *coup* the Yugoslavs had saved the soul and the future of their country, but it was already too late to save their territory.[29] On 6 April the Germans invaded, without a declaration of war, and eleven days later the Yugoslav Army surrendered. Even if they were defeated, the gesture was not without significance to the history of the Second World War. It delayed the beginning of Operation Barbarossa – the invasion of Russia – by at least four weeks. Its psychological value in inflicting a moral defeat on the Nazis and boosting the morale of their opponents may have been of greater value than its military importance.

NOTES

1 The Hungarian census of 1910 records the following populations for Baranja, Bačka and the Yugoslav portion of the Banat:

Serbs	381,872
Croats	6559
Bunjevci and Sokči*	62,904
Magyars	421,567
Germans	301,035
Romanians	75,806
Slovaks, Ruthenians, etc.	58,003
Others	12,152
	1,319,898

* These two groups are thought to be immigrants from the interior of Dalmatia, who entered Bačka and Baranja in the late fifteenth century.

2 Outside the town of Zara there were only 10,000 Italians in Dalmatia – the Slavs numbered over 600,000.
3 The Treaty of Rapallo, 12 November 1920.
4 In 1913 there was a small Albanian salient projecting towards Prizren which was transferred to Yugoslavia after the war, and there was a frontier rectification in Albania's favour in the Prespa area.
5 Montenegro coveted Scutari, and Serbia the port of Shengjin.
6 From the text released by the Foreign Office on 29 March 1920 and printed in the *Daily Telegraph* (30 March 1920).
7 In 1920 the Allied Supreme Council had offered northern Albania to the Yugoslavs, in the hope of persuading them to come to terms with Italy over Fiume.
8 *Manchester Guardian* (30 September 1921).
9 This settlement appears to have satisfied the friends of Albanian independence in London, for the redoubtable Mary Durham wrote in her scrapbook under the above cutting from the *Guardian*, 'I have kept my promises made in 1913. Albanian independence is recognised. We dissolved the Anglo-Albanian Association not long afterwards'.
10 A League financial adviser was appointed to assist the Albanian government.
11 *Prečani* – across the river: a term used of the Serbs separated from their homeland by the Habsburg frontiers along the Sava and Danube rivers.
12 P. Morača and D. Bilandžić, *Avangarda 1919–69* (Belgrade 1969).
13 See F. Tudjman, *Kritika*, 14 (1970), p. 14.
14 Pero Morača, *The League of Communists of Yugoslavia* (Belgrade 1966), p. 13.
15 Morača, *The League of Communists of Yugoslavia*, p. 13.
16 S. Pavlowitch, *Yugoslavia* (London 1971), p. 64.
17 Fran Zwitter, *Nacionalni problemi v Habsburski monarhiji* (Ljubljana 1972), p. 203.
18 The *banovine* were: Dravska (Slovenia), Savska (covering Slavonia, parts of Bosnia and Vojvodina, and the Adriatic coast between Fiume and Zadar), Primorska (central Dalmatia and part of western Bosnia), Dunavska (most of Vojvodina and part of northern Serbia), Drinska (central Bosnia and part of western Serbia), Vrbaska (northern Bosnia),

Zetska (Montenegro, Hercegovina and Kosovo), Moravska (central Serbia), and Vardarska (Macedonia and southern Serbia). Belgrade was a separate prefecture.

19 The other two members of the regency, Professor Stanković, a Serb, and Ivo Perović, a Croat, were worthy but little-known figures who played little part in politics.

20 Alexander had intended to do this on his return from France.

21 The *ban* of Primorska issued instructions that any official who did not vote for the government 'will be held responsible and punished without mercy'.

22 The Concordat was a legacy of King Alexander, but Stojadinović failed to secure its ratification in the face of fierce opposition from the Orthodox Church. See chapter 8.

23 Conversation quoted by J. B. Hoptner, *Yugoslavia in Crisis, 1934–1941* (London 1962), p. 13, n. 7.

24 Hoptner, *Yugoslavia in Crisis*, p. 24.

25 Quoted by Hoptner, *Yugoslavia in Crisis*, p. 24, n. 5.

26 A crowd of 5000 demonstrated at Kragujevac on 26 March.

27 Dragiša Ristić, *Yugoslavia's Revolution of 1941* (University Park, Pennsylvania 1966), p. 84.

28 Ristić, *Yugoslavia's Revolution*, p. 72.

29 *Hansard*, 3 May 1941.

6 Yugoslavia during the Second World War

It is not appropriate here to deal with the military history of Yugoslavia during the Second World War. It is a story of incredible heroism and of appalling atrocity and bestiality. It provides lessons in guerilla warfare which ought to have won a place in the instruction manuals of the army staff colleges of the major powers. The ability of bands of ill-armed guerillas to deny large areas of the country to the Germans and Italians, and to hold down thirty enemy divisions[1] at a crucial period in the war, constitutes an epic in the annals of war.[2] The unique forms of military organisation which the partisans evolved, combining regular military formations – the highly mobile Proletarian Brigades – with locally based guerilla bands, under the general control of a communist-led high command, exactly suited the conditions of occupied Yugoslavia. In a country unhappily divided socially and nationally, the Partisans offered in Tito's words a 'National Liberation Anti-Fascist Front of all the peoples of Yugoslavia, regardless of party or religion. In forming partisan detachments it is essential not to be narrow-minded, but to give wide scope to initiative and enterprise of every kind'.[3]

Our concern here, however, is with the political aspects of wartime Yugoslavia and with the consequences to the future development of the country of the political patterns which emerged.

The occupying powers successfully played a game of divide and rule, helped by the smouldering animosities which envenomed the relations between the Yugoslav peoples (see map 4). It has been estimated that 1,750,000 Yugoslavs[4] – almost 11 per cent of the population – died during the war, and that more than half of those were killed by other Yugoslavs. The

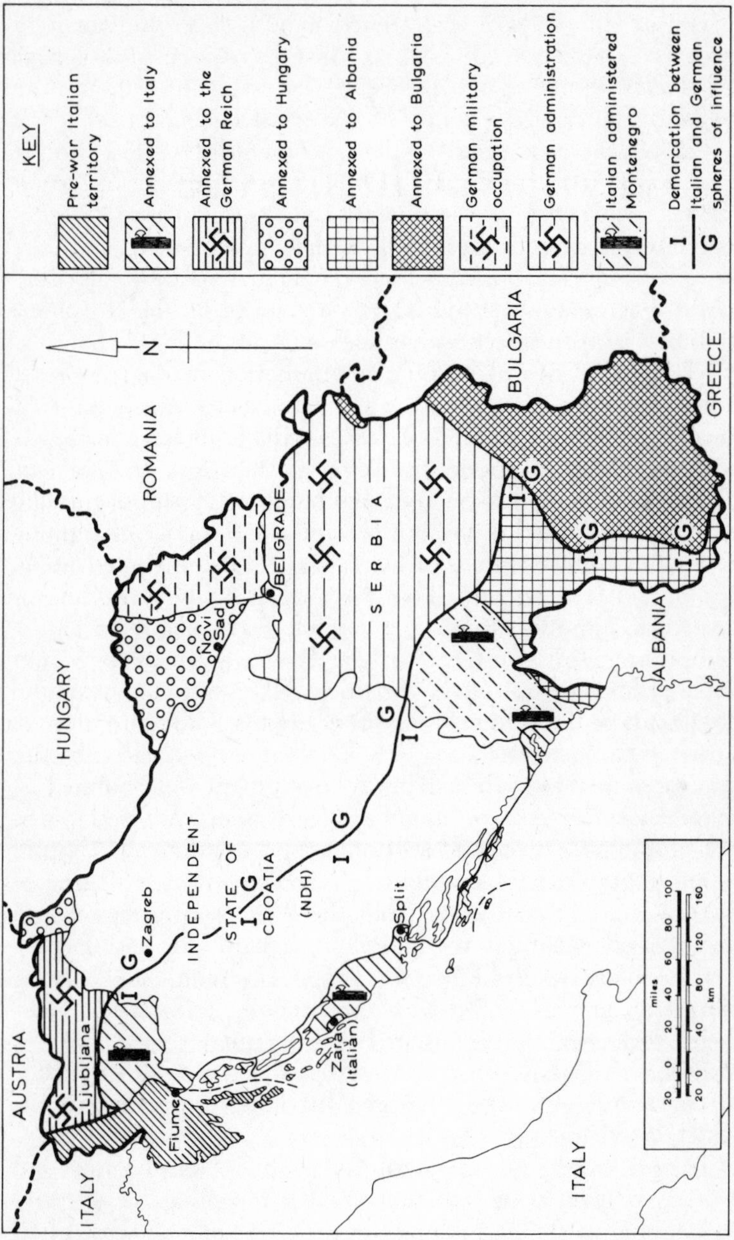

Map 4 The partition of Yugoslavia, 1941

worst fratricidal massacres occurred in the so-called Independent State of Croatia (NDH),[5] where Ante Pavelić ruled as führer (*poglavnik*). Some 350,000 Serbs were slaughtered by the *ustaša* during the three-and-a-half years of Pavelić's rule.

The NDH was not independent, it was hardly a state, and it was only 50 per cent Croat. This monstrous product of former wrongs, conceived in hatred and false national pride, represented the attempt by a group of warped extremists to revive the past glories of Croatia. It succeeded only in degrading the Croat name. The creation of the NDH was judged by the Nürnberg Tribunal to be a major war crime.

NDH came into being by a proclamation in Zagreb on 12 April 1941, two days after the Germans had entered the city. Pavelić had been allowed by the Italians to send his *ustaša* army across the frontier into Yugoslavia a few days earlier. Its frontiers were settled by negotiation with the occupying powers. In addition to most of present-day Croatia – excluding some Italian-held regions of Dalmatia – it also included Srem, Bosnia and Hercegovina. This 'state' of 6½ million inhabitants contained 750,000 Moslems, 2 million Serbs and over half a million others of non-Croat origin. It was given as 'king' the Duke of Spoleto, who took the title of Tomislav II,[6] to remind the Croats of the medieval glories of the first Croat kingdom of Tomislav I, formed in AD 924. NDH occupied roughly the same area as that of the medieval kingdom. It was hemmed in on all sides by Axis-occupied territory and was itself partitioned into a German and an Italian zone of influence. Despite its grotesque lack of credibility, NDH received a degree of international status. Apart from the Axis powers, Spain and Switzerland accorded it diplomatic recognition, and Pavelić was cordially received by the Pope. At home the Catholic hierarchy, led by the Archbishops Stepinac and Šărić, urged their flocks to support the Pavelič regime. Even Vlatko Maček, the leader of the Croat Peasant Party and a minister in the Royal government, urged his followers to accept the NDH.

There is no doubt that many Catholic Croats who were not Fascists welcomed the creation of an independent Croat state as a step towards the realisation of the nationhood which had been denied them by Hungary in the nineteenth and by Serbia in the twentieth century. Many joined the Croat defence forces (the Domobrani), and others, more extreme in their nationalism, joined the *ustaša*. The relationship of the *ustaša* to the Domobrani was similar to that of the SS to the German army. Just as many German generals were revolted by the brutalities of the SS, so the Domobrani recoiled from the worst atrocities of the *ustaša*.[7] Even the Germans and Italians intervened on occasions to restrain the *ustaša* from their more extreme brutalities, and at one time they toyed with the idea of trying to replace Pavelić with Maček, in order to prevent the chaos which *ustaša* madness was precipitating.

Croatia was not the only area where local quislings supported the occupation, although none of the others were rewarded with anything like the sham independence granted to the NDH. In Slovenia the former royalist governor, *Ban* Marko Natlačen,[8] attempted to create a separate Slovene state, but when he saw that the Axis leaders had other ideas, he settled for an advisory role to the Italian occupation forces in Ljubljana. A Slovene military force, analogous to the Domobrani, known as the Bela Garda (White Guards) was formed. Although Bela Garda did participate in actions against the partisans both in Slovenia and elsewhere, there is little said about any atrocities on the scale of those committed in Croatia. This may be because Slovenia is the most culturally homogenous area of Yugoslavia: 98 per cent of the pre-war population were Slovenes, and the vast majority were Roman Catholics. Most of the Croat atrocities were committed against non-Croats, as part of a policy of national 'purification'.

Serbia[9] was at first governed by a commissioner, Milan Aćimović, the former Belgrade chief of police. In August 1941 the 'commissioner government' was replaced by a puppet Serbian government under the premiership of General Milan Nedić. A state guard was formed of 5000 men, mainly from the police force, but the fascist leader Dimitrije Ljotić[10] was allowed to form a Serbian Volunteer Corps, recruited from his Nazi-minded followers. In addition there were three groups of Serbian *četniks*[11] who took their name from the old pre-war veterans' association led by Kosta Pečanac. The position is succinctly put in a German intelligence report:

> The *Četnik* units are divided into three groups, those of Kosta Pečanac which support the Nedić government, those of General Novaković which lean towards the Communists, and the anti-Communist units of Staff-Colonel Mihailović. Mihailović is against Pečanac and Novaković. His supporters are mainly officers. His organisation is purely military. He rejects the Communists because he is of the opinion that the time has not yet come for a general uprising. He would like first to organise the entire country and then to attack.[12]

Četnik groups were also formed among the Serbian inhabitants of Croatia, Bosnia and Montenegro. In some cases the excesses of the *ustaša* drove them into collaboration with the partisans, but more commonly they collaborated with the Italians in Dalmatia. Where the opportunity presented itself they wreaked vengeance on the Croat population for *ustaša* atrocities committed against Serbian villages. Many settlements in the Dinaric *polja* between the Adriatic and the Bosnian border are of mixed Croat and Serb population. It sometimes happened – as in the Sinjsko *polje* – that a village would change hands several times, falling alternately to the *ustaša* and to the *četniks*. In each case old scores would be paid off. The villagers even looked to the regular armies of the Italian or German occupiers to rescue them from the fury of their fellow Yugoslavs. Where the Partisans were active a policy of genocide was not practised, but rough justice was handed out to suspected collaborators.

In Montenegro a Provisional Administrative Committee of royalists and separatists came into being within a few days of the outbreak of hostilities. This body welcomed the Italian forces and later turned itself into a *sabor* (parliament) of a 'sovereign and independent' kingdom of Montenegro. It was, of course, neither sovereign nor independent. The *sabor* requested that Prince Mihailo, the grandson of King Nikola, the last Montenegrin king, should be offered the crown, but Mihailo refused. It soon became apparent that the *sabor* was unrepresentative of Montenegrin opinion. On 13 July 1914, the day after the proclamation of the 'Independent Kingdom', there was a mass insurrection in which Communist partisans and *četniks* co-operated. The Italians were almost thrown out, but by

December, with the help of Albanian troops, they had reasserted their control over the main centres of what was clearly an Italian-occupied puppet state. The Independent Kingdom was forgotten.

Further south, in Albania, another Italian satellite had come into being before the war. In 1941 its frontiers were enlarged at the expense of Yugoslavia by the incorporation of Kosovo, Metohija and the Albanian-speaking areas of western Macedonia into a Greater Albania. These areas had once been Serb, but during the Turkish occupation of the Balkans, Serbs had migrated north to Habsburg territory and had been replaced by Moslem Albanians.[13] In 1940, at its fifth Conference, the Yugoslav Communist Party re-affirmed a resolution of 1928 proposing that Kosovo should be handed over to Albania.[14] The Yugoslav Communists played an important part in establishing the Albanian Communist Party in November 1941, and they later collaborated in partisan warfare.

Albania had never been truly independent since its formation in 1913. Under King Zog, who seized power in 1924, it became a satellite state of Italy, and was occupied by Italy in 1939.

There developed both in Albania itself and in the occupied areas of Kosovo and Macedonia a situation analogous to that in Yugoslavia, with two resistance movements, one led by Communists, which wanted to convert the struggle against the enemy into a social revolution, and the other which was nationalist and hoped to maintain the pre-war social structure. A further complication, however, was that the Albanians were divided into two main linguistic and cultural groups, the Ghegs and the Tosks. The Ghegs inhabited the northern mountains and were predominantly Moslem; the Tosks lived in the south, were more urbanised and were predominantly Orthodox in religion. Some Gheg chieftains owned estates in Kosovo and Macedonia, and the majority of the Albanians in Yugoslavia were Moslems of Gheg origin. The Gheg chieftains acted independently of the two resistance movements. They were prepared to support the Italians, and later the Germans, in harassing the Serbs in Kosovo. In 1942 several of the Gheg chiefs, led by Abas Kupi,[15] made an alliance with the Communists to form a National Liberation movement (Levisija

Nacional Clirimtare), but broke with them after the Italian collapse in 1943. The Tosks provided the majority for both the Communist-led partisans and the conservative Balli Kombetar.

The situation was like that in Yugoslavia, with the Ballists drifting by way of parallel actions and tactical agreements into outright collaboration with the puppet regime established by the Germans[16] in Tirana in 1943, in similar fashion to Mihailović's collaboration with the Nedić government in Serbia. Albanian collaborators assisted the Italians in suppressing the Montenegrin rising in the autumn of 1941, and helped in the policing of Kosovo. The partisan forces worked closely together after 1943,[17] both in Kosovo and Macedonia. Thus, the wartime history of Albania has a place in the Yugoslav story.

What remained of Macedonia after the attachment of the western areas to Albania was annexed by Bulgaria, together with some parts of South Serbia.[18] The Macedonians had been treated by the Serbian-dominated royalist regime as 'South Serbs',[19] and many were at first prepared to accept Bulgarian rule in preference to Serbian. Even the Yugoslav Communist Party was unwilling in its early days to accept the Macedonians as a separate national group. The Slovenes and Croats were allowed to form separate parties in 1937, but it was not until 1943 that a Macedonian Communist Party was formed.[20] This was strange, as 15 of the 58 Communist deputies elected to the national parliament in 1920 were from Macedonia, and these 15 Communists were the largest single group amongst the 33 deputies from Macedonian constituencies. Internal dissension and the repression by the Serbian police undermined the Macedonian Communists during the 1920s and 1930s. When the Bulgarian occupation came in 1941 not only were the people at large uncertain in their allegiance, but so were the Communists. Eventually the clumsiness of the Bulgarians and the successes of the partisans swung the majority towards a Yugoslav orientation, and by 1943 the Macedonians were playing a full part in the resistance movement.

Amongst the non-Slav groups there were many who welcomed the break-up of Yugoslavia. The Albanians of Kosovo and the Hungarians of the Vojvodina and Prekomurje were satisfied by the frontier changes that brought them once again under the rule of their compatriots, and the German-speaking minorities in Slovenia and Vojvodina came into their own when the Reich extended its power into the Balkans.

After the collapse of the Royal Army and the flight of the king and his government, first to Jerusalem and then to London, resistance to the occupation continued in some areas. Remnants of the Royal Army joined Colonel Mihailović in the wooded Šumadija region south of Belgrade. Mihailović hoped to unify the various *četnik* groups that were in existence mainly in Serbia and the Serbian-speaking areas of Bosnia and Montenegro, and to build an underground organisation which would eventually play a part in the restoration of the monarchy. He became the officially recognised representative of the exiled royal government in London and in 1942 was made minister of war by the king and promoted to general.

In the same area during the summer of 1941 Communist-led groups were also operating. These partisans had completely different aims from those of the *četniks*. They represented Yugoslavs of all different nationalities and all social classes, whilst the *četniks* were predominantly Serbian and were led by royalists. The leadership of the partisans was composed of tough revolutionaries, familiar with underground operations after twenty years of illegal work against the royalist regime. They wanted to organise a massive guerilla operation against the occupying powers and their Yugoslav collaborators as a first step to creating a Communist society in Yugoslavia.

After the German invasion of the Soviet Union in June 1941 the German forces in Yugoslavia were reduced and an opportunity was afforded for both the *četniks* and the partisans to establish control over comparatively large areas outside the main strategic centres.

For a time in the summer and autumn of 1941 there seemed to be a possibility of collaboration between the two resistance groups. In September 1941 Tito and Mihailović met in the Ravna Gora and agreed to work together at local level, and some joint operations were carried out on a limited scale. A second meeting in October produced no practical results. By the end of October co-operation had effectively broken down. This was partly because of disagreement over ultimate political objectives. By this time Mihailović was in contact with Captain

Hudson, a British liaison officer, and had high hopes of receiving both political and military aid from the Allies. As the representative of the exiled royal government in London, he felt little need to make concessions to Tito, a man whom he regarded as being little better than a bandit. There was also serious conflict over the military strategy to be followed in resisting the Germans. In September Hitler had ordered his troops to take reprisals against the civilian population. For every German soldier killed 100 Yugoslav hostages must die. Mihailović was not prepared to risk the wholesale slaughter of innocent Serbs by conducting ambushes against the German troops. The appalling massacre of 7000 inhabitants of Kragujevac – including several hundred schoolboys – in October was an example of the terrible vengeance which could be expected. Mihailović's reaction was to lie low and to desist from provocations. Tito's was to extend the range of his operations.[21] The Germans sent in reinforcements and on 28 November forced Tito to give up the town of Užice, where in September he had established a partisan 'republic'. The policy of the partisans was to create a 'people's government' in the areas they occupied and to begin to apply their Communist principles whereever they had the power to do so. Even when their forces were driven out of an area, they attempted to maintain a Communist underground organisation in every occupied territory.

After the retreat from Užice in the winter of 1941 the partisans moved their headquarters via the Sandžak into Bosnia, capturing the town of Foča. In this period the military formations of the partisans were reorganised, and the first 'proletarian' brigades came into being. The statute establishing the First Proletarian Brigade states that: 'The proletarian people's liberation shock brigades are the military shock formations of the peoples of Yugoslavia under the leadership of the Communist Party'.[22] These units became the nucleus of the People's Army. Also at Foča the basic principles of the People's Liberation Committee were elaborated.[23] In November 1942, when they were in occupation of Bihać, on the western boundary of Bosnia, the first meeting was held of the 'Anti-Fascist Council for the National Liberation of Yugoslavia' (AVNOJ). The Bihać manifesto declared the aims of AVNOJ to be the liberation of Yugoslavia and the establishment of a broad democratic government, which recognised the rights of the different ethnic and religious groups in the country.

During 1943 the fortunes of the partisans fluctuated wildly. In the early part of the year they held some 45,000 square kilometres of the interior of Bosnia and Montenegro, had a hold on the Dalmatian coast, and had even begun to control parts of Slavonia. A series of offensives starting in January 1943 drove them out of Bihać and forced them to retreat to Montenegro. When Captains Deakin and Stuart as members of a British military mission were dropped by parachute to make contact with Tito in May they found the partisan high command almost encircled in the area of Mount Durmitor. Stuart was killed on 9 June, but Deakin, although wounded, escaped with the partisans, sharing with them their appalling privations on the long trek across Montenegro and Bosnia during the summer of 1943. This retreat included the epic crossing of the river Sutjeska, which has come to occupy in Yugoslav lore the same legendary significance that the Long March of the Chinese army holds in the annals of Chinese Communism. Within a few months Tito had snatched victory from the jaws of defeat. Helped by the collapse of the Italians in September, which provided him with captured arms and supplies – and even soldiers[24] – the partisan movement was able to establish an embryonic state. There were wholesale desertions from the NDH and the *četniks* to the partisans. Links across the Adriatic with the Allied forces in Italy established following Deakin's mission, helped to strengthen their position.

In November the partisans were in command again of large areas of Bosnia and Dalmatia. At Jajce, the old Bosnian capital, AVNOJ held its second meeting, and declared itself on 29 November to be 'the supreme legislative and executive body in Yugoslavia' – in fact, a provisional government. Dr Ivan Ribar, a well-known pre-war politician,[25] was elected president, and a declaration was issued that the king could not return 'until such time as the people, by their own free will, after the liberation of the entire country, decide the question of the king and the monarchy'.

The Allied powers were already beginning to withdraw support from Mihailović and to see in Tito the future leader of Yugoslavia. The British military missions to both partisans and *četniks* had for some time been sending back reports to British Intelligence in Cairo which both told the same story.[26] Mihailović was not effectively fighting the enemy but was, in fact, collaborating with them in order to destroy the partisans. The partisans, on the other hand, were an effective resistance movement, in control of large areas of the country. The matter was clinched by the report of the mission led by Brigadier Fitzroy Maclean, who arrived in Bosnia shortly after the Italian collapse, as the chief of an official British military mission and as the personal representative of Winston Churchill. At the Teheran conference, which took place at the same time as the Jajce meeting of AVNOJ, the allied leaders agreed to give their full support to the partisans. Churchill told the House of Commons in May 1944:

> The reason why we have ceased to supply Mihailović . . . is a simple one. He has not been fighting the enemy, and moreover, some of his subordinates have made accommodations with the enemy from which have arisen armed conflicts with the forces of Marshal Tito . . . We have proclaimed ourselves the strong supporters of Marshal Tito because of his heroic and massive struggle against the German armies.

In June 1944 a new royal government was formed in London, and its leader, Dr Šubašić, was sent to Dalmatia to meet Tito. The Šubašić government was created under pressure from the British government and was expected to make its peace with Tito. Support was withdrawn from Mihailović, and in September the king broadcast an appeal to all Yugoslav patriots to rally to Tito.[27]. In August Tito crossed to Italy to meet Churchill and confirmed the agreement previously reached that members of the Šubašić government should join Tito's provisional government.

Mihailović made frantic efforts during 1944 to wrest the political initiative from Tito. His answer to the Jajce declaration was the Ba Congress of representatives from various anti-Communist parties,[28] held 25–8 January in the presence of a representative of the United States military mission to the *četniks*. The Ba Congress called for the creation of a federal Yugoslavia, with three semi-autonomous units – Serbia, Croatia and Slovenia. Nothing was said of the Macedonians, whose national aspirations were not recognised by the pre-war politicians.[29] In any event, the Ba proposals looked half-hearted in comparison with the reality of the *de facto* provisional government created at Jajce. The Ba programme was not intended to be implemented until after the war, whereas Tito began to act on the Jajce proposals immediately in the areas he commanded.

As the tide of war moved in Tito's favour the various groups of anti-Communist politicians who had collaborated in various ways with the occupying forces began to look for escape routes. Those who were adroit enough to join the partisans in time were able to work their passage to patriotic respectability during the last year of the war.[30] Others tried to form pro-Allied movements and prayed for an Anglo-American landing in Dalmatia. In fact, Soviet troops entered Yugoslavia from Romania and Bulgaria and assisted the partisans in their liberation of Belgrade on 20 October 1944.

NOTES

1 According to the authors of *Yugoslavia in the Second World War* (Belgrade 1967), p. 69, there were at the end of 1941 sixteen Italian, six German, two Bulgarian and six Croat Domobran divisions engaged.

2 F. W. Deakin is at present engaged on a major history of the war in Yugoslavia. His personal account of his own experiences as a British officer attached to Tito's partisan headquarters has already appeared: see *The Embattled Mountain* (Oxford 1971).

3 Order of the day by Tito, quoted by S. Clissold in *A Short History of Yugoslavia* (Cambridge 1968), p. 216.

4 Davičo and Bogosavljević, *The Economy of Yugoslavia* (Belgrade 1960).

5 Nezavisna Država Hrvatska.

6 He was never crowned, and never visited Croatia.

7 The German general in Zagreb, assessing the poor morale of Domobrani sent to support *ustaša* units, writes of their 'spiritual revulsion against the struggle which the mass of the Croats regard as a fratricidal war. They regard the outbreak and extension of the insurrection [of Serbs threatened with genocide by *ustaša*] as a judgement . . . on the mad hatred of the *ustašas* for the Serbs'. Quoted from Vishaupt, in *Yugoslavia in the Second World War*, p. 66.

8 Natlačen was *ban* of the Drava Banovina, the administrative unit covering Slovenia.

9 The Serbia referred to here is what remained after the separation of the Banat (under German rule), Bačka and Baranja (under Hungarian rule), parts of South Serbia (under Bulgaria) and Kosovo–Metohija (attached to the Italian puppet state of Albania).

10 Leader of the *Zbor* movement.

11 *Četa* is the term used for an army company. A *četnik* is literally a member of a military company, but the term is used also to include the irregular forces who struggled against the Turks in occupied Serbia and the veterans' body – a cross between the British Legion and the Territorial Army – which operated after the First World War.

12 *Yugoslavia in the Second World War*, p. 63, n. 20.

13 Atanasije Urošević, *Kosovo* (Belgrade 1965), pp. 20–2.

14 N. C. Pano, *The Peoples Republic of Albania* (Baltimore, Maryland 1968), pp. 40–2.

15 See Julian Amery, *The Sons of the Eagle* (London, 1948), pp. 56–60.

16 The Germans took over from the Italians in September 1943 and established an 'independent' Albanian government.

17 For example, as early as September 1942 the Macedonian Communist leader Krste Crvenkovksi was arrested in Gostivar, then part of Greater Albania, and sent to jail in Tirana. He escaped with a fellow prisoner, Koçi Xoxe, who later became a minister in Enver Hoxha's government and was executed as a Titoist in 1949. Krste Crvenkovski, *Along New Paths* (Belgrade 1969).

18 In fact, Macedonia did not exist as an administrative unit. Between 1921 and 1929 it was divided into the *oblasti* of Bitolj, Skopje, Štip and parts of Vranje and Priština. After 1929 it formed part of the Vardarska *banovina*. The present republic of Macedonia was created after the Second World War.

19 For example, in 1927 the Macedonian-speaking areas sent to the parliament in Belgrade twenty Serbian-speaking deputies and only two Macedonians. K. Crvenkovski, *Twenty-five Years from the Formation of the Communist Party in Macedonia* (Skopje 1968), p. 10.

20 Crvenkovski, writing of the 1920s, stated that: 'The unenlightened and wrong standpoints of the CPY regarding the national question in general, and . . . the Macedonian question in particular were one of the basic obstacles for its closer connection with the nationally enslaved masses of the Macedonian people.' *Along New Paths*, p. 10.

21 According to F. W. D. Deakin, 'On 29th November Tito had telephoned to Mihailović, asking him what he proposed to do, and received the reply that the *četnik odreds* (companies) would "return to their territories, and carry out suitable guerilla action, until conditions for a general rising existed". This brief interchange marked the end of contact between the two men. On 30th November Mihailović held a meeting of his commanders on Ravna Gora, and it was decided to "legalise" the četnik units in agreement with Nedić and in common action against the partisans' (*The Embattled Mountain*, p. 145).

22 Quoted by Deakin, *The Embattled Mountain*, p. 101.

23 The Foča regulations 'laid down the basic principles for the setting up of a new peoples government; responsibility to the people; election rights; unity of authority; self government'. *Yugoslavia in the Second World War*, p. 103.

24 The Italians had been instructed to surrender to the partisans. Many

went even further and joined them, forming Garibaldi Divisions within the Liberation Army. P. Auty, *Tito* (London 1970), p. 218.

25 Ribar had been the Speaker of the Constituent Assembly which passed the Vidovdan Constitution of 1921.

26 See P. Auty, *Tito*, chapter 13, and F. W. Deakin, *The Embattled Mountain*, for accounts of relations between the partisans and the allies.

27 An account of the background to these events from a point of view sympathetic to Mihailović and King Peter is given in S. K. Pavlowitch's *Yugoslavia* (London 1971), pp. 155–62. The more commonly accepted interpretation of the situation is given in P. Auty's *Tito*, pp. 237–41.

28 The Congress was held in the Serbian village of Ba. It elected Živko Topalović, President of the pre-war Socialist Party, as its President. The Croat Peasant Party, the Democratic Party and the Slovene Alliance were also represented. Pavlowitch accords a greater significance to the Ba Congress than is given by other historians of the period.

29 After a slow start the Macedonian partisans went into action in 1943. Tito won the Macedonians over to a Yugoslav rather than a Bulgarian orientation by recognising their national aspirations.

30 Deakin, in *The Embattled Mountain*, writes of a general who had held commissions in the Austro-Hungarian, Royal Yugoslav, NDH and partisan armies.

PART II

7 The formation of the People's Republic

The first legislative and executive bodies of the new Yugoslavia were direct descendants of the AVNOJ Council and the National Liberation Committee which it elected at Jajce in 1943. As a concession to Allied opinion the provisional government was enlarged by the inclusion of non-Communist members. The provisional assembly of what was at the time called Democratic Federative Yugoslavia included some eighty non-Communists amongst its 318 members, and the provisional government included Dr Šubašić, former head of the royal government in London, as foreign minister, Milan Grol, leader of the Democratic Party, as deputy premier, and Juraj Šutej of the Croat Peasant Party. The main task of the new administration, which was formed in March 1945, was to prepare for the elections to a Constituent Assembly, which were to be held in November. Until the Constituent Assembly voted a new constitution, the country would be governed under legislation passed by AVNOJ and the provisional assembly. During this interim period certain important legislation was passed concerning agrarian reform and the expropriation of the property of collaborators, and a new electoral law was promulgated which extended the vote to all citizens over eighteen years and withdrew voting rights from alleged Fascists and quislings.

In fact, the day-to-day administration of the country was in the hands of the Communist Party, acting through the provisional government at national level and through the people's committees at local level. The non-Communist ministers were isolated and unable to organise their political supporters. In August 1945 a People's Front was formed which included, under Communist leadership, many of the non-Communist individuals and organisations which had participated in the

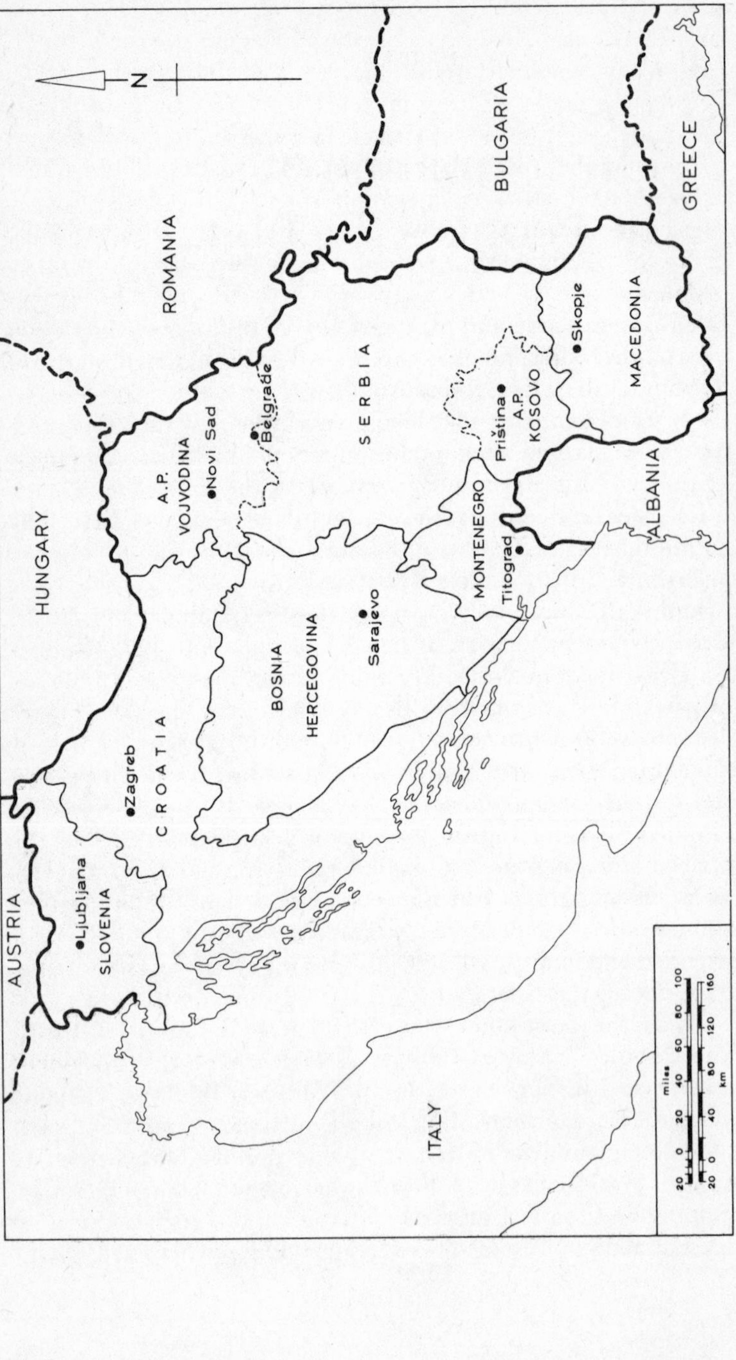

MAP 5 Present-day administrative boundries

work of AVNOJ and in the liberation movements in the various regions.[1] It was made impossible for parties outside the People's Front to campaign in the elections for the assembly, although the attempt was made by a group led by pre-war Serbian politicians under the title of the United Democratic Opposition and by some members of the Croat Peasant Party. In protest against the methods used to silence opposition, Grol, Šubasić and Šutej resigned from the government and decided not to take part in the elections. When the vote was taken on 11 November a single list of candidates approved by the People's Front was presented to the electorate. Less than 10 per cent of those who went to the polls rejected the official list. In the absence of opposition candidates the election was in reality a plebiscite. The first act of the newly elected Assembly was to depose the king and to give the state a new name – the Federative People's Republic of Yugoslavia (*Federativna Narodna Republika Jugoslavija* – FNRJ). A new constitution was approved on 31 January 1946 and the Constituent Assembly then turned itself into the first parliament of the People's Republic.

In the aftermath of victory the partisans meted out rough justice to any who were suspected of collaboration with the enemy, or merely of hostility to the Party. Many were shot or thrown in jail without trial by regular courts. In March 1946 Mihailović was captured, and three months later he stood trial in Belgrade along with a score of his associates. The Mihailović trial, which resulted in the death penalty for ten of those principally accused, was used as a show trial in order to incriminate not only the *četniks* but also Nedić, Ljotić and the Serbian royalists and Fascists. During the autumn of 1946 the Catholic Church in Croatia was similarly discredited when Archbishop Stepinac was tried and sentenced to sixteen years' hard labour.

The evidence of these trials is still a matter of controversy. Undoubtedly Mihailović had collaborated with the enemies of the new Yugoslavia – with Nedić and the Serbian quislings and with the Germans and Italians against the partisans. His supporters would claim that he was the last legal representative of the royal government and that he had acted in what he thought was the best interests of the Kingdom of Yugoslavia. But the Kingdom had disappeared, and a new revolutionary republic had come into being with a new kind of legality. In the eyes of the new regime he was as much a traitor as William Joyce or John Amery were in post-war Britain, and he suffered the same fate. Archbishop Stepinac had also compromised himself and his Church, both by his failure to condemn Pavelić and by his refusal to co-operate with the new regime.

As well as these leaders of the anti-Communist forces who had to be silenced, there were thousands of lesser figures who remained in Yugoslavia and who were purged during the first few post-war years. Thousands more had fled abroad as the Germans retreated. Some estimates give a figure of half a million, excluding the 350,000 Volksdeutsche who were either expelled or who fled to Austria and Germany.

Yugoslavia survived the winter of 1945–6 largely with the help of UNRRA, which contributed over $400 million in food, clothing, machinery, railway engines and technical assistance during 1945 and 1946.[2] By 1946, with the new regime firmly in control and accorded diplomatic recognition and founder-member status at UNO, the task of building a new society began in earnest.

The 1946 constitution was modelled on that of Stalin's Soviet Constitution of 1936. Although formally accepting the principle of federation, with the right of secession for the six federal republics,[3] it was in fact a highly centralised state. The Federal Assembly was made up of a Federal Council (*Savezno Veće*) elected directly by the people and a Council of Nationalities (*Veće Naroda*) chosen by the parliaments of the six republics and the two autonomous units of Serbia. The Presidential Council of the Assembly (*Prezidijum*), headed by Dr Ivan Ribar, had the attributes of a corporate head of state. Marshal Tito was the first premier of the first government appointed under the 1946 constitution.

The ruling principle of the new regime was that of 'revolutionary statism', or the dictatorship of the proletariat, exercised by the Party in the name of the workers. The controlling hand of the Party was evident at all levels of political, economic and cultural life,[4] but the Party was not mentioned in the constitution.

The long road from the early post-war stage of centralized administrative state socialism to the pluralistic form of 'market socialism' which was reached in the late sixties can be divided into three phases. The introduction of workers' self-management in the early fifties and the constitutional law of 1953 marked the end of the first period. There followed a decade during which the concept of workers' self-management evolved. In the early sixties major changes in the management of the economy and the constitution of 1963 ushered in the period of 'market socialism'. A fourth phase began in the early seventies, when important changes were initiated, culminating in the Tenth Congress of the LCY and the introduction of a new constitution.

As yet the basic outlines of the economic system have not been radically changed, although there are signs that the enthusiasm for the market which was apparent in the sixties is now waning.

NOTES

1 The Slovene Liberation Front (OF) for example, included representatives of the Sokol national sports movement and the younger, left-wing Clericals.

2 See J. Tomasevich in *Yugoslavia*, ed. R. J. Kerner (Berkeley, California 1949), p. 391.

3 The six republics were Bosnia–Hercegovina, Croatia, Macedonia, Montenegro, Serbia and Slovenia. Serbia was divided into three units – Serbia Proper, the Autonomous Province of Vojvodina, and the Autonomous District of Kosovo–Metohija.

4 On the whole, however, the Yugoslav Communist Party did not impose as heavy a hand on writers and artists as did Zhdanov in the later years of Stalin's rule in the USSR.

8 The first phase in post-war development

The first phase of socialist Yugoslavia's development can be traced back to the middle of the Second World War. Long before Tito led his victorious partisans into Belgrade in October 1944, many Yugoslavs had experienced life under the rule of the Communist Party. In the islands of liberated territory that emerged from time to time throughout the war the partisans established 'people's liberation committees' to run the civil administration of the towns and villages they held. The local government units which were later formed corresponded both in areas of authority and in functions to these embryonic people's committees of the war years. This fact is explicitly affirmed in the 1946 constitution, which gave legal status to the people's committees. Article 6 states that the committees 'had been set up during the struggle for national liberation, and represented the principal achievement of the struggle'. The General Law on People's Committees that was promulgated on 1 April 1952 also stresses their significance: 'The People's Committees which were created and built up by the working masses in the People's Liberation War and the Socialist Revolution shall be the bases of the State authority of the working people . . .'[1]

In a speech on the twentieth anniversary of the formation of the National Liberation Committee (*de facto* the provisional government) at Jajce, Mijalko Todorović stated that: 'In fact, the People's Liberation Committees represented, both in essence and form, the new democratic and revolutionary workers' and peasants' authority.'[2]

The statutes of individual communes usually acknowledge in their preambles their descent from the wartime people's liberation committees and their debt to the Communists who led the partisan struggle. Thus, the Statute of the Commune of Požarevac,[3] a commune of 73,000 inhabitants in north-east Serbia, states that: 'the League of Communists of Yugoslavia acts in our Commune . . . as the basic initiator of political activity . . .', and it speaks of the contribution of 'The working people of Požarevac' to the revolutionary struggle, 'in the War of People's Liberation and in the socialist revolution under the leadership of the Communist Party of Yugoslavia'. Reference is also made to the 'Socialist Alliance of the Working People'. In fact, when one examines the individual articles of the Požarevac constitution, the League of Communists is never referred to by name,[4] whereas the SAWPY (Socialist Alliance of the Working People of Yugoslavia) is accorded a definite constitutional status – e.g.:

> (Art. 167) The Commission (on Personnel, Election and Appointments) shall number 9 members, including 5 to be nominated by the Assembly . . . 2 to be delegated by the Communal Committee of the Socialist Alliance.
> (Art. 203) The meeting of electors shall be convoked by the president of the Communal Assembly and also when so required by the *Communal Committee of the Socialist Alliance* or by a group of at least 50 citizens. . . .

The Socialist Alliance is the lineal descendant of the People's Front, created to mobilise what are referred to in Marxist jargon as 'the broad masses of the people', in contrast to the Communist Party, which is the 'vanguard'.[5]

National liberation committees began to appear in areas held by the partisans as early as 1941, and by February 1942 there were several hundred in existence throughout Yugoslavia. The 'Foča regulations' of February 1942 laid down the principles under which the committees should operate. Amongst other things, they insisted on the '*unity of authority*, *democratic centralism*, equal rights for men and woman. . . .'

At Bihać in November 1942 fifty-four representatives of the committees met[6] and founded the Anti-Fascist Council of the National Liberation of Yugoslavia (AVNOJ). AVNOJ's Executive Board acted as a government, establishing departments for internal security, economy, health, religious affairs, social welfare, etc., and issuing regulations that it was able to enforce in territories under partisan occupation.

The meeting of AVNOJ which took place in the old Bosnian capital of Jajce in November 1943 established a provisional government for Yugoslavia and sketched in the outlines of the federal system by recognising the regional councils as 'supreme organs of the people's authority on their respective territories'. Although many individuals who participated in the work of AVNOJ were not Communists, including the president, Dr Ivan Ribar, the real control of both AVNOJ at national level and of the people's liberation committees at local level lay in Communist hands. Under the Foča regulations, drafted by the veteran communist Moša Pijade, the socialisation of the means of production had already begun.[7] One of the regulations, for example, declared that 'all confiscated property, both movable and immovable, is to become social property and to be entered in the People's Liberation Fund, administered by People's Liberation Committees at communal and district level'.[8]

In 1944 AVNOJ passed regulations nationalising all enemy property. In 1945 this sequestration was extended to include the property of war profiteers, collaborators and 'absent persons', so that by the end of the war 80 per cent of industry, as well as transport and banking, was in state hands.[9] Agricultural land was not, however, nationalised.

All these various measures of state socialism were given regular constitutional form under the constitution passed by the Constituent Assembly and by a series of laws subsequently passed by the Federal Assembly. One of the most important was the Basic Law of State Economic Enterprises, which made explicit the administrative system of regulating the economy. State enterprises were placed under the direct control of a hierarchy of ministries and directorates, to whom the director of the factory was responsible. The rights of trade unions were limited to those of advisory and consultative bodies.[10] The trade unions were, in fact, part of the machinery for transmitting state directives to the workers. In the words of Vukmanović-Tempo, trade unions showed their concern for the workers' interests 'not so much by representing them as by educating them'.[11]

During this period of state administrative control there was, as Tito put it some years later,[12] 'a high degree of concentration of authority in the central organs of the state, and the direct management of the state mechanism by the party'. This was, in fact, the classical Stalinist form of state capitalism, which apologists for the system sought to identify with Marx's phase of 'the dictatorship of the proletariat'. The Party, acting in the name of the proletariat, not only initiated policies, but also directly administered all aspects of the execution of those policies from federal to communal and enterprise level. In later years the dangers of this system were spelled out in the programme presented to the Ljubljana Congress of the League of Communists in 1958:

> Our experience, as well as the experience of other socialist countries, has shown that the management of the economy and of the whole of social life by way of the State apparatus exclusively leads, perforce, to greater centralisation of power, to an ever closer merging of the State and Party apparatus, to their further strengthening, whereby they tend to become independent and impose themselves as a force over and above society.
>
> These are the roots of the specific phenomena of the period of transition: bureaucracy and the bureaucratic–statist deformities in the developments of socialist relations.[13]

Apart from the anti-democratic tendencies of this system, which at its worst could lead to a Stalin-type personality cult, it was ultimately inefficient, as Bičanić pointed out:

> In the Stalinist centralised type of economic system, government machinery was completely merged with party organisation and business management into one monolithic system, run by authoritarian, centralised command through the medium of directives. That is, orders issued from those above to those below in the hierarchical system were not binding on those above, but had to be implemented without question by those below. This inefficient system blocked initiative from underneath and placed responsibility for numerous operational decisions – and mistakes – on top party leaders.[14]

The same point was made by Grozdanić when he stated that: 'Efforts to carry out efficient control of the development of the economy from one centre proved useless and unrealistic'.[15]

THE FIRST FIVE-YEAR PLAN

These doubts about the effectiveness of the state-centralist administrative machinery were afterthoughts, expressed a decade or more after the system had been abandoned. At the time such opinions would have been regarded as heretical, or even treasonable. The five-year plan, 1947–52 was conceived in the spirit of the centralist philosophy. It is probable that it would have failed through a combination of bureaucratic self-strangulation and the inexperience of those who attempted to implement it, but it never had the chance to prove itself. In June 1948 the Cominform expelled the Yugoslav Party, and a Soviet-led economic and propaganda war was initiated with the objective of overthrowing the Yugoslav leaders. As the plan had been based on the assumption of Soviet economic support, it was doomed to fail once Stalin had kicked away its main prop.

The planning machinery established by a law of 25 May 1946[16] was controlled by a federal planning commission to which were subordinated a hierarchy of republican, district and communal planning commissions. The lower echelons took their orders from above and had no initiative in varying the proposals that emanated from the all-powerful federal commission. At the point of production the enterprise director was in the same position as that of the Soviet manager under Stalin: he was told what his target was to be, and his job was to meet it. As the chief planner of the day Boris Kidrić wrote at the end of the first five-year plan, the enterprise 'had virtually nothing to plan, everything being planned from above. The enterprise collaborated, it is true, in the elaboration of operational plans, but these plans depended directly on the basic plans which were dictated from above, in great detail, by the state apparatus that is to say, by the bureaucrats'.[17]

The only plan to be implemented under this centralised system was the five-year plan, 1947–51, which was later extended to 1952. It failed to reach many of its targets, largely because it depended upon trade and aid from the eastern

European countries, especially USSR and Czechoslovakia, and this was interrupted by the expulsion of Yugoslavia from the Cominform in 1948. Nevertheless, a great deal was achieved. The concentration of resources on the rapid development of industry produced a doubling of industrial output and an increase of 75 per cent in non-agricultural employment (see table 9).

Table 9 Indexes of industrial production by sectors, 1946–52 (1939 = 100)

	1946	*1947*	*1948*	*1949*	*1950*	*1951*	*1952*
Total industry	79	121	150	167	172	166	164
Electricity	98	124	176	189	205	217	230
Coal	83	115	129	147	153	143	144
Oil	58	88	152	242	377	416	422
Iron and steel	78	123	147	152	151	160	176
Chemicals	69	120	144	159	160	163	164
Textiles	80	124	156	159	152	132	120
Food	85	131	159	142	131	136	114

Source: Statistički Godišnjak (1962)

The investment pattern reflected the concentration on basic industrial development to the disadvantage of the consumer goods industries and agriculture: 22 per cent of national income was reinvested, and of this 42 per cent went to mining and manufacturing and less than 10 per cent to agriculture (see table 10).

In judging the success or failure of the plan it must be borne in mind that external factors over which the Yugoslavs had no control intervened after 1949 to frustrate the aims of the planners. The arbitrary suspension of trade by the Cominform countries was a major factor. It not only cut off essential supplies, but it also forced the Yugoslavs to divert resources into military expenditure. The severe drought of 1950, which cut agricultural output to below pre-war levels, was also an unforeseen disaster. There were also inherent weaknesses in the planning strategy. The flagrant neglect of agricultural investment in a country where over 65 per cent of the population lived from the land certainly made the effects of the harvest failures in 1950 and 1952 more severe. The inexperience of the planners led them to attempt too much too quickly: factories were started in areas which lacked the material and human resources to sustain them; much investment was wasted; there was no regional strategy of economic growth, so that in spite of the intention to promote more rapid growth in the less developed areas, regional disparities grew.

Table 10 Percentage investments by sector, 1947–52

	1947	*1948*	*1949*	*1950*	*1951*	*1952*
Agriculture	9	12	11	9	8	10
Forestry	2	3	2	1	1	0
Mining and manufacturing	34	32	38	42	46	61
Construction	1	2	3	3	3	2
Transport	21	22	13	13	17	9
Social investment	26	27	30	29	22	16
Other	7	2	3	3	3	2

Source: Statistički Godišnjak

In spite of all its shortcomings, the plan did provide the basis for the rapid industrial growth of the 1950s, and it laid the foundations for Yugoslavia's emergence as a modern industrial society.

AGRARIAN REFORM

The Yugoslavia that the Communist leaders inherited at the end of the Second World War was one of Europe's least developed agrarian countries. There were some 2½ million peasant holdings, of which almost three-quarters were under 5 hectares (12·35 acres) in area.[18] In addition, there were many hundreds of thousands of landless peasants – especially in the Vojvodina – and about 3 million former peasants who had not found permanent employment in other occupations.[19] They formed the reservoir for the flood of migrants who left Yugoslavia for work abroad. The dwarf holdings of the majority of Yugoslav peasants were worked with the minimum of agricultural machinery. According to Dr Vučković, 182 out of every 1000 holdings depended on wooden ploughs, and 379 had no ploughs at all. In addition, a large proportion of the holdings did not really belong to those who farmed them, 'since the debt-ridden peasant owners tilling the land were actually controlled by their creditors, i.e. the village usurers and the city banks'.[20] The position has been summarised by Jozo Tomasevich:

> Yugoslav agriculture during the interwar period was characterised by predominantly peasant subsistence farming, by primitive techniques of production, by dearth of capital and small capacity to save and invest, by a growing agricultural overpopulation which had a tendency to lower the living level of those occupied in agriculture, by a primitively organised market for agricultural products, by an unsolved problem of agricultural credit, and by a heavy taxation burden.[21]

The Yugoslav Communist Party's attitude to the peasantry was to bring about a 'socialist transformation of agriculture' by encouraging the formation of co-operative farms and by persuading peasants to join them. They recognised that they could not at once introduce wholesale collectivisation and that, for an interim period, help would have to be given 'to small and medium peasants in order to increase the productivity of their farms'.

However, the Party did not really trust the peasants, as Tito hinted when in 1948 he reminded the delegates to the fifth Party Congress of Lenin's views on the peasantry:

> The peasant holding continues to remain small-scale production. It is here that we have a boundlessly broad and very deep-rooted basis of capitalism. It is on this basis that capitalism preserves itself and regenerates in the fierce struggle against the state buy-up of grains (and other products) and against the state distribution of supplies in general.[22]

The ultimate aim of collectivisation could not be realised, however, until the ravages of war were repaired and the food shortages of the immediate post-war years had been overcome. Collectivisation in some form was seen as a necessary accompaniment to the modernisation of agriculture. Yugoslavia's industrial revolution needed the support of an agricultural revolution that would enable fewer hands on the land to feed more mouths in the growing industrial towns. In the short run it was necessary to produce more food from the existing peasant holdings and to alleviate the situation of the landless peasants.

The first major step affecting agriculture which the new regime took was the passing of the Law on Agrarian Reform and Resettlement on 23 August 1945.[23] Article 1 stated:

> With the object of allocating land to farmers having no land or having an insufficient quantity thereof, agrarian reform shall be carried out on the whole territory of Democratic Federal Yugoslavia[24] in realisation of the principle: The land belongs to those who cultivate it.

Article 5 laid down that:

> The maximum agricultural holding to remain the property of the farmer cultivating it with his family shall be established by provincial laws, with the proviso that it may not be under 20 nor over 35 hectares of cultivable land. Within these limits the establishment of the maximum shall be effected in each individual case, with due regard to the number of members of the family, the quality of the soil and the type of crop.

Exceptions to the upper limit of 35 hectares were permissible in special circumstances (e.g. where the soil was very poor). The new law provided for the expropriation of the land of certain categories of owners,[25] and its distribution to landless peasants, war veterans and poor peasants from the karstic *polja* behind the Dalmatian coast. The dispossessed included private owners of large estates; banks; churches and monasteries; and Germans. Table 11 shows the number of the various types of owners, and the area of land taken from them and put into the land fund.

The area of land made available for redistribution through the land fund was approximately one-tenth of the total pre-war cultivated area. Individual peasants received 51 per cent of the land thus reallocated. More than half of these newly created farms were given to the 65,000 families who were moved from the poorer agricultural regions and resettled on the rich Pannonian lowlands of Vojvodina and Slavonia,[26] and

Table 11 Land transferred from private owners to land fund under 1945 Law

Type of owner	*Number*	*Area (hectares)*
Large estates	2633	235,000
Banks and joint-stock companies	837	78,000
Churches and monasteries	2625	164,000
Private farmers owning more than legal maximum	8836	122,000
Non-farmers	14,131	32,000
Germans	96,874	673,000
Other	42,584	189,000
Total	168,520	1,493,000

Source: J. Tomasevich, *Collectivization in Eastern Europe*, (Kentucky 1958)

to veterans of the partisan army who were allocated former German lands in Vojvodina. The second largest slice of the expropriated land (24·3 per cent) went to the state. This included areas of existing forest and land capable of re-afforestation. The rest was allocated to state institutions, except for 2·6 per cent which was made available to agricultural co-operatives. Table 12 shows the way in which the land fund was disbursed:[27]

Tomasevich regards the 1945 Law on Agrarian Reform as 'a radical and important piece of legislation for the future development of land tenure in Yugoslavia, but of limited significance as a means of alleviating agricultural overpopulation in the country'.[28]

The law certainly left the door open for collectivisation, but the opportunity was not immediately followed up. In 1951 Yugoslavia was still a land of small peasant proprietors farming plots of less than ten hectares – co-operative farms of all types covered little more than 20 per cent of the total cultivated areas. This was at the height of the campaign to achieve the 'Socialist transformation of the village', which began with the Central Committee resolutions of January 1949. Before this campaign was launched a few hundred voluntary collectives

Table 12 Disbursal of land fund under 1945 Law

Type of new owner	*Area (hectares)*	*Percentage of total area*
Individual peasants	797,400	51
State farms	287,700	18·3
State enterprises	39,700	2·5
Health and educational institutions	20,100	1·3
Nationalised forests	380,300	24·3
Agricultural co-operatives	47,000	2·6
Total	1,572,200	

Source: J. Tomasevich, *Collectivization in Eastern Europe* (Kentucky 1958)

had been established, most by ex-partisans who acquired former German lands in the Vojvodina.[29] During the period 1946–8 the number of collectives grew from 454 to 1318, and the area which they covered from 121,000 to 324,000 hectares (2·4 per cent of the total farm area). The dramatic effect of the collectivisation drive launched in 1949 was to increase the number of collectives to 6626, with a total area of 1,839,978 hectares. At its greatest extent, in 1950, collectivisation covered almost 2½ million hectares, or 17 per cent of all farm land. If one adds to this figure the area of the state farms and other publicly owned agricultural land it appears that, even at the maximum extent of the drive to socialise the village, 78 per cent of Yugoslavia's agricultural area remained in private hands.

I have used the term 'collective' in the foregoing account, but it is necessary to define the term more precisely. The Yugoslav expression *seljačka radna zadruga* (peasant work co-operative)[30] was used to describe four main types of collective farm. In two of these the income of the peasant was related partly to the amount of land he brought in to the collective. He either leased his plot and received an agreed annual payment for it, or he drew interest on the value of his investment of land. In both cases he also received additional payment for the work he performed as a member of the collective's labour force. In the two other main types no interest or rent was payable, remuneration being solely based on work done. In most cases a proportion of the payment was in produce rather than in cash. In all four types the peasant who took his land into a collective was able to retain up to a hectare as his private family plot, and he or his wife could sell any surplus in the local town market. Table 13 shows the distribution of different types of collectives in 1950:

Table 13 Distribution of collective farms, 1950

	*Number of farms**
Land leased by owner at fixed rent	1021
Owner paid interest in respect of capital value of land	2212
No payment made for use of land by collective	3400
Land fully collectivised (cf. Soviet *kolkhoz*)	328

Source: J. Tomasevich, *Collectivization in Eastern Europe* (Kentucky 1958)

In addition to the various forms of peasant work co-operatives there were several hundred large state farms (*poljoprivredne dobre*) which resembled the Soviet *sovkhozi*, and a smaller number of specialised farms belonging to state welfare and educational institutions. In all, farm land in the state sector amounted to about 500,000 hectares.[31]

* Total land area of all types – over 2,000,000 ha.

The collectivisation drive began after the expulsion of the Yugoslav Communist Party from the Cominform and may even have been a response to it. In the bitter exchanges between Moscow and Belgrade during the year before the public denunciation of Tito by Stalin, the question of Yugoslavia's agricultural policy was raised on several occasions. The Yugoslavs were accused of tenderness towards the *kulaks*, and of failing to wage the class war vigorously in the countryside. A comparison of the Yugoslav situation with that of other People's Democracies shows how unjustified were the Cominform's allegations. The Yugoslav land reforms of 1945 fixed the maximum holding of cultivable land at between 25 and 35 hectares,[32] whereas the first post-war reforms in Hungary permitted a maximum of 400 hectares, later reduced to 100. In Poland the maximum varied, from 100 hectares in the regained territories to 50 elsewhere, and similar limits were set in Czechoslovakia. Romania had a general maximum of 50 hectares. It is true, however, that at the time of the Cominform resolution only 2·4 per cent of the Yugoslav farm land was cultivated by the 1300 peasant work co-operatives, and the state sector accounted for a further 3.5 per cent. However, these figures compared favourably with those from other People's Democracies which, at this time, had hardly begun to collectivise.

The resolution of the Second Plenum of the Central Committee of the CPY on 29 January 1949, passed six months after the publication of the Cominform resolution, almost looked like an attempt to prove Stalin wrong. Its implementation certainly sharpened the class conflict in the villages, if by this is meant the intensification of various pressures on the richer farmers. Hitherto, collectivisation had been a voluntary affair, occasionally pushed forward by local party zealots. The main objective of the government was to get food out of the villages and not to harass the more successful peasants into sullen non-co-operation. Inducements were offered to persuade peasants to enter collectives,[33] and if an isolated individual stood out against joining a collective when his neighbours had formed one, he could, in certain circumstances, be compelled to abandon his farm.[34]

Although the 1949 resolution stressed that the peasants were free to refuse entry to collectives, the zeal of young Party members often led to *de facto* compulsion.[35] Apart from social pressure and veiled threats, the taxation system discriminated heavily against the larger private farmers, and their obligations under the system of compulsory deliveries of produce were extremely onerous.

In its first two years the collectivisation drive led to an increase in the number of households in the collectives from 60,000 in 1948 to 418,000 in 1950. The area under collectivisation increased during the same period from 324,000 to 2,400,000 hectares.

This hasty and ill-thought-out scheme failed to produce more food than before or to utilise more efficiently the large labour force available. By the end of 1950 it was clear to the Party leaders that a mistake had been made,[36] but it was not until November 1951 that the policy was officially changed.[37]

The new policy declared that 'the consolidation and gradual enlargement of collective ownership . . . in the hands of the *general agricultural co-operatives* . . . becomes the basic method of further socialist transformation of the village'.

NOTES

1 Article I, General Law on People's Committees: A. General provision, *Službeni List* (Official Gazette) (22 November 1952).

2 Speech on 29 November 1963 at a joint meeting of the Federal Board of SAWPY and of the Federal Assembly, reprinted in English in *Two Decades of Socialist Yugoslavia.* (Belgrade 1964).

3 English text, 'Statute of the Commune of Požarevac', *Collection of Yugoslav Laws*, XII (Belgrade 1965).

4 It presumably appears under 'socio-political organisation'.

5 In 1967 the League of Communists had 1,013,000 members, but SAWPY had over 8 million.

6 Seventy-one delegates were invited, but the Slovenes and some others were unable to reach Bihać in time.

7 'Explanations and instructions for the work of People's Liberation Committees in Liberated Areas'.

8 Quoted in *Workers' Management in Yugoslavia*, no. 16 (Belgrade 1970), p. 11.

9 Law for the Protection and Control of National Property (May 1945); Law Concerning Confiscation and its Execution (9 June 1945); Law for the Confiscation of Enemy Property by the State, and the Sequestration of the Property of Absent Persons (July 1946).

10 S. Grozdanić, 'Administrative Management of Public Enterprises in

Yugoslavia, report presented to the Thirteenth International Congress of Administrative Sciences, Paris 1965.

11 Report to the Fourth Congress of Trade Unions (Belgrade 1959).

12 J. B. Tito, *Forty Years of the C.P.Y.* (Belgrade 1959).

13 Draft programme of the LCY, 1958.

14 R. Bičanić, 'Economics of Socialism in a Developed Country', *Foreign Affairs*, 44 (1966), p. 635.

15 Grozdanić, in report to Thirteenth Int. Cong. of Administrative Sciences

16 *Službeni List*, no. 45 (1946).

17 Boris Kidrič, 'Proposals for New Economic Laws', *Komunist* 4–5 (1951), p. 2.

18 P. Marković, 'Posedovna Struktura Jugoslovensko Poljoprivrede', *Ekonomist*, 1 (1960), pp. 108–27. The figures of size of land holding are for 1949.

19 Dr Mihailo Vučković, Foreword to *The Legal Status of Agricultural Land* (Belgrade 1962).

20 Vučković, *The Legal Status of Agricultural Land.*

21 Jozo Tomasevich, 'Collectivization of Agriculture in Yugoslavia', chapter 7 in *Collectivization in Eastern Europe* (Kentucky 1958), p. 166.

22 J. B. Tito, *Political Report of the Central Committee of the CPY* (Belgrade 1948), p. 124.

23 *Službeni List*, no. 64 (1945).

24 This was the title used by the provisional government in 1945. With the coming into force of the 1946 constitution the country became known as the Federal People's Republic of Yugoslavia.

25 Article 3, para (e): 'The excess of cultivable land over 3–5 hectares whose owners' principal occupation is not farming, and which is not tilled by themselves and their families, but through leasehold or hired labour'.

26 Dr M. Vučković, *The Legal Status of Agricultural Land*, p. 86.

27 The discrepancy between the figure of 1,493,000 hectares confiscated and 1,572,200 distributed is explained partly by the existence of forest and farm land already in state ownership before the expropriations.

28 Tomasevich in *Collectivization in Eastern Europe*, p. 167.

29 The author visited such a farm near Sremska Mitrovica in 1948.

30 The term *zadruga* also has a special meaning to historians of Yugoslav society.

31 In 1945 the state sector covered 388,000 hectares; by 1957 it had grown to 750,000 hectares.

32 The maximum varied according to local conditions.

33 In Sremska Mitrovica in 1948 the author saw one example of the type of inducements offered. Yugoslavia had at this time, in common with other People's Democracies, a two-price system for clothing and other consumer goods. Items in the shops bore one tag showing the 'free market' price of the commodity and another, four or five times cheaper, showing the price to be paid by holders of ration coupons. (Peasants who joined the collective were given extra coupons, enabling them to buy more shoes, household utensils, etc., at these lower prices.) Collective farmers

were also included in health and welfare schemes on a similar basis to industrial workers, whilst private peasants had to fend for themselves.

34 If, for example, a private holding prevented the consolidation of a nearby collective, compulsion could be used. Compensation was offered, but often at a very low price, and frequently in the form of an allocation of an equivalent amount of land.

35 The author knows of an eighteen-year-old Party member who was sent into his home village in Macedonia to order his father to join a collective.

36 An indication that the steam had gone out of the drive was the slight drop during 1951 in the number of collectives. The figures are: 1950 – 6964 collectives with 418,659 households; 1951 – 6797 collectives with 417,958 households.

37 Directive of the Central Committee of the CPY, 'Regarding further ways of Socialist transformation of the village'. Report in *Borba* (25 November 1951).

9 The second phase in post-war development

The halting of the collectivisation drive at the end of 1950 was one manifestation of a change of direction in the policies of the Communist Party over the whole field of economic and political affairs. In the late 1950s the changes were interpreted retrospectively by many Yugoslav spokesmen as logical extensions of Marxist theories concerning the 'withering away of the state' – as, for example, at the Ljubljana Congress of 1958 – but more recently there has been a tendency to admit that they were in part a response to the severe economic crisis that followed the expulsion from the Cominform. As Pero Morača wrote in 1966:

> The USSR and East European countries broke off all agreements on cooperation with Yugoslavia and carried out an economic blockade against her . . . This pressure had a particularly adverse effect upon Yugoslavia's economy and reconstruction, because the USSR and East European countries were to have accounted for 50 per cent of her total trade and an even greater part of the planned import of industrial equipment.[1]

The trade deficit increased tenfold between 1948 and 1950.[2] Further disruption to the economy was caused by the need to increase defence expenditure, which by 1950 absorbed 23 per cent of the national income. Finally, there was a severe drought in 1950, which cut agricultural output back to pre-war levels (see table 14). The effect of all these severe blows to the economy was reflected in the drop in industrial output that occurred between 1949 and 1953 (see table 15).

The psychological shock of the break with the Cominform

Table 14 Indexes of agricultural production in Yugoslavia, 1948–57 (1930–9 = 100)

1948	*1949*	*1950*	*1951*	*1952*	*1953*	*1954*	*1955*	*1956*	*1957*
103	103	75	106	75	106	94	116	97	140

Source: Statistički Godišnjak, 525 (Belgrade 1962)

Table 15 Indexes of industrial production, 1946–52 (1939 = 100)

1946	*1947*	*1948*	*1949*	*1950*	*1951*	*1952*
79	121	150	167	172	166	164

Source: Statistički Godišnjak (1962)

and the severe economic setback that followed stimulated a re-examination of the theoretical basis of Yugoslav Communism. In Morača's words:

> The analysis of Yugoslav social reality clearly showed that the system of revolutionary statism (étatism) which had come to the fore in the years immediately after the war, acted as a fetter upon development and was a source of serious bureaucratic deformations.

As early as May 1949 there were signs of a shift away from the centralist methods of administration. The Law on People's Committees (May 1949), which gave greater powers, both political and economic, to the organs of local government, was the first legislative enactment that weakened the power of the central state machinery. Speaking in the debate on the new law in the Federal People's Assembly, Edvard Kardelj stated that:

> The development of socialism can follow no other road but that of the continuous strengthening of socialist democracy,

> implying broader autonomy of the working masses, their enlistment on an ever wider scale in the operation of the state machinery from lowest to highest level, and their growing participation in the management of every enterprise, institution, etc.

During the same year a number of federal economic ministries were replaced by councils at federal and republican level, 'as new bodies of state management of the economy'.[3] These minor administrative changes in no way weakened the power of the Party over the state apparatus, and their significance should not be over-stressed. More important in the long-term development of the Yugoslav concept of socialist democracy were the first experiments in workers' self-management, which began in 1949. In December 1949 over 200 large enterprises established advisory bodies on which the workers were represented. By June 1950, when the first law on workers' self-management was enacted by the Federal Assembly,[4] there were 520[5] such bodies in existence, covering 12 per cent of all industrial enterprises. Immediately after the passing of the Basic Law, arrangements were made for the election of workers' councils in all industrial enterprises employing more than thirty workers,[6] and by October 1950 6319 enterprises, with a total working force of 974,932 workers, had established workers' councils.

The Basic Law defined the concept of workers' self management:

> Factories, mines, carriers, transport, trade, agricultural, forest, public utility and other state economic enterprises, as the general people's property, shall be managed by working collectives on behalf of the social community, within the framework of the state economic plan . . . The working collectives shall exercise this right of management through workers councils. . . .[7]

When first established the workers' councils had little more power than the pre-June advisory bodies that had been established under a set of 'Instructions for the Establishment and Work of Workers' Councils in State Economic Enterprises', issued on 23 December 1949 under the signatures of Boris Kidrič (Minister–President of the Economic Council) and Djuro Salaj (President of the Trade Unions). These instructions speak of the 'consultative functions' of workers' councils: 'The Instructions emphasised that the creation of workers' councils did not reduce the director's role in running the enterprise . . .'[8]

The Basic Law spelled out in detail the rights and prerogatives of management:

> A director shall organise the process of production in an enterprise and directly conduct the realisation of the plan and the operation of the enterprise, enforcing the laws and other prescriptions, the conclusions of the managing board of the enterprise and the orders and instructions of the appropriate state organs, as well as of the managing board and the director of the higher economic association.
>
> A director shall be directly responsible for the enforcement of the laws, or other legal prescriptions and the orders of the appropriate state organs, and he shall ensure their application in an enterprise. Within the economic plan and conformably to the conclusions of the managing board of an enterprise, the director . . . shall make contracts and allocate the working assets. A contract shall be valid as soon as made by the director. A director shall represent an enterprise before the state organs and in the legal relations with different physical and legal persons. He may authorise another person to represent the enterprise in determinate legal matters.
>
> The director of an enterprise shall hire workers and appoint other employees in the enterprise, except those concerning whom it was otherwise decreed by the special prescriptions, and he shall issue the decisions relating to their labour relations with the enterprise. The director . . . shall make decisions relating to the termination of employment of the workers and office employees, unless this power was delegated to other persons in the enterprise on the basis of general prescriptions.
>
> The workers and office employees have the right to file objections and appeals with the managing board of an enterprise against every decision relating to termination of

employment or assignment to another job, and final decision shall rest with the managing board. The director . . . shall assign the workers and office employees to the individual jobs and determine their duties. The workers and office employees . . . shall be accountable to the director for their work in the enterprise. The director . . . shall ensure discipline in the work and operation of the enterprise. The director need not consult the workers' council in routine matters but he does consult them when major changes in policy are envisaged.

In practise the workers' councils of 1950 had little real power over the managers, who in turn were agents of the state and, ultimately, of the Party. The economy was still managed from the centre, and as long as this situation remained there was no possibility of achieving either autonomy for the enterprise or workers' control within the enterprise. One of the key questions of workers' control was the power of the workers' council to distribute incomes.

In the period immediately after 1950 the management board of the enterprise – not the workers' council – made the first draft of income scales. The workers' council had the right to make comments and raise objections. The draft scale, together with any modifications proposed by the workers' council, was then sent to the people's committee of the commune, which, in consultation with the trade unions, would settle the final allocation of incomes and send the approved scale back to the enterprise. If there was serious disagreement between the parties involved in these procedures, provision was made for arbitration by a commission set up by the government of the Republic.[9]

An important principle that was established from the outset was that income distribution within an enterprise was not the sole responsibility of the workers in the enterprise. The people's committee of the commune (*opština*) had a major role to play in this, as in other matters affecting the economy of its *opština*.

The local people's committee nominated the director of an enterprise on the recommendation of a commission, 50 per cent of whose members were elected by the workers' council. The workers' council could recommend to the *opština* that a director should be dismissed, but the final decision rested with the people's committee. The director has been described as

> a representative, an organ of the local community in the enterprise. . . . The local community, through the law, has entrusted him with seeing that all the decisions and actions of the bodies of workers' management are within the framework and the spirit of the law and other regulations enacted by the authorities.[10]

During the 1950s a number of laws were enacted by the Federal Assembly which gave wider powers to the people's committees of the communes, and which made adjustments to their structures in order to accommodate the evolving system of workers' self-management. The law of 1952[11] stated that: 'The people's committees as the local organs of *State* authority shall be the organs of popular self-government in the communes . . .' (Art. 1), and that the duty of the committee was to 'safeguard the economic, social and cultural development of a commune'.

The people's committees were composed of two groups of elected councillors. The people's chamber was directly elected by all adult citizens, but the producers' council was composed of members indirectly elected by two electoral colleges. One of these colleges represented 'industry, trade and arts and crafts', and the other 'the group of agriculture, which shall include farmers affiliated to farmers' co-operatives and the members of their households engaged in agriculture, workers and office employees in state farms, workers and office employees of farmers, co-operatives and other agricultural workers'.[12] The councils of producers at first constituted 50 per cent of the total membership of the people's committees, but this proportion was later raised to 75 per cent.[13] The representation of an enterprise on the electoral college that chose the members of the producers' councils was determined in relation to its 'contribution to the social product'. Thus, the weight of decision making was made to depend on the representatives of the organised industrial workers, in the larger enterprises operating under the self-management system. The private peasants, who outnumbered the industrial workers by two to one, could vote only in the direct election of the people's councillors, who constituted only one-quarter of the membership of the people's committees. In addition to this, the factory worker had a second vote for the much more powerful producers' councils. The influence of the peasantry was further reduced in 1959 as a result of a boundary reorganisation which enlarged the communes. The number of communes was reduced from 1193 to 760,[14] and their boundaries were redrawn to create units in which an urban area was linked to its adjoining rural hinterland. The town disappeared as a separate administrative entity, and the previous differentiation between urban and rural communities was abolished.[15]

RELATIONS BETWEEN ENTERPRISE AND THE COMMUNE

The various constitutional changes referred to above represent the first steps towards the decentralisation of economic decision making and the weakening of central state power (or destatisation). Former state monopolies became 'social property', administered but not owned by working collectives.[16] The commune replaced the federal or republican government as the political body responsible for the general direction of economic policy, and through the producers' councils the government of the commune was intimately linked to the workers' councils of the enterprises operating on its territory.

The role of the commune became particularly important in the founding of new enterprises, although legally new undertakings could also be established by the federal or republican governments, trade unions, co-operatives or other 'socio-political organisations'. In most cases the approval of the people's committee of the commune was required. The ILO report *Workers' Management in Yugoslavia* stated that:

> In practice communes and districts generally take the initiative in founding new undertakings, while the federal authorities or the republics only do so in the case of particularly large projects. Normally, undertakings are founded in accordance with the requirements of the plan. They are usually financed by advances from public investment funds or by bank loans.[17]

During the period between the founding of a new enterprise and the constitution of the workers' council the undertaking was managed by a director appointed by the commune. When the preparatory stage was completed the commune was required to approve the constitution before a workers' council could be established. Enterprises that were established before 18 December 1953[18] were required to submit their constitutions to the commune for approval. Even after the approval of the constitution the enterprise was still subject to regular 'social control' by the commune.

The most important sphere in which the commune exercised control was over the distribution of the funds of the enterprise. The accounts passed by the workers' council were examined by the financial and labour-planning departments of the commune and then brought before a full meeting of the producers' council. The ILO report states that:

> The Commune producers' councils must carry out a general study [of the reports of the workers' councils] at the end of each half year . . . and are entitled to make recommendations to the workers' councils concerning the distribution of the net income and other aspects of the economic management of the undertaking directly related to the targets of the national economic plan, investment programmes, vocational training schemes, etc. . . . The representatives of the workers' councils are also normally entitled to attend the sitting of the producers' council at which the position of the undertaking is discussed. . . . The workers' council . . . must then meet once more and consider the recommendations of the producers' council.[19]

If the workers' council disputed the recommendations of the people's committee it could appeal to the producers' council of the district or the republic and, in certain circumstances, to the courts. During the 1950s this rarely happened.

THE WORKERS' COUNCIL AND THE MANAGEMENT OF THE ENTERPRISE

The working collective, in which the rights of management theoretically reside, include all those employed in an enterprise from the director down to the floor sweeper, but for electoral purposes only those over eighteen years old who enjoy full Yugoslav civil rights are able to participate.[20] In enterprises with fewer than thirty workers the whole work force constituted the workers' council, but in larger collectives a workers' council was elected to exercise the functions of self-management. At its first meeting the workers' council elected a management board of from three to eleven members. In enterprises with less than seven workers, the whole working force constituted the managing board.

In 1952 there were 8800 enterprises within the system of self-management, and of these 4187 had fewer than thirty workers. The average size of work force was 114 members. By 1958 the average size had increased to 146, and the proportion of enterprises with less than thirty workers had dropped from 47 to 43 per cent of the total. In the manufacturing industry, however, the size of units was considerably larger than the average, as the majority of the very small undertakings were in catering and handicrafts. In 1958 the average size of a collective in industry was 336 members. There was also a wide regional variation in the size of collectives. In Croatia the average was 180, whilst in Macedonia it was only 110. Nevertheless, despite these differences between sectors and regions, the typical working collective was small enough for most of the members to know each other. Only 80 industrial concerns (3 per cent of the total) and 26 building enterprises (also 3 per cent) employed more than 2000 workers in 1959. Over 50 per cent of industrial enterprises had between 30 and 250 workers.[21] The functioning of the self-management system during the first decade since its introduction in 1950 should be seen in the context of these figures. The changes that occurred in the system during the second decade, 1960–70, were partly adaptations necessitated by the changing structure of industry. Technological change and the demands of efficiency, especially after the reforms of 1965, resulted in mergers and amalgamations, and the average size of enterprises steadily grew. The channels of communication appropriate in an enterprise with 100 workers employed in a single factory are no longer relevant when the labour force has grown to tens of thousands, dispersed in several centres of production.

NOTES

1 Pero Morača, *Savez Komunista Jugoslavije* (Belgrade 1966), p. 52.

2 From 600 million dinars to 6000 million dinars.

3 *Radničko Samoupravljanje u Jugoslaviji*, ed. S. Grozdanić and M. Radosavljević (Belgrade 1970), p. 25. They were abolished in 1952.

4 Basic Law on the Management of State Economic Enterprises and Higher Economic Associations by Working Collectives (27 June 1950).

5 The first 'pilot' workers' council was elected at the Prvoborac Cement Factory at Solin on 31 December 1949. Grozdanić and Radosavljević, *Radničko Samoupravljanje u Jugoslaviji*, p. 22.

6 In units with below thirty workers, the whole working force (the working collective) constituted the workers' council.

7 Basic Law, Article 1 (English text from *Social Government in Yugoslavia*, Information Service, Belgrade 1957).

8 Grozdanić and Radosavljević, *Radničko Samoupravljanje u Jugoslaviji*, p. 20.

9 T. Tomić, *Radni odnosi u privredi* (Belgrade 1957).

10 M. Bogosavljević and M. Pesaković, *Workers' Management of a Factory in Yugoslavia* (Belgrade 1959), p. 65

11 General Law on People's Committees, 1 March 1952, *Službeni List*, No. 22 (1952).

12 Law Amending and Supplementing the General Law on People's Committees, Art. 35, *Službeni List*, no. 40 (1953).

13 *Statistički Godišnjak* (1959, 1960).

14 *Statistički Godišnjak* (1959, 1960).

15 Amendments to the General Law of 1955, *Službeni List*, no. 24 (1959) and no. 47 (1959).

16 Fundamental Law of 13 January 1953 Art. 6. *Službeni List*, no. 2 (1953).

17 International Labour Organisation (ILO), *Workers' Management in Yugoslavia* (Geneva 1962), p. 58.

18 This was the date on which two ordinances were issued under the terms of the Constitutional Law of 1953. They laid down precise rules for the foundation, management and liquidation of enterprises.

19 *Workers' Management in Yugoslavia*, pp. 238–9.

20 In 1952 5·8 per cent of the working force did not have a vote. By 1957 the percentage had fallen to 2·5. These figures are calculated from the tables in the *Statistički Bilten* by subtracting the number of registered voters in the workers' council elections from that of the total work force.

21 Figures calculated from *Statistički Bilten*, 137, (1959) and 143 (1959).

10 From Party to League

At its Sixth Congress in November 1952 the Communist Party changed its name to that of the League of Communists (Savez Komunista). This symbolic act registered the intention of the Communist leaders to change the relationship between the Party and the State. Under the system of administrative socialism, 'Government machinery was completely merged with party organisation and business management into one monolithic system, run by authoritarian, centralised command through the medium of directives.'[1]

The shortcomings of this system were becoming increasingly apparent to the Party leaders. As Bičanić wrote in 1966, 'This inefficient system blocked initiative from underneath and placed responsibility for numerous operational decisions – and mistakes – on top party leaders'.[2]

Under the 'new system' the position of the party organisation was that of arbiter, without formal responsibility for running current affairs; this made criticism and even personnel changes in government possible without directly engaging the authority of the Party.[3] The framework for the new system was set up by the resolutions of the 1952 Congress and by the new federal constitution enacted in 1953.[4] It was some time, however, before the reality of these changes became apparent at grass-roots level. There were doubts among the Communist leaders about how far they should go in relinquishing administrative control over the state machinery and the economy. Some, like Djilas, went to the extreme of advocating a second, albeit socialist, party.[5] The report of the Seventh Congress of the League refers to two other categories of deviationists. It criticises 'the habits acquired during the period of centralised economic administration which are still apparent in the resistance of some executives to the principles of workers' management – which they have not understood and sometimes treated as a mere formality'. At the other end of the scale from these supporters of 'the old idea that final decisions should lie with the Communists' were those who felt that 'they were not bound by the policies and decisions of their organisations and of the leaders of the League'.[6]

At its Seventh Congress, held in Ljubljana in 1958, there was an attempt to construct a new theory of communism, based on the experience of the decade since the expulsion of the Yugoslav Party from the Cominform. The argument put forward was that: 'centralised forms of state management of the means of production' can play 'a positive role in the development of socialism', particularly in the early stages of industrialisation and 'until the principal factors of backwardness have been overcome'. But in exercising its control over the economy there is a danger that:

> . . . the state may turn into a factor of stagnation, into a fetter of social development. . . . Our experience has shown that the management of the economy and of the whole of social life exclusively through the state apparatus inevitably leads to greater centralisation of power, to an ever closer merging of the State and Party apparatus, strengthening them to the point where they tend to become independent and impose themselves as a force over and above society.[7]

These 'bureaucratic–étatist deformities' can lead to personality cults, and to the betrayal of the revolution. The way out of this cul-de-sac is to initiate, as soon as possible, forms of direct democracy. Gradually the State will begin to wither away as socialist consciousness develops and as new forms of social and economic organisation evolve. The evolutionary process will be a long one, however, and during the transitional period the State will still have vital functions to perform: 'It will be less an instrument of force, and more and more an instrument of social self-government, based on the consciousness of the common material interests of working people and on the concrete needs of their producing organisations.' The task of the League of Communists is 'to give ideological guidance in the process of socialist development; in doing so it is in the vanguard. . . . But this does not confer any special prerogatives or privileges on the members of the League'.[8] The question as to whether, if the State eventually withers away, the League will go the same way is one to which the communist leaders have given no clear answer – or rather, they have given a variety of different answers. In any case, this is not a question of immediate practical concern. The State and the League are likely to be there in some form for many years to come, but the form will undoubtedly change.

During the 1950s the Communists began to adjust themselves to their new role. They no longer held private meetings to brief their members as to how they should vote on every item of the agendas of the public bodies on which they served. The resolutions were couched in general terms and were concerned with broad principles rather than with detailed instructions. They had more initiative to act on their own judgement, but they were nevertheless expected to act within the policy of the League, and could be disciplined for not doing so. Also, on matters of vital concern it was still possible for the League machinery to be used in order to obtain a decision in a workers' council or producers' council on a specific resolution. Communists were expected to be activists, playing a leading role in public life. The percentage of Communists serving on workers councils varied from place to place, and any statistics should be treated with caution. However, there is no doubt that during the 1950s, in all key sectors of the economy, the workers' councils of the major enterprises were led by members of the League, and that the majority of members of managing boards were Communists.

PEOPLE'S FRONT TO SOCIALIST ALLIANCE

The Communist Party was not the only political organisation which functioned in Yugoslavia after the revolution. There was also the People's Front, an organisation which was entirely subordinate to the Communist Party in its political line, but with a much larger membership. The Party worked through the Front, and was in fact accused by the Cominform of losing its identity within the amorphous mass of the larger body. The Cominform strictures in 1948 were unjust to the Yugoslavs, whose practice with regard to the People's Front was entirely in harmony with the Soviet line.

In February 1953, two months after the Party had changed its name, the Front became the Socialist Alliance of the Working People of Yugoslavia (SAWPY). Its membership was enlarged until, by 1960, a majority of the adult population were, at least nominally, members.[9] It is doubtful, however, if most of the members were active, or even if many realised that they were members, for SAWPY was made up of a number of affiliated organisations – trade unions, veterans' associations, cultural, youth and women's organisations, and above all the League of Communists. After the 1953 Congress the activities of SAWPY were directed principally towards the strengthening of self-management at commune level. It, rather than the League of Communists, called public meetings to discuss major political issues, and to mobilise public opinion at election times.

THE TRADE UNIONS

The early post-revolutionary trade unions in Yugoslavia were modelled on the Soviet pattern. Initially fourteen unions were established. These were financed mainly by the federal and local governments, and the task of the 3500 salaried officials[11] was to 'mobilise' the working masses to produce more. In addition to their role as transmission belts of State and Party directives, they also performed a number of welfare functions for their members. After the introduction of workers' self-management the unions saw their principal function as being the protector and guardian of the new system.

'We show our concern for the workers' interests not so much by representing them as by educating them and helping them to settle their problems at first hand, to share in the management of undertakings, the regulation of internal relationships within each collective . . .,' declared Svetozar Vukmanović at the 1959 Trade Union Congress. He claimed that there was no need for the unions 'to perform a protective role in the classical meaning of the term, because there is no wage earning relationship vis-à-vis private capitalists or the state as a public capitalist'.[12]

Although the League remains paramount in the sphere of political decision making, it has gradually withdrawn from direct management of the economy. Politically, Yugoslavia is closer to the original concept of 'People's Democracy' than to the west European model of liberal parliamentarianism. It is true that there is a far greater freedom of expression and of movement than has ever been permitted in the Soviet-style 'People's Democracies', and the methods by which political decisions are taken are more open to public pressure, but the intention of the League is to maintain the role as defined in the classical Stalinist concept: '. . . Even when there exist several parties and social and political organisations, [People's Democracy can succeed] on the one indisputable condition that the only leading and directing force of all political life is the Communist Party, which does not and cannot share leadership with anyone.'[13]

The problem for Yugoslav Communists is to know how it is possible to determine the broad strategic aims of the society in a political sense without interfering in the day-to-day management of the economy. In a complex society that has close economic relations with both socialist and capitalist economies, drawing the line between economic and political decision making or between strategic and tactical decisions becomes increasingly difficult. Contradictions are encountered at all levels within Yugoslav society. They manifested themselves in the struggle within the League which led to the purging of Ranković in 1966, and in the 'conflict between the autonomy of the enterprise and the central allocation of investments'. According to Professor Samardžija, this conflict 'led to resistance by the enterprises towards the plan, and particularly of decentralised units towards the centralised, federal plan. The more the system developed, the more acute this conflict became, and a crisis was reached in 1965'.[14]

THE NEED FOR REFORM

According to Rudolf Bičanić, the reform of 1965 was 'an integration of short-term and long-term economic objectives and the implementation of the 1963 Constitution'.[15] In one sense it can be seen as a further stage in a process of evolution towards the objectives set by the League of Communists at its 1958 Congress. Bičanić spoke of the four *D*'s – Decentralisation, De-étatisation, De-politicisation and Democratisation.

These were seen as the goals of the self-management system. When their ultimate fulfilment is achieved, the State will have withered away, and society will consist of a commonwealth of self-managed, autonomous socialist enterprises and institutions.

In another and more mundane sense the reform was an attempt to find a way out of the economic crisis of the early 1960s. That there was a crisis in the early 1960s is readily admitted by Yugoslav economists, and indeed the official figures spell out the details. The causes of the crisis and the remedies to be applied are not so readily agreed.

One school of thought, that of the reformers, sees the survival of 'étatist' and centralist tendencies, in conflict with the basic tenets of self-management, as the culprit:

> . . . from 1961 onwards the system of planning described above (i.e. the 1957–61 and 1961–5 plans) has been involved in a crisis culminating in the economic reform, and an ever more frequently advanced demand that the system and method of planning be adapted to the changes that have occurred in the self-management system . . . It consists . . . in an intensification of two contradictory tendencies in planning at the level of enterprises and in the global macroeconomic spheres that are under the control of the state. The system of planning contained two contradictory series of economic decisions and impulses, of which one had its voice in the administration and the other in the self-management bodies of the enterprises.[16]

After giving a number of detailed examples of the 'organisational and economic disharmony between planning at the levels of micro- and macro- economy', Maksimović concludes that:

> the central topic of criticism was the still strong influence of the administration and bureaucracy in the adoption of macro-economic decisions concerning the orientation of the economy, as well as the strong participation of administrative control in the formation of accumulation and the distribution of investments.[17]

If this view is accepted, the remedy seems to be to remove the remaining vestiges of centralism and bureaucracy, in order to give the self-management system the freedom to solve its problems in its own way. Another analysis might lay the blame on the too rapid development of self-management, and look to a restoration of many of the elements of the State centralist system. As Peter Wiles points out in his comments on Maksimović's paper, whatever sociological, psychological and political advantages the self-management system may have,

> . . . when we turn to economics we find little if any advantage. On the macro-level the sheer productive performance of self-administered Yugoslavia is excellent, but growth was no slower during the 'administrative period', and the performance of Soviet-type economies continues to be at least as good. Even certain capitalist countries do as well or better. Again, inflation and rising prices are as rampant as nowhere in Europe. . . .[18]

Wiles does not, of course, recommend a return to centralism, but some Yugoslavs, accepting his argument that self-management did not *per se* lead to higher growth and did tend towards inflation, were in favour of curbing its further development. Politically this group was defeated with the fall of Ranković in 1966. Nevertheless, its view was that self-management, whilst in itself a desirable goal, should not be allowed to get out of hand:

> One line represents those economists who view with a certain scepticism the possibilities for a rapid practical organisation of such a concept as self-management planning. They express their misgivings that one might prematurely begin with the abolition of the existing functions and prerogatives of the state in planning and the creation of a special kind of 'institutional vacuum', without leaving enough time for a period of transition . . . [during which] the anomalies perceived in the course of the last decade of self-management [can be corrected]. They are especially alarmed due to the emergence of monopoly structures, the autonomous effect and differentiation in the creation of personal incomes, the existence of informal groups in enterprises which are against

the co-ordination and integration of their business activity with other, less developed enterprises. This is why it is apprehended that – without a long-term co-ordination – consultations on co-ordination of planning activity will be futile.[19]

The performance of the Yugoslav economy since the reform will be examined later, but it is appropriate at this stage to observe that the fears expressed above were reawakened during the crisis that led to the 1971 devaluation of the dinar. The reform was intended to prepare the way for the final step from extensive to intensive methods of production. It was to give priority to the mechanism of the market as the main determinant of economic policy, and to reduce to a minimum the role of the State. By introducing the concept of 'the international division of labour' it finally killed the notion of economic autarchy, and opened the Yugoslav market to competition from the industrially developed capitalist economies of western Europe.

NOTES

1 R. Bičanić, 'Economics of Socialism in a Developed Country', *Foreign Affairs*, no. 44 (1966), p. 634.
2 Bičanić, in *FA*, no. 44 (1966).
3 Bičanić, in *FA*, no. 44 (1966).
4 Constitutional Law, 13 January, 1953.
5 The Third Plenum of the League's Central Committee, January 1954, argued that, by denying the guiding role of the League, Djilas was taking the path of petty bourgeois *laissez-faire* and anarchy.
6 *VII Kongres Saveza Komunista Jugoslavije* (Belgrade 1958), p. 143.
7 Draft programme of the LCY 1958, *VII Kongres SKJ* (Program SKJ) (Belgrade 1958), p. 326.
8 From President Tito's closing speech to the Fifth Congress of SAWPY, reported in *Borba* (23 March 1960).
9 There were 6·5 million members in 1960. The economically active population was 8·3 million.
10 For a further survey of the role of the unions, see F. Singleton, 'Workers' Self Management and the Role of the Trade Unions in Yugoslavia', in *Trade Union Register* (London 1970), pp. 231–47.
11 The figure of 3500 for the number of salaried officials is given by Stamenković in *Naša Stvarnost*, 11, no. 10 (1957), p. 337.
12 'Cetvrti Kongres Saveza Sindikata Jugoslavije' (Report of the Chairman to the Fourth Congress of Trade Unions) (Belgrade 1959).

13 *Great Soviet Encyclopaedia* (Moscow 1954), p. 134
14 Miloš Samardžija, 'The Yugoslav Economic System and Contemporary Socialist Economic Theory', *Ekonomist* (English issue) (1969), p. 51.
15 R. Bičanić, in *Foreign Affairs*, no. 44 (1966).
16 Ivan Maksimović, 'The Economic System and Workers' Self-Management in Yugoslavia', in M. J. Broekmeyer, *Yugoslav Workers' Self-Management*, (Dordrecht, 1970), p. 143.
17 Maksimović, in *Yugoslav Workers' Self-Management*, p. 145.
18 P. Wiles, 'A Descent Towards Particulars', in Broekmeyer, *Yugoslav Workers' Self-Management*, p. 154.
19 Maksimović, in Broekmeyer, *Yugoslav Workers' Self-Management*, p. 147.

11 The third phase in post-war development

In almost every aspect of economic, social and political life, Yugoslavia in 1960 bore little outward resemblance to the country as it existed in 1950. Workers' self-management had been firmly established throughout the public sector of industry and agriculture. The Party, under its new name, no longer sought to regulate every aspect of the life of the society. By abandoning the cruder forms of centralised control over the economy, greater flexibility and realism had been introduced into the methods of planning. Objectives were defined in general terms, in contrast to the rigidly set targets of the first five-year plan. Perhaps even more significant than these structural changes, the climate of thinking in which decision making operated had been transformed. Nevertheless, many vestiges of the old system remained. If the Communist Party had withdrawn from the direct exercise of administrative control, it still had enormous influence as the only centre of political power. Members of the League of Communists held key positions at all levels of economic and social life. Their informal influence was probably as great as it had ever been, even though its formal powers had been given up. The workers' councils were restricted in their freedom of manoeuvre by legal constraints and informal pressures. The banking system was still centralised and was subject to government control. Through its control over investment, the State was still able to determine the pattern of economic development. The state also retained direct control over foreign trade, and many prices of essential commodities were centrally regulated.

The performance of the economy during the 1950s was in many ways impressive. Between 1952 and 1959 the average annual growth of industrial production was 13 per cent. This rapid growth in itself created problems, especially in the balance of payments. In the period 1954–6 the average deficit on the foreign trade account was 12,805 million dinars. By 1958 it had reached 47,984 million dinars. At this time there was no large balancing flow of invisible exports from tourism or from the remittances of Yugoslav workers abroad. Not only was the size of the trade gap increasing in amount, but there was a fall in the ratio of exports to imports. In 1954 97 per cent of the cost of imports was covered by export earnings. In 1961 this had dropped to 62 per cent. Table 16 shows the trends during the late 1950s and early 1960s.

Table 16 Value of exports as a percentage of imports, 1954–61

1954	97	1958	64
1955	78	1959	69
1956	68	1960	69
1957	60	1961	62

Source: Statistički Godišjnak (1962)

Yugoslavia was spared a major economic crisis arising out of this dismal performance owing to the massive United States aid received during this period. Between 1953 and 1958 the inflow of US aid was 61 per cent above the value of the trade deficit.[1]

'A deficit in the trade balance', wrote Kresimir Džeba, 'is not by itself a negative trend, since it means in practice that our development is financed by other countries.'[2] He did, however, go on to admit that the enormous size of the deficit and the poor performance of Yugoslav exports was a matter of great concern. Economic factors apart, it cannot have been a happy situation for the industrial development of socialist Yugoslavia to be dependent upon the goodwill of the United States.

The changes of the 1950s may have produced a vast increase in industrial output, but it was at enormous cost. The problem was now to improve the productivity of labour and to concentrate on quality and price rather than on sheer volume of output. Already, in the second five-year plan (1957–61) the concept of '*rentabilnost*' (rentability) of investments had been introduced. This was an attempt to prevent the wasteful investment of large sums in 'political factories', especially in the less developed regions. The policy was, however, only partially and half-heartedly applied. In a sense it ran counter to certain deeply rooted concepts in Yugoslav social thinking. One of these was the idea that a society could not be truly socialist if there were large regional differences between the living standards of the people. Legal equality between the nationalities was meaningless when income differentials between the poorest and richest areas were as high as 1 to 5.

The new policy also implied some form of central control over investment, and this was contrary to the tendency towards decentralisation which workers' self-management encouraged. How then could Yugoslavia develop her concept of socialist self-management and at the same time solve her economic problems? The answer was to induce efficiency through the discipline of the market. Autonomous public enterprises, operating within the system of workers' self-management, were to compete with each other, and ultimately on the world markets, with the minimum of central direction. In order to carry out such a policy of 'market socialism', and to share in the 'international division of labour', it was necessary to make fundamental changes in the political and economic framework. The first stage was the introduction of a new constitution in 1963.

THE 1963 CONSTITUTION

The constitution was promulgated on 7 April 1963, after a lengthy process of debate in political and social organisations throughout the country. In introducing the preliminary draft to a joint meeting of the Federal Assembly and the Socialist Alliance[3] Edvard Kardelj spoke of the role of the State:

> (It) reflects the socialist order but does not conserve it . . . , defends the achievements of the revolution, but simultaneously encourages the democratic evolution of society. . . ,

> co-ordinates trends, but does not seek their uniformity. . . . The highest aim of the socialist state is finally to cease to be an instrument for the governing of people, and to become a joint organisational instrument to enable free people to manage things.[4]

The 1953 constitutional law had made possible the development of workers' self-management in the enterprises; the 1963 constitution moved a stage further in providing for the extension of self-management to all other areas of society. Educational, cultural, health, social welfare and administrative bodies were all to participate in the social self-management of the society.

The Federal Assembly was reorganised so that it had five chambers, each with 120 members, and one, the Chamber of Nationalities, with 70. The deputies to the Federal Chamber were to be elected by all citizens, on the basis of territorial constituencies. The remaining four chambers – the Economic Chamber, the Chamber of Education and Culture, the Chamber of Social Welfare and Health, and the Political–Organisational Chamber – were to be elected on the basis of a limited and indirect franchise from special electorates representing the interest groups in whose name they were to act, e.g. workers' councils, public employees, teachers, doctors. Finally, the Chamber of Nationalities was composed of ten representatives of the republican assemblies of each of the six republics and five each from the assemblies of the two autonomous provinces. It must discuss all changes in the constitution. Members of all chambers served for four years, half of them retiring every two years, and no member could sit for two consecutive terms in the same chamber. Members of republican and provincial assemblies could not sit in the Federal Assembly unless they had been nominated to the Chamber of Nationalities. The executive arm of government was the Federal Executive Council, which functioned as a cabinet, although its members did not have departmental duties in the same sense as members of a British cabinet.

The comparable post to that of prime minister in Britain was the presidency of the Federal Executive Council. The president was chosen by the head of state, and must then receive the approval of the Federal Assembly for the list of FEC members which he presented to them. The president of the republic was elected at a joint meeting of all the 670 members of the chambers of the Federal Assembly. He had the usual functions of a titular head of state, such as representing the country in the relations with foreign countries, appointing Yugoslav ambassadors and receiving the credentials of foreign ambassador's exercising the power of granting pardons, and acting as commander in chief of the armed forces. He also had the right to initiate discussions in the FEC and to preside at its meetings. In 1967 a new body, known as the Council of the Federation (Savet Federacija),[5] was set up, and the head of State also presides over it as well as over the Council of National Defence. In all these legislative functions the president was not simply a figurehead. He had the power to bring forward proposals and, indeed, frequently did so.

The principle of rotation was applied to all elected offices, although not to President Tito. It was also forbidden for any individual except Tito to hold high office simultaneously in the government and the League of Communists. In fact, until the purges of 1972, a small group of senior national figures played a game of musical chairs around the top table, whilst beneath them there was a steady circulation of lesser personalities between republican and federal offices. This made more difficult the formation of interest groups which might crystallise into opposition.

The selection of candidates for any of the elective offices was strongly influenced by the League of Communists and the Socialist Alliance, but the process was not as monolithic as in the 1940s and 1950s. In the 1960s the League moved away in practice from the Stalinist concept of 'democratic centralism' and no longer required absolute obedience from its members on all questions. Regional and national differences frequently found expression through the machinery of the League, and on many issues the Communists were divided between the 'centralists' and the 'reformers'. For example, in the 1967 elections the minister of foreign trade was defeated in the Lazarevac constituency of Serbia by an ex-partisan general, whose views were more 'fundamentalist' than those of his younger reformist opponent.[7] Theoretically, any group of citizens could promote a candidate for any office, but in practice the leading role of the League and SAWPY was safeguarded. Kardelj, addressing a meeting of the Federal Assembly in February 1964, made it clear that the League would remain paramount in political life:

> The pivot of the working man, deputy and Assembly, in this respect, are all the manifestations of social thinking and culture, and all the social organisations, particularly the League of Communists – as the leading ideological and political force in the building of socialism, and the Social Alliance of the Working People – as the organised large-scale socialist and democratic platform of the citizens and social organisations. The two organisations, mutually interlinked, are under the present conditions, the main political–organisational and educational agent. Without their activities it would be impossible for the broad sections of the working people consciously to perceive the objective and long-term needs of social progress, and to unite their thoughts and efforts in the common socialist action of society.
>
> The specific position of the League of Communists in our political system is, of course, the political expression of the power of the working people in given historical conditions, that is to say, as a given level of intensity of class antagonism. This, undoubtedly, invests its social activities with exceptional political authority.[8]

NOTES

1 All figures in the above section are based on *Statistički Godišniak*.

2 K. Džeba, 'Principal Objectives of Socio-economic Development', *Narodna Armija* (4 September 1964), p. 5, col. 2.

3 E. Kardelj, 'On the principles of the preliminary draft of the new constitution', report of a speech on 21 September 1962. (Jugoslavija, Belgrade Documentation Series, no. 2003, October 1962).

4 Kardelj, Beograd Documentation Series, no. 2003 (1962).

5 This body was composed of equal numbers from each of the republics and contained some of the leading 'old guard expartisans', e.g. Kardelj, Crvenkovski, Gošnjak, Marinko, Ziherl. The principle of duplication of offices and of rotation did not apply.

6 Communists still spoke of 'democratic centralism', but the extent to which they had in practice abandoned it was revealed in 1972 when Tito, Dolanc and others urged the need for a tightening of Party discipline.

7 General Radivoje Jovanović was later recalled by his constituents, after being disciplined by the League of Communists.

8 Edward Kardelj, 'The New Yugoslav Federal Assembly', *Federal Assembly Series*, II (Belgrade 1964), pp. 12–13. The meeting was a joint session of all chambers of the Assembly, to which were invited representatives of 'socio-political organizations' (e.g. LCY, SAWPY, trade unions, etc.). This type of meeting, which has no constitutional status, is often used for making important political pronouncements. For example, Tito made his proposals for constitutional reform in October 1970 to the Zagreb *aktiv*, a conference of republican assembly deputies and local political, trade union and workers' council leaders.

12 Economic decentralisation

THE 1965 ECONOMIC REFORM

The first major steps towards decentralisation of economic decision making began with the 1957–61 five-year plan, although they had been foreshadowed by the development of the self-management system during the previous few years. As often happens in Yugoslavia, the declared objectives of the system were often at variance with the reality of day-to-day economic relations. These contradictions arise partly because of the struggle within the decision-making bodies, between the reformers and the more conservative elements who see their positions threatened by the abandonment of the old policies. They also arise because the implementation of reform policies is inhibited by the restraints imposed on the decision makers by the harsh realities of the current economic situation. For example, as early as 1957 a speaker at the Congress of Workers' Councils was able to state that: 'Under our system . . . it is for the market to tell the enterprise whether or not it has succeeded in obtaining social recognition for its labour.'[1] Had what Dugonić called 'the justice of the market' applied in 1957, many Yugoslav enterprises would have closed down, and many of the investments that have been made since that time would not have been sanctioned. In fact, the State frequently interfered with the operation of the market – for example, by subsidising failing enterprises, directing investment resources according to social and political rather than economic criteria, fixing prices of some commodities, and so on. The second and third five-year plans (1957–61 and 1961–5) were exercises in what Stanovnik has called 'planned guidance of the economy'.[2]

The devolution that occurred in the late 1950s was primarily from the federal authorities to republican and local government organs (*srezovi* and communes) in relation to major policy decisions regarding location of new industries, and to enterprises where detailed decisions on production methods, marketing and production planning were concerned. A key question was the allocation of investments, which were still under indirect central control. Enterprises were far from autonomous in the disposal of their resources.

> However, even in these respects, their decisions cannot be regarded as being independent from the government and especially from banks, which control the allocation of a substantial proportion of investment funds. The significance of this influence becomes apparent if one considers that, as late as 1964, enterprises have been transferring as much as 80 per cent of their earnings before tax (*akumulacija*) to the government.[3]

Although theoretically free to invest their own funds, enterprises were unable to accumulate sufficiently large resources to make this freedom effective. Enterprise funds were mainly used for 'simple reproduction' (i.e. depreciation).

> Until 1957 the use of these funds was strictly determined by end purpose (i.e. they could only be used for the reconstruction and replacement of the assets available). The regulations were modified in 1957, thus enabling the depreciation funds to be used also for the repayment of investment loans, and in 1959 all restrictions regarding the use of depreciation funds and other financial resources of working organisations were abolished.[4]

In practice, however, enterprises continued to derive most of their investment resources from social investment funds. The most important of these was the General Investment Fund, which was formed by means of a levy of 6 per cent on the capital of enterprises. This fund was administered by three specialised federal banks, one each for investment, agriculture and foreign trade, which had been established in the late 1950s. Local investment funds were administered through communal banks, but in both cases the managements of these banks were directly appointed by either the federal or the local political authority, communal banks being little more than the financial arm of their founding communal authority, and restricted to dealing with enterprises of a local character only.

Enterprises requiring finance for investment submitted plans to these banks, which would allocate their inevitably scarce resources on the basis of numerous criteria, the most important of which was the extent to which the proposed investment fitted the current five-year plans. Other criteria included '*rentabilnost*' (rentability) and economic factors such as the percentage of the required funds which the enterprise could raise itself and the current profitability of the enterprise concerned. Many political factors also entered the equation, however; at the federal level there was the desire to redistribute investment funds in favour of the underdeveloped south, and at the local level the desire to promote the local commune, with little regard to the optimal location of a particular industry. Indeed, the main weakness of the system appears to have been the fact that most projects were considered in isolation, with little or no co-ordination between projects, despite the plan.[5] Though this system produced a degree of decentralisation in that the responsibility for initiating investment projects were placed in the hands of enterprises, the methods of decision making were long-winded and complex, and a great deal of political and bureaucratic pressure influenced the decisions made.[6] The parochial nature of local bank management has been a problem ever since. Further, the acute shortage of social funds for investment led certain enterprises to apply with insufficiently drafted plans, just in case they should ever need them.

In 1961 the banking and investment system was streamlined. Every commune was to have a communal bank, and all credits to enterprises were to pass through them. The National Bank ceased to credit the economy directly, and its business was passed over to the communal banks. Republican banks were set up, so that each government authority had a corresponding bank through which to make its investments. Each of these banks was limited in its activity to enterprises on its own territory, thereby preventing any competition between banks.

The years between 1961 and 1965 were of great importance to Yugoslav banking, as most of the changes made in this period foreshadowed the 1965 reform. Whereas prior to 1961, banks, especially communal banks, had been used as a means of social control by their founding commune (that is, more to check on the legality of enterprise accounts than their economic rationality), banks now became entities in their own right, and many of the functions of social control were passed to the new Social Accounting Service.[7] More important, representatives of the local economy were co-opted on to the management boards, alongside the political appointees. Perhaps most important of all, in an attempt to depoliticise the process of investment allocation, government investment funds were transferred to the banks, to become a part of the banks' own resources.

Although this was at first only a bookkeeping transaction, since banks had always dealt with social investment funds, it signified a new attitude to the allocation of investment; in future it was to be an economic rather than a political process. Though a local authority could still require a bank to provide finance for a certain project at a low rate of interest, it had to pay the bank the difference between that and the interest the bank might have received elsewhere. Apart from this, the banks' decisions on investment were final.

Banks also became progressively more independent of the National Bank. All banks were required to place in the National Bank a very high proportion of their total deposits (sometimes as high as 40 per cent). This could be lent back to the banks for specific projects. The importance of this process as a means of central supervision of banking activity can be gauged from the fact that in 1961 70 per cent of all credits granted by banks were covered by loans from the National Bank. By 1965 however this proportion had fallen to 43 per cent (see Table 17),

Table 17 Percentage of credits given by banks covered by loans from the National Bank, 1961–5

	1961	*1962*	*1963*	*1964*	*1965*
Communal banks	68·5	60·0	57·5	51·2	47·0
All banks	70	57	55	48	43

Source: Statistički Bilten Služba Društvenog Knjigovodstva, (22 February 1966), pp. 16–17, 22

indicating that banks were increasingly financing the credits they gave out of their own resources.

Banks were therefore prepared for the changes brought upon them by the upheaval of 1965 and 1966. In fact, the significance of these reforms for the banking system lay not so much in any sudden changes in business activity as in the fact that the principles under which the economy had been attempting to operate since 1961 were at last clarified, while the re-alignment of prices and the devaluation of the dinar parity, which were also part of the reform, allowed something of a fresh start to be made. While this is not to detract from the importance of the reform, table 18 indicates the relative stability

Table 18 Sources of investment finance, 1961–8 (percentages)

	1961	*1962*	*1963*	*1964*	*1965*	*1966*	*1967*	*1968*
Government*	61·7	59·6	56·4	36·5	26·7	15·7	17·7	15·7
Enterprises	29·5	29·7	27·8	25·9	28·8	39·8	32·7	31·2
Banks	0·9	2·9	9·1	31·4	36·7	37·3	44·9	47·2
Other	7·9	7·8	6·7	6·2	7·2	7·2	4·7	5·9

Source: Statistički Bilten Služba Društvenog Knjigovodstva

of sources of investment over the reform period. It shows a sudden jump in investment financed by enterprises following the extensive liberalisation in 1965 of regulations concerning the distribution of earned enterprise income, but an equally rapid fall to the previous level in the following year. Overall, the extent of self-financing has remained remarkably constant since 1954. The main feature of the table is the steady and undisturbed rise in the proportion of investment financed through banks, and the equivalent fall in the role of political authorities.

The laws relating to banking brought into effect on 1 April 1966 abolished the concept of 'territoriality', which had been

* 'Government' applies to all socio-political authorities, federal, republican and communal.

the keynote of the previous system. All former federal, republican and communal banks were to compete equally over the whole territory of Yugoslavia. Only banks of a certain size were allowed to undertake investment business; there were eight of these in 1966, but by 1970 all banks were conducting both investment and short-term business.

Most important, however, was the new concept of the place of a bank in a socialist market economy. No longer were banks to be the financial arm of the political authority. The new concept was that banks were special organisations of the economy to be managed by those enterprises or socio-political bodies having deposits in a special founders' fund. Voting strength on the management boards was to be proportional to the size of the deposit, to a limit of 10 per cent of the total for any one depositor. This restriction applied also to socio-political authorities, reducing them to the same level as enterprises. The workers in the bank would also usually have one representative.

This system of 'users' management' was designed to keep the bank in its proper place in a socialist market economy. Workers' self-management on the part of the bank would mean that enterprise money placed in a bank would be manipulated gainfully by people (the bank workers) other than those who had created it. This would constitute undesirable appropriation of surplus value from the workers in the depositing enterprise, and would be contrary to socialist theory. This problem has been solved in the past by the controlling influence of the State, which as the true representative of the entire working class was not in a position to exploit workers, but the idea behind the whole of the 1965 reform was to remove the influence of the State from the workings of the market as far as was possible.

A bank is thus seen as an extension of the group of enterprises comprising its founders. The profits made from banking activity still belong to these founding enterprises, and they control the credit policy of the bank. Banks are, in Yugoslav parlance, servants of the economy, rather than equal members of it or powers over it.[8]

However, the specific manner in which banking had developed prior to 1965 led to a continuation of the problems that had characterised investment allocation before 1961, namely the excessive localisation of funds. Banks whose custom had in 1964 been restricted to enterprises in their own commune naturally came in 1966 to be managed by these same highly localised enterprises. The bank mergers that have reduced the numbers of banks from 112 in 1966 to 67 in 1969 and 25 in 1972 have hardly ameliorated the situation; for apart from the former federal banks, mergers have involved banks in neighbouring territories. The former federal banks have merged with banks in all regions and continue to do business over the whole territory of Yugoslavia, but most other banks remain locally orientated and in some cases are even assuming the character of spokesmen for their particular republics.[9] For instance, Bosnia–Hercegovina and Montenegro have only one bank each, while single banks or associations of banks dominate over 90 per cent of banking business in both Croatia and Slovenia.

This regionalisation is especially relevant in the light of federal government policy on interest rates. The federal Executive Council has the power to impose a ceiling on interest rates, which in recent years has often been less than the rate of inflation. In 1971, for example, the rate of inflation was 17·5 per cent, while the maximum interest rate chargeable on investment loans was 10 per cent.[10] Even when the 'real' rate of interest has been positive, it has certainly been below the level that might equate the supply and demand for credit. In consequence, the rate of interest cannot act as an allocative mechanism, and other factors must influence the credit committees of banks when they decide which projects to finance. In short, though in theory banks consider any project on its economic merits, much as before, they are bound – and consider it in some respects their duty – to favour the projects of their own members in their own republic. The three former federal banks are important exceptions to this rule.

It is consequently alleged that there is insufficient capital mobility in Yugoslavia. Savings in, say, Slovenia, are accumulated in Slovenian banks and used to finance the projects of Slovenian enterprises. The interest rate is unable to entice it to a second republic, where returns in real terms might be higher, since the interest rate is fixed well below the real return to investment and cannot reflect differentials in rates of return.

Apart from the former federal banks, there are only minimal inter-republican flows of banking funds.[11]

This leaves the federal government's fund for the development of the underdeveloped republics and Kosovo as the main instrument for the geographical redistribution of funds, for even the branches of the former federal banks in separate republics tend to balance their accounts in the long term. The extent to which this federal redistribution occurs is indicated by table 19.

Table 19 Deposits of government bodies as a percentage of the total assets of banks

SFRY	13·4
Slovenia	4·6
Croatia	4·6
Vojvodina	6·1
Serbia Proper	10·6
Bosnia–Hercegovina	25·6
Montenegro	32·6
Macedonia	33·1
Kosovo	55·5

Source: Jugoslovensko Bankarstvo, 7–8 (1972) pp. 28–31

The relative importance of government funds in the banking system of the less developed regions is obvious, as is the fact that any decrease in federal allocation of funds would be highly disadvantageous to these regions.

Yet such a decrease might well result from the proposals to establish a capital market which were discussed in 1971. Few business people were satisfied with the system, whereby investment allocation and banking were almost completely free from overt political direction[12] and no longer bound by comprehensive plans of future long-term investment needs, yet equally, for reasons expressed above, were unable to follow pure market criteria through the interest rate. The banking system exists in limbo between plan and market, unable to make proper use of either system for determining the rationality of investments, or rather using an inadequate combination of both. Arguments for and against a freer interest rate, the role of interest in a socialist market economy, and the effect of a possible higher rate of interest on inflation were matters of public controversy in the early seventies. (For example the protracted debate between Kavčič and Kardelj in 1971–2, with regard to the possibility of private investment.) An increasing number of bankers and government economists began to argue – mainly in private – that a free capital market with a free interest rate must come. To some extent this debate has been pushed under the surface by the reassertion of democratic centralism.

The bases on which a capital market may be built already exist. The practice of issuing 'bonds' (*Hartije od vrednosti*) has recently been revived, and is no longer confined to socio-political authorities.[13] Certain enterprises, sometimes under-written by banks, sell three-year bonds carrying the maximum rate of interest and offer price concessions on their products and lotteries or easy credit facilities to subscribers, which raise the effective interest rate above the legal maximum.[14] Though at present there have been few such issues, the practice is expected to spread, and it is generally admitted that there exist large savings held privately by households which could be tapped, given sufficient incentive.

The emergence of a capital market would mark the final stage in the process of decentralisation and depoliticisation of economic decision making; the final transfer from plan to market. The effect of this for the Yugoslav economy could well be considerable. Perhaps most important would be the effect of a market on the geographical distribution of investment. It is generally accepted that the investment needs of the south are radically different from those in the north; the south needs considerable long-term investment in infrastructure, sources of power, and other basic industries. The north already has this infrastructure, and can thus make good use of shorter-term investment credit, aimed at improving existing capacities or diversifying existing industries. It is just this sort of investment that would be favoured by a capital market. One of the most important considerations to a would-be investor in Yugoslavia would be the speed with which his investment could be repaid, especially given the exceedingly volatile nature of the Yugoslav economy. Few investors would be willing to tie their capital in a twenty-year development programme in Kosovo if there was the possibility of a three-year investment in Slovenia.

In other words, a transfer from plan to market would mean a shortening of the time horizon; private investors can never afford to take as long a view as can government planners. This would almost without doubt benefit the north, running directly counter to the government's oft-stated but feebly executed policy of greater aid to the south, with the eventual aim of bringing its living standard up to that of the north. Other problems have to be solved, most notably the justification for a capital market in terms of socialist economics, but these could doubtless be overcome; the Yugoslavs have rarely let ideology impede pragmatism for very long, and their ideology is remarkably malleable.

There remain, however, economists who realise these implications, and who believe that the free market system went too far in the early 1970s. The shelving of progress in this direction in 1974, and the return of democratic centralist tendencies, also has the support of some who were, only three years previously, strong supporters of even further liberation of the market.

THE REFORM OF THE PRICE SYSTEM

The ultimate intention of the reform was to free prices from administrative controls, and to substitute market forces as the main determinant of prices. This could not be achieved in one step. There had been an attempt to free some prices in 1958, but during the economic crisis of 1960–1 there was a reversion to price controls over a wide range of goods on which controls had previously been relaxed. At the beginning of 1964 about 6 per cent of industrial products were subject to price controls. The inflation of 1964, during which the cost of living rose by 20 per cent, caused the federal government to intervene still further. On 25 March 1965 a general price freeze was ordered on all industrial goods. This was a holding operation to stabilise the position until the reform legislation was passed by the Assembly. In July the reform – a collection of some thirty laws relating to the economy – was passed. As a direct result there was a general rise in the price of industrial goods of 39 per cent, food prices by over 50 per cent,[15] rents by 100 per cent and the cost of living by 44 per cent (see table 20). Farmers were given guaranteed minimum prices for a large range of agricultural products.

Having sanctioned the price increases the reform imposed price controls on most goods.[16] The government's powers over prices are, however, limited and often ineffective, especially over consumer goods and food. In October 1970, for example, a price freeze was decreed, but retail prices rose by 1 per cent per month during the next three months, which was approximately the same rate as for the previous three months.[17]

Table 20 Movement of prices, 1960–6 (chain index)

	1960	*1961*	*1962*	*1963*	*1964*	*1965*	*1966*
Industry							
Retail	105	106	103	103	112	139	108
Producers'	104	103	101	100	106	120	103
Agricultural							
Retail	109	117	114	108	126	151	104
Producers'	110	117	110	111	133	142	115
Services	141	113	105	104	113	153	106
General retail	108	109	104	105	113	144	107
Cost of living	110	112	107	105	118	150	107

Source: Annual report of the National Bank (1966), p. 15

The long-term objective of establishing market relations as the determinant of prices still eludes the reformers. Time after time the exigencies of the immediate economic crisis force the federal authorities to intervene. Always they protest that their intervention is a temporary measure and that the ultimate aim is to free the economy from administrative constraints. Thus, Prime Minister Ribičič, in presenting his stabilisation programme to the Federal Assembly on 26 November 1970, stated: 'We know that by these measures . . . we are exposing ourselves to the risk of being called centralists and étatists – because we are cutting into the autonomous rights of the socio-political communities . . . However, at this moment there is no other choice'. On prices, he said:

> We have adopted for the time being the policy of keeping them at the present level, except that we will allow necessary corrections where obvious disparities exist between internal prices and those on the foreign market. These corrections will be made on the basis of consultations. It will be made possible to eliminate certain illogical trends in connection with the prices of bread, coal, newspapers, etc. We have also decided that prices in the infrastructure and in the sphere of services (electricity, post and telegraph, rents and rail charges) should not be increased in the months ahead. However, in this respect, too, we are well aware that solutions should be sought elsewhere – in liberalisation and in a freer influence of the forces of supply and demand on price formation.[18]

Clearly, Yugoslavia has a long way to go before prices can be freely determined by the market, but the reform of 1965 and subsequent measures removed some of the anomalies in price structure that existed previously. The criteria used since 1965 are described in the OECD *Survey* for 1966:

> The prices established in 1965 are based on thorough prior study using matrix techniques. Three desiderata were considered before final decisions were reached: bringing prices nearer to those on international markets; using prices as instruments of development policy in combination with customs duties; creating as far as possible 'equal conditions for the formation of incomes, by the various categories of producers.[19]

The inflationary crisis of 1970 which necessitated the intervention of the federal government, with its 'stabilisation programme', was the third such crisis in the decade 1960–70.[20] In 1974 Yugoslavia still headed the inflationary league table in Europe with a rate of 30 per cent. It has been suggested that these phases of too rapid expansion of demand and prices are inevitable because of 'the ability of enterprises freely to decide price and wage levels'.[21] The self-management system has no built-in regulator, although theoretically the aim is to introduce free competition – both domestic and foreign – as the ultimate determinant of prices. International experience does not suggest that inflation is in practice held in check by competition:

> The brake which competition might provide in this respect could have only little effect, in view of the smallness of the Yugoslav market and the size of enterprises imposed by modern technological conditions. Foreign competition might be more effective, but would still not be enough, as is proved by the example of several Western economies which, though wide open to foreign competition, are nevertheless troubled by serious inflationary pressure.[22]

INCOMES POLICY

The above quotation from the OECD *Survey* hints at a problem that is fundamental to the whole economic and social policy of Yugoslavia. If workers' councils are free to determine the distribution of the enterprises' resources, will they not be tempted to allocate a larger share to personal incomes and to neglect the need for accumulating savings for investment? The economists can justifiably argue that it is in the long-term interests of the workers to restrain the desire for immediate advantages because, unless adequate investment levels are maintained, tomorrow's living standards will be threatened. This argument was put forward by Professor Korać in 1969:

> Working collectives aim towards a permanent rise in the standards of living. As this is the real stimulus for the working people to associate in collectives of commodity producers – and as this aim cannot be realised without extending production – it will be obvious that it is in the subjective interest of the working collectives to ensure conditions for a permanent rise in the standards of living, i.e., a permanent increase in consumption, by allocating a part of the earned income for capital formation (in order to extend production). If the total current income is used for personal consumption, the collectives would not be able to extend production, which in turn is the only way of ensuring a permanent increase in personal income. This leads us to conclude that it is in the interest of the working collectives to allocate a part of the earned revenue for capital formation . . . and to use only the

remaining part of the income for their current personal consumption.[23]

Arguments that sound convincing to academic economists may be looked at in a different light by the shop-floor worker when he comes to cast his vote in favour either of jam today or pie in the sky. Professor Korać claims that the danger of workers voting themselves excessive personal incomes receded when the enterprises were given control over the allocation of investments, as well as over income and depreciation funds. The first steps along this road were taken in 1957[24] and were further advanced by the Law on the Determination and Distribution of Income in Working Organisations, in 1968. As soon as workers realise that they have the responsibility for allocating funds for 'extended reproduction'[25] they abandon 'the mentality of wage labour' and adopt 'the mentality of self-management'. 'Although it might appear strange, the Yugoslav experience shows that the mentality of wage labour is changed as soon as the workers are given the opportunity to make decisions on expanded reproduction . . .'[26] Other observers are not as optimistic as Professor Korać. The post-reform period has been characterised by a lack of long-term investments and a steadily accelerating inflation, which, in the winter of 1970, forced the federal government to intervene. Between 1965 and 1970 the cost of living index rose by an average of 10 per cent per year, whilst incomes rose at approximately twice this rate. It would appear that, despite Professor Korać's optimism, workers' councils have in fact paid out an unjustifiably high rate of personal incomes.

There is also evidence that income differentials are growing. 'Unwarranted disparities also appeared in income levels between individual work organisations, branches and sectors of the economy.'[27] This is surely to be expected if enterprises are given a degree of autonomy in determining the levels of income. The successful will have larger funds available for distribution, and they would be unusual men if they did not take advantage of their position. Self-management is supposed to lead to higher living standards. Who can blame the workers for striving to attain this goal? The self-managed enterprise operates as a closed system, and the workers' council cannot be expected to take into account the wider implications of their decisions on income distribution. In a sense the whole trend towards greater autonomy for the enterprise has weakened the influence of the forces that previously restricted the freedom of the individual enterprises in the name of the community at large. Initially these constraints were imposed by administrative decrees of the State. As the direct links between enterprise and State were loosened, the influence of socio-political bodies such as the League of Communists, the Socialist Alliance and the trade unions began to play a more important role. Since the reform, however, the intention – if not yet the accomplished fact – is to use the discipline of the market to regulate the economy. The greatest good for the greatest number is apparently to be achieved when the laws of supply and demand are allowed to operate without state intervention. The commonwealth of self-managed, worker-controlled enterprises, each aiming at producing as high an income as possible for itself, will ultimately create a prosperous socialist society.[28] There is apparently no conflict 'between the interests of the working collectives as commodity producers and those of the social community as a whole. Working collectives, as well as the social community, are interested in increasing their personal incomes'.[29]

NOTES

1 R. Dugonić, 'Economic Cadres and Producers' Self-Management', report to the Congress of Workers' Councils.

2 Janez Stanovnik, 'Planning Through the Market – the Jugoslav experience', *Foreign Affairs*, January, 1962), p. 255.

3 T. Hočevar, 'The structure of the Slovenian economy', in *Studia Slovenica* (New York 1965), p. 186. The figure of 80 per cent is quoted from Mara Bešter, 'Razmišljana ob pripravah zakona o družbenem planiranju', *Gospodarski Vestnik*, XIII, 15 (1964), p. 2.

4 V. Pejovski, 'Yugoslav investment policy', in *Investiciona Politika Jugoslavije, 1966–70* (Belgrade 1967), p. 7.

5 This point is made by V. Bakarić in *Aktuelni Problemi Izgradnje Našeg Privrednog Sistema* (Zagreb 1963).

6 See F. E. I. Hamilton, *Yugoslavia – Patterns of Economic Activity* (London 1968), pp. 144–51, for a detailed study of specific decisions.

7 However, the law on banking of 1971 still provided for an individual working in a bank to be fined if he or the bank allowed an enterprise to make an illegal payment (i.e. to use short-term loans for investment purposes).

8 See, for example, 'The Law on Banking', in *Official Gazette of SFRY*, 58 (1971).

9 Privredna Banka Sarajeva, the only bank in Bosnia–Hercegovina, dealt with 76 per cent of total deposits and 92 per cent of short-term credits for working capital in that republic in 1971. *Ekonomska Politika* (13 March 1972), p. 11.

10 For a table showing the 'real' rate of interest in Yugoslavia since 1962, and a discussion of interest rate policy, see *Jugoslovensko Bankarstvo*, no. 4 (1971), p. 7.

11 A conclusion also reached by *NIN* (27 August 1972), p. 11.

12 The only way the government of the National Bank may implement their monetary policy is by means of open market operations, discount policy and the level of the (substantial) compulsory deposits of commercial banks in the National Bank. These instruments are similar to those used in the West. See also Dimitrije Dimitrijević, 'Monetary System and Policy', in *Ekonomist* (1969), pp. 85–6.

13 See *Jugoslovensko Bankarstvo*, no. 3 (1972), pp. 41–7 for full details of all bond issues to date. Notable also are the government bond issues for public works and projects such as the Belgrade–Bar railway.

14 So successful was a flotation of bonds purchasable only in foreign currency by a Novi Beograd tractor firm in 1972, which offered tractors on credit to subscribers with only a six-month wait (normally three years), that the amount of the issue was doubled. See *Ekonomska Politika* (12 June 1972), p. 15.

15 Average food prices August–December 1965 were 52 per cent more than the annual average for 1964.

16 OECD *Report* (1966) states that 90 per cent of goods were subject to price controls in 1965.

17 The rise was, however, uneven. Retail prices remained steady in August and September and jumped sharply in October. Index of retail prices (1969 = 100): August, 111; September, 111; October, 114. *Source Indeks* no. 11 (1970), p. 34 *Indeksi Cena*.

18 *Borba* (27 November 1970) p. 1.

19 OECD *Survey* (1966), p. 8.

20 The others were in 1960–1 and 1964–5. A fourth began on 1 January 1973.

21 OECD *Survey* (1966), p. 29.

22 OECD *Survey* (1966), p. 29.

23 Miladin Korać, 'The Socio-Economic Basis of the Yugoslav Economic System', *Ekonomist* (1969), p. 28.

24 See p. 145 above.

25 The phrase *proširena reprodukcija* (literally, 'expanded reproduction') is a favourite with Yugoslav economists. It is borrowed from Marx, and is used in contrast to *prošta reprodukcija* (simple reproduction), i.e. the replacement and maintenance of existing means of production. Expanded reproduction relates to new investment for expanding the means of production.

26 M. Korać, in *Ekonomist*, p. 27, notes 13 and 14.

27 Milentije Pesaković, '*Dve decenije samoupravljanja u Jugoslaviji*, (Belgrade 1970), p. 34.

28 'The direct target of the working collective is its orientation towards higher income.' Korać, in *Ekonomist*, p. 26.

29 Korać, in *Ekonomist*, p. 27, note 11.

13 Foreign policy and foreign trade

In the modern world there are few countries which possess within their own borders all the sources of food, raw materials and power that are necessary to the development of manufacturing industry. Even if the potential is there, the problems of accessibility of resources are often such that it is economically advantageous to import significant amounts of essential raw materials and food. A far greater problem to the industrialising country is the need to import technological know-how and capital goods from the more developed nations. Largely for political reasons, the USSR during the inter-war period, and the People's Republic of China more recently, have attempted to industrialise without participating greatly in world trade.[1] They are both large enough and well enough endowed with natural resources – including huge reserves of manpower – to make self-sufficiency a credible, if expensive, basis for industrialisation. Small countries like Yugoslavia cannot afford the luxury of autarchy if they are to move rapidly into the ranks of the developed nations. As we have seen in chapters 2 and 3, Yugoslavia does not possess the geographical conditions for self-sufficient industrial development. Her fuel and power production is inadequate and, although she is an important producer of non-ferrous ores, she lacks many essential mineral resources. Throughout the greater part of the post-war period Yugoslavia has been a net importer of raw materials, fuels, iron and steel products, and capital equipment. There was also a great technological gap between Yugoslavia and the developed world, which could only be narrowed quickly with outside help.

Yet, despite these geographical and human handicaps, the Communist leaders of Yugoslavia decided to follow the Soviet model in their initial plans for industrialisation. Their decision was based primarily on political considerations. They had been brought up in a country in which industrial development was synonymous with exploitation by foreign capital.[2] They had before them the example of the USSR, which had industrialised from its own resources, without recourse to foreign aid and with foreign trade occupying an insignificant role in the economy. In conversation with young Yugoslav Communists at the time of the Fifth Party Congress in 1948, I was struck by the supreme self-confidence with which they assumed that, armed with little more than the sword of dialectical materialism, they could overcome the physical and human obstacles to industrialisation. If the Soviets could make the great leap forward from the era of the wooden plough to that of the mass production line in a generation of socialist development, so could the Yugoslavs. This self-confidence was not shattered by their expulsion from the Cominform. It was several years before the realisation came that a small, under-developed country like Yugoslavia could not industrialise in isolation from the rest of the world's economy.

In the words of Professor Adamović, 'The whole sector of foreign trade was treated as an 'unavoidable evil' in the period of centralised planning, rather than as a major factor of economic development'.[3] Foreign trade was controlled entirely by the State, and was confined almost entirely to commodity exchange, often organised on a bilateral basis. Invisibles played virtually no part in the balance of payments. In 1948 57 per cent of imports and 52 per cent of exports were as a result of trade with the Cominform countries.[4] Rates of exchange were manipulated by the State within the framework of a centralised planning system, and

> . . . the difference between prices in the country and on the world market were covered by a special fund set up for this purpose.[5] The enterprises thus ran no risks, their role being mainly reduced to the technical implementation of administrative programmes. They were often compelled to deal with diverse aspects of trade, because their work depended entirely upon permits and upon the competent administrative body. The earnings of economic organisations were determined by margins fixed by the administrative body.[6]

FOREIGN TRADE POLICY BEFORE 1948

The foreign trade policy followed during the first post-war years was a reflection of two fundamental political principles in which the Party at that time had implicit faith. One was the desirability of industrialising as far as possible from internal resources, within a closed economic system. Whatever the cost, if it was at all possible goods would be manufactured in Yugoslavia even if they could be imported more cheaply from abroad. Exports were simply a device for obtaining essential imports.[7] There was no policy of capturing export markets for goods that Yugoslavia might be able to sell competitively on world markets. As a result, the total volume of foreign trade was small, representing less than 10 per cent of GNP. At this low level, visible trade was in balance until 1948.[8]

The second principle was that, if it should be necessary to trade, this exchange of goods should be on a bilateral basis with other socialist countries. Before the war over two-thirds of trade was with western Europe and less than one-fifth with eastern Europe. Almost all the east European trade was with Czechoslovakia. After 1945 there was a complete reorientation towards the USSR and eastern Europe.

The assumptions on which these policies were based were completely shattered by the expulsion of Yugoslavia from the Cominform in 1948. For five years trade with the socialist countries came to a dead stop. In several cases where trade agreements were broken Yugoslavia had already delivered her share of the bargain, but never received either the goods to which she was entitled or any form of compensation for non-delivery.

THE EFFECTS OF THE COMINFORM DISPUTE

The immediate effect was, of course, a dramatic slump in the total amount of foreign trade. Between 1948 and 1950 the value of exports almost halved, and imports fell to 75 per cent of the 1948 figure. It was not possible for Yugoslavia suddenly to reverse the flow of trade and to revert to the pre-war pattern of regional orientation, in which western European countries formed the major trading partners. Apart from any technical factors, there were also major political obstacles. In addition to her general support of the Soviet line on all major issues at the United Nations, Yugoslavia was involved in several international disputes with her non-Communist neighbours. In all cases the United States and her west European allies were involved.

The most serious dispute was over Trieste. Yugoslav partisans entered the city in 1945 and were forced to withdraw under Anglo-American pressure. The Paris Peace Conference of 1947 was unable to reach a final agreement upon the Italo-Yugoslav boundary in this area. Although Yugoslavia gained Istria and a large part of the Julian region from Italy, she also laid claim to the city and port of Trieste. Pending the establishment of a Free Territory of Trieste, under a governor appointed by the UN Security Council, the Trieste area was divided into two occupation zones: zone A, including the city, was placed under Anglo-American military occupation; zone B, including the small ports of Koper (Capo d'Istria) and Piran (Pirano), was occupied by the Yugoslav army. The Soviet Union was unwilling to support Yugoslav claims, partly because of its fear of offending the Italian Communists, but did not openly oppose them until after the Cominform resolution of 1948. There was deadlock in the Security Council over the appointment of a governor and the establishment of a Free Territory.

The Western powers, no doubt with an eye on the chances of Signor de Gasperi's Christian Democrats defeating the Socialist–Communist front in the Italian general elections, hinted that they would be happy to hand over Trieste to a suitably pro-western Italian government. The Yugoslavs were thus left without friends. This did not prevent them from pressing their claims, even to the point of shooting down a United States plane which strayed over the border.

An equally tense situation existed on the southern borders with Greece. Here again the Yugoslavs were left on a very dangerous limb by the defection of their former Soviet ally. The Greek partisans under the Communist Vafiades (General Markos) were conducting a civil war against the Anglo-American-supported royal government. Until 1948 the northern neighbours of Greece, all members of the Cominform – Bulgaria, Yugoslavia and Albania – provided a safe haven for any Greek partisans who were hard pressed by the enemy. After 1948 the Soviet Union stopped supporting Markos, accusing him of Titoist deviations, and the Bulgarian and Albanian frontiers were closed to fugitives, but Yugoslavia continued to give support to the Greek rebels.

On the Slovene–Austrian border, where Yugoslav territory adjoined the British zone of occupation, there was another dispute, less serious than the Greek or Italian imbroglios but nevertheless a hindrance to good relations. In Carinthia there was a Slovene population in the country areas around Villach (Beljak) and Klagenfurt (Celovec). The Yugoslavs always claimed that the 1921 plebiscite administered by the League of Nations was a fraud, and after the Second World War they revived their claims to the Slovene-speaking areas of Carinthia. A recent American writer considers that the Soviet Union's refusal in July 1949 to continue supporting Yugoslavia at the United Nations on this issue marked the real turning point in Yugoslav foreign policy.[9] 'The last lingering illusion about Stalin's intentions dispelled, the Yugoslav leadership began now to systematically counter Soviet charges and Cominform hostility'. Shortly afterwards Yugoslavia changed her policy towards the Greek partisans, closing the frontier on 27 July.

There is some evidence to suggest, however, that economic pressures were already working to force the Yugoslavs to moderate their hostility to the West. They had applied to the World Bank for a $200 million credit, and to the Export–Import Bank for $50 million.[10] They were not likely to get this much needed economic aid unless they showed signs of a more co-operative spirit in their relations with the West.

TRADE AND AID FROM THE WEST

The Western nations – particularly the United States and Britain – realised the value of sustaining Yugoslavia in the face of the systematic attempts of the USSR to overthrow Tito and his supporters. The amounts Yugoslavia received in 1949 are listed in table 21.

During 1950 the Export–Import Bank gave another $35 million at 3·5 per cent, and Britain, Belgium and West Germany gave further substantial short-term credits at rates of interest varying from 4 to 7.5 per cent. In 1951 came the first long-term loan from the International Bank and a huge gift of $417 million over five years from United States, Britain and France.

Regular US military aid began in 1952. Later, credits were granted for the purchase of agricultural surpluses, and these continued until 1957.

Table 21 Credit given to Yugoslavia, 1949

Source	*Amount*
International Monetary Fund (for purchase of primary materials)	$9 million
US Export–Import Bank (for capital equipment)	$20 million (at 3·5 per cent interest)
Britain	£8 million (at 5 per cent interest)
plus Midland Bank (for financing Yugoslav imports to UK)	£2·5 million
Holland (for shipbuilding industry)	10 million DFL (at 5·5 per cent interest)

Source: Yugoslav Encyclopaedia

Throughout the 1950s the Yugoslav economy was sustained by credits and grants from the United States and western Europe. According to a French writer, United States aid to Yugoslavia up to 1961 was greater than that given to India and was surpassed only by that provided for Greece and Turkey.[11] This enormous volume of aid enabled Yugoslavia to run a massive trade deficit during a period of rapid industrialisation. In the period 1965–74 exports averaged 70 per cent of imports, but in 1972 and 1973 there was a balance of payments surplus, thanks to tourist earnings and *gastarbeiter* remittances.[12] Since 1948 Yugoslavia has never had a visible trade surplus. Throughout the 1950s the proportion of exports as a percentage of imports averaged 62 per cent, at a time when GNP was growing at a rate of over 10 per cent and industrial output at almost 13 per cent per annum (see table 22).

This rapid industrial growth required huge imports of raw materials, fuel and capital equipment – particularly machinery and transport equipment – most of it from hard currency areas (see table 23). It was made possible by the various forms of foreign aid.

Table 22 Rates of growth of GNP, 1947–62 (percentages)

	1947–52	*1952–60*	*1960–2*	*1947–62*
Industry	4·6	12·8	6·8	9·2
Agriculture	3·3	7·5	0·8	2·6
National economy	2·0	10·1	5·3	6·7

Source: Branko Horvat, *Note on the Rate of Growth of the Yugoslav Economy* (Belgrade 1963), p. 9

Table 23 Imports, 1956–8 (percentages)

	1956	*1957*	*1958*
Raw materials and semi-manufactures	51·0	55·1	52·2
Capital goods	14·0	18·3	23·7
Consumer goods	35·0	26·6	24·1

Source: Statistički Godišnjak (1962 and 1970)

RELATIONS WITH COMECON

In 1955, following the visit of Khruschev and Bulganin to Belgrade, relations with the Soviet Union began to improve. Trade with the COMECON countries was re-established, and in 1964 Yugoslavia signed an agreement that enabled her to participate in the work of COMECON, although not as a full member. By the time relations were resumed Yugoslav foreign policy had moved a long way from the positions of 1948. Remembering the disruption to the economy caused by the Cominform blockade, the Yugoslavs were not disposed to rely too heavily on Soviet promises. Nevertheless, they were prepared to normalise relations and would not refuse any credits that might be offered. In 1955 and 1956 the Soviet Union, Czechoslovakia, Poland and the GDR all granted credits, amounting in total to $440 million, at rates of interest considerably lower than the normal World Bank rates. After the Hungarian revolt of 1956 relations between Yugoslavia and her eastern neighbours went through a period of strain, and as in 1948 the agreements were not honoured.[13] When Mr Khruschev toured Yugoslavia in 1962 he offered new credits and ordered several ships to be built in Yugoslavia yards. The revival in commercial relations stimulated a growth in COMECON's share of Yugoslav foreign trade from under one quarter in 1963 to over one-third in 1965 (see table 24).

Table 24 Yugoslavia's trade with COMECON, 1963–5

	Value of trade (m. dinars)	*Percentage of Yugoslav trade*
1963		
Exports	2636·2	26·6
Imports	2998·8	21·9
1965		
Exports	5722·8	41·9
Imports	4594·2	28·5
1974		
Exports	24,676	38·1
Imports	28,781	22·4

Sources: Statistički Godišnjak (1968). *Indeks* (1975/2), p. 29

Between 1948 and 1953 Soviet and eastern European spokesmen frequently attacked Yugoslavia for selling out to the Western capitalists and quoted figures of US military aid to prove their point. There is no doubt that Yugoslavia modified her foreign policy to remove the worst sources of friction with the West, but although contriving not to provoke unduly the governments that were sustaining the economy, she did not abandon the basic principles of her foreign policy.

RELATIONS WITH NON-COMMUNIST NEIGHBOURS

During 1949 support for the Greek partisans was quietly dropped, and in 1953 the Bled Treaty brought Greece, Turkey and Yugoslavia together in a Balkan Pact which contained military clauses. This brief episode in which Yugoslavia entered into an alliance with two members of NATO bore little fruit. The deterioration of relations between Greece and Turkey because of the Cyprus situation undermined any possibility of their co-operation in the Balkans, and Yugoslavia's need for reinsurance diminished after 1955 when Khruschev reversed Stalin's anti-Yugoslav policy.

After the signing of the Austrian State Treaty in 1955, the problem of the Slovenes in Carinthia was allowed to recede into the background, but it was not completely forgotten. The Yugoslavs make no territorial claims, but they insist that the Austrian government should implement the clauses of the State Treaty relating to the rights of national minorities. From time to time an incident occurs when, for example, a road sign in Slovene is defaced by right-wing Austrian nationalists. In 1974 the Yugoslavs also raised the problem of the rights of the Burgenland Croats, descendants of migrants who settled in Austria 500 years ago. Here the issue was the status of the Croat language in the schools. In acrimonious exchanges the Austrians accused the Yugoslavs of interference in their internal affairs, and the Yugoslavs alleged that the Austrian authorities took no action to restrain chauvinists from such nationalist groups as the *Heimatdienst* in their attacks on Slovenes. Another source of friction with Austria arose from the presence on Austrian soil of former *ustaše* members. In 1970 an armed group crossed into Yugoslavia and made an attack on local security forces in Bosnia.

The Trieste issue also flared up again in the 1970s. Most people assumed that this matter had been satisfactorily settled by the agreements reached after the crisis of 1953. The Paris Peace Treaty of 1947 envisaged the creation of a Free Territory of Trieste, but this section was never implemented. Meanwhile, the proposed territory was divided into zone A under Anglo-American and zone B under Yugoslav occupation. In 1953 the Western powers proposed to hand over zone A, which included the city of Trieste, to the Italians. The Yugoslavs mobilised along the frontier and threatened to march in to Trieste if Italian troops were permitted to enter zone A. The crisis ended with the signing of the London Memorandum of 1954, in which the *de facto* position of Yugoslav occupation in zone B and Italian occupation of zone A was recognised. Italy and Yugoslavia then got down to negotiations on practical issues concerning trade and the regulation of traffic across the border, and within a few years Italy had become Yugoslavia's chief trading partner.[14]

In 1974 the Italian government, under pressure from right-wing elements, suddenly reactivated the issue by protesting at the erection of road signs by the Yugoslavs announcing to travellers that they were entering *SFR Jugoslavija–SR Slovenija* when they crossed the border into the former zone B. The Italian note stated that 'Yugoslav territory has never been extended to the Italian territory described as zone B in the unrealised Free Territory of Trieste'. The Yugoslavs reacted angrily, and there was a wave of protest meetings throughout the country. The government even raised the matter at the Geneva conference on European security as a threat to world peace. The dispute rumbled on inconclusively for the rest of the year. It would seem that internal political reasons in the two countries explain both the initial Italian note and the somewhat dramatic Yugoslav overreaction. Neither country can hope to gain from a reopening of an issue which has lain dormant for over twenty years.

In her relations with West Germany political differences did not seriously hinder the development of trade. Yugoslavia recognised the GDR in October 1957, despite warnings by the Federal Government that, under the terms of the Hallstein Doctrine, West Germany would sever diplomatic relations with any government which recognised the Ulbricht regime. Despite a break in diplomatic relations which lasted until January 1968, West Germany's share of Yugoslav foreign trade rose during this period from 10·5 to 14 per cent.

NON-ALIGNMENT

Despite her economic dependence on the West, Yugoslavia's most important demonstration of political independence was her championing of the cause of non-alignment. There was little direct economic benefit to Yugoslavia in this policy. The proportion of Yugoslav trade with the non-aligned group has actually fallen since the 1950's. In 1958 it accounted for 17 per cent of foreign trade, but by 1969 the percentage had fallen to 6·6 per cent and by 1971 to under 6 per cent (see table 30).

The Agreement on Preferentials signed in 1967 between Yugoslavia, India and the United Arab Republic provided for a lowering of customs duties between the three countries and was intended to be a model for international trade relations between the countries of the Third World. At the non-aligned nations' summit conference at Lusaka in 1970 the emphasis in the resolutions had shifted from the preoccupation with nuclear disarmament and colonialism, which characterised the Belgrade (1961) and Cairo (1963) conferences, towards a concern with problems of economic development. The Algiers conference of 1973 also stressed economic co-operation, although support for the 'Arab cause' was equally important. At UNCTAD, and in the meetings of UN agencies, Yugoslavia's voice has consistently been raised in support of the developing nations, often in defiance of the big powers of both East and West.

The policy of non-alignment was the obvious one for Yugoslavia to take when she was cast out of the Cominform. It has been particularly associated with President Tito, who was clearly the inspirer of the series of non-aligned summit conferences. His tireless personal diplomacy, which included long journeys to Africa, Asia and Latin America during the 1960s,[15] indicates the great importance he attaches to Yugoslavia's role in the Third World. Nevertheless, there are signs that Yugoslavia's interest may be waning as the pull of ever-closer economic links with the EEC countries begins to affect her foreign policy. The big figures of the early conferences have left the stage – Nehru, Nasser, Sukarno. It was perhaps symbolic that President Tito did not attend the funeral of his old friend Nasser in 1969 because he was acting as host to President Nixon.[16]

Although non-alignment may have produced no spectacular economic benefits to Yugoslavia in a direct and measurable way, it is probable that the volume of aid that was received during the 1950s and early 1960s was indirectly related to the enhanced political prestige and influence which the posture of non-alignment conferred on Yugoslavia. It became a major concern of United States policy to prevent Yugoslavia from slipping back into the Soviet embrace. It was also important to the United States and western Europe that they should counter Soviet and Chinese influence in the Third World. Both objectives required that they should support the integrity and economic survival of Yugoslavia. More recently, a third opportunity had opened up. Yugoslavia's willingness to admit foreign capital has been seen by United States and West German businessmen as offering a springboard for new markets in both eastern Europe and the Middle East. Factories based in Yugoslavia will, it is hoped, be able to produce goods for these new markets, using cheap Yugoslav labour. The position was expressed by John Whitney, the leader of a US trade mission to Yugoslavia, when he said in a broadcast on his return home: 'We consider that the geographical position of Yugoslavia is most favourable, that she is situated in close geographical proximity to the Eastern countries, and that she has been maintaining very good relations with them and with the developing countries.'

He therefore urged United States businessmen to consider investment in Yugoslavia and assured them that new Yugoslav laws relating to foreign capital gave adequate guarantees against the risk of expropriation.

Yugoslavia would not have been so attractive to such Western interests if she had been aligned on either side in the cold war. To point out these possible indirect economic benefits from non-alignment is not to doubt the sincerity of the President and his colleagues in the great efforts they have made in international politics. The constant procession of world political figures to Belgrade in order to confer with Tito is an indication of the influence which a small nation can have in international relations, and no one would deny that such influence as Yugoslavia has been able to exert has been in the cause of peace.[17]

The non-aligned policy was the cornerstone of Yugoslavia's foreign relations during the decade between the early 1950s and the early 1960s, and its high watermark was the Belgrade conference of 1961. Since the mid-sixties, whilst still maintaining non-alignment as an essential pivot of her relations with the rest of the world, Yugoslavia has moved closer to the West. The dynamic for this steady shift has come from the new economic policies that were introduced in 1963 and 1965.

THE INTERNATIONAL DIVISION OF LABOUR

The Reform of 1965 proclaimed Yugoslavia's intention to enter fully into the 'international division of labour'. The implication of this slogan was that foreign trade barriers would be removed and the Yugoslav market would be opened to competition from abroad. This competition would act as a spur to greater efficiency of domestic industry and would enable Yugoslavia to compete in world markets as an equal partner. The Social Development Plan 1966–70 looked forward to the achievement of convertibility of the dinar by 1970: 'Until convertibility of the dinar has been achieved, a portion of commodity imports will be regulated through a combination of foreign exchange and external trade measures. . . . Exports of commodities will in principle become free.'[18]

It was realised that the transition to a market economy could not be achieved at a stroke, and that state intervention, including 'a policy of moderate protection of domestic industry,'[19] would be necessary for a time. The objective, however, was to free enterprises as rapidly as possible from any restraints, except those of the market, on their ability to deal directly with foreign partners. By a process of 'natural selection' aided by the State the Yugoslav economy would adopt a policy of comparative advantage, selling on world markets those goods it could produce competitively and ceasing to produce what could be more cheaply imported. It was foreseen that this policy would, if successful, involve a radical restructuring of industry. The dislocations that followed would include a shake-up on the labour market. Many inefficient firms that had hitherto hoarded labour would be forced to reduce their payrolls. As part of the intention was to force Yugoslav industry to adopt modern technology, the brunt of the burden of redundancy would be borne by the unskilled workers.

Gastarbeiter

To ease the tension which was bound to arise from an increase in unemployment Yugoslavia must again, as in pre-war days, become an exporter of surplus labour. This involved a relaxation of the old restrictions on freedom of movement. Gradually in the early 1960s the policy of issuing visas to would-be migrants was liberalised. The removal of the restriction led to a flood of Yugoslav workers leaving to find jobs in western Europe. In some rural areas whole villages were depleted of their active working population. For example, in the Sinj region, inland from Split, the majority of the male population between twenty and forty years of age went abroad after 1965. Figures given by the deputy from Sinj at a meeting of the socio-political chamber of the Federal Assembly show that in the seven underdeveloped *opstine* of Dalmatia, for every 100 Yugoslavs employed at home, 86 are working abroad.[20]

Estimates as to the number of Yugoslavs who have found work abroad vary. The figure given in the 1971 census is obviously too low, as it is only slightly higher than the numbers recorded by the West German authorities for Germany alone. It is probable that at the end of 1971 there were 1 million Yugoslavs working abroad, and of these over half were in Germany. German records of entrants, based on the issuing of labour permits, show that the number of Yugoslavs in the Federal Republic increased almost forty-fold during the 1960s: in 1960 there were under 10,000; in 1970 there were almost 400,000. The Yugoslav share in the total number of foreign *gastarbeiter* has risen from 3·2 per cent in 1960 to 21·2 per cent in 1970.

The attitude of the Yugoslav authorities to this mass migration has changed rapidly. Until the early 1960s it was actively discouraged. As the unemployment figures climbed, there was a grudging acceptance that it was perhaps better to let a man go abroad rather than have him living on the dole at home. There was however no policy of protecting the worker from exploitation in Germany. Once he got abroad he was on his own. After the reform of 1965 there was a conscious policy of encouraging workers to go abroad. The Yugoslav government and the trade unions made agreements with the authorities abroad to regularise methods of recruiting and to ensure that the workers were given fair conditions of employment. More recently there has been some concern at the number of workers who are leaving Yugoslavia and there are definite policies to encourage the repatriation of certain classes of migrants.

The numbers abroad fluctuate according to economic circumstances in the host country. For example, the temporary slowing down of the German economic boom in 1966–7 was dramatically reflected in the figures of Yugoslav migrants leaving during 1967. The oil crisis of the early seventies produced an even more dramatic effect on the rate of employment in Germany, and in 1974 the federal government introduced restrictions on the admission of further *gastarbeiter*. It is too early yet (1975) to measure the consequences of these developments on the Yugoslav economy, but clearly they contain serious implications for the future.

Apart from relieving pressure on the Yugoslav economy, the migrant workers also make a valuable contribution to the balance of payments. In the years 1970–2 the percentages of remittances from West Germany were: 67 per cent (1970), 68 per cent (1971) and 72 per cent (1972).

Table 25 Invisible earnings, 1965–73 ($ million)

	1965	*1966*	*1968*	*1969*	*1970*	*1971*	*1972*	*1973*
Remittances of migrants	59	95	122	206	500	650	870	1209
Tourism	81	116	182	241	274	360	432	595

Sources: 1967–71 figures issued by National Bank and quoted in OECD surveys. 1972 figures from *Ekonomska Politika* (January 1973), p. 23. 1973 figures from *Privredni Vjesnik* (17 January 1974), pp. 2–3

Tourism

The relaxation of frontier controls which enabled Yugoslavs to find jobs in western Europe came a few years after the beginning of a drive to attract foreign tourists from convertible currency areas. Yugoslavia possesses a coastline and a climate which give it an enormous advantage in competing with other tourist areas. In relation to other forms of investment, tourism produces a quick return in foreign currency. It not only benefits those directly employed in the hotel, catering and related service industries, but also stimulates activity in the building industry, food manufacturing, agriculture and handicrafts, often in areas remote from the holiday centres. It may distort the economy to some extent, creating a demand for luxury imports to satisfy the needs of the tourists. The modern tourist likes to enjoy the Dalmatian sun, but he often expects to find Dortmund beer, Soho-style gambling machines, Coca-Cola and similar products from home when he returns to his hotel from the beach. The Yugoslavs have now begun to cater for those needs by entering into licensing agreements with German, Danish and Austrian breweries, and with the ubiquitous Coca-Cola company. Certain hotels are now equipped with casinos, 'playmates', strip clubs and similar entertainments to help Western tourists to feel at home.

Although Yugoslavia has been very successful in exploiting its tourist potential (see table 25–6), it can be dangerous for a developing country to rely too heavily on tourism. The tourist industry is subject to seasonal fluctuations and is also highly sensitive to forces completely beyond the control of the host country – for example, international crises, whether political or monetary, economic recessions in the countries from which the visitors come, and changes in holiday fashions.

Table 26 Foreign tourists and their overnight stays, 1953–71 (thousands)

	Tourist	*Overnight stays*
1953	245	855
1954	321	1104
1955	485	1833
1956	394	1333
1957	499	1966
1958	598	2509
1959	835	3433
1960	873	3511
1961	1080	4523
1962	1242	5270
1963	1755	7650
1964	2272	10,085
1965	2658	11,240
1966	3437	14,720
1967	3678	16,107
1968	3887	17,210
1969	4836	22,400
1970	4748	22,560
1971	5260	25,873

Source: Statistički Godišnjak

The majority of foreign tourists come from West Germany, Italy and Austria.[21] During the early sixties the steadily increasing flow of tourists began to impose strains on the hotel and catering industry. Investment in tourism was not one of the priorities of the policy makers during the period of rapid industrialisation. There was a shortage of both accommodation and trained personnel. In order to cope with the influx the authorities at first turned a blind eye to private initiative in tourism. In resorts like Split the absurdly bureaucratic regulations regarding the registration and taxing of guests staying in private homes were ignored, at least during the tourist season.

By the mid-sixties official encouragement was given to persons wishing to modernise their homes in order to cater for tourists. The State also invested large capital sums in improving transport facilities. The Adriatic highway, the Magistrala, provided a access by motor car to the whole of the Dalmatian coast. The relationship between the completion of the road and the rise in the number of foreign tourists is illustrated in table 27.

Table 27 Relationship between completion of the Adriatic highway and the rise of tourism, 1961–5

	Overnights of foreign tourists				
	1961	1962	1963	1964	1965
Biograd na Moru (road completed 1962)	30,116	42,923	65,842	92,751	118,332
Kaštel Stari (road completed 1964)	22,071	31,433	35,794	34,940	52,205
Umag (road completed 1964)	32,371	39,648	69,634	99,769	120,634

Source: Statistički Godišnjak (1962–6)

The sudden rise in the number of car-borne tourists created new pressures on the Yugoslav economy. Service facilities were inadequate, and again the authorities responded firstly by turning a blind eye to private enterprise in this field and later by licensing and encouraging it.

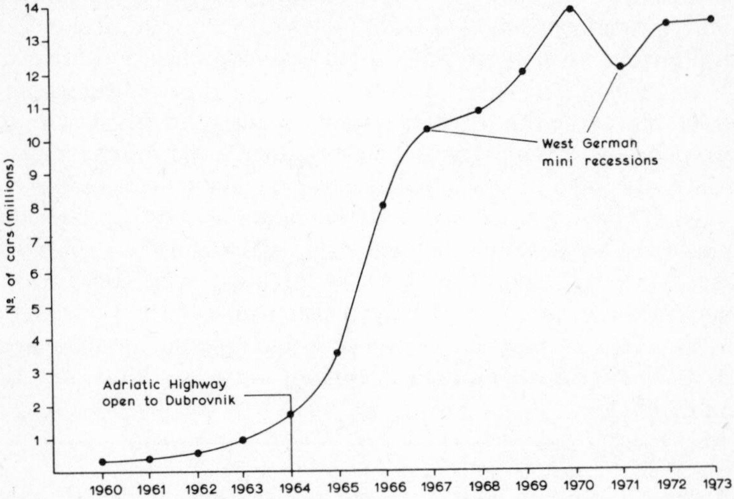

FIG. 1 Foreign cars entering Yugoslavia, 1960–9

The opening of frontiers, both to allow Yugoslavs to work abroad and to admit foreign tourists, had profound social and political as well as economic consequences for Yugoslavia. The generation that made the revolution looked eastward, if it looked abroad for guidance; the rising generation of the 1970s looks to western Europe – and above all to Germany – for its models. Its life style, its ambitions, are directed to the affluent societies from whence come the tourists with their large cars, caravans and motor boats and their well filled wallets.

The rapidity with which the children of the ex-partisans have abandoned the attitudes of their parents towards the former enemy is remarkable.

Foreign Capital

One aspect of this relationship is the attempt to attract foreign investment. It is a curious example of Yugoslavia's pragmatism that a foreigner can invest private capital in the Yugoslav economy and receive a profit on his investment on terms which are not available to a Yugoslav citizen. The Yugoslavs hope to import modern technology with the foreign capital and also to attract investment to the less developed areas of the country. There have been modest successes towards attaining the former objective, but as table 29 shows, very little foreign capital has been attracted to the less developed areas.[23]

The passing in 1967 of the first law permitting the investment of private foreign capital allowed the investors to share in joint ventures with Yugoslav enterprises, provided that the foreigners share did not exceed 49 per cent of the total investment. In practice, the average share of foreigners in joint ventures is only 18 per cent. Since 1967 the regulations have been amended several times, usually with the intention of making joint ventures more attractive to foreigners.

In addition to the joint ventures, Yugoslav industry has developed other forms of co-operation with western European and American firms – e.g. manufacture under license and joint marketing arrangements. The main areas of operation are in the field of motor cars (where Fiat's co-operation with the *Crvena Zastava* firm at Kragujevac leads the field), electronics, chemicals, plastics and textiles. The chief Western participants are Italy and Federal Germany, both members of the EEC.

Yugoslavia's close involvement with western Europe inevitably raises the question of her relationship with Western trading and financial organisations. She joined GATT in 1966 and a year later entered in negotiations with EFTA and the EEC. In March 1970 the first non-preferential trade agreement between Yugoslavia and the EEC was signed. This was renewed in 1973. Yugoslavia's main concern has been to ensure that she can export to EEC countries the agricultural produce which will help to pay for her industrial imports from these countries. Meat and wine have been the subject of special agreements.

Although Yugoslavia's unique relationship with COMECON began in 1964, some years earlier than that with the EEC, trade with COMECON countries is less in total and is growing more slowly than her trade with the EEC. Although in 1974 it may seem that Yugoslavia is looking towards the East with more friendly eyes than in earlier years, the realities of her economic situation mean that she will continue to need her trading partners in the West, and that the trend towards closer economic ties with the EEC is likely to continue. So far the Yugoslavs have shown that economic dependence need not mean the loss of political independence.

Table 28 Yugoslav workers in Federal Germany, 1954–71*

	Yugoslavs	*All foreign workers (including EEC members)*	*Percentage of Yugoslavs*
1954	1801	72,906	2·4
1955	2085	79,607	2·5
1956	2297	91,293	2·5
1957	2778	108,190	2·6
1958	4846	127,083	3·7
1959	7310	166,829	4·4
1960	8826	279,390	3·1
1961	12,858	475,722	2·7
1962	23,608	655,473	3·6
1963	44,428	811,463	5·4
1964	53,057	932,932	5·7
1965	64,060	1,164,364	5·5
1966	96,695	1,314,031	7·3
1967	97,725	1,023,747	9·5
1968	99,660	1,014,776	9·8
1969	226,290	1,372,059	16·0
1971	411,503†		

Source: Erfahrungsbericht auslandische Arbeitnehmer 1969 der Bundesaustalt fur Arbeit (Nürnberg 1970), Ubersicht 4

* Figures for 1954–60 give situation at end of July; figures for 1961–9 give situation at end of June in each year.

† Figures for 1971 based on Yugoslav census, March 1971.

Table 29 Foreign investments in Yugoslavia: contracts on joint ventures concluded and registered

	Yugoslav company and location	*Foreign investor*	*Industry*	*Total investment ($)*	*Foreign investment ($)*	*Date contract was concluded*
1	Crvena Zastava (Kragujevac)	FIAT (Italy)	automobiles	47,500,000	5,000,000	3 April 1968
2	Beogradski Grafički Zavod (Belgrade)	Printing Development Int'l (USA)	artist's colours	325,000	159,250	17 May 1968
3	Cinkarna (Celje)	Lacke und Farben (German Democratic Republic)	titanium dioxide	22,608,000	11,064,000	24 April 1968
4	Tvornica Olvnih i Aluminijskih Proizvoda (Zagreb)	Tubettificio Ligure (Italy)	aluminium packaging	508,000	152,400	11 Sept. 1968
5	Idrija (Idrija)	Kautt und Bux (Federal Republic of Germany)	electrical	877,688	430,067	28 Aug. 1968
6	Kamen (Pazin)	Ilma (Italy)	marble products	2,675,451	1,329,451	30 May 1969
7	Crvena Zastava (Kragujevac)	FIAT (Italy)	automobiles	63,372,278	17,000,000	11 June 1969
8	Elektrosrbija (Belgrade)	Financière des Applications d'Electricité (Belgium)	lighting equipment	240,000	117,600	18 April 1969
9	Konus (Slovenske Konjice)	Masny Promysl (Czechoslovakia)	leatherwear	10,784,000	4,768,000	5 June 1969
10	Chromos–Katran–Kutrilin (Zagreb)	Major Prodotti Dentali (Italy)	dental products	279,656	87,650	23 May 1969
11	Progres–Invest (Belgrade)	Pechiney–St Gobain (France)	chemicals	180,000	88,200	14 March 1969
12	Energoinvest (Sarajevo)	Cie Francaise d'Étude et Constructions (France)	petroleum refineries	202,550	66,841	20 March 1969
13	Unis (Sarajevo)	SKF (Sweden)	ball bearings	13,296,000	3,000,000	14 March 1969

	Yugoslav company and location	*Foreign investor*	*Industry*	*Total investment ($)*	*Foreign investment ($)*	*Date contract was concluded*
14	VEGA (Ljubljana)	Maruman Co. (Japan)	measuring instruments	100,000	49,000	15 Feb. 1969
15	Elektrosrbija (Belgrade)	Messwandler–Bau (Federal Republic of Germany)	electrical equipment	300,000	90,000	24 Feb. 1969
16	Vesna (Sjenica)	Halstenbach Co. (Austria)	underwear	628,415	300,546	26 Sep. 1969
17	Crvena Zastava (Kragujevac)	International Finance Corp. (IFC–affiliate of the World Bank)	automobiles	8,000,000*	8,000,000	12 March 1970
18	Kamen (Pazin)	General Cave (Italy)	marble products	320,240	128,240	5 Feb. 1970
19	General export (Belgrade)	AGIP (Italy)	oil pumps, hotels	6,400,000	640,000	18 Dec. 1969
20	Sloga (Zrenjanin)	Ets Lipig (Switzerland)	knitted goods	265,395	130,037	24 March 1969
21	Natron Maglaj (Belgrade) General export	Centroproduct (Italy)	chemicals	667,000	266,000	29 Aug. 1970
22	FAP-FAMOS (Belgrade)	Daimler–Benz (Federal Republic of Germany)	trucks	60,160,000	9,280,000	15 July 1970
23	Meblo (Nova Gorica)	Harvey Guzzini (Italy)	furniture	128,470	51,392	4 May 1970
24	Chromos–Katran–Kutrilin (Zagreb)	Hempel's Marine Paints (Denmark)	ship paints	576,000	224,000	9 Sept. 1970
25	Jugotutun (Skopje)	Baumgartner Papiers (Switzerland)	chemicals	800,000	392,000	29 May 1970
26	Regeneracija (Zagreb)	Helsa Werke (Federal Republic of Germany)	chemicals	128,560	62,880	15 June 1970
27	OHIS (Skopje)	Produits Chimiques Pechiney (France)	chemicals	22,545,000	2,250,000	16 April 1970
28	OLT (Osijek)	Wendel–Emailfabrik (Federal Republic of Germany)	chemicals	1,984,000	496,000	14 Nov. 1970

29	Tobacna Tovarna (Ljubljana)	Reemtsma (Federal Republic of Germany)	tobacco	376,970	150,788	16 June	1970
30	TAM (Maribor)	Klöckner–Humboldt–Deutz (Federal Republic of Germany)	commercial vehicles	21,788,707	2,732,240	9 Oct.	1970
31	IKL (Belgrade)	SKF (Sweden)	ball bearings	5,272,731	1,475,250	29 Jan.	1971
32	MIP (Ljubljana)	Richard Daniel (Federal Republic of Germany)		191,257	59,836	8 March	1971
33	Obrtni centar (Koper)	Giuseppe Mazzucco (Italy)		140,000	48,300	12 Feb.	1971
34	Fadip (Bečej)	Dunlop Limited (England)					
	Jugohemija (Belgrade)	The International Investment Corp. for Yugoslavia (England)	hydraulic hoses	2,490,533	1,080,000	15 April	1971
35	Interprodukt (Umag) Intercommerce (Umag)	Atko Handels AG (Switzerland)		180,600	88,500	19 April	1971
36	Lek (Ljubljana)	Bayer AG Leverkusen (Federal Republic of Germany)	pharmaceuticals	3,153,007	1,544,973	17 Nov.	1970
37	ETA (Cerkno)	EGO—Elektrogeräte (Federal Republic of Germany)	electrical	1,517,534	743,533	7 April	1971
38	IPLAS (Koper)	Hoechst GmbH (Austria)		1,126,866	552,266	4 Jan.	1971
39	TAM (Maribor)*	International Finance Corporation (USA)	commercial vehicles and motors	1,588,320	1,588,320	20 June	1971
40	Unioninvest (Sarajevo)	Marlo SpA (Italy)		3,200,000	640,000	29 June	1971
41	Iskra (Trbovlje)	Knapic (USA)		1,224,490	600,000	13 July	1971
42	Socijalen borec (Bitola)	Luxill AG (Lichenstein)		2,133,333	800,000	30 July	1971
43	Lesnoindustrijsko Podjetje (Slovengradec)	Credex Handels GmbH und Co. (Federal Republic of Germany)	wood processing	7,558,231	1,000,000	6 May	1971

	Yugoslav company and location	*Foreign investor*	*Industry*	*Total investment ($)*	*Foreign investment ($)*	*Date contract was concluded*
44	Klemos (Lenart v Slovenskih Goricah)	Kunster Ehringeschaussen (Federal Republic of Germany)		208,333	100,000	24 Nov. 1971
45	Sava (Kranj)	Semperit Aktiengesselschaft (Austria)	tyres	21,343,199	6,314,133	8 Jan. 1971
46	Meblo (Nova Gorica)	Feltrobex (Switzerland)	furniture	1,888,235	923,529	15 Dec. 1971
47	Sladkogorska (Sladki Vrh)	Tragergesellschaft (Federal Republic of Germany)	fine tissue paper	10,249,411	1,552,941	24 Nov. 1972
48	Jugodent (Novi Sad)	Arman di dario (Italy)	electro-mechanical equipment	1,740,570	812,041	18 Feb. 1972
49	Dečani (Dečani)	Freund, SUC (Italy)	metal	283,965	99,388	13 March 1972
50	UNIS (Sarajevo)	Volkswagenwerk AG (Federal Republic of Germany)	passenger cars	5,058,823	2,482,353	6 March 1972
51	FAP–FAMOS (Belgrade)†	IFC (USA)	commercial vehicles	2,170,588	2,170,588	23 March 1972
52	Astra (Zagreb)	IRET, SpA (Italy)	telecommunications	930,292	325,605	31 Dec. 1972
	Total			361,665,111	93,505,561	

Source: International Investment Corporation for Yugoslavia, London

* Additional foreign investment in joint venture listed under no. 30 above

† Additional foreign investment in joint venture listed under no. 22 above

Table 30 Yugoslav trade with non-aligned countries, 1968–73*

	1968		*1969*		*1970*		*1973*	
	Exports	*Imports*	*Exports*	*Imports*	*Exports*	*Imports*	*Exports*	*Imports*
India	327·8	252·2	494·5	434·8	569·1	539·2	467·2	451·7
Indonesia	99·6	11·4	42·0	9·1	20·1	11·0	59·0	5·7
Iraq	39·5	150·0	53·2	234·0	38·9	360·1	108·2	413·3
Malaysia	28·8	84·7	11·5	158·8	27·8	150·4	6·4	300·0
Pakistan	297·1	73·1	169·1	141·1	134·2	118·3	283·6	175·1
Algeria	16·7	50·6	43·9	49·1	21·9	29·6	26·9	187·9
Ethiopia	6·2	7·1	12·1	21·0	3·5	4·2	6·8	152·6
Sudan	26·4	26·9	69·5	51·0	74·7	37·6	155·4	37·1
Ghana	40·2	48·7	42·3	57·0	37·0	143·5	83·6	151·8
Morocco	20·7	17·4	26·3	44·3	26·3	85·7	98·8	447·1
Tunis	39·6	66·8	54·0	77·3	33·1	64·9	92·7	19·9
UAR	348·3	196·6	270·2	371·3	327·5	297·8	182·6	152·6
Cuba	77·1	64·7	28·7	37·9	21·7	11·7	34·6	84·0
Total	1368·0	1050·2	1317·3	1686·7	1341·8	1834·0	1605·8	2578·8

Sources: *Statistički Godišnjak (1971)*. *Statistika Spoljne Trgovine* (1974), pp. 21–4

* 1971 – 1$ = 12·5 new dinars; 1974 – $1 = 17 n.d.

NOTES

1 Imports as a percentage of GNP 1968:

USSR	3·7 per cent
UK	23·5 per cent
Yugoslavia	18·8 per cent

2 According to S. Dimitrijević, *Foreign Capital in the Economy of Old Yugoslavia* (Belgrade 1958), the proportions of foreign capital in certain industries were as follows: 'Cement 97 per cent; chemicals 67 per cent; textiles 81 per cent; food industries 51 per cent. In addition the main non-ferrous ore mines were in foreign hands. Bor copper was French owned and the lead–zinc–silver mines of Trepća were in British hands.

3 Ljubiša Adamović, 'Foreign Trade Policy in Yugoslavia', *Ekonomist*, English edition (Zagreb 1969), p. 72.

4 'Jugoslavija 1945–64', *Statistički Pregled* (Belgrade 1965).

5 The Foreign Trade Equalisation Fund was abolished in 1951, and was replaced by the system of multiple exchange rates.

6 J. Daviĉo and M. Bogosavljević, *The Economy of Yugoslavia* (Belgrade 1960).

7 'It is necessary to secure, by an increase of exports, sufficient foreign currency to pay . . . for the raw materials, machines and equipment bought.' N. Petrović, *Spoljna Trgovina Jugoslavije* (Belgrade 1947), p. 13.

8 In 1946 there was a surplus of 176·8 million dinars. The deficits in 1947 and 1948 were small, representing only 0·75 and 1·5 per cent, respectively, of the total value of foreign trade.

9 Alvin Z. Rubinstein, *Yugoslavia and the Non-Aligned World* (Oxford 1970).

10 The full amounts were not granted. See table 21.

11 Kruno Meneghello-Dincic, 'Les expgriences Yougoslaves d'industrialisation et planification' (Paris 1970), p. 67.

12 OECD Economic Surveys Yugoslavia 1974 and 1975, and *Statistički Godišnjak.*

13 The position was not as bad as in 1948, when only $20 million worth of the promised credits of $400 million had been paid at the time of the rupture. See K. Meneghello-Dincic, *Les Expériences Yougoslaves*, pp. 63–7.

14 A position she was to lose to Federal Germany in the 1960s.

15 President Tito is the most widely travelled head of state in the world. His visits abroad have taken him to the Far East, Africa, Latin America, the Middle East, to all six of the original EEC members, to the United States, Canada, Britain, the USSR, Poland, Czechoslovakia and Romania. China is the only important country he has not visited.

16 His close personal friendship with President Nasser began in the late 1950s. The two presidents met on a score of occasions either in Yugoslavia or in Egypt during the last ten years of Nasser's life. No such close relationship has developed between Tito and President Sadat, although they have exchanged visits. Yugoslavia has vigorously supported the 'Arab cause'.

17 Visitors to Belgrade between 1970 and 1972 included: President Nixon, Mr Brezhnev (September 1971), U Thant, Kurt Waldheim, Haile

Selassie, Chou En Lai, Willy Brandt, Presidents Pompidou, Saragat, Jonas and Ceauşescu, Queen Elizabeth, Queen Juliana and Prince Sihanouk.

18 'Yugoslavia's Social Development Plan 1966–70' English text from *Yugoslav Survey* (1966), no. 27. p. 3881.

19 *Yugoslav Survey* (1966), p. 3881.

20 Of the 1550 who migrated from Sinj between 1965 and 1968, 74 per cent were male and 54 per cent were under thirty years. See Ivo Baučić, *Porijeklo i Struktura Radnika iz Jugoslavije u S. R. Njemačkoj.* (Zagreb 1970), p. 127. For a breakdown of the migrant population according to national republics, the figures for 1969 were given by Ivan Kojundžic, Deputy from Split, in a debate in the socio-political chamber, reported in *Privredni Vjesnik*, 21 May 1970, p. 6:

Total of Yugoslavs working in western Europe		520,000
According to nationality		per cent
	Croats	63
	Serbs	24
	Slovenes	5
	All others	8
According to national republic		
	Croatia	53
	Serbia	26
	Bosnia–Hercegovina	9
	Other republics	12

21 In 1970 these three countries accounted for 60 per cent of all tourists.

22 In 1967 I had the opportunity of questioning the children in a village in Sinjsko Polje about their ambitions. In the upper class of the local elementary school 90 per cent of the children declared their ambition on leaving school was to find employment in Germany. My host was an ex-partisan leader in an area that had seen heavy fighting against the Germans, and had named one of his sons Orel, in honour of the Red Army's victory in 1944.

23 See also OECD ,'Foreign Investment in Yugoslavia' (Paris 1974).

14 Religion and the State

There are three major religious communities in Yugoslavia – the Roman Catholic and Orthodox Christians and the Moslems. The 1948 and 1953 censuses recorded the religious allegiance of the whole Yugoslav population as follows:

	1948	*1953*
	%	%
Orthodox	49·53	41·2
Roman Catholic	36·7	31·7
Moslem	12·52	12·8
Other religions	1·25	2·2
Non believers	–	12·6

The curious fact that in 1948 all Yugoslavs were stated to have some religious belief, although the Communist Party claimed at that time to have a million members, arises from the way in which the census was taken: the 1948 figures show the religious tradition in which the respondents were brought up, rather than their active participation in religious life at the time of the census. In Yugoslavia religion is not simply a matter of one's personal faith – it is also a badge of national identity. Slovenes and Croats have inherited the Roman Catholic tradition, whilst the national cultures of the Serbs, Macedonians and Montenegrins are rooted in Orthodoxy.

There are two main Islamic groups – the Slavic-speaking Moslems of Bosnia and the Albanians and 'Turks' of Kosovo and western Macedonia. In areas of mixed nationality – for example, in Bosnia – the identification of nation and religion has often had the same impact as exists today between Catholic and Protestant in Northern Ireland. The problem of relations between the State and the religious communities has therefore great importance in Yugoslavia, both under the pre-war kingdom and the present regime.

The royal house of Yugoslavia was formerly that of Serbia and its members were all adherents of the Serbian Orthodox Church. Although the Vidovdan Constitution proclaimed the equality of all religions, the Orthodox Church had a special position as the established Church of the old Serbian kingdom. Old Serbia had six Orthodox dioceses, under a metropolitan in Belgrade. After the formation of Yugoslavia there were seventeen dioceses under a patriarch, whose title, according to a statute of 1929, was that of Archbishop of Ipek (Peć), Metropolitan of Belgrade and Karlovci[1] and Serbian Patriarch.[2] The patriarch was elected by a council composed of bishops, the rectors of the universities and seminaries, representatives of the clergy, the prime minister, certain state officials and mayors and some members of the Skupština. The lay element composed almost half of the electorate, and the numbers of the *ex-officio* state representatives indicate the closeness of Church–State relationships. The king was, of course, head of the Church.

The power of the Orthodox Church was demonstrated during the Concordat crisis of 1937. King Alexander, before he died, had taken the initiative in starting talks between his government and the Vatican, with a view to regulating the relations between the Yugoslav state and the Roman Church. Before the formation of Yugoslavia agreements had existed between the Vatican and the various governments responsible for parts of the Yugoslav lands. That with the Serbian government was taken as the model for the Concordat which was signed by the Stojadinović government in July 1935, less than a year after the death of the King. Two years later a government bill incorporating the terms of the Concordat was passed by the Skupština in the face of bitter opposition.[3] The Holy Synod of the Serbian Orthodox Church excommunicated most of the ministers and members of parliament who supported the bill, and some ministers resigned or were expelled from the ruling party (JRZ, or Yugoslav Radical Union). Stojadinović gave way to Serbian pressure and withdrew the bill before it was due to be sent to the Senate. Although the Serbs made a great issue of the Concordat, the Croat political leaders were not greatly involved in the affair. The Slovene Clericals supported the Concordat, as members of the government coalition, but did not seem deeply troubled by its withdrawal. The Moslems, also supporters of the Stojadinović government did not concern themselves with the affair, being satisfied with the relations which then existed between the Islamic community and the State.

After 1937 no further moves were made to regularise the relations between the Roman Catholic Church and the Yugoslav state until after the Second World War, although the *Sporazum* of 1939 was a sincere attempt at reconciliation with the Croats as a national group. There was too little time left, however, to allow this initiative to succeed before Yugoslavia became involved in the Second World War.

THE RELIGIOUS COMMUNITIES DURING THE SECOND WORLD WAR

The Orthodox Church leaders, under their patriarch, Gavrilo, played an active role in the *coup d'état* of March 1941, when the regency and the government were overthrown. When the Germans took Belgrade in April Gavrilo refused to flee the country with the king and his ministers. His courageous defiance of the occupiers eventually provoked the Germans to arrest him, and to imprison him in the notorious concentration camp of Mauthausen, near Linz, and later in Dachau. He returned home, unbroken in spirit, in 1946, and led his Church during the first, difficult post-war years.[4]

Despite Gavrilo's anti-Nazi stand, and the fact that many clergy joined the *četniks* and some the partisans, the Orthodox Church in Serbia was not persecuted during the occupation. Its plight in Croatia and Bosnia, however, was quite different. In the Independent State of Croatia (NDH) only about one-half of the 6·7 million inhabitants were Roman Catholics of Croat origin. There were also 2·2 million Orthodox Serbs, 750,000 Moslems, 70,000 Protestants and 45,000 Jews.

The formation of the Croat state under its leader (*poglavnik*), Ante Pavelić, was openly welcomed by Roman Catholic Church leaders. Archbishop Šarić of Sarajevo had been a member of the *ustaša* organisation since 1934, and Bishop Garić of Banja Luka was also believed to be a member.[5] Archbishop Stepinac of Zagreb, the Primate of Croatia, appeared to accept the religious policy of the quasi-fascist state.

An extract from his diary, referring to a meeting with Pavelić on 16 April 1941, a few days after the NDH had been proclaimed, states that Pavelić intended to 'uproot the sect of Old Catholics, which was nothing more than a society for divorce', and that 'he would not show tolerance to the Orthodox Serbian Church because . . . it was not a Church but a political organisation'. The Archbishop had the impression 'that the Poglavnik was a sincere Catholic and that the Church would have freedom of action . . . '.

Although there is no evidence that Stepinac approved of the brutal savagery of the *ustaše* towards Orthodox Serbs, and although he did issue guarded warnings to his clergy against indiscriminate acceptance of the *ustaše* policy of forced conversions, there seems no doubt that he looked on the new Croat State with benevolence. He forbade his priests to don *ustaše* uniforms but he did nothing publicly to censure his fellow bishop, Ivan Šarić of Sarajevo, who for example wrote odes in which the Poglavnik was compared to Christ. Šarić wrote in *Katolički Tjednik* (the Catholic weekly) that 'it was stupid and unworthy of Christ's disciples to think that the struggle against evil could be waged in a noble way and with gloves on.'[7]

Some of the worst atrocities against Orthodox believers were committed by followers of the gentle St Francis of Assisi. About 800 of the 1800 diocesan priests in the NDH were members of the Franciscan order. They included Miroslav Filipović, the boss of the concentration camp at Jasenovac, where 200,000 prisoners died, and Božidar Bralo, who 'was accused of having taken part in a massacre of 180 Serbs at Alipašin Most, and of 'having danced a macabre dance round their bodies in his soutane, with the Ustaše militiamen'.[8]

The policy of the NDH government was that the Serbs were unwelcome and uninvited visitors to Croatia, who must either 'submit or get out'. The choice which the *ustaše* offered the Serbs, of accepting the faith or being put to the sword, is associated in Christian legend with the followers of Mahomet, but it was pursued with enthusiasm by some of the Croat Catholic extremists.

The Moslems, however, were treated with far greater consideration than were the Orthodox. A memorandum of the Moslem leaders of Banja Luka, sent to the NDH government in November 1941, protested against 'the slaughter of the priests . . . the mass shootings of people often entirely innocent, the expulsion of entire families . . . and their forced conversion to the Catholic faith'. These events

> filled honest people with dismay and left the worst possible impression on us Moslems in the regions concerned. . . . Religious toleration, which had attained a high level in Bosnia and Hercegovina despite the multiplicity of beliefs, has been shattered. . . . Some of the Catholic clergy hold that their hour has come, and they are exploiting it without scruple. Propaganda for Catholicism has become so intense that we are reminded of the Spanish Inquisition. . . .[9]

The Moslems did not, however, complain that massacres against their believers had occurred, although they protested against *ustaše* murder gangs wearing the fez when attacking Orthodox churches and of their insulting behaviour towards Moslems. In fact, the NDH regarded Croatia as a 'state of two faiths – the Catholic faith and Islam',[10] and they made efforts to placate the Moslem community.

The attitude of the Vatican to the NDH was ambiguous. The Holy See maintained diplomatic relations with King Peter's government in exile in London, and the King's representative lived as a guest at the Vatican. Nevertheless, the Vatican was anxious to maintain contact with the Croatian authorities. When Pavelić asked for a papal representative to be appointed, a Benedictine, Mgr Ramiro Marcone, was eventually sent to Zagreb as apostolic legate – a personal and temporary post, without diplomatic status, and implying a *de facto* recognition only. This was a great disappointment to Pavelić, who had hoped for at least an apostolic delegate.

Pavelić's first representative in the Vatican, Dr Rusinović, explained the Holy See's position regarding recognition in a report of an interview with the Papal Secretary of State, which he went to Zagreb on 8 February 1942:

> Cardinal Maglione was very cordial. I greeted him in the name of the Poglavnik, and emphasised the Catholicism of

> the Croatian people. . . . He thanked me . . . and asked me to return his greeting to the Poglavnik. He added that the Holy See cannot recognise the NDH *de jure*, since, for at least a century, they have adopted the procedure of not recognising political situations created during a war. In this connection he reminded me that Abyssinia has not yet been recognised as an integral part of the Roman Empire. However, the Holy See does not forget its sons who are undergoing difficult trials during the war. . . . The Holy See has Croatia constantly in mind, since Croat is synonymous with Catholic, and the Holy See cannot imagine a Croat who is not a Catholic. . . .[11]

This remained the official position of the Vatican throughout the war, although Pius XII showed himself on several occasions to be willing to go out of his way to show favours to individual representatives of the NDH.[12] The *de facto* recognition granted in June 1941 was not publicly announced until February 1942. The *ustaše* authorities accorded the apostolic legate diplomatic honours and attempted to give the populace the impression of full recognition, but the correctness of the Vatican's position became apparent in 1943 when the tide of war turned against the NDH and its allies. The *ustaše* ceased to be represented in the Vatican at the time of the Italian surrender, and although Mgr Marcone stayed on in Zagreb until the end of the war he no longer acted in a quasi-diplomatic role. When the Holy See made its first tentative contacts with the new Yugoslavia, it was through the American, Mgr Patrick Hurley.

The position in Slovenia was quite different from that in Croatia. There was no significant non-Catholic minority and, apart from the German-speaking enclaves round Kočevje and Maribor, there was no national minority either. There was, therefore, no basis for a 'holy war' against alien elements such as that which was conducted by the *ustaše* against the Serbs. During the period of the Kingdom of Yugoslavia the Slovene Catholic hierarchy had supported a conservative clerical party (the Populists) under Mgr Korošec. Korošec was regarded as the spokesman of Slovene national interests in pre-war Yugoslavia, and he served as a minister in several governments, including a brief spell as premier in 1928.

There were many Catholics, including some clergy, who did not support the political line of the hierarchy but who had little opportunity to express their opposition until 1941. When Slovenia was partitioned Ljubljana came under Italian occupation. Bishop Rožman, the head of the Slovene Church, collaborated with the Italian administration[13] and later with the Slovene Alliance, a conservative nationalist body that had contacts with Mihailović and the royal government in exile.[14] Despite the collaboration of the bishop and many of the clergy in the Ljubljana diocese with the Italians, there were Catholics in the Italian-occupied areas who played an active part in the resistance movement. The Osvobodilna Fronta (OF), formed in April 1941, was a broadly based movement which included from its inception clergy, lay Catholics of various political colours, and Communists. The role of the Catholics in the Slovene resistance, at least in the early stages of the war, was closer to a genuine partnership with the communists than that which existed in other regions.[15]

THE POST-WAR PERIOD

The co-operation of Christians with the liberation movement – whether on the Slovene pattern or as individuals in the partisan armies operating elsewhere – could not erase from the minds of the Communists the role of the Church leaders who collaborated with the enemy. As the partisans swept to victory there were summary trials and executions of priests in many of the newly occupied areas. The attacks on Catholic clergy in Croatia was particularly virulent. Many of the more notorious collaborators, including Archbishop Šarić of Sarajevo and Bishop Rožman of Ljubljana, fled abroad, but the head of the Croatian Church, Archbishop Stepinac, remained in Zagreb. He was detained for a short time in May 1945, after denouncing the way in which alleged collaborators were being treated by the authorities.

Although Stepinac recognised the new government as the secular authority at his meeting with Tito shortly after the fall of Zagreb to the partisans, he made a clear distinction between acceptance of a government's existence and recognition of that government's right to tamper with the privileges of the Catholic Church. He opposed the separation of Church and State, the secularisation of education, and the nationalisation of Church property. Relations were not made easier by the Pope's denunciation on 2 June 1945[16] of partisan attacks on the clergy. The speed with which Stepinac and the Vatican denounced the excesses of the new regime stands in sharp contrast to their attitude to the far more horrible atrocities committed by the *ustaše*.

The government at first attempted to win the co-operation of Stepinac, despite his wartime record, but they completely misjudged him. In 1946 he was arrested and sentenced to sixteen years' imprisonment for collaborating with the Pavelić regime. The Vatican replied by excommunicating all who were involved in the trial – in itself not a very serious punishment to men who were actively supporting a Communist-led government. Relations between the government and the Vatican became progressively worse, and in 1952 there was a complete break in diplomatic relations.

The Orthodox Church fared rather better than the Roman Catholic Church. It was led by a patriarch whose anti-Fascist record was impeccable. It has always been regarded as a national Church and, unlike the Roman Catholic Church there was no hint of treasonable links abroad.[17] There had been no religious war against Catholics in the areas with an Orthodox majority, and although Church leaders had collaborated with the Nedić regime, and many clergy had supported the *četniks*, nothing happened in Serbia to be compared with the wholesale collaboration of Catholic clergy with the NDH. There were also Orthodox priests who served with the partisans.

The Orthodox Church found it easier to accept the role in society which the new regime was prepared to allow it, and despite some difficulties a *modus vivendi* between Church and State was possible.

The Moslem community also proved to be willing to co-operate with the State, after a change of leadership under government pressure in 1947. Some of its more traditional members objected to the formal abolition of the veil in 1950 and to the liberal attitude to women professed by the socialist state. Some Albanian and Turkish Moslems took the opportunity to migrate to Turkey during the 1950s, when improved relations between the Yugoslav and Turkish governments made this possible. On the whole, however, the Moslem community co-operated with the State in the same way that it had done in pre-war days.[18]

The constitution of 1946 guaranteed freedom of religion to all Yugoslav citizens and at the same time declared that there should be a complete separation between Church and State. Religious instruction in schools was forbidden, and only civil marriages were regarded as legal. The religious communities were allowed to train their own clergy in schools, seminaries and *medrese* which they financed themselves. They lost most of their income when their lands were nationalised, but the law provided for state aid to religious bodies and individuals. This included direct subsidies to the Churches, the maintenance of the fabric of historic churches and monasteries, and the payment of salaries and pensions to priests registered as members of officially supported unions of clergy.

The view of the Communist Party at this time was that religion, as an outworn superstition, would wither away and that there was no point in persecuting believers. Anti-religious propaganda in the schools, youth organisations and the army would ensure that the young were not drawn towards religion, and the natural processes of mortality would take care of the old. Incitement to religious hatred was banned as part of the general policy of 'brotherhood and unity' among all Yugoslavs. This was interpreted to mean that, for example, Catholics should not attack Orthodox believers, but it did not stop Communists from attacking Christians.[19]

Relations between the Churches and the State passed through four main phases after the war.[20] Until the passing of the Basic Law on the Legal Position of Religious Communities, in 1953, which implemented the principles expounded in the constitution of 1946, there was a period of all-out conflict, especially directed against the Roman Catholics of Croatia. This was, perhaps, understandable, in view of the behaviour of the Catholic Church during the war, 'and the suspicions of Marxists that the Churches always tended to support the entrenched order . . . at least when it came to the Roman Catholic and Orthodox Churches'.[21]

During this period there is no doubt that some local party officials paid off old scores against the parish clergy and that persecution of Christians did occur. The trial and imprisonment of Stepinac and the break in relations with the Vatican occurred during this first phase.

With the passing of the 1953 law a new phase began, to which Mojžeš refers as being one of de-escalation. Party spokesmen began to hint that there were humanist elements in Marxism and that there was no necessity for head-on conflict. Tito even rebuked Party zealots for overstepping the law in their attacks on priests. Marxist sociologists began to study religion as a sociological phenomenon and to attempt to understand the role of religion in society, rather than merely to denounce religious beliefs.[22]

Relations between the State and the Orthodox and Moslem communities improved steadily during this period, but there was little change as far as the Catholics were concerned until the 1960s.

The attitude of the state authorities towards the Moslem community was cautious but not hostile during the 1950s. Both sides were digesting the consequences of the government's victory over an anti-Communist group elected in 1945 to the leadership of the Moslems. In their clash with the IVZ (Moslem Religious Community) leaders in 1947 the authorities cut off all state support and effectively prevented the Moslems from collecting voluntary contributions.[23] This financial pressure, combined with the arrest of one or two Moslem leaders on charges of anti-state activity, induced the Vakufski Sabor to give way. A new constitution for the government of the Moslem community was introduced, which satisfied the government that the IVZ would not again, as in 1945, elect a strongly anti-Communist leadership. The government then resumed its payments to the Moslems, and they in their turn co-operated with the authorities in agreeing to changes in the traditional Moslem way of life – e.g. the abandonment of the veil after 1950 – and in keeping strictly away from any activity that might be construed as political.

The government attitude during the 1950s was to regard the Moslems simply as a religious community and not as a separate ethnic group. In the 1953 census, for example, Moslems in Bosnia were recorded as Yugoslavs, whilst in 1948 they had been called '*neopredeljeni muslimani*' ('undifferentiated Moslems').

Those in Kosovo, Macedonia and Serbia registered as Albanians or Turks or under their appropriate Slav national titles. In the 1961 census, however, the term 'ethnic Moslem' was permitted. The change in attitude came towards the end of the 1950s, although the first public sign was in late 1960, during the discussions on the rules for taking the census. In 1963 a new constitution for Bosnia–Hercegovina was promulgated, which recognised the special status of the Moslems as an ethnic group. An article in the Sarajevo journal *Pregled* in 1964 argued that 'the overwhelming majority of the Bosnian–Hercegovinian Moslems have made clear their feeling of belonging to the Moslem community as an ethnic, and not religious, group'.[24]

The first public demonstration of a change in the attitude of the government to the Catholics came in February 1960, when President Tito conferred a high state decoration to honour the eightieth birthday of Mgr Ujčić, the Archbishop of Belgrade. The following month the Bishop of Skopje, Mgr Čekada, was convicted of currency offences. He admitted to receiving 14 million dinars from the Congregation de Propaganda Fidé for use in the dioceses of Skopje and Sarajevo. The Bishop argued in court that the smuggling of the money would have been unnecessary if Church–State relations had been on a proper basis. The court handed down a surprisingly light punishment – a suspended sentence of eighteen months, which the Bishop never served. Had it occurred a few years later the whole transaction would have been sanctioned by the authorities. Throughout the Catholic areas of Yugoslavia today one can see old churches restored and new ones built with the help of funds sent from abroad.

The day after the award to Mgr Ujčić, Cardinal Stepinac died in the village of Krašić, where he had lived in restricted residence since his release from prison in 1951. The authorities agreed to allow the funeral service to be conducted in the Cathedral in Zagreb. A huge congregation came to honour a man who was regarded by many as a great Croat patriot as well as a great Church leader. His tomb has since become a place of pilgrimage for Croat nationalists. The apostolic administrator, Mgr Franjo Šeper, who had been in charge of the Croatian Church during the exile of Stepinac, was created Archbishop. He governed a Church whose leading personnel had been almost completely renewed during the previous decade. The time was now ripe for a cautious advance towards a more realistic understanding between the Roman Catholic Church and the State.

The turning point came with the brief pontificate of Pope John XXIII. The deliberations of the Second Vatican Council made a deep impression on both Catholics and Communists. On both sides there was a realisation that a *modus vivendi* was possible and desirable. There was a relaxation of controls on the religious press and journals like *Glas Koncila* (The Voice of the Council) in Croatia, and *Družina* (The Family) in Slovenia steadily increased their circulation. In 1969 the twenty-nine religious journals published throughout the country printed almost 10 million copies, 8 million of which were produced by the Catholics.[25] The religious press has been careful not to use its new-found freedom provocatively and has been less harassed by the authorities than have some of the Marxist philosophical journals like *Praxis* and *Gledišta*. Some of the more petty forms of discrimination against practising Christians were quietly dropped. The production began, by Yugoslav enterprises, of Christmas and Easter greetings cards, religious calendars and gramophone records of religious music, despite occasional protests from party dogmatists.[26]

At the official level talks began between the Yugoslav government and the Vatican, which led to the signing of an agreement in April 1966, providing *inter alia* for an exchange of envoys.[27] In 1970 the status of the envoys was raised to ambassadorial level, and in 1971 President Tito was received in audience by the Pope.[28] Yugoslav Catholics have since then acted as hosts to an International Mariological Congress, and there has been a relaxation in contacts at all levels between them and the world Catholic community.

The dismissal of Ranković in July 1966 and the subsequent purge of the police helped still further to relax the tension between Church and State. The dialogue that had developed between groups of Marxist and Christian (mainly Catholic) intellectuals during the early sixties now came fully into the open. There was almost a cult of 'dialogism', and it became fashionable to publish studies by Marxist sociologists and philosophers in the religious press and by Christians in Marxist periodicals. The Bishop of Split was invited in November 1970 to give a lecture in the Law School, and in return the professor of sociology spoke to students at the Theological School. An entire issue of the educational journal *Školski Vjesnik* was devoted to the theme 'School, Religion and Church in Self-Managing Society'.[29]

The theme of many of the contributions to the 'dialogue' was that Christians have a role to play in a socialist society and that Christianity and Marxism both have something positive to offer. The Marxists have ceased to quote the slogan 'Religion is the opiate of the people', and the Christians have discovered that their teaching of 'love thy neighbour' springs from the same spirit of humanism as the socialist's faith in the brotherhood of man. Few would go as far as Branko Lukšić,[30] who describes himself as a Christian Marxist, but many more would use the terms Christian humanist and Marxist humanist. In 1971 the Croat League of Communists even discussed whether practising Catholics could be admitted to membership. Ten years earlier the mere suspicion that a comrade observed Christmas at home would have led to dismissal from the League.

The 'dialogue' is not a purely Yugoslav phenomenon, but is part of a world-wide movement[31] which owed much to the initiative of John XXIII in changing the attitude of the Catholic Church to Communists. The encyclical of Pius XI, *Divini redemptoris*, which forbade any co-operation with Communists, even in pursuit of noble ends, was forgotten. In their turn, the Communist leaders responded. In the words of the Macedonian leader, Krste Crvenkovski, 'the Communist movement around the world has justifiably become more tolerant toward the religious feeling of the masses. It is self-evident that this is connected with a certain reformation within the Churches'.[32]

In the easier atmosphere of the late sixties the Churches made rapid progress, especially in Catholic Slovenia and Croatia, and the Communists turned a blind eye to developments which a decade previously would have been the subject of administrative action. Sunday school attendance, especially in Catholic villages, increased rapidly, and the number of religious schools in 1970 was double that of pre-war years. In a survey conducted in Slovenia 60 per cent of adults declared themselves to be practising Catholics, although only half of these were regular church attenders. In some villages all the children attended Sunday school, and the Church's influence was also felt in various social welfare organisations. This situation worried some Communists, who feared the emergence of the Church as a political force. The Socialist Alliance formed a series of co-ordinating committees, 'intended to enable religious members of the Alliance to discuss the problems of their religious communities in a democratic manner'.[33]

During the same period the Serbian Orthodox Church made less spectacular progress. It had never been subjected to severe political pressures such as those that were directed against the Catholics, and there was therefore less lost ground to recover, for example in the training of new priests to replace those who had been killed or who had fled abroad. Unlike the Catholic Church, it did not have a strong appeal to young people or to intellectuals,[34] and although it had the character of a Serbian national church it did not become involved, as did the Croatian Catholic Church, with the more extreme forms of nationalism. Its greatest problem in the recent past has arisen over the secession of the Macedonian Church.

The history of the Orthodox Church in Macedonia is inextricably bound up with the Macedonian national movement. After the abolition of the Archbishopric of Ohrid in 1767, the Macedonians were placed under the jurisdiction of the Patriarchate of Constantinople. During the next century resistance developed to the Greek influences which stemmed from Constantinople, and the Macedonians made common cause with the Bulgarians in demanding an independent Slav Church. This was achieved in 1870 by the creation of the Bulgarian Exarchate, which included the eparchy of Veles, the territory of which covered most of modern Macedonia. The first demand for an independent Macedonian Church was made in 1891 by the Metropolitan Teodorij of Skopje, but Macedonia remained under the ecclesiastical jurisdiction of the Bulgarian Exarchate until 1918. With the formation of the first Yugoslav State, the administration of the Macedonian Church passed into the hands of the Serbian Orthodox Church. Serbian bishops were appointed, although the majority of the parish priests were Macedonian, except in the Kumanovo region along the present Macedonian–Serbian border. In 1941 the Bulgarians expelled the Serbian bishops and replaced them with Bulgars. The creation of the People's Republic of Macedonia gave encouragement to the Macedonian autonomists in the Church, but the first Macedonian demands were met with an absolute refusal to negotiate by the leaders of the Serbian Church. The new Macedonian government also gave strong support to the movement for a 'Macedonian National Orthodox Church'. The Metropolitan Josip of Skopje, who was a Serb, incurred the disapproval of the government because of his opposition to the separation of the Macedonian Church. When his name was put forward as a successor to the Serbian Patriarch, Gavrilo, the government put heavy pressure on the Church to ensure the election of another candidate, Vikentije, who was thought to be more pliant. In fact, Vikentije temporised, and when he died in 1958 the Macedonian problem remained unresolved. Some progress towards the formation of a Macedonian Church had been made, however. In 1951 the Auxiliary Bishop, Dositej, who although a Serb was personally very popular with the Macedonians, paid an official visit to Macedonia with the approval of the Patriarch. The enthusiasm with which he was received gave rise to hopes that the dispute could be amicably resolved, but despite Dositej's good offices the gulf between the Macedonians and Serbs remained as wide as ever. In 1954 the talks were held between Serbian Church leaders and representatives of the Macedonian clergy during which the Serbs accepted in principle two of the Macedonian demands – the use of the Macedonian language for administrative purposes and the appointment of Macedonian born bishops to replace the Serbs who had been removed in 1941 and who had not since been allowed by the government to return to their dioceses. A practical difficulty arose concerning the appointment of Macedonian bishops, because all the candidates proposed by the Macedonians were married men with families. The canon law of the Serbian Church forbids the election of married clergy to the office of bishop, although there is no rule of celibacy for the lower clergy. Thus the Serbian Sabor continued to reject all the candidates proposed by the Macedonians. On the language question the Serbs eventually made concessions, under heavy pressure from the government. After 1957 the Macedonian language was permitted for administrative purposes and in sermons, but Old Church Slavonic was retained for the Liturgy. Patriarch Vikentije expressed his 'special gratitude to the Federal Executive Council for the assistance extended in consolidating the Church in the People's Republic of Macedonia'.[35] When the Patriarch made a canonical visitation to Macedonia in 1957 he was received with full state honours by the Macedonian government, but beneath this outward show of harmony the Macedonians remained dissatisfied by the continued rejection by the Serbian bishops of the Macedonian candidates. In 1958, with the public support of the Macedonian government, a conference of Macedonian clergy re-established the historic Archbishopric of Ohrid, with three autonomous dioceses, but they continued to recognise the Serbian Patriarch as the supreme head of the Church. Bishop Dositej was elected Archbishop of Ohrid and Metropolitan of Macedonia, although he did not have the permission of the Serbian Church to assume this office. The newly elected Serbian Patriarch, German, accepted the *fait accompli*, and in 1959 he went to Macedonia to join Dositej in the consecration of another Macedonian bishop. Canon law requires the participation of two bishops in the consecration of a third, and once the Macedonians had their second bishop regularly appointed there were no canonical obstructions to the creation of others. The Serbian Holy Synod continued to oppose the movement towards Macedonian independence, and in 1966 they passed a resolution declaring that an autocephalous Macedonian Church would be regarded as 'a dissident religious organisation'. The Serbian Church also opposed the efforts of the Macedonians to secure the canonically necessary recognition of three sister Orthodox Churches for their autocephalous status.

In 1967, 200 years after the suppression of the Archbishopric of Ohrid, the Macedonian Church declared itself to be autocephalous and elected Archbishop Dositej as its head. This move had the full support of the Macedonian and Yugoslav governments,[36] but was vigorously opposed by Patriarch German and the Serbian Synod.

No other Orthodox Church has yet recognised Macedonian

autocephaly. The Greeks are bitterly opposed, whilst the Bulgarians welcome separation from the Serbs, but cannot approve of Macedonian Church independence lest this implies recognition of the Macedonian nation. The Patriarch of Moscow warmly welcomed a Macedonian Church delegation in 1968 but withheld his official recognition of the separate Church. The Serbs have stopped short of declaring an official schism, probably under government pressure, but relations between the Serbian Bishops' Sabor and the Macedonian Church have been severed. In Macedonia the breakaway Church enjoys a more favoured position than any of the Churches in other parts of Yugoslavia. The hierarchy is regarded as a part of the official government protocol list and appears in prominent positions at state functions. In 1971 the archbishop and the vice-president of the Macedonian Assembly participated in a joint Church–State delegation to Rome, where celebrations were taking place in honour of the Apostles of the Slavs, Cyril and Methodius.

The good relations which exist between a Christian Church and Communist government in Macedonia are possible because both can find common ground in the expression of Macedonian aspirations. The reassertion of Communist influence over all aspects of Yugoslav society which occurred after 1971 inevitably affected the religious communities. In view of the close identification between religious and national allegiance in Yugoslavia, it was to be expected that some religious leaders would be involved in the nationalistic ferment which reached its peak in the Zagreb demonstrations of November 1971 but which also manifested itself in less dramatic ways in other republics.

Although Communist spokesmen have frequently attacked the religious communities for indulging in nationalistic propaganda, there is little evidence that religious leaders played any significant role in initiating the upsurge of nationalism which occurred throughout Yugoslavia. In April 1972 a Serbian government official complained that church publications displayed 'an ever increasing involvement of religious groups and individuals in nationalistic and chauvinistic propaganda'[37] but he produced no evidence to support his claim. On the contrary, there are signs that the responsible leaders of the religious communities have moved away from the sterile religio-nationalistic quarrels of the past. As the dialogue between Communists and Christians, which flourished in the period before 1971, dwindled into insignificance in the new political climate, the Orthodox and Roman Catholic Churches began to talk to each other and to work together in ways which would have been inconceivable a generation earlier. Leaders of both Churches co-operated in the formulation of proposals regarding the rights of religious communities for presentation to the commission which was drafting the 1974 constitution. In October 1974 the Catholic bishop of Maribor organised an ecumenical colloquium in which leading theologians from both communities participated. At lower levels, despite occasional examples of primitive religious chauvinism, the ecumenical spirit is beginning to affect the followers of the two main Christian Churches. It seems possible that attacks by Communist leaders such as Mr Dolanc may help to strengthen this co-operation.

Much of the recent criticism has been directed at those religious leaders who have sought to put forward a view on the positive role of believers in a secular socialist society which steps far beyond the circumscribed limits within which Communists are prepared to tolerate the practice of religion.

The approach by the Catholic bishops to the constitutional commission in the autumn of 1973, requesting stronger guarantees of religious freedom, was taken by Mr Dolanc and others to imply that the Christians were asking for 'free competition' on an equal footing between the ideologies of Christianity and Communism. The Slovene Church was in the front line during 1973 and 1974 for alleged 'political clericalism'. In November 1974 the staffs of the two Slovene religious papers *Družina* (Family) and *Ognjišče* (Hearth) were accused of financial misdemeanours and of illegal contacts with Slovene anti-Communist exiles in western Europe and America. Issues of the Croat Catholic paper *Glas Koncila* have been banned from time to time on the grounds that articles in them were of a political character. It would seem that the Communists suspect that the Churches took advantage of the relaxation of Party vigilance during the late sixties to consolidate their position and to offer a rival centre of ideology, especially to the young. In the words of Mr Bilić, the Croatian leader, the Party will not allow 'religious feeling to be exploited in order to oppose the system of socialist self-management'.[38] Article 174 of the 1974 constitution defines the rights and duties of religious communities:

> Profession of religion shall be free and shall be the individual's private affair.
>
> Religious communities shall be separate from the State . . .
>
> Religious communities may found religious schools for the training of clergy only.
>
> Abuse of religion . . . for political purposes shall be unconstitutional.
>
> The social community may provide financial help to religious communities.
>
> Religious communities may have the right to own real property within limits determined by statute.[39]

'To achieve the status of a religious community a group must be officially registered and must meet only on premises officially licensed for the purpose. Foreigners are not allowed to establish religious communities and religious meetings in private houses are not permitted'.[40]

Although the new regulations are stricter than those previously in force, they are not designed to prevent the practice of religion, but to confine it to officially known channels which are strictly religious in the narrowest sense of the term. The interpretation of what are unconstitutional political activities is being defined in more restrictive terms, especially in relation to social and educational activities amongst the young. The new cadres policy of the LCY will ensure that people with known religious allegiances will find it difficult to obtain responsible positions, especially in education. The chances of a practising Catholic becoming the headmaster of a school or a university lecturer in Yugoslavia have always been at least as remote as the possibility of known communists achieving similar positions, for example, in Spain. It seems likely that the discrimination will increase. Nevertheless, many young people and intellectuals maintain their links with the Churches. This is particularly so amongst Catholics in Croatia and Slovenia, and it is here that one may expect further friction between State and Church. The Orthodox Churches in Serbia and Montenegro are less active and have been less successful in attracting new adherents, and the Macedonian Orthodox Church appears to operate in close partnership with the authorities. The Moslem community in Bosnia has been only slightly identified with the concept of Moslem ethnic group, as has that in Kosovo with the Albanian national revival.

It is too early since the reaffirmation of the role of Communism in Yugoslav society to predict whether the religious communities can expect to be subjected to further pressures. It seems unlikely, however, that there will be a reversion to the crudities of the early post-war policies, as both sides have learned to live together, however uneasily.

NOTES

1 During the Turkish occupation of Serbia Proper the patriarchate at Sremski Karlovci was a focal point for Serbian nationalism.

2 In 1766 the Serbian patriarchate had been abolished by the patriarch of Constantinople.

3 The voting was 167 to 127. As the government parties at the time of the 1935 elections held 300 seats to the opposition's 67, the vote amounted to a moral victory for the opposition.

4 He died in 1950.

5 See Carlo Falconi, *The Silence of Pius X*;; (London 1970), part III, pp. 259–351, for an account of the Roman Catholic Church in Croatia during the war. He is perhaps over-critical, and he seldom gives the benefit of the doubt to the Church when the evidence is in dispute.

6 Ibid., p. 273.

7 Ibid., p. 294.

8 Ibid., p. 298. This incident is probably exaggerated, or even untrue. The truth about the *ustaša* is sufficiently appalling without embroidery.

9 Ibid., p. 287.

10 Ibid., p. 277.

11 Quoted in Ibid., p. 327.

12 For example, by being willing to receive officials like the mayor of Zagreb and ministers of the NDH in audience at short notice, and without undue ceremony.

13 Outside the cathedral in Ljubljana stands a monument erected to commemorate an incident in 1943, in which the wives and children of hostages taken by the Italians pleaded with Rožman to intercede with the authorities. Rožman refused and the supplicants were forcibly removed. The monument, erected in 1953, represents a hand with an accusing finger pointing to the bishop's palace. Shortly after it was erected a priest took a hammer and broke off the finger.

14 In 1944 Rožman contacted the Vatican on behalf of the Slovene

Alliance. There were hopes of establishing an autonomous Slovene unit within a Yugoslav federation under King Peter. The Slovene Alliance was represented at the Ba Congress called by Mihailović in 1944 (see above pp. 96–7).

15 The Slovenian Liberation Front apparently guaranteed a more equal standing to Marxists and Christians than was the case in the People's Front in other states in which the Marxists were more clearly dominant.' Paul Mojžeš, 'Christian–Marxist encounter', in *Journal of Ecumenical Studies*, 9, no. 1 (1972), p. 5.

16 'Unfortunately, in more than one region we have had to deplore the killing of priests, the deportation of civilians, the massacre of citizens without trial or for motives of private vengeance; no less sad than this is the news that has to come to us from Slovenia and Croatia.' Pope Pius XII, quoted by Falconi, *The Silence of Pius XII*, p. 351.

17 Tito is reputed to have attempted in the spring of 1945 to persuade Stepinac to 'co-operate with the new government in running the Catholic Church in Yugoslavia more independently of Rome'. S. Pavlowitch, *Yugoslavia* (London 1972), p. 184. The links with the Vatican were regarded with great suspicion by the Communists.

18 The Moslems in pre-war Yugoslavia benefited from the divisions between Serbs and Croats. Under the leadership of Dr Spaho the political support of the Moslem organisation was used as a bargaining counter to win concessions for the Moslem community of Bosnia. Spaho and the Slovene Catholic leader Korošec often acted together, and both held ministerial office. Under the NDH the Bosnian Moslems were treated with respect whilst the *ustaše* slaughtered Orthodox Christians.

19 The only case I can recall in which an atheist was prosecuted for attacking religious beliefs was in Slovenia in 1967; when the poet Gajsek was tried because of his anti-religious poem 'The Holy Family'.

20 I have adopted the periodisation suggested by Paul Mojžeš in his article, 'Christian Marxist Encounter in the Context of a Socialist Society', *Journal of Ecumenical Studies*, 9, no. 1 (1972): (1) all-out conflict (before 1953); (2) de-escalation (1953–62); (3) suspension of hostilities and de-escalation (1962–7); (4) constructive rapprochement and dialogue (1967–72). Since 1972 there has been a noticeable increase in tension between the authorities and the religious communities.

21 Mojžeš, in *JES* (1972), p. 6.

22 Among serious works published during this period Mojžeš lists: Gajo Petrović, *Lenjin o Religiji* (1953); Oleg Mandić, *Od Kulta Lubanje do Kršćanstva* (Zagreb 1954); Ante Fiamengo, *Faktori Koji Podržavaju Religioznu Svijest* (Belgrade 1958); and Mihailo Marković, *Dialektička Teorija Značenja* (Belgrade 1961).

23 The IVZ tried to institute a scheme for collecting two dinars per month from all Moslems, but the authorities vetoed it.

24 Quoted by P. Shoup, *Communism and the Yugoslav National Question* (New York 1968), p. 216.

25 In 1970 the following circulation figures were given in an article in *NIN* (20 December 1970, p. 5):

		No. of copies per issue
Roman Catholic:	*Glas Koncila*	230,000
	Mali Koncil	50,000
Orthodox:	*Pravoslavije*	20,000
	Pravoslavni Misionar	48,000

One million copies of the annual Orthodox Calendar were distributed.

26 When records of Christmas carols were first produced by the Yugoton enterprise in Zagreb, the local LCY secretary wrote an angry letter of protest to a Zagreb paper, complaining that the label bore a statement that the recording had been blessed by a priest. When the Party official had demanded an explanation from the Yugoton director, he was calmly told that the seal of religious approval helped to boost sales!

27 The Vatican, an apostolic delegate and the Yugoslavs, a special envoy.

28 The meeting was originally arranged for 1970, but Tito's visit to Italy was cancelled because of national protests by right-wing parties.

29 *Školski Vjesnik*, 19, no. 5–6 (1969).

30 Branko Lukšić is one of the editors of the Split Catholic periodical *Crkva u Svijetu.*

31 The Paulus–Gesellschaft of West Germany sponsored several dialogues between Christians and Marxists, beginning in 1965.

32 'Samoupravljačko Društvo Jamstvo Ravnopravnosti i Slobode', *Svesći*, no. 13 (1968), p. 94.

33 *NIN* (21 March 1971), p. 18.

34 Orthodox believers have played little part in the Christian–Marxist dialogue, which has really been a Catholic–Marxist exchange of views.

35 Quoted by Palmer and King, op. cit., p. 68, from a report in *Borba* (19 April 1957).

36 This was a year after the fall of Ranković. Crvenkovski has argued that Ranković was the main stumbling block to an earlier attempt to gain government support for the Macedonians.

37 *Večernje Novosti* (1 April 1972).

38 *Delo* (2 November 1974) quoting an article by Mr Bilić in the Zagreb student journal *Ideje.*

39 Constitution of the SFRY, English text, Article 174 (Belgrade 1974).

40 *Borba* (5 March 1973).

15 Nationalism

THE DEMOGRAPHIC PICTURE

When the first Yugoslav kingdom came into existence three national groups were recognised in its title – Serbs, Croats and Slovenes. The Slav peoples of Macedonia, Bosnia and Montenegro were not recognised as being of separate nationality. Most were regarded as being Serbs, except for the Croat speakers of Bosnia. The non-Slav inhabitants of the new state – the Magyars, Germans, and Romanians of the Vojvodina, the Albanians of Kosovo, Montenegro and Macedonia and the Turks of Macedonia – were regarded as alien elements. There were also several Slav-speaking groups who were of non-Yugoslav origin. The largest of these were the Czechs and Slovaks of the Vojvodina, who numbered over 115,000 in 1921. In all there were over 2 million, or 17 per cent of the population who did not belong to the three main Yugoslav groups. As the census of 1921 did not distinguish between Serbs and Croats, it is possible only to estimate the respective populations of those included within this broad heading. Using the figures for religious allegiance recorded in the census, it would appear that there were over 6 million Serbs[1] and under 3 million Croats (see table 31).

During the inter-war period the effects of differential rates of natural increase, combined with unequal rates of migration between different regions, altered the balance between the various groups. The populations of Slovenia, Croatia and the Vojvodina grew more slowly than those of the less developed southern regions, although the higher rates of natural increase in the south were partly counteracted by a high rate of migration during the 1920s. With the onset of the world economic crisis and the political disturbances of the 1930s opportunities

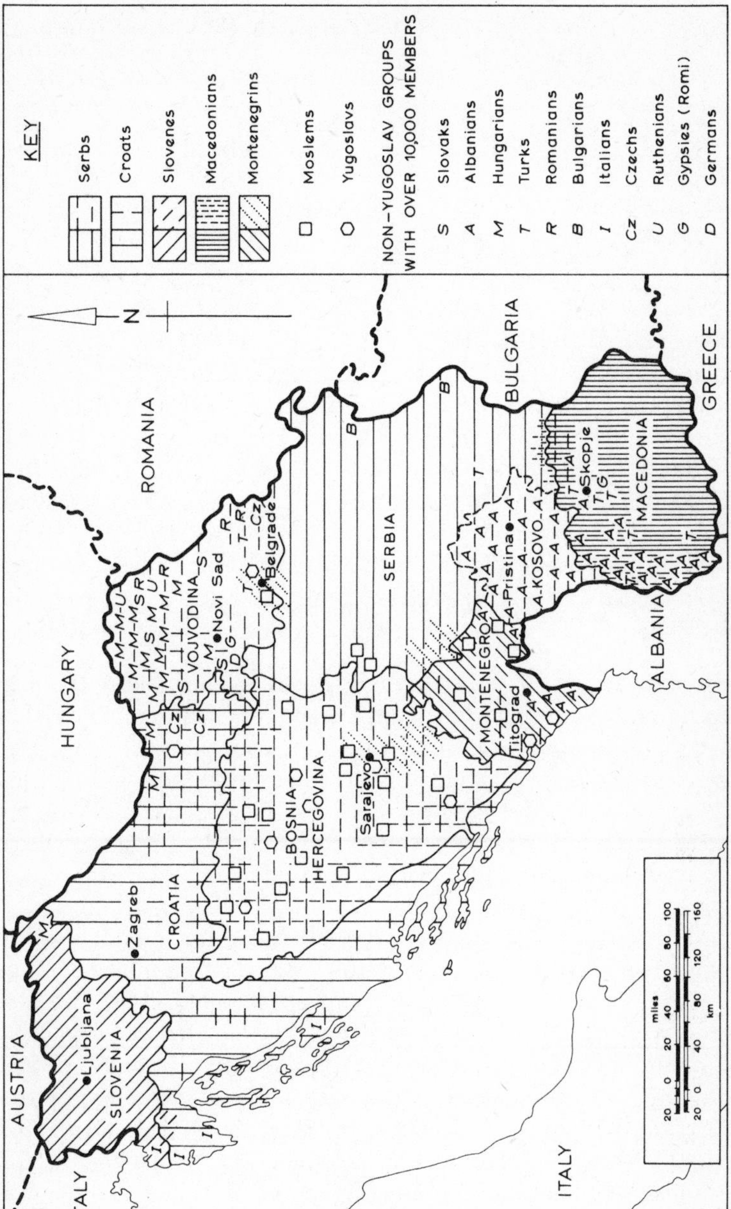

MAP 6 Present-day distribution of nationalities

Table 31 The population of Yugoslava, 1921 (main language groups)

Yugoslavs	
Serbs and Croats	8,911,509
Slovenes	1,019,997
Total	9,931,506
Non-Yugoslavs	
Germans	505,790
Magyars	467,658
Albanians	439,637
Romanians	231,068
Turks	150,322
Czechs and Slovaks	115,532
Other non-Yugoslavs	143,378
Total	2,053,385*
Total population	11,984,911

Source: Admiralty Handbook, III (London) chapter 1

for migration out of Yugoslavia declined, but there was still some drift of population from the poorer south to the richer north. Montenegro, for example, had approximately the same proportion (2·45 per cent) of the Yugoslav population in 1939 as in 1921, despite a rate of natural increase well above the 1939 national average of 11 per thousand. The populations of Macedonia, Bosnia and Serbia continued to grow faster than those of the northern regions, as table 32 illustrates:

The Second World War resulted in significant changes in the demographic patterns of the Yugoslav population. It is probable that 1·75 million people were killed, and hundreds of thousands more fled the country at the end of the war. The Volksdeutsche, of whom there were over half a million in 1921, were reduced to 55,000 in 1948. The German-speaking population of Kočevje and Maribor in Slovenia, which numbered almost 30,000 before the war, were ejected or fled to Austria. The 300,000 Germans[2] of the Vojvodina were reduced in 1948 to a mere 31,000, and their numbers have since dropped to

* Non-Yugoslavs comprised 17 per cent of the total population

Table 32 Birth and death rates, 1939 (per thousand)

	Birth rates	*Death rates*	*Natural increase*
Bosnia	37·2	17·0	20·2
Montenegro	29·3	13·3	16·0
Croatia	25·5	16·3	9·2
Macedonia	34·9	18·8	16·1
Slovenia	22·1	14·2	9·9
Serbia	27·4	14·6	12·8
Vojvodina	21·1	16·9	4·2
Kosovo	36·3	19·4	16·9
Yugoslavia average	25·9	14·9	11·0

Source: Boris H. Mikolji, 'Current Demographic Trends in Yugoslavia', a paper delivered to the American Sociological Association Annual Meeting (New Orleans 1972)

7243 according to the 1971 census. Of the other large non-Slav groups, the number of Magyars remained approximately the same as pre-war, i.e. half a million, and the Romanian population fell from 231,000 in 1921 to 166,000 in 1948.[3] One group that has steadily grown both in its total numbers and in its share of the population of Yugoslavia is the Albanian (formerly Shiptar) group: in 1921 they were 440,000 in number, or 3·7 per cent of the population; in 1948 the numbers had increased to 750,000, or 4·8 per cent and in 1971 they had reached over 1·3 million, or 6·7 per cent.

Another great change that is reflected in a comparison of the census returns of pre- and post-war years is the differentiation of the various Yugoslav groups. In 1921 there were Serbo-Croats, Slovenes and the non-Yugoslav peoples. In 1948 and subsequent years five Yugoslav nations – Montenegrins, Croats Serbs, Macedonians and Slovenes – were recognised. A sixth group appeared at different times as:

> *neopredeljeni muslimani* (1948) ('undifferentiated Moslems'); *Jugosloveni neopredeljeni* (1953) ('undifferentiated Yugoslavs'); *muslimani u smislu etničke pripadnoste* (1961 and 1971) ('Moslems in the ethnic sense').

These six divisions of the Yugoslav peoples correspond to the six constituent republics of the Yugoslav federation, the 'ethnic Muslims' being the Slavic-speaking Moslems of Bosnia. The 1946 constitution describes these six federal units as: 'A community of peoples equal in rights, who on the basis of self-determination, including the right of secession, have expressed their will to live together in a federative state'. The non-Yugoslav nationalities and the national minorities[4] were also recognised as having equal rights with the 'nations' and in the development of their national cultures and languages, but the right to republican status within the federation was not granted. The People's Republic of Serbia was divided into three administrative divisions: Serbia Proper (*Uže Područje Srbije*), with 92 per cent of its population of Serbian origin; the Autonomous Province (*Autonomna Pokrajina*) of Vojvodina, in which there was a Serbian population of 50·6 per cent, and several other national groups, the largest of which were the Magyars, with 25·8 per cent; and the Autonomous Region of Kosovo–Metohija (*Autonomni Oblast*), in which 68·5 per cent were Albanians and 23·6 per cent Serbs.

The only republics in which there were no substantial national minorities were Slovenia (97 per cent Slovene); Serbia Proper (92 per cent Serb); and Montenegro (90·7 per cent Montenegrin). Over 20 per cent of the inhabitants of Croatia were non-Croats, the largest minority being the 14·5 per cent of Serbs. Almost one-third of the people of Macedonia were not even of Slav origin: 17·1 per cent were Albanians 8·3 per cent Turks, and there were significant minorities of gypsies and Vlahs. The Republic of Bosnia–Hercegovina contained 44·3 per cent Serbs, 30·8 per cent 'Muslims' and 24 per cent Croats.

During the period between the 1948 and 1971 census reports there have been further changes in the distribution of the nationalities, and these have had important political consequences. In general, the growth of population by natural increase has been lowest in the more developed regions and highest in the economically backward south (see table 33). This has meant a shift in demographic balance in favour of the peoples of the less developed areas, which has been reinforced by the effects of migration of workers abroad in the 1960s.

The only exception to this generalisation is that there has been a fall in the numbers of Montenegrins, and in the percentage of Montenegrins in the total population during the inter-censal period 1961–71.[5]

Table 33 Birth and death rates, 1950–70 (per thousand)

	1950–4			*1960–4*			*1970*		
	Birth rates	*Death rates*	*Nat. incr.*	*Birth rates*	*Death rates*	*Nat. incr.*	*Birth rates*	*Death rates*	*Nat. incr.*
Less developed regions									
Kosovo	43·5	18·0	25·5	41·7	13·1	28·6	36·0	8·6	27·4
Bosnia	38·2	13·9	24·3	31·7	9·1	22·6	20·9	7·0	13·9
Montenegro	32·1	10·0	22·1	26·9	7·3	19·6	19·8	6·5	13·3
Macedonia	38·4	11·7	26·7	29·4	9·7	19·7	23·3	10·2	13·1
Yugoslav average	28·8	12·4	16·4	22·1	9·5	12·7	17·8	9·0	8·8
More developed regions									
Serbia	26·1	11·3	14·8	16·6	8·7	7·9	15·0	9·2	6·2
Slovenia	22·8	10·9	11·9	17·9	9·6	8·3	16·4	10·5	5·9
Croatia	23·2	11·7	11·5	17·2	9·7	7·5	13·9	10·2	3·7
Vojvodina	23·3	12·4	10·9	16·3	9·7	6·6	12·6	10·1	2·5

Source: Statistički Bilten, 727 (1972) table 3

In 1948 41·5 per cent of all Yugoslavs were Serbs; this percentage had fallen to 39·7 per cent in 1971. The proportion of Croats fell from 24 to 21·8 per cent, and of Slovenes from 8·6 to 8·3 per cent during the same period. On the other hand, the proportion of Albanians has risen from 4·9 to 6·4 per cent; of 'ethnic Muslims' from 5·2 to 8·4 per cent; and of Macedonians from 5·6 to 5·9 per cent.

Within the same republics and autonomous provinces the demographic changes have been more dramatic than the national percentages might suggest. The rapid advance of the 'ethnic Muslims' in Bosnia from 30 per cent to almost 40 per cent of the population of the republic has been accompanied by a relative decline of the Croats (from 24 to 20·6 per cent) and of the Serbs (from 44·3 to 37·2 per cent). The Albanians of Kosovo now form 73·7 per cent of the population of the province, compared with 68·5 per cent in 1948, whilst the Serbian population has fallen from 23·6 to 18·4 per cent. In the more developed areas, the Serbs of Vojvodina have increased from 50·6 to 55·8 per cent, and the Magyars have fallen from 25·8 to 21·7 per cent. During the period 1961–71 there was even an absolute drop in the numbers of Magyars, Czechs, Slovaks and Germans in the province. In the case of these last non-Yugoslav groups, there seems to have been a process of assimilation at work. Children of mixed Magyar–Serb marriages, for example, often attend Serbian schools and become Serbianised. Assimilation is assisted by the migration of young people from rural areas, where Magyar influences are strong, to towns like Novi Sad, where Serbian culture predominates. Of the towns of over 60,000 inhabitants, only Subotica has a predominance of Magyars (see table 34).

Table 34 National composition of towns of over 60,000 inhabitants in Vojvodina, 1971 (percentages)

Town	*Population*	*Serbs*	*Croats*	*Magyars*	*Romanians*
Novi Sad	213,000	63·4	7·0	13·4	—
Subotica	146,000	13·0	31·6	49·5	—
Zrenjanin	129,000	69·9	1·2	17·0	2·9
Pančevo	110.000	67·1	2·5	6.0	6·0
Sombor	98,000	49·8	19·4	22·7	—
Sremska Mitrovica	78,000	83·2	7·3	1·7	—
Kikinda	69,000	75·7	—	19·0	—
Vršac	60,000	67·1	1·0	8·1	16·5

Source: 'Popis Stanovništva i Stanova 1971', *Statistički Bilten*, 727 (1972)

Migration

Throughout the post-war period there has been a steady migration of Yugoslavs from rural areas to the growing industrial towns. The ratio of rural to urban population throughout the country has changed from 70:30 in 1948 to 40:60 in 1971. There has been a marked concentration of population in the capital cities of the republics and autonomous provinces, especially in the less developed regions. In Macedonia, for example, the net inward migration into Skopje between 1953 and 1961 was 14,146, and between 1961 and 1971, 53,896. Of thirty other settlements in Macedonia with populations of over 15,000 all recorded a net loss by migration. Skopje increased its population by 180 per cent during the eighteen-year period.[6]

In the 1950s most of the migration was within republics,[7] but in the 1960s there were important changes in the patterns of movement. Firstly, the relaxation of frontier controls made possible the movement of hundreds of thousands of workers out of Yugoslavia, to work in western Europe. The first to take advantage of this new freedom were those whose contacts with western Europe were historically and geographically the closest – the Croats and Slovenes. Before 1965 over 50 per cent of those seeking work abroad were from Croatia, and a further 14 per cent were from Slovenia. In the period 1965–71 the proportion of migrants from Croatia fell to 33 per cent and the proportion from Slovenia to 6·6 per cent, whilst Bosnia and Macedonia, whose contributions before 1965 were negligible, provided between them almost 30 per cent.[8]

A second phenomenon was the increase in inter-republican migration within Yugoslavia. In the late 1960s labour shortages began to trouble the Croatian and Slovenian economies, and a drift of workers from the south began. The numbers of Albanians and Bosnian Moslems in Croatia and Slovenia, and of Montenegrins in Serbia, increased significantly during this period. Most of the less skilled construction workers in the northern republics and many in Dalmatia are migrants from the south, and they occupy a similar position in the urban societies of Ljubljana and Zagreb to that of the first-generation Asian migrants in British cities.

In the early post-revolutionary phase the Yugoslav communists believed that they had solved the problem of nationalism in their country. They admitted that 'vestiges of the past' would remain, and that true national equality could not be achieved until the regional inequalities in economic development had been eliminated. However, this was only a matter of time – and not a very long time at that. They are today sadder and wiser men. The phenomenon of nationalism is not cured by proclaiming the legal equality of nations and by affirming the brotherhood and unity of all the Yugoslav peoples. In 1967 Dr Jončić could write that, thanks to the policy of the Party towards the nationalities question, not only was there no problem, but the national diversity formed 'one of the strongest factors of unification of the Yugoslav peoples'.[9] In 1970, however, Stipe Šuvar admitted that 'Nationalism occurs amongst all Yugoslav nations today, and it is an illusion to think that the problem will be solved by repressive measures, propaganda or by refusing to discuss it'.[10]

He analysed the causes of nationalism in contemporary Yugoslavia and concluded that two of the primary causes of dissension were the economic inequalities between republics and the intervention of the federal authorities in the interests of the weaker nationalities.

Croatia

The outburst of Croat anger in November and December 1971 was the culmination of a long period of discontent, much of it grounded in genuine economic and social grievances. As with most nationalist movements, it was the middle-class intellectuals and the students who were the front-runners, but the unrest penetrated below the surface to the less articulate peasants and workers.

When the students took to the streets in November 1971 their protests were at first limited to the economic problems of Croatia. The hiving off of foreign currency from Croat enterprises by the centrally controlled bank was deeply resented. An enterprise was able to retain only 10 per cent of its foreign currency. The rest was deposited in the National Bank in Belgrade. Croatia earns more foreign currency than any other republic. Its industries are more export-orientated than those of any republic except Slovenia, and it sends more workers abroad and receives more foreign tourists than any of its neighbours.[11] Zagreb is the great commercial centre of Yugoslavia, with a per capita income from foreign trade greater than that of any other city of Yugoslavia. Over 80 per cent of the seaborne trade of the country passes through Croatian ports, with Rijeka and Split accounting for 9·3 million of the 12 million tons handled in 1969.

The economic grievances of the Croats had been the subject of complaint for several years before 1971. As the area of permitted dissent widened during the late sixties Croat journals were able to publish articles drawing attention to the alleged economic discrimination against Croatia. For example *Kritika*, in July 1971, estimated that 30 per cent of Croatia's national income was being transferred to other republics. It was argued that the maintenance of an artificially high value for the exchange rate of the dinar increased the plunder of Croatia, and that a devaluation to 18 dinars to the dollar would be more realistic.[12] A few weeks earlier the same journal had stated that 50 per cent of Zagreb's national income was 'drained away', half of this by the federal government.[13] The same author complained that, although Croatia's capital/output ratio was better than that of any other republic, investment resources were being dissipated in places where the returns were much lower than in Croatia (see table 35). This, it was argued, is contrary to the principles of market socialism.

Table 35 Capital/output ratios, 1966–8

Underdeveloped republics and provinces		*Developed republics and provinces*	
Montenegro	13·09	Croatia	1·46
Kosovo	9·34	Slovenia	1·96
Macedonia	7·62	Vojvodina	3·14
Bosnia–Hercegovina	4·84	Serbia	3·96

Source: Federal Planning Bureau in *Kritika*, 13 (1970), p. 490

Another aspect of Croatia's economic situation that was given a thorough airing during the late sixties and early seventies was the steady draining away of Croatian workers abroad. The publication in August 1971 of the results of that part of the census relating to workers abroad gave further impetus to the fears of some Croats that the nation faced the possibility of a demographic decline. The figures showed that 5·2 per cent of the total population was abroad.[14] Of these, 50·7 per cent were under thirty years old and 63·2 per cent were men.

Nationalist-minded writers made great play with these figures, stirring the deep-rooted anxieties about the survival of the nation.[15] It was implied that Croatia's best young men were being forced to leave their motherland because there was no economic future for them at home. If Croatia were not being bled by Belgrade for the benefit of the Serbs, the Macedonians and the Albanians, she might be able to provide for her own sons.

The Croats were fully aware of the economic disadvantages to them of belonging to Yugoslavia. The amount of foreign currency earned by Croatian enterprises, the taxes paid to the federation, the number of tourists arriving and workers leaving can all be measured, and the cost can be stated in finite terms. What was not discussed were the compensating advantages which Croatia derived from her association with Yugoslavia.

Croatia's ability to earn hundreds of millions of dollars a year from foreign tourists depends partly on the investment in the late fifties and early sixties of large sums by the federation in highways, hotels and transport facilities. There has also been heavy federal support for the shipbuilding industry, 90 per cent of which is in Croatia.[16] Croatian industry has derived benefits from the less developed areas in the importation of cheap raw materials and food, as the terms of trade between the developed north and the less developed south have generally been to the advantage of the north.

It is virtually impossible to draw up a balance sheet and to determine the profit and loss to Croatia of its participation in the Yugoslav economy. The significant political fact is that most Croats believe that they have been exploited, and during the last ten years enough statistical evidence has been selected by nationalist-minded writers to provide convincing evidence to support their suspicions.

Most Croats will publicly declare that they are not opposed to the principle of giving economic aid to the less developed regions. They point out, however, that they are opposed to wasteful, uneconomic investments which simply impoverish the whole federation. It is undeniable that the return on investment in the more developed areas is far greater than that for the underdeveloped. The northern areas have a greater infrastructure, better access to markets and a more highly trained labour force. But if cost–benefit is the only criterion, then virtually no investment would be made in the less developed areas. To say 'I believe in helping Kosovo as long as it can be shown that the return on the investment is as high as it would be from investing the same resources in Croatia', would be equivalent to opposing the diversion of investment from Croatia to Kosovo.

Another argument that is used by the Croats is that their first duty is to assist in the raising of the levels of underdeveloped regions within Croatia. There are twenty *opštine* in Croatia – mainly in the hinterland of Dalmatia – where the per capita income is below 50 per cent of the Croatian average.[17] Several of these, along the old military frontier, are inhabited by Serbs.

Nationalist sentiments are not based solely on economic arguments. The sense of national identity is the result of a complex interplay of historical, linguistic, religious and cultural factors, but economic inequalities add to the tensions which already exist within a multi-national state.

Slovenia

The Slovenes share many of the resentments of the Croats. Slovenia contributes a higher per capita share to federal funds than any of the other republics, simply because Slovenia's per capita income is the highest. It also has the highest proportion of its population employed in industry and the lowest rate of unemployment, and the value of its exports in per capita terms is greater than that of the other republics. Slovenes have made less of their grievances than have the Croats, but they are nevertheless convinced that they have been exploited by the less developed republics. Slovenes also fear, but less stridently than do the Croats, the possibility of 'biological impoverishment'. 21 per cent of the Slovene labour force in 1970 was drawn from other republics,[18] whilst over 10 per cent of Slovene workers were working abroad.[19] Great efforts have been made to persuade the skilled workers to return to Slovenia. The target set in the autumn was for the immediate return of 30,000 and the eventual return of 60,000.[19] The campaign has been of limited success, however, as the pull of higher wages and better working conditions is as strong for the skilled Slovenes who go to Germany as it is for the unskilled Albanians who move into Slovenia. Only a recession in Germany is likely to reverse the flow, and the first signs of this became apparent in 1973 when Germany ordered a temporary ban on the importation of foreign labour.

Economically, Slovenia has much to gain from being the most advanced region in a developing economy that is moving closer in its trade relations to Slovenia's neighbours, Austria and Italy. Any form of separation from Yugoslavia would lead eventually to its becoming a less developed adjunct to the economies of its wealthier neighbours. Also, the Slovenes feel no cultural threat from any other Yugoslav nations, whereas the Croats feel that they have to struggle to assert their distinct cultural identity against the Serbs. Slovene national feeling during the post-war period has been directed more to the problems of Slovenes in the border regions of Italy and Austria than against their fellow South Slavs: 95 per cent of Slovenes in Yugoslavia live in the Slovene republic, whilst only 78 per cent of Croats live in Croatia. It is perhaps understandable that the Croats feel the need to assert their individuality in more forceful terms than do the Slovenes.

Both Croats and Slovenes have taken a lead in pressing for the implementation of the economic reforms and for the 1971 constitutional amendments. With their stronger economic position they have nothing to lose from the development of 'market socialism'. The less central the control of the economy, the more they will be able to seize the opportunities which their comparative advantages offer them in relation to the weaker developing republics.

Occasionally the realisation that the decentralisation works to the advantage of the stronger regions breaks through into print in the less discreet organs of the press. For example, in April 1971 the Belgrade student paper *Studentski List* published an article that reported the proceedings of a staff meeting in the Belgrade Law Faculty. Several speakers described the constitutional amendments then under discussion as part of a monstrous Croatian plot against the Serbs.[21]

Serbia

Serbian nationalism is rooted in the historic traditions of Serbia as the torch-bearer of Slavism against the Turks. The Kingdom of Yugoslavia was, as we have seen (pp. 72–5), founded on the Greater Serbian principle which underlay the Vidovdan Constitution. The linguistic affinities between Serbs and Montenegrins, and the existence of Serb-speaking groups in Bosnia and Hercegovina, lend colour to the claims of Serbian expansionists who would like to see a Serbian outlet to the sea. The Belgrade–Bar railway, now (1975) under construction, is a symbol of this historic desire for the Serbs to re-establish their contact with the Adriatic. In a country that lives with its history it should be remembered that the medieval state of the Nemanjić dynasty united Zeta (which includes Bar) with the lands south of Belgrade, and that both were within the Serbian Patriarchate of Peć. If it seems that historical analogies are being stretched too far, one has only to read the discussion in the Belgrade journal *NIN*, in which Orthodox clergy are taken to task for denying the existence of the Montenegrin nation. Patriarch German himself is attacked for regarding Montenegrins as Serbs and also for opposing the establishment of an autocephalous Macedonian Church. He was quoted as opening a speech in Montenegro with the words 'We Serbs – of course, I believe that Montenegrins are also Serbs – all Serbs, wherever we are . . .'.[22]

An extreme manifestation of Greater Serbian sentiments came to light with the arrest in December 1971 of the president of the Serbian and Montenegrin Bar Association, Slobodan Subotić. Subotić was a supporter of the Nedić regime and was an active *četnik* during the war. Although he was imprisoned for a time in connection with war crimes, he was able to return to his legal practice and eventually to become president of the Bar Association, which was regarded as a stronghold of Serbian nationalism. Leaflets found in his office were quoted in *Politika*.[23] They urged Serbia to prepare for the day when: 'Yugoslavia breaks up and Croatia becomes a sovereign state', because, unless Serb committees are set up in Dalmatia and in other Serbian areas of Croatia, there will be no alternative to war with the Croats in defence of Serbian interests.

Serbian nationalism has always been closely linked with the

Orthodox Church, just as Croat nationalism has a deep association with the Catholic Church. Reminders of these historic links on occasion produce bizarre results. In Smederevo the local committee of the LCY sacked a prominent member and censured several others for 'singing nationalistic and orthodox songs' at the instigation of a priest during the celebrations for the opening of extensions to a local factory. *Borba* reported that 'the celebration was turned into a real "*Ivkova Slava*", and a demonstration of Serbianism combined with orthodoxy'.[24]

Another manifestation of Serbian national feeling which occurs at the individual level is the refusal to receive communications written in Latin characters. This attitude was publicly defended by the well-known Serbian painter, Milić of Mačva, who returned a letter sent to him by the National Museum of Valjevo with a covering note stating that: 'the Milić of Mačva Atelier receives no letter written in the Latin alphabet from the Socialist Republics of Serbia, Bosnia–Hercegovina, Montenegro or Macedonia. . . . If you wish to write to me in the Latin alphabet, please do so from Croatia or Slovenia'.[25]

Assertion of Serbian nationalism is often accompanied by anti-Croat feelings. After the troubles in Croatia in 1971 there was a wave of hostility towards Croatia amongst Serbs in Belgrade. The president of the Union of Belgrade Youth warned that it was wrong to assume that youth is immune from nationalism and that, in a multi-national city like Belgrade, it was particularly important not to encourage anti-Croatian feeling amongst young people.[26]

Serbian nationalism has no great public 'cause' with which to rally the people. 'In Serbia,' wrote Stevan Pavlowitch, 'culture and religion took over the old structures left unoccupied by politics, and private nationalism became wordy and lachrymose.'[27] The Serbs, as the largest national group within Yugoslavia, have no reason to feel threatened by the cultural or economic domination of any other group. In fact, they are often seen as the source of hegemonistic tendencies towards the Croats and others. To understand these feelings one must look back again into the historical circumstances which thrust Serbia into the leadership of the Yugoslav movement and provided the opportunity for Serbian nationalists to impose the centralist Vidovdan Constitution on the Yugoslav

Kingdom. There is some evidence – as distinct from Croat-inspired rumour – that Serbs were over-represented in the state administration of socialist Yugoslavia, both at federal level and in the autonomous provinces. This was particularly so in Kosovo before the fall of Ranković in 1966. The fact that Belgrade is both the capital of Serbia and the capital of Yugoslavia increases the identification of the federal government apparatus with Serbia. It is inevitable that a high proportion of middle- and lower-rank federal civil servants are drawn from the surrounding Serbian population, although efforts are made to ensure that higher posts are distributed according to a formula which ensures fair representation for all national groups.

Vojvodina

The Serbs have strong historic ties with the Vojvodina, for it was here, during the long period of Turkish occupation of Serbia Proper, that Serb refugees kept alive the national culture. The academies and cultural societies of Novi Sad and the Orthodox monasteries in the Fruška Gora were the centres from which the Serbian renaissance of the early nineteenth century drew its inspiration. During the late nineteenth century the Serbs of Vojvodina were subjected to a process of Magyarisation,[28] and again, as in the previous century, the Orthodox Church and the Serbian cultural organisations kept alive the Serb spirit. The Serbs were again forced to defend their national culture during the Second World War, when Hungary occupied the Vojvodina.

Since the war the Hungarian element has steadily declined, although it is still predominant in the rural areas between Novi Sad and the Hungarian border, and in the towns of northern Bačka.[29] Although as a recognised nationality the Magyars have the right to educate their children in their national language and culture, many Hungarian peasants send their children to Serbian schools. The number of primary school pupils in Hungarian schools fell by over 10 per cent between 1964 and 1969, and although there was an increase in grammar school pupils from 1078 to 1452 the total number is still well below the average for the province.[30]

The virtual disappearance of the Volksdeutsche population at the end of the war also gave the Serbs an opportunity to advance their position in the province. The Germans of the Vojvodina were mainly descendants of the colonists who were encouraged by the Habsburgs to settle the lands, which until the eighteenth century had been under Turkish rule. They settled the rich farm lands of the Banat and southern Bačka, founding their own villages and maintaining their own culture. Over the years numbers of them settled in Novi Sad and other towns, where they formed an important element in the business community. Although many were unsympathetic to Nazism, when the occupation came in 1941 there were those amongst them who collaborated, and when the war ended the majority were forced to flee. This left a vacuum in the social and economic life of the Vojvodina, which was quickly filled by immigrant Serbs and Croats.

The dwindling number of Croats include two main elements. The older established settlers, known as Bunjevci and Sokči,[31] were reputedly migrants from Dalmatia who entered the Vojvodina in the late seventeenth century. A second wave of Croats entered as agricultural colonists under a state sponsored scheme of resettlement after the Second World War. Many of these originated in the Lika, Kordun and Sinjsko Polje, the poor karstic depressions inland from the Dalmatian coast. The Hungarian census of 1942 gives a figure of 61,000 for the Bunjevci and Sokči and 9000 for the Croats. In 1948 all three groups together numbered 134,232. This suggests a migration of some 60,000 under the post-war colonisation schemes. Since 1961 the number of Croats has fallen from 145,341 (7·8 per cent) to 138,561 (7·1 per cent). The figures for workers abroad suggest that Croats from the Vojvodina are over-represented in this migration, but not to a sufficient extent to account for the decline in their numbers. There may also have been a substantial migration to other parts of Yugoslavia – most probably to Croatia – or it may be that the sudden increase in 'Yugoslavs' in the census returns (from 3174 in 1961 to 46,928 in 1971) includes many formerly registered as Croats.[32]

Of the other nationalities in the Vojvodina only three – Slovaks, Romanians and 'Rusnjaks'[33] comprise more than 1 per cent of the population each, although there are villages where

Czechs and Ukrainians are locally in a majority. The Montenegrins are mainly post-war migrants, whilst the other groups are either relics of historic folk movements during Habsburg times or the families of peasants who were left on the wrong side of the frontier in 1918 and preferred to stay with their farms. Like the Magyars, their numbers are declining as the older folk die off and the younger ones become assimilated into the predominantly Serbian culture of the towns.

The preponderance of Serbs in the government of the Vojvodina has been overwhelming throughout the post-war period. It has also been paramount in the League of Communists and the Socialist Alliance. Table 36 shows the extent to which the Serbs were over-represented in the League of Communists in the 1950s. The position today is substantially the same.[34]

Table 36 Membership of the League of Communists of Vojvodina, 1953–8 (percentages)

Nationality	*1953*	*1958*	*Percentage of nationality in region's population, 1953*
Serbs	74·6	73·5	51·1
Croats	5·6	5·9	7·5
Macedonians	1·4	1·2	0·7
Magyars	7·4	8·4	25·4
Montenegrins	6·1	6·4	1·8

Source: P. Shoup, *Communism and the Yugoslav National Question*, p.72

The multi-national character of the Vojvodina might suggest that the province provides a fertile ground for friction between the nationalities, but in fact there has been less public dissension here than in other areas of mixed nationality. At a meeting of the provincial conference of the Socialist Alliance in May 1972 a Hungarian speaker from Subotica complained that the press gave the impression that 'Subotica was some kind of centre of Hungarians and Croats in which nationalist phenomena were manifested to the highest degree', and that the impression was given that other forms of nationalism (e.g. Serbian) did not exist. This was one of a number of oblique references to the Serbian-controlled press, which tended to take a 'holier than thou' attitude towards the alleged nationalist activities of the minority groups and to pretend that Serbs were immune from the taint of nationalism.

During the anti-nationalist campaigns of 1972 a number of Croat teachers and university lecturers were dismissed for nationalist activities, and attacks were made on the Catholic Church for discouraging mixed marriages between Croat Catholics and members of other nationalities.

In December 1972 the public prosecutor reported that only nine citizens of Vojvodina were in detention for political offences, including nationalism, compared with fifty-two in Croatia and forty-two in Bosnia–Hercegovina. He implied that nationalism is not a major problem in the province.

Kosovo

Under the 1946 Constitution the predominantly Albanian-speaking areas of Kosovo and Metohija became the Autonomous Region (*oblast*) of Kosmet within the Serbian republic. The distinction between autonomous province and autonomous region was never clearly defined. Vojvodina, as an autonomous province, had its own supreme court, and peoples assembly but in other respects the relationship of the two areas to the Serbian and federal governments was similar. However, the implication was that Kosmet was of lower status. In 1968 the region was renamed the Autonomous province of Kosovo and was given equal status with the Vojvodina.

Undoubtedly the Albanians of Kosmet, who in 1948 formed 68·5 per cent of the population, were economically and culturally at a lower level of development than the Serbs.[35] There is evidence also that many were unenthusiastic about their inclusion in Yugoslavia, and would have preferred to remain within the Greater Albania which had been created by the Italians during the war. In December 1944 a revolt against the partisans began in Uroševac and fighting continued for several months. Previously there had been incidents in which partisans had fought with Albanian separatists, in one of which 200 Albanians were killed.[36] After 1948, when Enver Hoxha's

Albania joined in the Cominform attacks on Yugoslavia, there were fears of subversion from across the border, and the authorities became suspicious of any manifestations of Albanian nationalism.

These facts help to explain the dominance of the Serbs in the economic and political life of Kosovo and lend colour to Albanian accusations that the region was little more than a Serbian colony. In 1958 Serbs and Montenegrins formed 49·6 per cent of the Party membership although constituting only 27·4 per cent of the population, and the Albanians with 64·9 per cent of the population formed only 48 per cent of the Party. In government offices the Serb/Montenegrin domination was even greater, especially in the police and security forces. The economic life was similarly controlled by Serbs. In education Serbian teachers were in the majority, and higher education was under the control of Belgrade University, with visiting lecturers and professors flying down from Belgrade to teach students on a part-time basis.

The fall of Ranković in 1966 provided the opportunity for redressing some of the grievances of the Albanians. In the months following the famous Brioni Plenum, at which the decision to expel Ranković and his associates was taken, several Serbian police officials were tried for ill-treating and even murdering Albanians in police custody, and the harassment of Albanian students and teachers came to an end.

The easing of pressure only stimulated the more militant Albanians to press for greater autonomy. In 1968 riots occurred in Priština and also in the Albanian-speaking areas of Macedonia. These were led by teachers and students, several of whom were tried and sentenced to terms of imprisonment. At the same time political concessions were made. The region became an autonomous province, entitled to its own flag[37] and national anthem. Belgrade's control over higher education was given up, and the independent University of Priština came into existence in 1969. There was a rapid Albanianisation of teaching posts and student places. A *numerus clausus* was even proposed at the university, in which twice as many Albanians were to be admitted than members of other nationalities, although only 2873 Albanians graduated from high school in 1970, compared with 3085 Serbs and Montenegrins. Visiting lecturers from Tirana began to replace those who had formerly travelled down from Belgrade. Many Serbian-speaking students chose to go to Niš or Belgrade, and young Albanians from Macedonia preferred to study in Priština rather than Skopje. Many Serbian and Montenegrin specialists working in Kosovo left after 1971 and were not replaced.[38]

The results of the 1971 census, which showed that the proportion of Albanians in Kosovo had increased from 67·2 per cent in 1961 to 73·7 per cent in 1971 whilst the proportion of Serbs and Montenegrins had declined from 27·5 to 20·9 per cent,[39] gave a psychological boost to the more extreme nationalists. In some areas Serbs and Montenegrins were forced to leave their homes because of the hostility of their Albanian neighbours. According to the secretary of the League of Communists in Vitina, there was 'a mass exodus of Serbs from the Kosovo–Morava valley' following incidents which included 'the breaking of Serbian and Montenegrin gravestones'.[40]

The deterioration in relations between Serbs and Albanians in the late sixties may have been a temporary phenomenon, resulting from the relaxation of pressure on the Albanians after several years during which they were treated as second-class citizens by the dominant Serbs. It is disturbing to note, however, that there was at the same time an increase in tension between Albanians and Macedonians. The spectre of an Albanian Republic within Yugoslavia, taking in Kosovo and western Macedonia and eventually linking with the Albanian State to form a 'Greater Albania', may seem a distant nightmare to the Yugoslavs, but it is one that has some appeal to the more extreme Albanian nationalists. One of the factors that will determine the future of Kosovo within Yugoslavia is the degree of success which the Yugoslav federation has in solving the economic and social problems of its most backward region.

Bosnia–Hercegovina

The Republic of Bosnia–Hercegovina is the only one of the six federal republics in which there is no clear majority of any one of the recognised Yugoslav nations. In 1948 the Serbs were the largest group, with 44·3 per cent, but by 1971 the 'ethnic Muslims' had become the largest group, with 39·6 per cent compared with the Serbian figure of 37·2. During the same period the proportion of Croats declined from 24 to 20·6 per cent.

The concept of an 'ethnic Muslim' group is one which has been deliberately encouraged by the Yugoslav authorities, and was particularly associated with the Bosnian Communist leader Avdo Humo, who was a member of the federal government and of the Party leadership until December 1972 when he fell victim to the purge instituted in that year.[41]

Montenegro

The establishment of a Montenegrin republic was justified on historical and political grounds but was less well founded on ethnic criteria. Montenegrins speak the same language as the Serbs and are descended from the same roots, but historical circumstances separated them during the Turkish occupation and they developed separate political institutions.

In 1918 the Montenegrin Assembly deposed the Petrović–Njegoš dynasty and voted for union with Serbia. Despite allegations that the vote was taken under duress, it would appear to have represented the wishes of the majority of Montenegrins.[42] During the inter-war period the cultural and religious ties between Serbia and Montenegro were strengthened. Young Montenegrins looked to Belgrade as their cultural centre, and many, like Milovan Djilas, became students of Belgrade University. Communist sympathies were strong among the Montenegrin intellectuals, encouraged by the long traditions of Montenegrin reverence for Russia.[43] Many of the Montenegrin partisan leaders during the Second World War were men who had joined the Party in Belgrade. In addition to the flow of students and young workers from Montenegro to Serbia, there was also a return flow of teachers and priests from Serbia.

Despite these close ties the Montenegrins were recognised as a separate nation by the 1946 Constitution, and a People's Republic of Montenegro was established. It has been suggested that the creation of a Montenegrin republic, rather than the inclusion of Montenegro in Serbia, was intended to allay fears of Serbian hegemony in other republics. The close relations between the Serbs and Montenegrins that existed before the war have continued in the post-war period and have been very much to the economic advantage of Montenegro. The per capita investment in Montenegro has been well above both the national average and the average for the less developed republics throughout the post-war period (see p. 249). Montenegrins had a disproportionate share of seats on the Central Committee and the Executive Committee of the Party during the period 1948–63.[44] During this period the percentage of Montenegrins on those bodies varied between 9 and 15, compared with the 2·7 per cent of Montenegrins in the total population and the average of 6·5 per cent of Montenegrins in the Party.

The great symbol of the Serb–Montenegrin community of interests is the Belgrade–Bar (B–B) railway, first planned in the 1950s and now (1975) well on the way to completion. The project made slow progress until work came to a temporary halt because of the investment squeeze of the early sixties. In 1963 agreement was reached between the Serbian and Montenegrin Central Committees to develop closer cultural and economic co-operation. A statement issued by the two bodies said that:

> the documentation and analyses prepared up to this time convincingly confirm the economic justification of building the Belgrade–Bar line. They show that this is not only a matter of helping Montenegro and the inadequately developed regions of Serbia, but concerns the construction of a communications link which has great economic significance for the country as a whole. . . .[45]

Despite this strong political backing, economic problems again delayed the completion of the line. In the late sixties a bond issue was launched to raise 500 million dinars from the public in order to save B–B. In fact, 900 million dinars were raised, most of it in Serbia. The completion of the line in the mid-seventies will further strengthen the economic co-operation between Serbia and Montenegro and will be of great benefit to the Montenegrin economy.

Although cultural ties and economic interests draw Serbs and Montenegrins together, there are also forces working towards a Montenegrin 'localism'. One element in this process is the tendency for policy makers and officials to develop a loyalty to the institutions in which they operate and to strengthen their own positions within the institutional hierarchy by emphasising its historical and cultural antecedents. In 1969 the Montenegrin Party decided to erect a new mausoleum to contain the tomb of Peter II, the last of the prince–bishops (*vladikas*) of the Petrović–Njegoš dynasty (see p. 36). The Serbian Orthodox Church, which owned the site of the shrine, protested vehemently and was accused by the local Party leaders of attempting to deny the existence of a separate Montenegrin nation. This was the beginning of a campaign to promote Montenegrin national culture, and even to suggest that there was a distinct Montenegrin language. These manifestations were part of the general movement throughout Yugoslavia during the late sixties to emphasise national differences. It culminated in the 1971 constitutional amendments, which gave greater powers to the national republics. By the end of 1971, and especially after the Zagreb demonstration, there was a recoil against the more extreme forms of nationalism, which was reflected in Montenegro, as in other republics, by a purge of nationalist elements and a withdrawal from the more extreme positions.

Macedonia

The Macedonian Republic, which came into existence at the end of the Second World War, contains several national groups. The largest, the Macedonian Slavs, comprised 68·2 per cent of the population in 1948, and 69·3 per cent by 1971. The largest non-Slav group, the Albanians, are heavily concentrated along the western side of the country, bordering on the Republic of Albania and the Autonomous Province of Kosovo. In the communes of Tetovo and Gostivar they form over 60 per cent of the population and in Debar, Kičevo and Struga, between 40 and 50 per cent of the population are of Albanian origin. The third largest group, the Turks,[46] who formed 6·6 per cent of the population in 1971, are also most numerous in western Macedonia, their strongest concentrations being in Debar (35·6 per cent), Kruševo (21·2 per cent), Gostivar (16 per cent), and Brod (15 per cent).

As the Albanians of Kosovo began to assert themselves after the fall of Ranković, their brothers in Macedonia also began to stir. They had genuine grievances, which were easily played upon by the minority of educated nationalists who led the movement. The Macedonians had been so busy establishing their own national language and culture that they had ignored the rights of their Albanian minority. In 1959, for example, at the third Congress of the Macedonian League of Communists, Lazar Koliševski pointed out that there would be considerable delay in promoting higher education for Albanians if instruction was to be given in the Albanian language. He suggested that the Albanians should learn Macedonian or Serbo–Croat: 'Every nationality in the course of its development transcends the exclusiveness of its own language because that presents an obstacle to its further development and its ability to master the modern achievements of science and culture.'[47]

Although this may make pedagogic sense, one wonders if the Macedonians would have accepted the same argument ten years earlier if it had been put to them by Serbs or Bulgarians. The minority of educated Albanians did not see the situation in the same terms. They pointed to the lack of higher education facilities, economic opportunities, and share in government from which the Albanians suffered. Until the riots in Tetovo in 1968 there were seldom any but Macedonians in the leading bodies of the party and government. Between 1954 and 1965 all members of the Executive Committee of the League of Communists were Macedonians, and there was never more than one Albanian in the government.

There were, of course, real problems for the Macedonians in dealing with their Albanian minority. It was hardly to be expected that the inequalities arising from historical circumstances could be eliminated overnight. With the best will in the world one could not suddenly create Albanian intellectuals and skilled workers from illiterate peasants. The suspicion of some of the Albanian leaders, however, was that the will was lacking.

The riots that broke out in Priština in November 1968 spread a month later to Tetovo. They were started when a Macedonian attempted to remove the Albanian flag from his neighbour's window. After two days of flag flying, slogan shouting and window breaking order was restored, and the leaders – mainly teachers, students and professional men – were tried and imprisoned for periods of up to thirty days. Some concessions were made to the grievances of the minority, but there has been little real long-term change in the situation in which the Albanians are a depressed minority within Macedonia.

The recognition of the existence of a Macedonian nation, and the development of its language and culture, was one of the major acts of post-war Yugoslav policy regarding the national question. The emergence of the Macedonian nation was bitterly contested by the Bulgarians after the death of Georgi Dimitrov in 1949. Dimitrov had favoured a Balkan federation, comprising the Yugoslav republics and Bulgaria, in the context of which the 'Macedonian Question' would have been amicably resolved. His death, shortly after the expulsion of Yugoslavia from the Cominform, was followed by an abrupt change in Bulgarian policy. Since then the Bulgarians have persisted in regarding the Slav peoples of Macedonia as Bulgarians and in refusing to recognise a Macedonian minority in Bulgaria. Events in Macedonian history such as the Ilinden Rising of 1903 are treated in Bulgarian journals as 'brilliant chapters in the history of the Bulgarian people',[48] and the Bulgarian Writers' Union insists that there is no separate Macedonian language and literature.

The Greeks have similarly denied the existence of a Macedonian national group in the Salonika area, and the more extreme have even laid claim to all Macedonia as part of the Greek heritage.

In the face of internal problems related to the growing nationalism of the Albanians and external pressures from their neighbours, the infant Macedonian nation has the strongest incentive to cling to Yugoslavia, which has given it so much in the three decades of its existence as a republic. Although it has advanced culturally and economically at a staggering pace compared with the centuries of stagnation before the Second World War, Macedonia shares with the other former Turkish areas many of the classic features of underdevelopment.

PROBLEMS OF REGIONAL ECONOMIC INEQUALITIES[49]

Yugoslavia is not unique among the nations of Europe in having within its borders some regions that are industrially

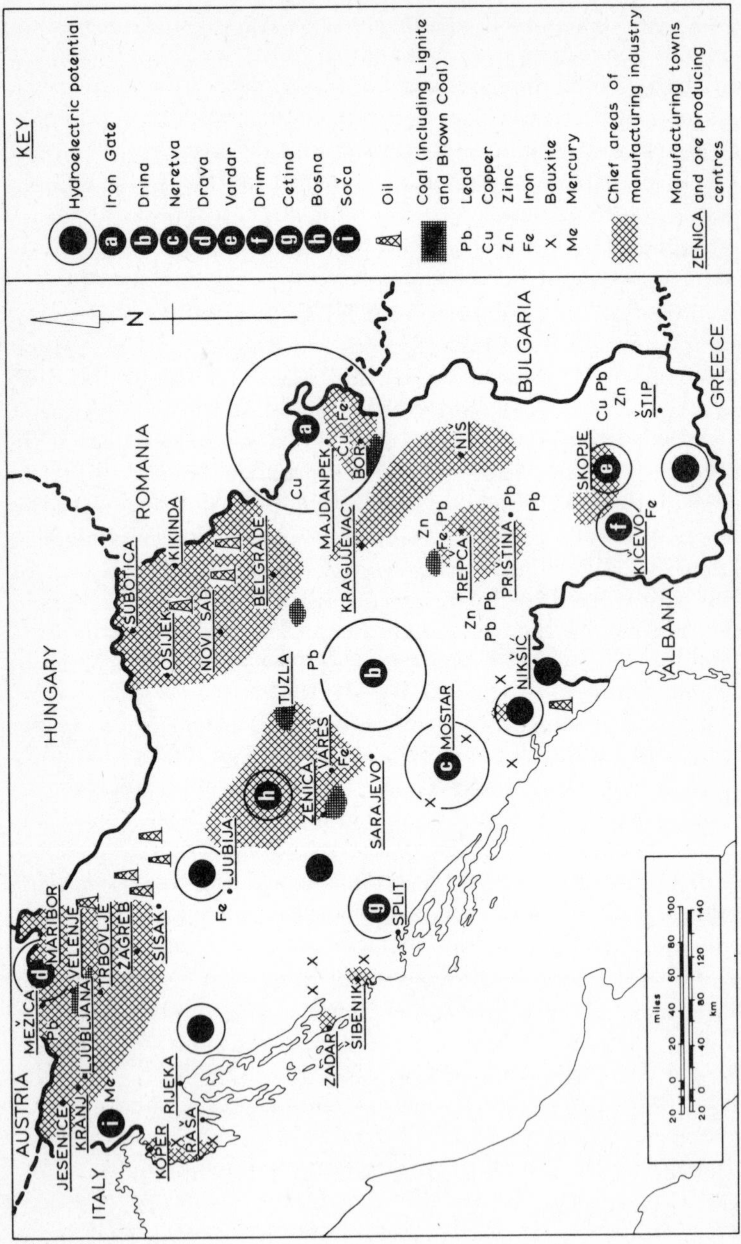

Map 7 Distribution of industries

developed and others where industrialisation has only just begun.[50] Italy, for example, has its problems of the industrialised north and the backward Mezzogiorno. Yugoslavia is unique, however, in that the regional differences in economic development are reinforced by cultural, linguistic and religious differences between the peoples of the different parts of the country. One can explain these differences in terms of historical development. The areas that are least developed are those which were under Turkish domination for several centuries; the more developed areas were formerly part of the Habsburg Empire.

The efforts of the Yugoslavs since the end of the Second World War have raised the general level of economic development throughout the country, but despite the sincere desire to narrow the gap between the rich and poor areas the distance between them remains approximately the same today as it did in 1945. Indeed, it would be little short of miraculous if the Yugoslavs had solved the problem in twenty-five years, for no other country has yet done so. In essence the problem is the same as that which exists between the affluent nations of the temperate latitudes of north-west Europe and America and the underdeveloped tropical world of Africa, Asia and Latin America. In this sense, Yugoslavia presents a microcosm of the world problem of relations between developed and underdeveloped regions. It may be an exaggeration to say, in the words of a Belgrade economist, that Yugoslavia has India and West Germany in one country, but it is not far from the truth if one substitutes Austria and Syria. In respect of living standards, cultural development and historical experience, Ljubljana has more in common with Graz or Salzburg than it has with Priština, and the Moslem peasant from Kosovo would feel more at home in Damascus than in Ljubljana.

The size and nature of the gap

Statistics that enable us to measure the size of the gap between developed and underdeveloped republics[51] are readily available, and comparisons can be made, for example, between the national income per head of Slovenia and Kosovo at various points in time. However, these figures disguise differences between smaller regions within the national republics. Croatia, for example, is officially regarded as a developed republic, but between 1961 and 1964 parts of Croatia were classified as under-developed, e.g. the karstic *polja* of Gorski Kotar and Lika. Even within the underdeveloped republics there are areas that are considered sufficiently backward to require special assistance. In Macedonia, for example, the communes of Debar, Kičevo, Brod, Kriva Palanka and Kratovo[52] are in this category. However, if we are to compare levels of development over the whole post-war period we can only use the coarse mesh of republican units, supplementing these where possible by the finer grading of micro-regions within republics.

The simplest and most obvious yardstick for measuring levels of development is income per head of population.[53] If we take only total national income, we ignore the effect of the wide differences in the rates of natural increase of the population.

Thus Kosovo's total national income went up by 320 per cent between 1947 and 1966, whilst Slovenia's during the same period increased by 360 per cent. The respective percentages for income per capita are 274 and 311. Kosovo, although increasing its total income by three times in twenty years, slipped back in relation to Slovenia, both in total income and even more in income per head. If one then looks at the difference in actual levels of income per head at the beginning of the period, the Slovene figure is three times that of Kosovo. At the end of the period the ratio is 5:1 in favour of the Slovenes. I have taken the most extreme examples, but table 37 shows that the areas with an income per head below the national average in 1947 have remained in this position throughout the period. The only changes in position have been that by 1952 Croatia had overtaken Vojvodina and moved into second place, and that Montenegro took fifth place from Bosnia–Hercegovina in 1966. Of the developed group, only Vojvodina has declined, and, of the underdeveloped group (including Serbia Proper, which is in a marginal position between the developed and underdeveloped groups) the relative improvement in Serbia, Montenegro and Macedonia has been small (less than 3·5 points), compared with the large relative decline in Kosovo (15 points) and Bosnia–Hercegovina (12·4). There is little sign, therefore, that the underdeveloped regions are catching up with their richer northern neighbours.

Regional variations in the structure of the economy

At the end of the war, Yugoslavia was primarily an agricultural country. In 1948 the population of farmers and their dependants was 10,600,000 or 66 per cent of the total population of 15,772,000.[54] By 1961 the number dependant on agriculture had fallen to 9,198,000[55] or 49 per cent of the population. It has since fallen to 36 per cent.[56] During this period the contribution of agriculture to the social product fell from 40 per cent in 1948 to 21·5 per cent in 1970, and is estimated to be 18·3 per cent in 1975. At the same time the proportion of the population dependent on the manufacturing industry rose from 7 per cent to over 20 per cent in 1971, and there were even greater increases in those gaining their livelihood from service industries, such as transport, commerce and tourism. The contribution of manufacturing industry to the social product reached over 35 per cent in 1957.[57] The pace of economic transformation was not evenly distributed throughout the country. Although there were spectacular industrial growth rates in some of the less developed republics and a fundamental change in the structures of the economies in these areas, their income per capita did not improve in relation to the more developed areas as can be seen from a comparison of tables 37 and 38 below.

Table 37 Indexes of national income per head at 1960 prices, 1947–66 (all Yugoslavia = 100)

	1947	*1952*	*1957*	*1962*	*1966*	*Rank order*
Group I: *above national average, 1947*						
Slovenia	175·3	186·7	181·5	198·5	188·5	(1)
Croatia	107·2	116·4	120·3	121·3	121·5	(2)
Vojvodina	108·8	89·3	109·2	103·4	107·4	(3)
Group II: *below national average, 1947*						
Serbia Proper	95·6	92·3	94·5	96·0	98·4	(4)
Montenegro	70·8	63·6	64·3	66·3	74·2	(5)
Bosnia–Hercegovina	82·9	87·6	74·2	72·7	70·5	(6)
Macedonia	62·0	59·3	60·8	57·1	64·3	(7)
Kosovo	52·6	49·3	42·5	34·0	37·6	(8)

Source: Statistički Godišnjak

Table 38 Structure of GNP, 1947–66 (percentages)

	1947			1966			1966
	Agriculture	*Industry*	*Other econ. activities*	*Agriculture*	*Industry*	*Other econ. activities*	*Rank order*
Yugoslavia	40·7	25·1	34·2	21·8	44·3	33·9	
Group I: *more than 30 per cent from industry, under 35 per cent from agriculture in 1947*							
Slovenia	27·4	36·9	35·7	11·8	52·1	36·1	(1)
Croatia	34·9	30·9	34·2	17·5	46·8	35·7	(2)
Group II: *more than 35 per cent from agriculture, under 22 per cent from industry in 1947*							
Bosnia	36·4	21·4	42·2	21·0	46·8	32·2	(4)
Serbia Proper	42·5	20·4	37·1	24·0	41·5	34·5	(5)
Montenegro	47·2	9·8	43·0	17·3	43·2	39·5	(3)
Macedonia	54·3	17·6	28·1	25·5	40·3	34·2	(6)
Kosovo	56·3	21·0	22·7	32·5	37·6	29·9	(7)
Vojvodina	60·7	17·8	21·5	38·8	34·4	26·8	(8)

Source: Statistički Godišnjak

A comparison of table 38 with table 37 shows a remarkable change of status for Vojvodina, which appears in third place as regards income per capita but at the bottom of the league as regards percentage of GNP from industry. This is because Vojvodina is a rich agricultural area, with a high output of farm produce from large-scale farming on fertile lowlands. The only other anomaly is the remarkable increase in the percentage of Montenegro's GNP derived from industry. This shot up from 9·8 per cent in 1947 to 43·2 per cent in 1966. All the others have kept their relative positions, but among the regions in group II Kosovo has seen the smallest switch in the relative contribution of agriculture and industry to the GNP. All the others in group II have at least doubled the percentage derived from industry. Kosovo has had an increase of only 52 per cent, a change of similar proportions to that which occurred in Slovenia and Croatia.

From these figures, one can conclude that the rate of industrial growth in the less developed regions has been faster than the national average, and this is borne out by figures produced by the Federal Bureau of Statistics, which show an average for 1947–66 of 10·1 per cent for all Yugoslavia, with Montenegro heading the list at 16 per cent, followed by Macedonia at 11·7 per cent; Bosnia at 11·1 per cent and Serbia Proper at 10·9 per cent. All the others are below 10 per cent, with Kosovo again at the bottom of the list with only 9.4 per cent.

Throughout most of the period before 1966 industrialisation policies favoured the building up of centres of heavy industry in each of the six republics, usually around the capital cities. This meant that the developing city regions around such centres as Zagreb, Skopje and Sarajevo drew in people from the underdeveloped areas outside the direct economic influence of the metropolitan agglomeration. The objective may have been to 'make full use, as quickly as possible, of existing reserves in productive enterprises and infrastructure', but it emphasised the already 'considerable disharmonies, both in respect of the degree of development of individual areas and of available economic potentials'.[58]

The problem was equally acute in both developed and underdeveloped republics, with the exception of Slovenia, where the industrial supremacy of Ljubljana was less obvious, and to a much lesser extent Croatia, where Rijeka was an important centre of development with a per capita income greater than Zagreb.[59] As Mihailović points out:

> The adverse influence of the concentration of industry in the suburbs and surroundings of Zagreb is obvious. With its great magnetic power the city discourages and subordinates the development of its surroundings. Skopje has overnight become a town of 200,000 inhabitants. In a republic which has been relatively lagging in development, this means that most economic activities have become associated with this centre. The attractiveness of living in Skopje and the possibility of employment have drawn great masses of people from all parts of Macedonia, particularly from the peripheral areas which will certainly therefore have additional difficulties in their future development.[60]

The problem is not only in the fact that certain existing centres received a concentration of industry, but also in the nature of the industries they received. By 1966, for example, the less developed areas were producing 35·5 per cent of the country's electric power, 48·5 per cent of its coal, 56 per cent of steel, and 77 per cent of lead. The proportions for consumer goods, however, were much lower – e.g. 30·8 per cent of cotton yarn.

In some cases the creation of centres of heavy industry was justified by the presence of raw material and fuel supplies in the underdeveloped areas, but in many cases the motivation was political or strategic, rather than economic. The Nikšić steel works in Montenegro was an outstanding example of this policy. Dr I. Hamilton writes that 'Two projects . . . the Sevojno copper-rolling mill[62] and the Nikšić steel works were located at great distances from their materials . . . Administrative haste led also to the location of the coke plant at Lukovac [Bosnia] . . . near materials which later proved useless for manufacture'.[63]

Dr Hamilton also draws attention to the influence of 'the system of uniform prices', which, 'in disregarding transport costs, encouraged many inefficiencies in the centralised allocation of flows before 1952, as for example in the 400 mile two-way exchange of lead concentrate between Slovenia and Kosovo'.[64]

The investment in Nikšić explains the very high per capita investment figures recorded for Montenegro, a republic with a population of only approximately half a million, compared with the underdeveloped regions (see table 39).

Table 39 Per capita investment indexes, 1947–63 (Yugoslavia = 100)

Slovenia	157
Montenegro	131
Croatia	110
Bosnia	83
Macedonia	81
Kosovo	54

Source: Statistički Godišnjak

Another example of the development of heavy industry within an underdeveloped area is the steel works at Skopje. 'Železara' Skopje draws on locally obtained materials to a greater extent than Nikšić. The iron ore – of low grade – comes from Tajmište, Demir Hisar and Kičevo, all within Macedonia, but over fifty miles away across difficult terrain, inadequately provided with means of transport. The fuel (lignite from the large Kosovo field) cannot be used directly in the smelting process. Only the limestone is from a source to the steel works.

The Skopje plant was one of the projects included in a development plan for the Yugoslav steel industry proposed in 1958, which was intended to increase the national output to 3·2 million tons by 1972, of which 80 per cent was to come from two centres – Zenica in Bosnia and Skopje in Macedonia. By 1968 output at Skopje was 600,000 tons, compared with an original target figure 900,000 tons. In addition, costs of production were higher than expected. As market considerations became more important after 1965 steel-using industries, such as the shipyards of Dalmatia, were forced to look to cheaper imported steel to meet their needs. Also, there were demands for the construction of steel mills in Dalmatia. In a speech during an official visit to Split in August 1969, Tito warned the Dalmatians that capital investment for such projects would not be favoured by the Federal Government.[65]

This particular issue was one facet of a much wider controversy concerning the whole concept of regional economic development in Yugoslavia. Like all other issues in Yugoslav economic policy in recent years, there are nationalist undertones implicit in the arguments used by the protagonists of the various alternative policies.[66] The two main arguments were put by Dr Kosta Mihailović (Serbian)[67] and Professor Rudolf Bičanić (Croatian).[68]

(1) Mihailović proposed a concentration of resources along the main river valley routes – Sava–Danube–Morava–Vardar. At the same time, he envisaged the development of a few selected centres of population growth in the interior area covering Bosnia, western Serbia, Kosovo and Montenegro, and the separate development of the Adriatic littoral mainly for tourism and service activities.

(2) Professor Bičanić proposed an Adriatic orientation, in which industry would be developed in relation to growth points along the Adriatic coast, centred on Split. 'Under Adriatic orientation in economic development of Yugoslavia is understood an inclusion of Yugoslavia in the international division of labour by the sea.' Bičanić criticised the Danubian concept as being orientated too closely to COMECON, and he favoured a Western orientation – 'It is not a question of underdeveloped regions along the sea . . . but of how to draw the entire continental area of Yugoslavia to the sea.'

It would appear that, in so far as there is a federal planning policy in relation to this controversy, a typical Yugoslav compromise has been reached, in which parts of both policies are being implemented. The Iron Gate hydroelectric scheme, which will provide an enormous increase in electrical power in Serbia as well as improving the navigation along the Danube, appears to be in line with the Mihailović policy, while the development of the Aluminium Kombinat at Titograd and Šibenik favours the Bičanić view. The Dalmatians have been advised, however, that their immediate future lies primarily in the expansion of tourist facilities in the coastal resorts.

Changing policies of regional economic development

The first post-war five-year plan stated that a major objective was 'to ensure a faster rate of development of economically backward republics and to remove all consequences of uneven development'. This was to be achieved by the rapid industrialisation of the backward republics.

It was expected, for example, that by 1951 industrial production would be 10·5 times above 1939 figures in Bosnia and 26·3 times above them in Macedonia. In fact, the rate of growth of industrial production fell far short of these objectives. It was not until 1966 that the underdeveloped areas approached the attainment of the 1951 targets – except for Montenegro, where, starting virtually from scratch, it was possible to reach startling figures of percentage growth (see table 40). Most of this

Table 40 Industrial production in underdeveloped republics, 1966

	times 1939 figures
Yugoslavia	7·8
Macedonia	18·9
Montenegro	40·0
Kosmet	6·5

Source: Čolanović, *Yugoslavia's Industrialization and the Development of the Underdeveloped Regions*, p. 6

expansion occurred during the period up to 1952, as can be seen from the figures for the growth of industrial output between 1952 and 1965. In this later period the underdeveloped areas increased their industrial production to 5·6 times above 1952 levels, compared with a national average of 5·5 times.

The policy regarding the financing of industrial development has undergone important changes since the early period of centralised administrative planning. As Srebrić puts it:

> At first industrialisation was carried out in a rather simple and ineffective way . . . New industries in underdeveloped areas

lacked connection with the market, and, therefore, could not operate efficiently . . . The industrialisation of underdeveloped areas was quite unconnected to other economic processes . . . The simplified system of economy management was matched by a simplified financial mechanism. The overall budget dealt with all monetary flows.[69]

The planners in Belgrade decided that a steel mill or a chemical works should be built in an underdeveloped region, and the money was found from the central budget. Between 1947 and 1952 57·4 per cent of total investment in ferrous metallurgy and 64·6 per cent of the investment in chemicals went to the underdeveloped areas. Between 1953 and 1956 the figure went up to 80·5 per cent for ferrous metals and 87·5 per cent for chemicals. The efficiency of investments in the less developed areas remained well below the national average even after the 1965 reforms and the emphasis on rentability (see table 41).

Table 41 Efficiency coefficients, 1964–7 (Yugoslavia = 100)

	1964	*1967*
Slovenia	126	126
Croatia	104	105
Bosnia and Hercegovina	99	101
Serbia Proper	98	94
Macedonia	73	74
Kosovo	64	69
Montenegro	56	49

Source: Turčić, *Regionalni i granski aspekt eficanosti ulozenih sredstva Jugoslovenske industrije, 1964–67*

Yet, despite the massive allocation of resources to the building of heavy industry in the underdeveloped areas, their share of investment per capita over the period 1947–63 was below the national average (see table 39). The only exception was Montenegro, with a per capita index of 131. It became obvious that much of the investment in heavy industry in the less developed areas was being wasted because of the weak infrastructure base of the underdeveloped areas and their lack of trained personnel at all levels from policy makers and planners to managers and skilled workers.

Table 42 Investment required to produce 1 kWh of electricity, 1947–56 (dinars at 1956 prices)

	1947–52	*1955–6*
Slovenia	55·2	36·3
Croatia	104·3	92·4
Serbia	177·1	113.0
Bosnia	241·7	88·0
Macedonia	353·9	219·7
Montenegro	729·3	541·9

Source: J. T. Bombelles, *The Economic Development of Communist Yugoslavia* (Stanford 1968), p. 100

Whilst great emphasis was placed on the development of heavy industry, with a tendency to encourage economic autarchy within each republic, little was done for agriculture, which employed the majority of the population. The rural economy of Yugoslavia before the Second World War was characterised by overpopulation and underutilisation of human and material resources. After the agrarian reform of 1945,[70] which redistributed land among the peasantry and expropriated the largest estates, the number of peasant proprietors increased. An attempt was made to organise large-scale migration of surplus agricultural population from the poorest areas. Peasants from Montenegro, Hercegovina, Gorski Kotar and the Dinaric *polja* behind the Dalmatian coast were moved to Vojvodina, often taking over farms vacated by dispossessed Volksdeutsche. Others moved into Zemun and Novi Sad, where they found non-agricultural employment. This policy of migration eased pressures on the poorest agricultural areas, but the total numbers involved were small, in relation to the farm population.[71]

Investment in agriculture was concentrated on the socialist sector which at its peak in 1950, before the abandonment of the drive to socialise agriculture, covered 2·5 million hectares out of 13·5 million hectares of farm land. Any assistance to private farmers was ruled out on political grounds. As Kardelj stated in 1959, 'Greater economic support to private farmers is out of the question – primarily because such support would strengthen capitalist relations in agriculture with all their negative social, political and economic consequences. . . .' The emphasis on the centrally controlled distribution of investment funds was almost wholly on industrialisation: 'The development of non-industrial sectors was given only nominal support.'[72]

Although the industrialisation policy achieved some shift of population from agriculture to industry in the underdeveloped regions, the majority of the population in these areas still depended upon agriculture for their income.

Table 43 Per capita income, 1947–63 (dinars at 1962 prices, 1947 = 100)

	1947	*1963*	*Percentage growth*
Yugoslavia	87·8	206·3	235
Republics with growth of per-capita income above the national average:			
Slovenia	142·6	401·9	282
Croatia	94·8	257·8	272
Republics with growth below national average:			
Macedonia	59·8	131·8	220
Serbia	84·9	185·4	218
Montenegro	62·5	132·7	212
Bosnia	70·0	140·9	201

Source: Statistički Godišnjak

The failure to invest adequate resources in the improvement of agriculture, and the inefficiency of investment in industry during a period of administrative control, goes some way to explaining why per capita income in the underdeveloped areas rose more slowly in the period 1947–63 than that in the more developed areas. The results are shown in table 43.

During the 1950s a degree of flexibility was introduced into the financing of economic development. There was some devolution of economic planning from the federal to the republican governments, but the major decision-making powers remained centralised. The General Investment Fund (Opći investicioni fond) was given larger resources and their total amount was guaranteed. Under the 1957–61 social plan, Macedonia, Kosovo–Metohija and Montenegro were the recipients of special federal investments as underdeveloped areas. For the first time, Macedonia and Kosovo received specific funds for agricultural development.[73]

These changes in methods during the late 1950s were temporary expedients, which modified but did not basically change the system of allocations of funds to underdeveloped areas.

Table 44 Designation of underdeveloped areas, 1947–70

Republic or autonomous province	*1947*	*1956*	*1957*	*1961*	*1964*	*1965*	*1970*
Macedonia	—	—	—	—	—	—	—
Montenegro	—	—	—	—	—	—	—
Bosnia–Hercegovina	—	—				—	—
Kosovo			—	—	—	—	—
Parts of Serbia, Bosnia and Croatia				—	—		

Source: Statistički Godišnjak

For a brief period in the early 1960s (1961–4) certain areas of south Serbia, east and south Bosnia and the Gorski Kotar region of Croatia were specifically designated as underdeveloped regions, although the republics to which they belonged were not considered to be underdeveloped. After 1965 this discrimination was abolished, and the title of 'Underdeveloped' was confined to whole republics or autonomous provinces (see table 44). It was left to the republican governments to make special plans for less developed areas within their own borders. This development should be seen within the context of the growing decentralisation of political and economic decision making.

The establishment in 1961 of the federal fund for the development of the underdeveloped areas was part of a series of economic measures that laid the foundations of the economic reform. The establishment of the fund was confirmed by Article 123 of the 1963 constitution, and subsequent legislation in 1965 modified its methods of operation. The Fund was formed by allocating 1·85 per cent of social income from all republics to be shared amongst the officially designated underdeveloped republics – at present Bosnia–Hercegovina, Montenegro, Macedonia and Kosovo.

The Fund was the major instrument but by no means the only one, for encouraging the development of the less developed areas. It has been used primarily to give credits for specific projects. These credits are administered by banks, investment associations and enterprises in the underdevelopment regions, and in general the projects which they support must be considered commercially viable. This principle is in keeping with the policy of the economic reform. Credits advanced under the Fund are given on favourable terms, compared with the normal regulations. Interest rates are lower, repayment is over a longer period, and the starting date for repayment can be delayed. Favourable terms are also offered to banks and enterprises in the developed republics that decide to invest in the underdeveloped regions. The same inducements apply to foreign investors, whether public or private. In addition, there are forms of federal investment outside the scope of the special fund.

> Federal financing in the reconstruction of the existing iron and steel mills already begun and the construction of a new iron works in Skopje is continuing from the previous period, the target being the completion of productive capacities which will yield 3·2 million tons of crude steel and finished steel products.[74]
>
> Non-repayable Federal investments in major communications account for 85 per cent of the calculated value of these projects, which include the construction of the Sarajevo–Ploče, Belgrade–Bar, Knin–Zadar, and Gostivar–Kičevo railroads, the inland section of the Adriatic Highway, the Županja–Opuzen motor road, and the new Sava bridge in Belgrade.[75]

For example, Macedonia received 23 per cent of the federal fund in the period 1964–8. One-third of the money has been used for infra-structure projects[76] and the rest made available to the investment banks, who allocate to enterprises on a strictly commercial basis. This emphasis on 'rentability' will accentuate the concentration of industry in a few already developed centres, especially Skopje.

In the light of the declared objective of the planners to increase income per head in the underdeveloped regions at a rate of 2 per cent faster than that of the developed regions, the figures in table 45 offer little encouragement.

Table 45 Indexes of national income per capita, 1966–70 (Yugoslavia = 100)

	1966	*1969*	*1970*
Slovenia	188·4	186	200
Croatia	121	133	125
Vojvodina	107	130	104
Serbia Proper	98·4	105	100
Macedonia	64·3	75	62
Montenegro	74·2	75	70
Bosnia–Hercegovina	70·5	73	66
Kosovo	37·6	43	30

Source: Statistički Godišnjak

The failure to close the gap in income level between the developed and underdeveloped regions has potential dangers in a multi-national state like Yugoslavia. It breeds resentment among the rich, who feel that their progress is held back by the need to sustain their poorer brethren, and it makes slogans about 'brotherhood and unity' seem hollow to the economically underprivileged. The development of decentralised 'market socialism' has tended to accentuate the regional inequalities. If the policy is pursued in a more thoroughgoing manner than hitherto, by the removal of the remaining central controls and the devolution of economic functions to the republics, the gaps will widen.

The 1971 constitutional amendments represented an attempt to contain the centrifugal tendencies of nationalism within a looser federal framework. The hope was that, if legitimate national aspirations were recognised, the republics would work together more readily for the common good of Yugoslavia. The events of 1971 called this hope into question. The outlines began to emerge of a series of six national economies, based on the republics, each with its own embryonic national bourgeoisie. The process went furthest in Croatia, where draconian measures by the central political machine were required to stabilise the situation; but similar tendencies were apparent in Serbia and Slovenia.

The expectation that agreement could be reached between the republics on the basis of distribution of the Fund for Assisting the Less Developed Areas[77] was proved to be a forlorn hope. After over a year of discussions no agreement had been reached by October 1972, although the deadline provided by the new law expired on 31 March. Eventually the Federal Executive Council invoked its powers under the Thirty-third Amendment, which enabled it to put forward provisional proposals for the distribution of the 700 million dinars which had accumulated whilst the republics were arguing amongst themselves. The necessity for this unprecedented federal intervention suggests that economic nationalism is still important, and that Yugoslavia has a long way to go before the equality of its nationalities is an economic reality as well as being a legal principle.

The 1974 constitution reiterates the obligations on the federation to determine which are 'the economically insufficiently developed Republics and Autonomous Provinces' and to establish a federal fund to assist them. Federal agencies are also empowered to float compulsory loans to assist the less developed areas and to give direct assistance for the maintenance of social services where these cannot be financed from local resources (Article 258). This last provision is of vital importance in view of the intention to place the responsibility for providing social services on the 'local communities of interest'. These bodies are expected to make agreements with local enterprises and communal agencies to raise the funds necessary for welfare, medical, educational and cultural purposes. Without some substantial outside help, this decentralised system will perpetuate inequalities of opportunity, because the poorer areas will be unable to raise adequate funds from their own resources and will be caught in a vicious downward spiral of deprivation. As one of the greatest handicaps to economic development is the lack of trained personnel, attention to the educational needs of these areas is of paramount importance. This is particularly true of Kosovo, where it is recognised that special problems exist and, according to a resolution of the Tenth Congress of the LCY, special treatment will be given from federal resources[78]. It is also hoped that agreements can be reached under which enterprise in the more developed republics can be associated with those in the less developed areas, thus providing the capital and technical expertise required. It is also hoped that foreign capital may be attracted to the poorer areas. Both these policies have been tried before, without conspicuous success.

The experience of other countries, as well as Yugoslavia's own recent history, suggests that inter-regional inequalities will increase for some time to come. J. G. Williamson, writing of the problem on a world scale, suggested that;

> Somewhere during the course of development some or all of the disequilibrating tendencies diminish, causing a reversal in the patterns of inter-regional inequality. Instead of divergence in inter-regional levels of development, convergence becomes the rule, with the backward regions closing the development gap between themselves and the already industrialised areas. The expected result is that a statistic describing regional inequality will trace out an inverted U over the national growth path; the historical timing of the peak level of spatial income differentials is left somewhat vague and may vary considerably with the resource endowment and institutional environment of each developing nation.[79]

Yugoslavia attempted by the various methods described above, to defy the trend to which Williamson refers: she may have succeeded in slowing down the whole pace of growth throughout the country in order to damp down the amplitude of the curve of regional inequality. The future may see a widening of regional differences before the process of convergence sets in.

NOTES

1 This estimate includes Montenegrins, Macedonians and Serbian-speaking Bosnians with the Serbs, as they were so regarded in pre-war Yugoslavia.

2 Estimate of 1931.

3 The 231,000 includes the Vlahs of the Timok area and Macedonia, as well as the Romanians of the Banat. The 1948 figure is the sum of the figures for Romanians and Vlahs. The Banat Romanians fell from 74,000 in 1921 to 60,000 in 1948. The number of Vlahs has fluctuated so wildly in the post-war census returns, that little credence can be given to the figures. In 1948 there were 102,953. This fell to 36,728 in 1953 and to 9463 in 1961. For some unaccountable reason it rose to over 23,000 in 1971.

4 In the 1974 constitution the term 'national minorities' (in the 1963 Constitution *nacionalne manjine*) was not used. The terms used are 'nations' (*narodi*) and 'nationalities' (*narodnosti*).

5 This fall in the number of Montenegrins from 514,000 in 1961 to 508,000 in 1971 (from 2·8 per cent to 2·5 per cent, of the Yugoslav population) is hard to explain. Official figures of workers abroad record only 5260 Montenegrins. It may be explained by the possibility that a substantial number who were recorded as Montenegrin in 1961 declared themselves to be Serbs in 1971. The Serbian population in Montenegro increased by over 25,000 between the censuses.

6 'Popis Na Naselenieto i Stanovite vo 1971 Godina', *Statistički Pregled*, 29 (Skopje, July 1972).

7 Except for the agricultural colonisation schemes, which moved thousands of farm workers from the Karstic *polja* of Croatia and Bosnia to the Vojvodina (see pp. 116–17 above).

8 Figures calculated from *Statistički Bilten*, 679 (1971), table 1·3. 40 per cent of the migrants from Bosnia–Hercegovina were Croats – almost double their share of the total population of that republic (table 1.10).

9 Dr Koča Jončić, *The Relations Between the Nationalities in Yugoslavia*, (Belgrade 1967), pp. 8–9.

10 S. Šuvar, *Nacije i Medjunacionalni Odnosi u Socialističkoj Jugoslaviji* (Zagreb 1970).

11 With 22 per cent of the population Croatia provided 28·5 per cent of Yugoslavia's exports in 1970. Slovenia, with 8·9 per cent of the population, contributed 17·8 per cent of exports, and Serbia, with 42 per cent of the population, had a 36·7 per cent share of the exports. *Ekonomska Politika* (2 November 1970), p. 15. Between 1967 and 1970 Croatia's share of the total number of foreign tourists entering Yugoslavia rose from 55 to 60 per cent (*Statistički Godišnjak*). According to the 1971 census Croatia, with 20 per cent of the Yugoslav population, contributed 33 per cent of the workers abroad. Of the total population of Croatia 5·2 per cent was employed abroad – the highest percentage of any European country except Portugal. 'Lica na Privremom Radu u Inostranstvu', *Statistički Bilten*, 679 (1971), p. 9.

12 *Kritika*, 17 (1970).
13 *Kritika*, 13 (1970).
14 *Statistički Bilten*, 679 (1971), pp. 9–10. The figure of 5·2 per cent refers to the population of Croatia and includes therefore some 30,000 (7 per cent) Serbs and others. If one takes the Croat population of other republics, the percentage of Croat workers abroad rises to 5·6 per cent of the Croat population. It should be stressed, however, that the census figures both for nationality and for workers abroad are controversial, and there are serious doubts as to their accuracy.
15 An article in *VUS* refers to the biological impoverishment of Croatia because the rate of emigration is higher than the rate of natural increase. Croatia's share of the Yugoslav population fell from 23·1 per cent in 1953 to 21·5 per cent in 1971. (The author states that it fell to 19 per cent in 1968, but the 1971 census records an apparent increase since 1968, to 21·5 per cent) *VUS* (18 February 1970), pp. 20–3.
16 When Mr G. Santo retired as director-general of the Yugoslav Foreign Trade Bank in 1970, it was alleged that he had favoured excessive investment in shipbuilding, which is mainly based in Croatia. The refutation of this charge in the Zagreb journal *VUS* was far from convincing. It stated that during the previous two years the bank had, in fact, invested 450 million dinars in shipbuilding but 1000 million in tourists. Croatia has about 75 per cent of the tourist capacity of the country. *VUS* (4 March 1970) pp. 10–11 and *Vjesnik* (8 May 1971), p. 7.
17 Fifty per cent of the Croatian average is still larger than the average for Bosnia–Hercegovina and Kosovo in 1969, when the national average per capita income was $650, the average per capita income for Slovenia was $1030; for Macedonia, $420; for Croatia, $740; for Bosnia–Hercegovina, $360; for Serbia, $520, and for Kosovo, $200. *NIN* (29 March 1970), p. 2.
18 *Borba* (1 September 1970), p. 9.
19 The 1971 census records 49,000 Slovenes working abroad. This amounts to 2·9 per cent of the total population and 10·6 per cent of the labour force.
20 *Privredni Vjesnik* (24 September 1970), p. 3. The figure of 60,000 given by the Slovene employment exchanges in September 1970 relates only to workers in Germany and Austria. It compares oddly with the census figure of 49,562 Slovenes working abroad and is one further example of the unreliability of the census figures.
21 *Studentski List* (20 April 1971), p. 4.
22 *NIN* (28 June 1970), p. 18; (19 April 1970), p. 32.
23 *Politika* (31 December 1971 and 1 January 1972).
24 *Borba* (4 November 1971), p. 5.
25 *Politika* (10 December 1971), p. 8.
26 *Borba* (11 December 1971).
27 Pavlowitch *Yugoslavia*, p. 339.
28 The Ausgleich of 1867 transferred administration of the Vojvodina from Vienna to Budapest – except for the Military Frontier region, which

passed to Hungary in 1873. Between 1880 and 1890, as a result of a Hungarian colonisation policy, the Magyar population of Bačka increased by 22 per cent.

29 The percentage of Magyars in 1971 in the main towns of Northern Bačka was: Subotica, 49·5; Bačka Topola, 72·2; Ada, 79; Senta, 85·4; Kanjiza, 88·6.

30 The Magyar speakers form 21·7 per cent of the population. Pupils in Magyar grammar schools form 9 per cent of the grammar school population.

31 The Sokči speak the Ikavian form of Croatian, which originates in central Dalmatia and western Bosnia.

32 An inquiry conducted in Novi Sad in 1971 suggested that a high proportion of children of mixed marriages were registered as Yugoslavs.

33 Until 1971 the 'Rusini' or Rusnjaks were included in the figures for Ukrainians.

34 One of the factors contributing to the over-representation of Serbs is that they are the most urbanised of the nationalities in the Vojvodina, and Party membership is always higher in the towns than in the rural areas, where the majority of Magyars and Croats live.

35 The illiteracy rate was more than double the national average, and the per capita income was 52 per cent of the national average.

36 Shoup, *Communism and the Yugoslav National Question*, p. 104, quotes Ranković's account of this incident, in which he blames the partisans for provoking the Albanians.

37 It chose the Albanian national flag.

38 According to *NIN* (27 June 1971), p. 12, '387 Serb and Montenegrin experts left recently, without any attempt to persuade them to stay.'

39

	1961	*1971*
Serbs	23·6%	18·4%
Montenegrins in Kosovo	3·9%	2·5%

40 Belgrade Home Service (11 February 1972), reported in BBC Monitoring Service (14 February 1972).

41 In 1959 he was a member of the Federal Executive Council and president of the Committee for the National Development Plan.

42 It has been argued that the arrival of 200 Serbian troops, on the day the Skupština met in Podgorica on 24 November 1918 to discuss the deposition of King Nikola, determined the outcome of the debate. The vote was taken on 26 November.

43 In the 1920 elections the Communists were the largest single party in Montenegro, with 34 per cent of the votes. In 1948 Montenegro was one of the areas in which support for the Cominform was strongest.

44 See Shoup, *Communism and the Yugoslav National Question*, appendix D, for numbers.

45 Quoted in ibid., from *Komunist* (6 February 1964), p. 1.

46 The fluctuation in the number of Turks, from 95,940 in 1948 (8·3 per

cent) to 203,938 in 1953 (15·6 per cent), and down to 108,552 (6·6 per cent) in 1972, is related to political factors – in the 1950s there was an agreement between Yugoslavia and Turkey concerning the repatriation of Turks and many Albanians classed themselves as Turks in order to qualify for emigration to Turkey. One-third of those declaring themselves to be Turks did not speak Turkish (see Frits Hondius, *The Yugoslav Community of Nations* (The Hague, 1968), p. 183).

47 Quoted by S. E. Palmer and R. R. King, *Yugoslav Communism and the Macedonian Question* (London 1971), p. 178.

48 *Trud* (Sofia 1 August 1968).

49 This section is based on the author's article, 'Problems of Regional Economic Development', in *Jahrbuch der Wirtschaft Osteuropas*, 2 (1971), pp. 375–95.

50 J. G. Williamson, in his essay, 'Regional Inequality and the Process of Natural Development', in *Regional Analysis*, ed. L. Needleman (Harmondsworth, Middx. 1968), points to the 'stubborn persistence of regional dualism at all levels of national development and throughout the historical experience of almost all presently developed countries'.

51 In this context 'republic' should also be taken to include 'autonomous region'. Serbian statistics are usually divided, separate figures being given for Vojvodina, Serbia Proper and Kosovo.

52 The underdeveloped communes of Croatia include many of those with a Serbian majority (see pp. 64n., 70 for details), and those in Macedonia include the areas where Albanians and Turks form a substantial proportion of the population (for details see pp. 239–40).

53 This is, in fact, the measure used by the Yugoslav government. See Branko Čolanović, 'Yugoslavia's Industrialization and the Development of the Underdeveloped Regions', UN Industrial Development Organisation, ID/Conf.1/G27. English text of a paper submitted by the Government of Yugoslavia to an International Symposium, Athens (29 November-20 December 1967). The Yugoslav approach to the problem is a pragmatic one. 'In determining what territories shall be considered as less-developed, the main criterion has been per capita income, but, quite naturally, some other characteristics of the areas in question have also been taken into account'.

54 Census figure, 1968.

55 *Statistički Godišnjak* (1968).

56 Census figure, 1971.

57 For a useful survey of the state of Yugoslav agriculture see OECD report, 'Agricultural policy in Yugoslavia' (Paris 1973). The term Social Product is used in Yugoslavia to cover only productive activities. As it excludes administration, defence, welfare services, education, and other non-productive activities it is lower than the normal GDP.

58 Kosta Mihailović, *Regional Aspects of Economic Development* (New York 1967), p. 39.

59 E.g. taking income per head for all 171 districts of Yugoslavia, in 1965 the rank order for the first eight was:

Kranj (Slovenia)	274,394 dinars
Maribor (Slovenia)	192,427 ,,
Rijeka (Croatia)	187,690 ,,
Ljubljana (Slovenia)	178,672 ,,
Zagreb (Croatia)	166,442 ,,
Belgrade (Serbia)	151,469 ,,
Celje (Slovenia)	133,636 ,,
Trbovlje (Slovenia)	115,410 ,,

Figures from table 9.4, p. 56 of ibid.

60 Ibid., p. 40.

61 Near Titovo Užice in south-west Serbia.

62 In the heart of Montenegro.

63 F. E. I. Hamilton, *Yugoslavia – Patterns of Economic Activity* (London 1968), p. 238.

64 Ibid., p. 239.

65 Speech to leaders of economic and political organisations in Dalmatia, 27 August 1969, reported in *Politika* (28 August 1969), p. 1, col. 3.

66 This was equally true of the controversy concerning investment in new roads, which erupted in the summer of 1969.

67 K. Mihailović, 'Problemi Privrednog Razvoja', *Ekonomska Biblioteka* (Belgrade 1962), pp. 40–7.

68 R. Bičanić, *Pomorstvo*, 9–10 (1964), pp. 38–9.

69 B. Srebrić, 'Policy Methods and Basic Results of Developing the Underdeveloped Areas of Yugoslavia,' *Ekonomist*, English issue, (Zagreb 1969), pp. 115–16.

70 Law on Agrarian Reform, passed by the Provisional National Assembly on 23 August 1945. See F. Ademović and M. Bašagić, *Agrarian Policy and Agriculture for Yugoslavia* (Belgrade 1968).

71 According to Ademović and Bašagić, 23,000 families were designated as republican colonists (i.e. families who moved to other areas within the same republic) and 42,000 families designated federal colonists (mainly war veterans and families dispossessed because of war devastation). The total number of agricultural holdings at this time was over 2·6 million.

72 Srebrić, in *Ekonomist* (1969), pp. 115–16.

73 Ibid., p. 117.

74 In 1969 output was 600,000 tons.

75 Vladimir Pejovski, *Yugoslav Investment Policy, 1966–70* (Belgrade 1968).

76 In 1969–70 a large proportion went to irrigation and drainage works and improvements to agricultural land.

77 In 1971 its title was changed to that of the Fund for Credits to Underdeveloped Areas.

78 An English text of the resolutions is given in the monthly journal *Socialist Thought and Practice*, Vol. 6–7 (June–July 1974), pp. 148–310. The reference to Kosovo is on p. 181.

79 J. G. Williamson, 'Regional development in particular countries', in L. Needleman (ed.), *Regional analysis* (London 1968), p. 108.

16 Constitutional changes, 1967 – 74

There have been five major constitutional statutes promulgated in Yugoslavia since the revolution. The first, in 1946, was modelled on Stalin's 1936 Soviet constitution. Although it provided a federal framework, with six sovereign republics and two autonomous units, it was in reality a highly centralised structure. The legislature, the Federal People's Assembly, consisted of two chambers, a Federal Council elected by direct suffrage and a Council of Nationalities, composed of delegates from the assemblies of the republics. There was no head of state, but a Praesidium, elected by the Federal Assembly. The Assembly also elected an Executive Council, whose chairman was the equivalent of a prime minister. Within the constitution power lay with the executive, whose first chairman was Marshal Tito. The Assembly simply approved the measures proposed by the executive. Outside the constitution, real power lay with the Communist Party, also headed by Marshal Tito as its secretary-general. There was considerable overlapping of personnel between Party and State offices, especially at the summit of the pyramid, where Tito headed both party and government and was also minister of defence and commander in chief of the armed forces.

The 1946 constitution was amended in 1953 to incorporate the concept of workers' self-management. It reduced the importance of the Council of Nationalities, which became merged with the Federal Council but could meet separately to debate certain issues. A new Council of Producers was created. This was elected indirectly by the producers' councils of the communes, and those chosen represented occupational groups – e.g. industry, commerce, agriculture. The office of president of

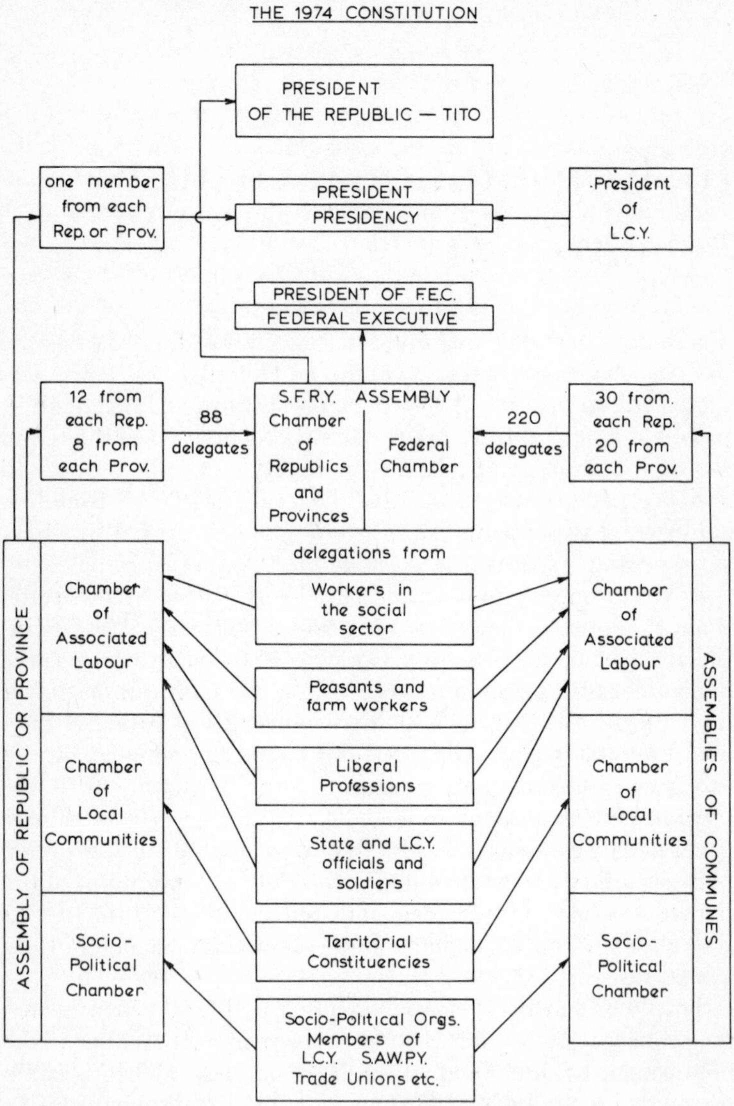

FIG. 2 The government of Yugoslavia, 1974

the republic was introduced and has been held continuously since 1953 by President Tito.

In 1963 a new constitution extended the concept of workers' self-management to that of 'social self-management'. More authority was given to communes and republics and to organs of self-management in the economy. The 1963 constitution created a new structure for the Federal Assembly by establishing indirectly elected chambers, representing various economic and social interests. The principle of rotation of office was introduced. This was intended to provide opportunities for new faces to appear at the top tables. The separation of the Party and the State was advanced by a rule that prohibited the simultaneous holding by one individual of high state and party office. This applied to everyone except Tito. The constitution also set up a constitutional court to safeguard 'socialist legality'.

THE 1967 CONSTITUTIONAL AMENDMENTS

The 1963 constitution was amended in 1967 to give a stronger voice to the Chamber of Nationalities in the Federal Assembly, and to give wider powers over internal security to the republics. These changes were initiated after several unconnected incidents which together indicated dissatisfaction in the republics over certain aspects of federal policies. The process for amendment began with a meeting of the Chamber of Nationalities on 27 January 1967, which was called by a group of delegates from Bosnia and Hercegovina. The original grievances of the Bosnians concerned the methods of allocating federal funds for economic development. This special meeting of the Chamber of Nationalities was unprecedented. Previously this body, composed of ten representatives from each of the six republican assemblies and five from each of the two provincial assemblies, was regarded as merely a formal symbol of the legal equality of the Yugoslav peoples. In 1967 the Bosnians showed that it could be used as an instrument for loosening federal control. At about the same time as the Bosnians were experiencing their troubles over the distribution of federal funds, a dispute in Slovenia brought into question the rights of the republics *vis-à-vis* the federation. The Slovene premier[1] Janko Smole, who was *ex officio* a member of the federal government, introduced a resolution in conformity with federal policy, which proposed a reduction in expenditure on social insurance. By an overwhelming majority the Slovene Social and Health Chamber rejected the proposal, and Mr Smole submitted his resignation. The affair was eventually resolved, but it brought into public discussion the problem of dual loyalty when republican and federal policies were in conflict. In Croatia the dispute over the use of the Croat literary language came to a head in March 1967 with the publication of the notorious 'Deklaracija'.[2] In Kosovo, the Albanian people were beginning to assert their rights after several years of subordination to Serbs during the period of Ranković's control over state security, which ended in 1966. The various causes of strain between the national groups in the republics and the federation in the centre, however different their origins, created a climate of opinion favourable to changing the constitution. This may explain the speed with which the 1967 amendments were approved by the federal parliament, for the whole process was completed by 18 April, less than three months after the issue had first been raised. In addition to widening the basis of representation and the powers of the Chamber of Nationalities, the 1967 amendments abolished the system whereby republican premiers had a place in the federal government, gave the republics power to appoint their own public prosecutors and gave the republics, through the Chamber of Nationalities, greater control over some federal officials.[3]

These changes did not, however, quieten the restiveness of the republics. Having used the legislative machinery to win a small degree of devolution, they began to press for more.

THE 1971 CONSTITUTIONAL AMENDMENTS

In 1971 even more radical constitutional reforms were proposed. They took the form of a further twenty-three amendments to the 1963 constitution, but the changes they proposed were so fundamental as to justify the term '1971 constitution'. There were three main elements to this new social contract. The first concerned the problem of the succession to the office of president, the second the future development of the system of self-management, and the third, which affected both of these issues, and in fact penetrates into every aspect of Yugoslav life, was the relationship between the nationalities.

The proposal for constitutional change came first from President Tito, in a speech he made in Zagreb on 21 October 1970. In it he warned of 'the very grave crisis that might face Yugoslavia' if he retired or died before arrangements had been made for the succession. In 1969 the League of Communists adopted the principle of a collective presidency, composed of a group of leading Communists, carefully chosen to provide a balance of representation for each of the six national republics and the two autonomous provinces. The president proposed a similar arrangement for the State. In the discussions which followed the issues were widened to include the whole question of the political and economic relations between the federal government and the republics, and also the enlargement of the rights of workers' self-management.

There was never any serious disagreement over the presidency. Amendment XXXV provided for the establishment of a collective presidency, composed of three members from each republic and two from each autonomous province. The twenty-two members of the presidency were to be elected by the republican and provincial assemblies, to serve for five years. From this body a president and vice-president were to be elected, to serve for one year. These officers were to be chosen according to a predetermined order, so that each of the national groups would in its turn provide the first citizen of Yugoslavia. An exception to the principle of annual rotation of office of president was made in the case of Josip Broz Tito. Amendment XXXVI, which makes the exception, refers to Tito's 'historic role in the national Liberation War, the socialist revolution, the creation and development of the Socialist Federal Republic of Yugoslavia', and to his status as a world statesman. There is no doubt that this remarkable man, then in his eightieth year, still had an important role to play in the history of his country. His re-election on 29 July was a demonstration of the affection and respect with which he was regarded by the majority of his people. It was also a recognition of the need for continuity at the top during the next few years, when the implications of the other constitutional changes were being worked out in the republics.

In the economic sphere the new constitutional amendments reaffirmed 'the right of the working people to dispose of the fruits of their labour', but they re-interpreted these rights in the light of the economic and social changes of recent years. The original concept of workers' self-management was introduced in the early fifties at a time when industrialisation was in its infancy. Enterprises were on a small scale, with scores rather than hundreds of workers, and the State still played a major part in the direction of the economy. The experience of the first decade of workers' self-management led in the early 1960s to the widening of the concept to embrace all aspects of public life. The term 'social self-management' was used to indicate that not only workers in publicly-owned enterprises but also participants in any form of social activity, whether cultural, political or recreational, had the right to govern themselves. This concept was incorporated into the 1963 constitution. Nevertheless, the State continued to play an important role in many spheres. For example, investment policies were still largely determined by the State, often indirectly. In 1971 Amendments XXI and XXII affirmed the right of workers to dispose of the wealth they had created through their 'associated labour'. In other words, workers' councils were given greater powers in deciding how to allocate the surplus funds of their enterprises between personal incomes, investment, social and welfare funds, and other purposes. In the past enterprises had been limited in their powers over investments for 'expanded reproduction' (a Marxist term for new investment, as opposed to 'simple reproduction' or investment for the replacement of existing plant and machinery).

The new laws stated that if an enterprise invested money in a bank, the profit made by the bank must eventually return to the investor. This is intended to prevent the emergence of a capital market, manipulated by banking institutions which made a profit at the expense of the investors. During the late 1960s there were signs that such independent financial institutions were beginning to develop. They were regarded as a threat to the basic socialist principle, 'from each according to his abilities, to each according to his work,' because the small number of employees of these financial institutions were able to enjoy high incomes made by the manipulation of funds acquired by the labour of others. Paradoxically, foreign investors have a specifically guaranteed position which is in some respects more favourable than that allowed to Yugoslav investors. This is a reflection of Yugoslavia's desperate need to attract foreign capital.

Amendment XXIII guaranteed private individuals the right to work with their own 'means of production' and to employ workers on a contractual basis. It also required private employers to make collective agreements with trade unions and economic chambers. There is a significant private sector in Yugoslavia, not only in agriculture, where 80 per cent of the land is in private hands, but also in catering, craft and service industries, road haulage, etc. The official limit of ten hectares of land privately farmed remains, but republics were given the right to permit larger private holdings in the light of local conditions (e.g. the quality of the land, especially in mountainous areas).

Throughout the amendments relating to the economy runs the principle of decentralisation. Enterprises were given greater power at the expense of republican and federal government agencies, and the federation lost powers to the republics. Certain basic unifying principles, however, were upheld. The unified market remained. Republics were not able to erect barriers between themselves to obstruct the free flow of capital, labour and goods. A common currency, common laws regarding foreign trade, customs duties, etc., were also retained. The basic principles of self-management and of the socialist economic and political system were also held to be common to all republics. The federal government was charged with responsibility for national defence and foreign policy and for assisting the economically backward regions, and was empowered to raise taxes to pay for these services. A complicated system of checks and balances was established, which required the agreement of the republics to any extension of federal power.

The working out of the new arrangements created many problems, and was accompanied by endless wrangling as the republics began to adjust their internal constitutions to conform with the proposed changes. The hope was that the open recognition of the differences between the Yugoslav nationalities, and the provision of constitutional machinery to settle these differences, would eventually lead to a voluntary co-operation, based on a mutual recognition of common interests. There were signs after the crisis of late 1971 that agreements between the republics on a number of important constitutional and economic matters were concluded more readily than had seemed probable when the constitution was passed in July (1971), but deadlock remained over some issues, e.g. allocation of funds to underdeveloped areas – until either the federal government or the LCY intervened.

The 1971 amendments represented a bold attempt to come to terms with the problem of relations between the nationalities. It almost created, at least in theory, a confederation of so-called sovereign[4] republics, but in reality the sovereignty of the individual republics was limited by the powers of the federation. It could be argued that the republics voluntarily surrendered part of their sovereignty to the larger entity, but as long as they retained the ultimate right of secession there was no permanent loss of sovereignty. The 1963 constitution explicitly gave to the peoples of Yugoslavia (not the republics)[5] the right of secession, and the 1971 amendments did nothing to change this. The arguments of constitutional lawyers about the meaning of sovereignty need not detain us here. What the 1971 constitution achieved was a *de facto* devolution of power to the republics. It was felt that in the past the imposition from above of an artificial unity simply exacerbated tensions to the point where the discussion of any public issue – political, economic, cultural or even sporting – was muddied by undertones of national rivalry. It was hoped that the 1971 amendments would pave the way for a healthier relationship between the nationalities and so provide a framework in which Yugoslavia's other problems could be tackled by mutual co-operation. If the legitimate aspirations of the nationalists could be met, they might come to see the value of working together for the greater good of socialist Yugoslavia.

In fact, nothing like this occurred. The advance towards autonomy simply whetted the appetite of the more extreme nationalists for even further devolution. In each republic there began to develop a local 'red bourgeoisie', each with its political power base in the republican League of Communists and its economic base in the local industrial enterprises and banks. This was particularly in evidence in Croatia, but it also affected the other republics. The demonstrations in Zagreb in November 1971 were the last straw. Tito and his close associates decided that it was time for drastic measures to remind the nationalists both of the Yugoslav dimension and also of the need to put the system of socialist self-management before all other considerations. Tito's famous Letter of September 1972, sent in the name of the executive of the LCY to all its branches, laid down guidelines for the future conduct of the party. In the letter (and in subsequent speeches by Tito, Dolanc and other high officials) four major forms of political deviation which had developed during the recent past were identified. The bureaucratic, *étatist* and unitarian forces were those which sought to strengthen the central power of the state apparatus, to oppose decentralisation, and in extreme cases to advocate a 'Cominformist' policy which looked back to the early post-war years in which the party directly administered the state. This tendency had been associated with deposed Serbian strong man Aleksandar Ranković. Often allied to this were the 'technocrats', who sought to undermine the system of self-management by concentrating power in the hands of managerial élites both in industry and banking. A third group were the nationalists, who sought to undermine the brotherhood and unity of the Yugoslav peoples, often with the intention of establishing centres of power within the republics for the bureaucratic élites which they served. Finally, there were the 'pseudo-liberals' and New Left intellectuals, who sought to undermine the role of the LCY under the cloak of spurious democratic slogans. It was not suggested that these various forms of political deviation operated within watertight compartments. Considerable overlap between the various groups was discerned, and in some cases the hand of the foreign interventionist was identified. All the groups were seen to have a common goal – to weaken the system of socialist self-management and to devalue the role of the workers in society. The reason for their influence in recent years was the weakness and lack of vigilance of the Party, which had been penetrated by deviationists who were using the LCY to further their own disruptive ends. The answer was for the Party to purge itself of the enemies of self-management and to return to the principles of democratic centralism. It must also operate an effective cadres policy to ensure that only true Communists held positions of responsibility in public life. The LCY, as the vanguard of the working classes, must become the watchdog, guarding the self-management system against its enemies. To facilitate this task, it was necessary to strengthen the constitutional framework of the system to ensure that the fundamental law of the state gave adequate expression to the aspirations of the working classes.

THE NEW CONSTITUTION OF 1974

The 1974 constitution established as the norm a system of election to the various legislative assemblies based on delegations drawn from occupational and interest groups (see figure 2, p. 266 above). The members of these delegations who sit in the legislative chambers of the assemblies are subject to immediate recall and replacement by another member, should they act against the wishes of the delegation which sent them. In Tito's words, 'A determined break has been made with all the remnants of so-called representative democracy which suits the bourgeois class.'[6]

Under the previous system there had been signs of the development of parliamentary practices similar to those in western Europe, e.g. the offer of resignation by the Slovene premier after an adverse vote in one of the chambers of the Slovene assembly and the skilful use of parliamentary questions by some deputies in the federal assembly. Such 'bourgeois' practices based on a concept of liberal parliamentary democracy will be virtually impossible under the delegation system. The delegations are formed at local level from six groupings (see figure 2).

(1) *Workers in the social sector.* These delegations represent members of 'organisations of associated labour' and 'work units' (*delegacije zaposlenih u organizacija udruženog rada i radnih zajednica društvenog sektora*). These are in effect the workers within self-managed enterprises, of whom there are 4·3 million in 21,000 organisations.

(2) *Peasants and farm workers.* 3·9 million active individual peasants.

(3) *Liberal professions.* 300,000 doctors, dentists, lawyers, etc.

(4) *State and LCY officials and soldiers.* These delegations are

formed from workers in the civil service, the socio-political organisations[7], and civilian employees of the armed forces as well as military personnel.

The above four groups send their delegates to the Chambers of Associated Labour (*Veće udruženog rada*) of both the communal and republican assemblies.[8]

(5) *Territorial constituencies* within each commune there are local units (*mestni zajendice*) of citizens resident in the area. The 500 communes contain approximately 10,000 such units. They send delegates to the Chambers of Local Communities within both the communal and republican assemblies.

(6) *Socio-political organisations.* The delegations mentioned under (4) above include only the paid officials of the socio-political organisations. The rank and file members also have a separate voice, through the delegates which they send to the socio-political chambers of both republican and communal assemblies.

When the first set of elections was over in May 1974, Tito told the Tenth Congress that over 700,000 citizens, or one in twenty of all eligible voters, were serving on some kind of delegation. Delegates serve for terms of four years, and no one may serve on 'a delegation of the same self-managing organisation or community for more than two consecutive terms' (Article 134). The electoral process is controlled by the Socialist Alliance or in some cases by the trade unions, except for delegations representing the army.

The federal institutions under the new constitution are composed of delegates chosen from the assemblies of the communes and republics. The Federal Assembly has two chambers: a 220 strong Federal Chamber chosen from the communal assemblies, with 30 members from each of the six republics and 20 from each of the two autonomous provinces; and an 88-member Chamber of Republics and Provinces, consisting of 12 elected by the republican assemblies and 8 by the provincial assemblies. These assemblies also send one member each to the federal presidency, to serve for a term of five years. The president of the LCY is also a member of this body ex *officio*.

The constitution continues the arrangement introduced in

1971 which provides for the presidency to elect its own president, to hold office for the period of one year. There is a strict order of rotation, which ensures that this position, which confers on its holder many of the attributes of a head of state, shall be held in turn by a representative of each of the republics and provinces (Article 327). During the lifetime of President Tito this post is superceded by that of the President of the Republic. Article 333 states that 'the SFRY Assembly may, on the proposal of the Assemblies of the Republics and the Assemblies of the Autonomous Provinces, elect Josip Broz Tito President of the Republic for an unlimited term of office'.[9]

On 15 May 1974 Tito was elected to this unique office, and two weeks later at the Tenth Congress of the LCY the honour of Life President of the League of Communists was also conferred on him. Despite his advanced years, he does not treat either of these posts as sinecures. He remains actively involved in the leadership of his country, exercising real authority in all spheres of public life.

The presidency elected under the new constitution is a smaller and more compact body than its predecessor established in 1971, and it appears also to be more powerful. Its formal duties include the nomination to the Assembly of the premier (President of the Federal Executive Council), the appointment of senior judicial and military officials and ambassadors, and the 'representation of the SFRY at home and abroad' (Article 313). It is also charged with the regulation of relations between the nationalities and with responsibility for state security (Article 313). It has the power to initiate proposals to the Federal Assembly on all policy matters.

In exercising its functions as a co-ordinator of the work of the republican administrations, the presidency frequently calls in the presidents of the republics and provinces,[10] as occurred at its sixteenth session on 12 December 1974. Tito once described the LCY as 'the connective tissue which binds socialist Yugoslavia together'. If this is true in the sense of political ideology, it would appear that the presidency fulfills this role in a constitutional sense.

Another function of the presidency is to nominate the candidates for election to the Council of the Federation (*Savet Federacija*), a body of 105 eminent 'socio-political and public workers' which first appeared in 1967, whose functions are somewhat obscure, and whose members are well paid for their past services and their present good behaviour. It has been described as a Yugoslav equivalent to the House of Lords, but it appears to have no legislative functions. It is mentioned in the constitution only under Article 315, section 7, which authorises the presidency to propose to the Federal Chamber the nomination and removal of its members. Those elected to the first Council under the 1974 constitution on 26 December 1974 included famous writers like Ivo Andrić and Oskar Davičo, the retired army commander General Gošnjak, the former Slovene president Miha Marinko, the Macedonian scholar Blaže Koneski, and a number of elderly ex-partisans who have retired from active politics.

One of the significant new departures in the 1974 constitution was that for the first time since the war both the LCY and the army had their roles in the legislative machinery written into the fundamental law of the state. At the top level, the president of the LCY is *ex officio* a member of the federal presidency, and this situation is repeated in the republican and provincial presidencies, where the local LCY leaders have a similar *ex officio* status. The LCY officials have a place in the delegations to the chambers of assemblies, and the rank and file members participate in the elections to the socio-political chambers. LCY members also have a strong voice in the election of the delegations by virtue of their leading position in the Socialist Alliance, as it is this body which draws up the lists of candidates for the elections.

The army's role in Yugoslav society has been greatly enhanced in recent years, both through the constitutional provision which enables soldiers to elect delegates to the chambers of associated labour, and by the changes in the statutes of the LCY, which have increased the number of army officers in the governing bodies of the party. It is also significant that the new public prosecutor is General Vuko Goče-Gučetić. Since 1971 Tito has often spoken of the role of the army in defending Yugoslav unity. In the aftermath of the Croat troubles, he emphasised the readiness of the army to 'defend the achievements of our revolution, if necessary from internal enemies . . . This should be known.'[11]

As both the LCY and the army are centralising agencies, with an all-Yugoslav rather than a republican character, the coming together of these two power groups provides a strong counter force to any centrifugal tendencies which may develop.

The legislative organs depicted in figure 2 and described above represent only the skeletal framework of the constitution. It is intended that the flesh which clothes the skeleton will be composed of the economic and social organs through which the concept of socialist self-management is to be realised. The driving force which gives life to the whole society is provided by the *avant-garde* of the League of Communists. Thus a large part of the constitution is devoted to outlining the rights and obligations and interrelations of a multitude of organisations. In this respect the Yugoslav constitution is unique, and many of the terms used will be unfamiliar to non-Yugoslavs, for a new terminology has had to be invented to describe new concepts in social relations.

One of the fundamental units is the 'organisation of associated labour'. This term includes industrial and commercial enterprises using publicly owned resources and organised on the basis of self-management, and also cultural, welfare, educational and other institutions within the public domain. Thus, an 'organisation of associated labour' could mean the workers' collective of a large factory, or a small work unit within the factory. If the latter, it is usually now referred to as a 'basic organisation of associated labour' and defined as 'a component part of an organisation of associated labour which makes up a technologically rounded whole, an independent economic and self-managing unit which can have the character of a legal entity'.[12] Within a non-economic organisation, e.g. a scientific institute, such a basic organisation would represent a separate department.

Another set of institutions unique to the Yugoslav constitution are the 'self-managing communities of interest'. These are of great importance in the sphere of public utilities, welfare and education. With a particular commune there would normally be five communities of interest, dealing respectively with education, science, culture, health and welfare. Others can be set up for housing, transport and public utilities. Each represents both the providers and the users of a particular service (e.g. teachers and parents, artists and audiences), and they have an equal status with the appropriate bodies of the communal assembly in arranging for adequate resources to be made available. They can make 'self-managing agreements' with fund-providing bodies, e.g. the commune, local enterprises or scientific foundations – to ensure that the service can be carried on. It is not clear whether this form of local financing for social services, which represents an extreme form of decentralisation, will mean that, for example, schools in poor rural communes will be unable to provide an education comparable to that of the wealthier industrial areas. There is obviously machinery, through the republican administration and ultimately through the federal funds for assistance to less developed areas, for equalisation, but past experience does not suggest that this will be adequate to remove anomalies. If it is to work, those who operate the system – and this means a vast number of ordinary citizens – must have a high level of civic consciousness and political idealism.

NOTES

1 His correct title was President of the Executive Council (*Izvršno veće*).

2 A group of cultural societies, led by 'Matica Hrvatska', demanded constitutional changes to protect the Croatian language against its subordination to Serbian, which they alleged was fostered as a 'state' language. Their manifesto, which provoked bitter controversy, was entitled 'Deklaracija o nazivu i položaju hrvatskog književnog jezika' (Declaration on the name and position of the Croat literary language).

3 For further discussion of the development of the Yugoslav constitution up to 1967, see Frits Honduis, *The Yugoslav Community of Nations* (The Hague 1968).

4 Yugoslav constitution makers have been somewhat indiscriminate in their use of the term 'sovereignty' (*suverenost*). Sovereignty has been held to be an attribute of the federation, of its constituent republics, and of the people.

5 Professor Djordjević, one of the authors of the constitution, interpreted this as meaning the 'constitutional right which the Republic has to leave the Federation'. Jovan Djordjevic, *Novi ustavni sistem* (Belgrade 1964), p. 566.

6 Speech by Tito at the Tenth Congress of the LCY. English text: 'Socialist Thought and Practice', Vol. 6–7 (June–July 1974), p. 46.

7 Socio-political organisations comprise the League of Communists, the Socialist Alliance, the trade unions, war veterans associations, and the Youth League.

8 In this description of the constitution the term 'republican assembly' also includes the assemblies of the two autonomous provinces, unless otherwise stated.

9 The constitution of the SFRY, English text, Article 333 (Belgrade 1974), p. 265.

10 In each republic and province there is a collective presidency analogous to that at federal level, and these bodies elect their own presidents.

11 Speech reported on Radio Zagreb (22 December 1971).

12 Explanation of some expressions and notions used in the SFRY constitution, English text, p. 308.

17 Yugoslavia today: problems of the 1970s

Yugoslav society has gone through many changes since the partisan leaders first took power at the end of the war. The society of the mid-seventies bears little resemblance to that which was envisaged in the blueprints of the 1940s, yet in the main the same leaders have been in charge during the period of transformation. Apart from Tito himself, there is a hard core of ex-partisans who have been continuously in office for thirty years. The application of the principle of rotation, which has applied for over a decade to all public offices except Tito's, has meant periodic changes, but these have been mainly a reshuffling of the pack, using the same cards. Replacements have had to be found from time to time when the occasional purges have occurred or when death has removed a leader.

The first group to be purged comprised those who, rightly or wrongly, were alleged to have taken the Cominform side in the great schism of 1948. These included Andrija Hebrang and Sretan Žujović, who were imprisoned, and General Arso Jovanović, who was shot while attempting to escape into Romania.[1] The trial of alleged Cominformists was the first public action against prominent party members during the post-war period. In 1954 Milovan Djilas and Vladimir Dedijer were expelled from the Party, and Djilas later suffered several periods of imprisonment for his persistent criticisms of Party policy. In the 1960s the fall of Aleksander Ranković and the expulsion of some of his associates was the only important upheaval in the League of Communists. In this case, although he was publicly denounced, there was no trial, and Ranković remains at liberty as a private citizen.

The purge in Croatia in 1971–2 removed from office a number of younger intellectuals and brought back into prominence several Party loyalists whose service goes back to the wartime period.

It was only in the autumn of 1972 that the purge, which had begun as an attack on nationalists, mainly in Croatia, suddenly widened to take in a broad spectrum of Communist leaders in all republics, whose alleged political offences ranged from liberalism to 'technocratic bureaucratism'. Many of these were respected leaders of the Party who had been members since pre-war days. Most of those leaders who have been forced to resign from public office or who have been expelled from the LCY have been allowed to slip quietly into obscurity. Only those lesser figures against whom there were charges of corruption have been brought to trial.

President Tito, although over eighty years old, took an active part in the conduct of the purge. In an interview with the editor of the Zagreb paper *Vjesnik* on 7 October 1972 he suggested that the trouble in the Party started in 1952, at the Sixth Congress.

> The role of the Party[2] was subdued in all important questions concerning social life. It was left only with the task of giving ideological guidance. The Party does have this role, but this is not enough. In its ranks it needs to have the kind of members and the kind of discipline which would prevent the class enemy from taking up positions which, in various forms, he already has in this country.

He and the others who supported his line in 1972 constantly referred to the need for 'democratic centralism' in the Party, and for the need to return to the earlier concept in which the Party was a watchdog that not only knew how to bark, but also had strong teeth.

The Leninist phraseology concerning the role of the Party is not new. What was new in 1972 was that action followed the words. It appeared that Tito was tired of listening to those who applauded him in public but who said to themselves, 'Let him talk, but we shall continue in our own way.' This time he intended to be listened to. It is also possible that, badly shaken by the evidence of disarray within the Party, he was determined to use the limited period of active life which remained to him to undo some of the changes which he had himself helped to initiate during the previous twenty years.

It is certainly curious how, during the twenty years after the Sixth Congress, Yugoslav leaders developed an ability to justify all the changes that were taking place in their country in terms of an unchanging Marxist phraseology. What was defended as socialist orthodoxy at one period was condemned as being harmful and contrary to the principles of self-managed socialism a few years later. The speaker was the same, the phraseology was the same; only the policy was different. Whilst the Communists successfully maintained a monopoly of political power, they were prepared to sanction a gradual development of centres of economic power which were independent of direct Party control. Democratic centralism remained, however, the essential principle of the Party's exercise of political power. In Tito's words, 'It is the only way to ensure success in building socialism.'[3]

This principle was strongly reaffirmed in speeches after the Croatian troubles of November–December 1971. Veljko Vlahović, at the Second Congress of the LCY in January 1972, spoke of the 'importance of the principle of democratic centralism, as well as the full significance of the LCY assuming a more consistent role as the initiator of the force of development in the self-managing socialist community'.[4] The role of the League of Communists as a prime mover in the political sphere was clearly demonstrated during the winter of 1971–2, when the Croatian state and Communist hierarchy was purged on account of its alleged nationalistic deviations. Tito addressed his attack on the 'rotten liberalism' of the Croatian leaders to a special session of the Praesidium of the LCY and not to the Skupština, and it was the LCY which was urged to assist the Croats in putting their house in order.[5]

In Serbia Marko Nikezić, a former foreign minister, was forced to resign from the presidency of the Serbian central committee in 1972, along with the secretary, Latinka Perović. In 1974, on the eve of the Tenth Congress, both were expelled from the LCY. Their offence was an over-liberal attitude to dissent within the Communist ranks, and they were particularly criticised for not behaving with greater severity towards the 'New Left' within Belgrade University. The withdrawal from public life of Koča Popović, once commander of the partisan army and a former foreign minister, at about the same time as Nikezić's removal from office was taken as a sign of silent protest against the purge by a highly respected veteran of the Party. A group of Communists in the Vojvodina, led by Mirko Canadanović, was also removed for alleged membership of a faction within the LCY which included Nikezić and Tepavac. Tepavac was replaced as foreign minister by Miloš Minić. Other casualties at this time included Slavko Milosavlevski, the secretary of the Macedonian Party, the veteran Moslem leader from Bosnia, Avdo Humo, and the liberal minded Slovene premier, Stane Kavčič.

Despite these purges, it was possible to identify within the ranks of the new central committee elected at the Tenth Congress in 1974 a core of some thirty veterans who had been continuously in high office since 1945. If one examines the lists of the government bodies under the new constitution of 1974 a similar continuity of personnel is apparent. Some of the 'old guard' slipped temporarily into less prominent positions during the sixties and were replaced in key positions by younger reformers and technocrats, but since the reassertion of the paramountcy of the Party they have recovered their positions.

The hold of the Communists over the political life of the country was not matched by a similar ascendancy over the machinery of economic life, although in the early seventies attempts were made to achieve this. Speeches and resolutions at the Tenth Congress no longer stressed the role of the market as the yardstick by which enterprises should measure their economic success. Instead emphasis was placed on the need for 'associated labour to gain control over the laws of commodity production and for society consciously and appropriately to guide and rectify market trends, thus diminishing the possibility of adverse influences being generated by the action of blind forces in socio-economic development and relations. The League of Communists must combat conceptions and tendencies to consider that market relations should be formed spontaneously, and socio-economic problems can be solved by the market's automatic operation.'[6]

During the sixties the separation of party, governmental and economic functions had developed as an important aspect of the process of decentralisation which accompanied the spread of 'market socialism'.

At first this was simply a division of labour within the ranks of the Communists, but as market relations began to replace administrative decisions as the main determinants of economic development, political control over the economy receded. The trained technocrat, who may or may not be a Communist, replaced the Party boss at factory level. Even if the managers were nominally members of the LCY, their day-to-day decisions were reached on the basis of commercial rather than political criteria. The growth of larger and larger enterprises through a deliberate policy of encouraging mergers and amalgamations produced a situation in which a relatively small group of firms dominated the oil-refining, chemical and heavy electrical goods industries.

There were many examples of ways in which 'the economy' moved in a direction contrary to the policies of the government. Resolutions of the various organs of Party and State, and of 'socio-political communities', were frequently ignored by workers' councils and boards of management whose decisions were reached in the light of sectional commercial interests rather than of long-term social and political objectives. The political decision makers may ultimately have had their way if the issue was of sufficient moment, but the consequent upheaval means that they will choose to enforce their will only when a crisis situation has been reached. The drive for decentralisation and the autonomy of economic units was carried to the point where only blunt instruments could be wielded by the politicians when they attempted to direct the economy. The pathetic failure of the Ribičič government's efforts to control prices in the winter of 1970 came about partly because enterprises deliberately evaded the regulations by a wholesale renaming of products.[7] The 'stabilisation programme' of 1971, which followed the price freeze, was equally ineffective in controlling inflation. Although economists argue about the causes of the Yugoslav inflation, which since 1965 has consistently run ahead of most other European countries, there is a strong body of opinion that accepts that the failure of the worker-run enterprises to limit income and price rises is a major contributory factor.[8] According to Branko Horvat, 'About four-fifths of the rise in prices can be explained in the rise of personal incomes above the rise in the productivity of labour. It follows that the inflationary mechanism in Yugoslavia is, for the most part, of the cost-push variety.[9] Other writers, however, argue that uncovered investments by the federation, and the political obligation on banks to grant short-term credits to cover wage payments in illiquid enterprises, were the major factors contributing to the inflation. If this interpretation is correct, then it is apparent that the economic decision makers were pulling in the opposite direction from that of the political leaders. As a writer in *Borba* put it in April 1971, 'The disparity between adopted economic policy and economic trends . . . has never been presented to our public in such a sharp form.[10]

There was also a sharp difference between the academic economists and the policy makers. The position is summarised in the following extract from Branko Horvat's article, 'Analysis of the economic situation', published in *Praxis*[11] in 1971.

> In February 1969 the Scientific Section of the Yugoslav Association of Economists again organised a conference in Kragujevac on the problems of stability. At the conference it was shown by empirical analysis that not one of the proclaimed goals of the reform (which can be quantified) was achieved, nor could be achieved. It was emphasised that, in so far as the policies announced by the then President of the Federal Executive Council were carried out, the number of unemployed would by 1975 exceed a million; half within the country and half abroad. (Today we know that this estimate was too optimistic, for the figure has already been surpassed.) Immediately after the Kragujevac Conference a closed meeting in the Central Committee of the Yugoslav League of Communists was held on the basis of material of two Economic Institutes, one in Zagreb and the other in Belgrade, which gave an identical judgement of the economic situation. One of the present Federal functionaries asserted that the judgement of the Belgrade Institute consisted of 'half truths'!
>
> All these, as well as numerous other attempts which I do not mention, had absolutely no effect except to bring unpleasantness to the authors of these judgements and proposals.

Throughout this entire period, the judgements of state and political functionaries differed diametrically from the judgements of scholars. From the statement of the then President of the Federal Executive Council in Parliament, in October 1966 ('I think that we can say unambiguously that the course of the reform up to now has been successful and that we can be satisfied with the results achieved') to the report at the meeting of the Praesidium of the Yugoslav League of Communists in May 1969, directly after the analysis of the cited economic institutes ('The course of the reform has stood the test . . . On a qualitatively new basis we have entered into a phase of dynamic growth of production and productivity of labour, employment and the standard of living') our country's public has been informed of the successful carrying out of the economic reform and the medium-term plan, of the successful fulfilling of strategic goals, of the qualitatively new structure of production and such. When the slowing of growth became evident, then it was begun to be emphasised (along with the ample assistance of unqualified economists) that slow growth represents the price of 'significant restructuring of the economy'. This slogan was launched and maintained until two young scholars showed, by a serious analysis, that it is false, and that slow growth checked the positive restructuring of the economy, which was anyway always known by experts on economic growth. Finally at the XIII session of the Praesidium of the Yugoslav League of Communists, in October 1970, it was emphasised that 'It is a matter of fundamental disequilibrium', which cannot be solved by practical daily measures, for it is 'a question of fundamentally changed relationships in the structure of the economy and the distribution of income'.

The question is posed: why, for a full five years did the judgements of political and state functionaries deviate to such a degree from the judgements of scholars? Why did all the attempts to communicate the results of scientific research remain unsuccessful? It is a matter of uninformedness (sic), ignorance, or something else? The answers to these questions are not of an academic nature. What will happen in the next five years depends on them.

The practical problems of managing the economy, controlling inflation, ending the liquidity crisis, and promoting faster economic growth in the less developed regions are being tackled on an *ad hoc* basis. Whatever the declared long-term objectives, day-to-day decisions are taken pragmatically under the immediate pressures of the moment and are often contrary to the principles on which policies are supposed to be based. In 1971 the tensions created by the pull of opposed interests within Yugoslav society produced a crisis that led President Tito to speak dramatically of the possibilities of civil war and foreign intervention. Referring to the events in Croatia and the measures taken to discipline the Croat League of Communists, he told the Praesidium of the Trades Union Federation on 18 December:

> Had we not now started this struggle, and prevented this – although it is not yet finished and we have much work to do – shooting and civil war would have perhaps have started in six months time, and you know what that would have meant . . . As Head of State and President of the LCY I could not have allowed someone else to come and restore peace and order . . . I would rather have applied extreme means, and you know what extreme means these are.[12]

Within a few weeks, however, this first reaction was considerably toned down. Speaking on 25 January 1972 to the second conference of the LCY, the President stated: 'There can be no question at all of any kind of crisis in our state. It is possible to speak of weakness, past weakness in the ranks of the League of Communists.'[13]

The weaknesses were soon shown to be more fundamental and more widespread than the local difficulties in Croatia. Nationalism is only one of the many problems which face the Yugoslavs, and it is not confined to Croatia. There are many other deep-rooted political, economic and social problems which remain to be solved. In the enormous task of directing an industrial revolution in a country which in 1945 was one of Europe's most underdeveloped states, the Yugoslav Communists have been battling on many fronts simultaneously. They have won some notable victories, but it is not surprising that at times they have appeared exhausted, confused and uncertain as to the way forward. They often appear to pit words and slogans against the harsh realities of life. The stubborn legacies of history, the constraints imposed by Yugoslavia's geographical situation, and the international pressures of the world power struggle are objective factors which limit the freedom of action of the Yugoslav Communists. Above all, there are the problems which arise from the social milieu in which they operate. Harold Laski once wrote of the tasks of revolutionaries and stated that their most difficult problem was not to change the machinery of government, but to change men's everyday habits of thought. The revolutionary *élan* of the early days soon evaporates in the face of the everyday problems of life.

Education, in its widest context, becomes a key problem in a society where over half the population is illiterate, as was the case in pre-war Yugoslavia. It is not simply a question of training the technicians, engineers, economists, teachers and administrators to run the emerging industrial society; it is also a question of winning the allegiance of millions of individualistic peasants to the values of a collectivist industrial society. It is even more difficult when the new society strives to develop as a self-managing Socialist community. As industrialisation and urbanisation progress, new social groups emerge. Social differentiation and the emergence of new élites pose serious problems for the upholders of egalitarian ideals. The Communists themselves, as a new political élite with a monopoly of power, are affected by these processes. There is a danger that their ranks are permeated with opportunists, who see Party membership as a step towards social advancement. The second generation after the revolution may lose contact with the roots from which they have sprung and become a new 'Red bourgeoisie', alienated from the workers in whose name they claim to act.

Yugoslav Communists are not unaware of these dangers. Veljko Vlahović, in his report to the second LCY conference in 1972, declared that 'The LCY had to free itself from ideological vacillation, opportunism, political inertia and rotten liberalism'.[14] Unfortunately, statements of this kind, which bear some of the marks of ritual self-criticism, do not always lead to action to redress the evils which are identified. The purge that was set in motion after the Croatian troubles of 1971 appears to be more far-reaching and serious than any since that which occurred after the expulsion from the Cominform in 1948. Its intention is to fulfil Tito's previously expressed aim of removing 'those elements who are impairing the ideological unity of the League of Communists',[15] and also to strengthen the role of Communists in society. Only when the Communists have achieved unity of purpose themselves can they hope to influence society. If they are divided into rival national parties – as seemed a possibility in 1970–1 – or are split ideologically into 'liberals' and 'conservatives', or if they are seen to be a corrupt oligarchy using political power for personal ends, the society will throw up new centres of power.

THE ROLE OF THE LCY

During the nineteen sixties Tito and other leaders often attributed the malaise within the ranks of the League of Communists to 'ideological confusion'. This is a condition which became increasingly apparent as attempts were made to construct a theory of 'market socialism', and to provide an ideological rationalisation for policies which were frequently determined by pragmatic adaptations to internal and external economic and political pressures. Although it is possible to find a theoretical basis for self-management in Marx's writing, it is difficult to justify 'market socialism' in Marxist terms.

Until after the break with the Cominform the Yugoslav leaders borrowed their theory and their programme directly from the Soviet Union, and especially from Stalin. As Dedijer wrote in 1951, referring to the devotion of Yugoslav Communists to Stalin, 'In no country in the world, in no Communist Party outside the Soviet Union, was that devotion so powerful as in Yugoslavia during the war'.[16]

Until its Fifth Congress, held in Belgrade a few weeks after it had been expelled from the Cominform, the Yugoslav Party did not even have its own official programme, and had never considered 'the possibilities and alternatives of a different path to socialism'[17] from that of the USSR. The author talked with delegates at the congress, and was impressed by their anxiety to demonstrate that they had not broken with Stalinism – Stalin had broken with them, and they earnestly hoped for a reconciliation. As if to prove their orthodoxy, the Yugoslavs intensified the drive against private traders, arbitrarily nationalising many small shops and tightening up the licensing regulations for those which were allowed to remain in business. They also began a collectivisation drive, as if to refute Cominform charges that they were 'a party of kulaks', and to show the Informbureau how unfounded their accusations were'.[18]

The emergence of a specifically Yugoslav road to socialism began with the development of workers' councils in the early fifties and became explicit at the Sixth Congress in 1952. The name of the Party was changed to that of the League of Communists, and its role began to shift from that of 'the direct operative leader of the entire life of society' to that of 'guiding the course of development by the methods of persuasion'.[19] The Seventh Congress, held in Ljubljana in 1958, further elaborated the concept of a Yugoslav road to socialism. It identified the evils of state capitalism which arose during the phase of revolutionary dictatorship that followed the overthrow of the old regime. Although state capitalism may be a necessary phase, there is no automatic transition from state capitalism to socialism. This can be achieved only by the conscious will of the working class. As the working class liberates itself from the fetters of bureaucratic *étatism* new forces will be released. It is not possible to chart in advance the exact forms that the socialist society will adopt as a result of the interplay of these social forces, but in the process of evolution the State will, as Marx predicted, begin to wither away.

The instrument that the Yugoslav leaders saw as being capable of achieving this evolution towards a truly democratic society was the system of self-management.[20]

The mass of Communists appeared to accept these new formulations, which were expressed in Marxist terminology, with frequent references to Marx and Lenin (but not to Stalin), as uncritically as they had previously accepted the Stalinism of the previous decade. For a brief period in 1953–4 there was an opening up of public debate in the columns of *Borba*. Between October 1953 and January 1954 Milovan Djilas, a prominent member of the central committee, wrote a series of articles in which he argued that the continued dictatorship of the Communist Party was holding back the development of a truly democratic socialism. He later openly advocated the formation of a second, socialist, party. It was not until Djilas published a bitter satire on the social pretensions of his Party comrades – and their wives – [21] that action was taken to remove him from the central committee and to expel him from public life. The immediate answer that Tito gave to Djilas's arguments concerning the withering away of the Party was that this could only be achieved when the last vestiges of the class enemy had been eliminated, and that the building of Communism was a lengthy process. To move in this direction too soon would be to destroy the achievements of the revolution. The official party historian dismisses the affair in a few sentences:

> At the end of 1953, he (Djilas) openly came forward with attitudes which meant the elimination of the guiding role of the League of Communists. The League's Central Committee, at its Third Plenum in January, 1954, explained the meaning of Djilas's ideas, and mobilised Communists in the struggle against petty-bourgeois laissez faire attitudes.[22]

Djilas was later imprisoned for publicising his heretical views abroad, and although many of his ideas were put forward in different forms by others who suffered no serious penalty, Djilas himself after 1954 had more influence outside Yugoslavia than within.

The ideological struggle that developed within the ranks of the Communists during the 1960s was of a more serious nature than that which was suppressed in the mid-fifties after the disgrace of Djilas. The solid core of pragmatists, led by such old guard ideologists as Kardelj, appeared to be giving a theoretical top-dressing to policies that had been decided on purely practical grounds. The economic reforms of the early sixties were introduced as a necessary step in the process of industrialisation. Until the economic crisis of this period Yugoslavia had been developing within a closed economic system, but the limits of expansion within this framework had been reached. The need was felt for a change from extensive to intensive methods of production, and for an opening up of economic relations with the rest of the world. Kardelj justified the economic aspects of the reform on purely pragmatic grounds.

> The economic aspect is no great discovery of ours, since it represents the sum total of measures which every society must take in similar situations. The measures are necessary when society is striving to effect the transition from extensive to intensive economic activity, to achieve a higher level of productivity, promote efficiency . . . increase competitive power in the international division of labour, achieve a higher degree of internal economic stability, convertibility of the dinar, etc.[23]

What was distinctive, in Kardelj's view, was that Yugoslavia's method of achieving these economic goals was through 'our system of self-managed social labour', which was based on the democratic participation of the working class. This was the safeguard against the development of managerial–technocratic distortions, and against the alienation of surplus labour by the State or by elements hostile to the interests of the working class. Paradoxically, Kardelj justifies the policy by claiming that it will transcend market relations and reduce income and social differences. Yet, as an essential part of the economic reform was the reliance on market forces rather than on administrative controls to determine the lines of economic development, it is difficult to see how 'market socialism' can accomplish the 'transcendance of market relations'. It is also difficult *a priori* to see why dependence on the market will reduce income differentials either between sectors of industry or between the developed and underdeveloped parts of the country. Kardelj admits that economic inequality is likely to remain a fact of life for some time to come:

> The opinion that conflicts of interest which are the outcome of economic inequality can be resolved through levelling, say, in the Chinese manner, or through a 'faster equalisation', as some subjectivist critics recommend, is a great illusion. Economic inequality is an objective fact not under man's control, that is to be found in the character of human labour.[24]

Kardelj sees in Yugoslav society a conflict between 'the working class' and 'bureaucracy'. He finds 'working class' easier to recognise than to define.

> I am therefore against any stereotype solutions when discussing of what and who the working class is in our country to-day. I personally find it hard to accept formulas which aim at introducing any physical criteria whatsoever into the category of working class . . . the working class is not homogenous and uniform . . . and has never been so in its history.[25]

The bureaucracy has two aspects. One aspect is that of 'controlled bureaucratism', which is a necessary feature of the transitional stage towards a socialist democracy, when elements of the old bourgeois society remain. This kind of bureaucratism is 'the lawful product of social relations' and is not an enemy of the working class.[26] The other, dangerous kind is the 'socio-economic bureaucracy', or in other words the managers and technocrats, who must be controlled lest they usurp the functions of self-management and alienate from the workers their right to dispose of their surplus production.

In the struggle against 'socio-economic bureaucratism' and the remnants of the bourgeois society, the working class must be led by Communists. There is no possibility of any other party leading the struggle. A multi-party system would imply the creation of political institutions to represent the interests of the groups against which the workers are struggling. Nor can elections be left to the haphazard interplay of conflicting personalities and groups; they must be controlled by the Socialist Alliance and the LCY, acting in the interest of the working class.[27] The monopoly of political power by the LCY is a theme to which Tito has frequently returned in recent times. Addressing the Belgrade *aktiv* in August 1971, he affirmed that: 'the Party is the main cohesive force in our country . . . what alternative force could hold it together?'

In his address to the Tenth Congress in May 1974 Tito elaborated at great length the necessity for the Communists to maintain their leading role in society. He attacked the tendency which developed in some circles after the Ninth Congress to convert the LCY into a 'federalistic coalition', and insisted that it must retain its centralised structure. At the grass roots level also, the party members must become more active in the basic organisation of associated labour in the factories and in local political and social organisations. It is only if the spirit of true Communism operates through the machinery of self-management that the new society will evolve.

Kardelj, in his articles in 1967 and 1968, did not look far beyond the horizon to see what sort of society did emerge when the workers had won their fight. He rejected world utopian visions about the future, and was concerned with the day-to-day struggle that he saw taking place around him. The essence of Kardelj's position is that a democratic socialist society *may* (not *will*) emerge from the interplay of forces released through the system of self-management. It will be based on the principle that the workers have the right to dispose of the fruits of their labour. There will be an end to the appropriation of surplus production, either by state or by private capital. 'Democracy and self-management are not a guarantee of freedom and humanism . . . but they are the most effective road towards freedom and humanistic relations among men'.[28]

The best surety that this goal can be achieved is that the class-conscious vanguard of the working classes – the LCY – provides undisputed leadership. The time to talk about the withering away of the Party will be when socialist consciousness has permeated all strata of society.

During the sixties differences within the LCY were frequently debated in public. The closing of ranks after 1971, and especially since the Tenth Congress, has led to a suppression of public debate on fundamental issues, and of the expulsion or resignation of dissidents.

In the winter of 1971–2 Kardelj and his fellow Slovene, Stane Kavčič, engaged in a discussion concerning private investments in the columns of the journals *Delo* and *Komunist*. Kavčič argued that certain people were acquiring large sums of money, which they either deposited in savings banks or used to purchase expensive consumer durables, or to pay for extravagant foreign holidays. He suggested that this money could be made available to enterprises if the owners could invest in 'some sort of shares'. 'Instead of going on holiday to the Fiji islands and spending a million there, the person concerned could give that money to an enterprise dealing with capital investment, which could give him interest and perhaps even something extra in addition, depending on the profitability of the investment concerned.'[29] He regarded this form of private investment as 'the most active form of past work', and believed that it did not conflict with the principles of self-managed socialism. Professor Janko Liska criticised Kavčič's proposals, on the ground that they would create a class of 'socialist rentiers'. He asked,

> Where did the people who are forced to go to the Fiji Islands get their money from? Was it really in accordance with the will of the people? Or was it a question of fraud, or of the misuse of public office . . . ? If the money they now spend on private swimming pools, Mercedes cars, profitable week-end houses and pleasure trips to Fiji is diverted to investment in enterprises, will they acquire self-management rights? According to the logic of shareholders they should have these rights . . . there is also another open question: who will inherit these shares?

Kardelj replied to this debate about private shareholding in a speech to the Third Conference of the Slovene League of Communists. He took the orthodox Marxist stand that private shareholding constitutes a form of exploitation of the labour of others. It is contrary to the spirit of the constitutional amendments, which whilst permitting some forms of private investment e.g. in the form of interest-bearing bonds, limits the period during which the investor can draw interest and confers no right of ownership. It is also contrary to the resolutions of the Ninth Congress of the LCY.

Despite Kardelj's pronouncement the debate continued for a few more months, but in October 1972 Kavčič was removed from office, along with other 'liberals' in Serbia and elsewhere. Previously debates of this kind, as for example that concerning private foreign investment a few years earlier,[30] had resulted in changes of policy, but in the political climate of 1972 the Yugoslav leaders were in no mood for risky experiments which would further extend 'market socialism'. The mood was one of caution and of a return to the ideological certainties of the past.

It is noticeable that these public debates amongst leading Communists were concerned with immediate policy questions. Although theoretical issues touching on the essence of Marxist philosophy are implicit, the context of the discussions related to the implementation of practical measures designed to deal with a concrete economic problem. The men who participated, although avowedly Marxists, were also men of affairs, grappling with day-to-day problems.

There are also in Yugoslavia Marxist philosophers – both within and without the ranks of the LCY – who are concerned with the long-term objectives of a socialist society. The group of sociologists, philosophers and political scientists associated with the controversial journal *Praxis*, founded in Zagreb in 1963, are one example. Until 1975, when the journal was silenced, *Praxis* stimulated debates on fundamental questions of socialist theory and practice which particularly influenced young Marxist intellectuals both inside Yugoslavia and in the West. It had little direct influence on the LCY, however. The officials often harassed and abused the members of the *Praxis* group, but they made no attempt to engage in debate with them, or to attempt to answer their arguments. There was seldom any meeting of minds between the officials of the Party and their Marxist humanist critics. From time to time during the sixties journals like *Praxis*, *Filosofija*, and more popular periodicals like *Književne Novine* and *Student*, were prosecuted. Authors who contributed critical articles were removed from public office or expelled from the LCY. The last two were brought into line by changing the personnel on editorial boards, and the first two were subjected to slow strangulation by the removal of subsidies. In February 1975 the *Praxis* board were faced with the refusal of their printers, under Party pressure, to produce their journal.

The long struggle in the philosophy faculty in Belgrade, which culminated in the dismissal of eight professors in January 1975, demonstrates the gulf between the party officials and their academic critics. The eight professors were all dedicated Marxists. Some, like Mihailo Marković, had been active partisans and had helped to further the cause of self-management throughout the post-Cominform period. They support the statement of principle which emerged from the 1958 Ljubljana Congress of the LCY, but consider that subsequent developments have led away from the path to a democratic socialist society which was envisaged in 1958.

Western commentators often see the struggle between different viewpoints within eastern European parties in terms of 'hard line conservative Stalinists' (e.g. Ranković in Yugoslavia) and 'liberal democratic revisionists' (e.g. Djilas), but the intellectuals who criticise the LCY leadership from the standpoint of Marxist humanism do not fit into these simple categories. For example, the official insistence on income differentials according to work performed leads to the widening of social differences. The humanists attack the growing social inequalities that arise partly from the income differences which 'market socialism' encourages. The official policy of decentralisation increases regional inequalities. The humanists advocate the establishment of self-managing institutions at federal level, which would then exercise certain essential centralising functions, for example in the allocation of funds to assist the less developed regions. They complain that genuine self-management is unrealised if it exists only at the micro-level, and is subordinated at higher levels to the power of state organs of coercion – e.g. the army, the police and the bureaucracy – which are not democratically self-managed.

The emergence of a managerial élite – the new 'red bourgeoisie' – was another target which drew fire from the *Praxis* group. Marković comments that in the early sixties, after a period of rapid economic growth,

> A substantial capital emerged in the hands of the state and it had to be decided whether a) to retain state control over the economy, b) to create a self-managing apparatus to take care of the co-ordination and direction of the economy, or c) to allow the managerial group to undertake the task; allowing the market to play the essential regulative role and keeping the state in the background, trying to preserve an overall control, always ready to intervene and to introduce order when needed.
>
> The first solution looked too conservative, the second too radical. The third was implemented. Whatever the advantages of that solution from the point of view of modernisation and efficiency, and although it still might be a better solution than the return to once abandoned state socialism, the

> consequences from the point of view of genuine socialist emancipation are rather grave.[31]

Criticisms of this kind can be found in newspaper articles and speeches by others during the late sixties, but their authors – some of whom are still active in politics – have not been removed from their posts. They have known when to withdraw and toe the line, but Marković and his colleagues have maintained their position. They have also drawn attention to the growing privileges of the new middle class.

> Another problem is to stop the new-born enriched middle class from being transformed into a myriad of small stockholders. Money made in speculations in land and 'week-end houses', from stealing and corruption and in hundreds of other illegal ways waits to be transformed into shares and to begin bringing in profits. There is a constant pressure to introduce the necessary legislation.
>
> The only chance for Yugoslav socialism to survive is to resist this pressure and to find solutions within a greatly transformed and integrated system of self-management.

It is ironical that Marković and the other seven Belgrade professors were dismissed only after the direct intervention of the State. Ever since the 1968 student demonstrations attempts had been made by the Party in Serbia to discipline them. These efforts were unsuccessful because, until 1975, the faculty council, which included staff and students, refused to vote for their expulsion. In 1974 the party organisation in the university established an anonymous committee which produced allegations that the dissident professors were unsuitable for their teaching posts on moral and political grounds. Eight commissions were established by the faculty council, one to investigate the charges against each of the accused professors. These commissions included scholars from other universities and a few lay members. In each case the integrity and competence of the person under investigation was unanimously vindicated. Despite this, attempts were made to persuade them to withdraw from teaching, either by accepting research posts or by taking leaves of absence to teach abroad. They always refused to make compromises which would imply the acceptance of easy terms for themselves at the expense of their student supporters. In the summer of 1974 several students were sentenced to terms of imprisonment of up to ten months on various charges of engaging in 'hostile activity'. In January 1975 the Serbian Assembly passed a resolution ordering that the jobs of the eight professors should be put at the disposal of the Federal Secretary for Education. In other words, having failed to achieve their removal from teaching duties by the normal processes of self-management within the university, the State stepped in to override the autonomy of the university. By this action the *apparatchiks* demonstrated the validity of the criticisms which the dissidents had been making. At about the same time, the appeals of the students against their sentences were granted by the Serbian Appeals Court.

The humanist critics represent the generation of intellectuals which came to adulthood in the early post-war years. Many were with the partisans whilst still schoolboys, and were at universities at the time of the break with the Cominform. Their faith in Stalinist orthodoxy was shaken, and they began to look again at Marxism, rejecting the dogmatic interpretations and ritual incantations which had passed for Marxist thought in the days when the Yugoslav Party was a slavish follower of Stalin. They discovered the humanist tradition in Marxism, and they read not only the lesser known writings of Marx himself, but also the works of Western philosophers who emphasised the rights of the individual against the crude *étatism* of the Stalinists. Ljubomir Tadić, for example, wrote of 'the animal like life of the community . . . which negates the human personality . . . That communism which looks from below shows its low level of understanding of human needs'.[32]

There is also a second post-revolutionary generation, the youth of today. Most of these appear to be completely indifferent to the polemics of their elders. They seem to be more interested in the material and cultural values of Western 'mid-Atlantic' society. Their view of life is perhaps expressed by Makavejev's film *W. R. The mysteries of the organism*, which was attacked by a writer in *Borba* because 'it treats all ideologies equally' and does not distinguish between Stalinism, Communism, anti-Stalinism and anti-socialism. It also advocates the emancipation of the human being through sexual freedom.

The minority of politically active youth is to be found in the universities – especially in Belgrade, Zagreb and Ljubljana. Their heroes are more likely to be Che Guevara or Herbert Marcuse than the ageing leaders of the Yugoslav revolution. In 1968 the Marxist critics of the older generation made common cause with the left-wing students when they demonstrated in Belgrade. Although the students did protest against the poor prospects of graduate employment and the need for university reform, these demands were within the context of a wider critique of Yugoslav society.

They confronted the LCY with its failure to live up to its own proposed objectives. They pointed to the credibility gap between the claims of the leaders for the virtues of the socialist self-managed society and the reality of unemployment, social inequality, corruption, bureaucracy and the lack of inner Party democracy.

In Croatia in 1971 the situation was somewhat different. It was not New Left socialism that moved the students in Zagreb, but Croat nationalism.[33] Their heroes were the group of Croat Communist leaders – many of whom were intellectuals – who appeared to be putting forward the grievances of the Croat nation over what they believed to be the economic and cultural discrimination practised against them by the Serbs. Shortly before the purge of the Croat leadership in the winter of 1971–2 the Croatian League of Communists enjoyed a brief and unaccustomed popularity amongst the young, but it was not based on dedication to Communism and did not produce a mass of new recruits. Tripalo was not proclaiming, like Dubček, 'Communism with a human face'; he was calling for Communism with a Croat face.

The feeling among many young Yugoslavs that the LCY has little to offer them is reflected in the decline in recruitment. In 1968 21,750 young people joined the Croat Party. The number dropped to under 6000 in 1969 and to under 5000 in 1970.[34] Recruiting campaigns give a temporary boost to membership but there is a rapid turnover, and many allow their membership to lapse after a few months. A writer in *Komunist* complained in August 1971 that many who joined as a result of the campaigns were ideologically unreliable, and that the Party needed to concentrate on the quality of its members rather than on mere numbers.[35] Although the total membership of the Party has remained steady at about a million since 1960, 525,180 new members were enrolled between 1960 and 1970; 223,600 resigned, died, or were expelled, and there is no record of what happened to another 196,174[36] who ceased to be members. Presumably they simply drifted out of membership through a lack of interest, or lost contact when they went abroad to work.

There has also been a decline in the proportion of peasants and workers in the Party. An article in *Naše Teme* in 1970 draws attention to the 'obvious fact' that the Party was losing contact with the peasantry. In 1961 10·4 per cent of members were peasants. In 1969 the proportion had fallen to 7·3 per cent. In Slovenia only 1 per cent of members were peasants, and in Croatia 4·3 per cent[37]. Although the decline may be explained partly in terms of the declining proportion of peasants in Yugoslav society, it is nevertheless a cause for concern that the peasantry, who then constituted almost 40 per cent of the population, should be so drastically under-represented. There has not been a corresponding rise in the proportion of workers. For some time Party spokesmen have been worried about the fact that 'the LCY has begun losing touch with ordinary workers and with ordinary people.'[38] As the proportion of industrial workers in the total population has risen, the proportion in the Party has fallen. If youth, peasants and workers are under-represented, whom does the Party represent? Does it contain a disproportion of functionaries, managers, intellectuals and members of the armed forces?

The meetings of the Praesidium and of the conference of the LCY, held in the winter of 1971–2 were accompanied by much self-criticism and by promises to do better in future. The first result was a purge of 'liberals', followed by a reassertion of the doctrine of 'democratic centralism'. Communists were urged to play a more active part in political and economic life and to act as a cohesive force in holding Yugoslavia to the path of socialism. The phraseology of self-management was frequently invoked, although often the practical policies which were advocated appeared to undermine its principles. One can more easily see what was meant in terms of social discipline than in terms of the ultimate political and ideological objectives.

NOTES

1 The attack on Hebrang and Žujović began before the Cominform resolution of June 1948. On 13 April a Party commission was set up to investigate charges that they had sabotaged the First Five-Year Plan. In 1949 Tito accused Hebrang of being an agent of the *ustaše*, and in 1950 Žujović signed a confession that both were Cominform agents. Žujović was released, but Hebrang, who refused to confess, died in prison.

2 The 1952 congress changed the name of the Party to that of the League of Communists. It is perhaps significant that Tito continues to talk of the Party.

3 Speech at Peć, 21 March 1967.

4 BBC East European Monitoring Service, EE/3898/C1/16 (26 January 1972).

5 Tito's speech to the praesidium of the LCY at Karadjordjevo (1 December 1971).

6 *Socialist Thought and Practice*, 6–7 (1974), pp. 43–4.

7 30,000 'new' products were registered with the Federal Price Bureau in the first three months of 1971, compared with 6000 for the whole of 1968.

8 In 1971 the rate of inflation was 12 per cent. It increased to 16 per cent in 1972 and to almost 30 per cent in 1974. The steep rise during the period 1972–4 was largely accounted for by the oil crisis and the subsequent world inflation.

9 Branko Horvat, 'Analysis of the economic situation', *Praxis*, international edition, 3–4 (1971), p. 557.

10 Rade Vojović, *Borba* (April 1971).

11 Horvat, in *Praxis* (1971), pp. 535–6.

12 Speech by Tito to the Praesidium of the Trade Union Federation, reported by *Tanjug* (18 December 1971).

13 Text of speech in BBC Monitoring Service, part II, EE/3998/C1/3 (26 January 1972).

14 Veljko Vlahović, reported in BBC Monitoring Service, EE/3898/C1/16 (26 January 1972).

15 *Borba* (1 May 1971), p. 1.

16 V. Dedijer, *With Tito through the war – partisan diary 1941–44* (London 1951), preface.

17 See Pero Morača and D. Bilandžic, *Avangarda 1919–1969* (Belgrade 1969), The authors worked for the Workers' Research Institute, and their view can be regarded as the official interpretation of this period of the Party's history.

18 Dedijer, *Izgubljena bitka J. V. Stalina* (Sarajevo 1969), p. 409.

19 P. Morača, *The League of Communists* (Belgrade 1966), p. 57.

20 '. . . the League of Communists endorsed self-management as the form of production relations that would effectively preclude the aforementioned deformations of bureaucratic–technocratic and state proprietorship type, and constitute a genuine factor of the emancipation

of labour and the working man . . .' E. Kardelj, 'The Class Position of the LCY', in *Socialist Thought and Practice*, no. 37 (December 1969), p. 4.

21 In the January issue of *Nova Misao.*

22 Morača, *The League of Communists*, p. 61. Svetozar Vukmanović in his memoirs, *Revolucija Koja Teče: Memoari* (Belgrade 1971), takes the Djilas affair more seriously, and accepts that Djilas was right in his *Borba* articles warning of the dangers of bureaucracy and the lack of inner Party democracy, but he attacks the *Nova Misao* article as extreme in its criticism of the leadership and dangerous in opening up the possibility of a multi-party system.

23 Kardelj, in *Socialist Thought and Practice*, no. 37 (December 1969), p. 5.

24 Kardelj, *Beleske o našoj društvenoj kritici* (Belgrade 1966), p. 180.

25 Kardelj, in *Socialist Thought and Practice*, no. 37 (1969), p. 13.

26 Kardelj could hardly say otherwise, as most of the members of this group are members of the LCY.

27 See Kardelj, 'Responsibility for elections', *Socialist Thought and Practice* (January–March 1967).

28 Kardelj, 'Radnička klasa, birokratizam i savez Komunista Jugoslavije', *Socijalizam*, 1–2 (1968), p. 6.

29 'Shares – Yes or No', *Komunist* (3 February 1972), p. 12.

30 The introduction of the law on foreign investments in 1967 was accompanied by similar socialist heart-searchings, and was eventually accepted on condition that the investor was hedged in by restrictions on the right to export his profits. Later many of the restrictions were relaxed.

31 Marković, *The contemporary Marx*, p. 135.

32 Lj. Tadić, *Poredak i sloboda* (Belgrade 1967), p. 272. Quoted in M. M. Milenkovitch 'Yugoslav Marxism in the Sixties', *Review*, Study Centre for Jugoslav Affairs, no. 9 (London 1970). Tadić was removed from his teaching post in Belgrade in January 1973.

33 Dražen Budiša, who became President of the Zagreb Students' Union in April 1971, was the first non-Communist to hold that office. He was removed in December 1971, and later tried and imprisoned for his part in the Zagreb disturbances.

34 *Borba* (March 1971), p. 11.

35 *Komunist* (5 August 1971), p. 2.

36 Figures from *Borba* (2 March 1971), p. 4.

37 *Naše Teme* (19 November 1970), pp. 1993–2006.

38 Interview given by Stane Dolanc to the youth newspaper *Mladost* and reported in *Borba* (23 November 1971), p. 7.

18 Conclusions

In the foregoing pages I have traced the economic and political development of Yugoslavia since the Second World War and have attempted to place the modern Yugoslav state in its historical and geographical context.

The Yugoslav revolution is now thirty years old. It has been in a constant state of dynamic change, and the society we see today is almost unrecognisable to those who knew the country a generation ago. Because of the constant movement on the surface, it is often difficult to discern underlying trends. There have been five major constitutional enactments since the end of the war. New methods of economic planning and industrial organisation have been introduced. Foreign policy and foreign trade have been completely realigned since the expulsion of the Yugoslav Communists from the Cominform in 1948. Yugoslavia began her revolution under the material and psychological domination of Stalin's Soviet Union. In a world divided into two camps, Yugoslavia was firmly committed to the Soviet side. Today foreign policy is based on the principle of non-alignment and foreign trade is dominated by the EEC countries and especially West Germany and Italy.

Many of the changes have been made under the pressure of external events over which the Yugoslavs have had no control. Others have come from within as a result of conscious attempts to solve deep-rooted problems within the multinational Yugoslav society.

The Communists assumed leadership in a war-ravaged country that had formerly been one of Europe's least developed peasant communities. They have wrought a great economic and social change through industrialisation. Before the war 75 per cent of the population depended upon agriculture, and they contributed 54·6 per cent of the national income; 70 per cent of agricultural produce was consumed on the farms. By 1954 manufacturing industry had surpassed agriculture in its share of the national income, and it now contributes almost three times as much as agriculture.[1] The mass exodus from the countryside reduced the farming population to 49 per cent of the total population by 1961, and to 36 per cent by 1971. The per capita income has risen from $70 in 1939 to over $700 in 1971. The more developed northern areas are now approaching the income levels of the neighbouring states of Italy and Austria.

Unfortunately, the economies of less developed areas have not grown at a faster rate than the national average, so the gap in living standards between, for example, Slovenia and Kosovo remains as large in 1971 as in 1947. These economic differences reinforce the cultural gap between the rich and poor areas and so add to the strains which exist between the various national groups.

As Yugoslavia emancipated itself from the rigid Stalinist framework of the early post-war years, it evolved new forms of economic and social organisation based on the concept of self-management. This process involved a revision of the role of the Communist Party in Yugoslav society and a reinterpretation of the Marxist theory on which its policy was based. It seemed as if these developments would lead towards a commonwealth of self-managed social and economic groups, interacting with each other within a decentralised market economy.

The reforms of the sixties were intended to prepare Yugoslavia for membership of the 'international division of labour'. This implied a breaking down of the economic and social barriers which formerly isolated Yugoslavia from outside influences. These influences have come flooding in, especially from western Europe. In the economic sphere, Germany and Italy account for almost 30 per cent of Yugoslavia's foreign trade. Western private capital is invested in Yugoslav enterprises, and many Yugoslav firms operate under licensing agreements with Western companies. Over 800,000 Yugoslavs are employed in western Europe as temporary migrant workers, and the majority of the foreign tourists are from EEC countries.[2] The economic consequences of these links with the West are of major importance to Yugoslavia, but so also are the social and political implications. The aspirations of many Yugoslav young people are directed to the successes of the capitalist states of the EEC, rather than to the ideal of a self-managed socialist society, about which their leaders talk. Yugoslavs employed abroad may learn new industrial skills, but they also acquire new social and political attitudes. Several local Communist leaders, concerned about the decline in the populations of their areas, have suggested that 'a better attitude to private work'[3] would discourage their citizens from leaving the country. It is curious that the prophets of a new social order should seek to persuade their citizens not to go to capitalist countries by promising them better opportunities for private enterprise at home.

Private enterprise in catering, service industries, handicrafts and small-scale manufacturing is steadily growing. In some areas the stimulus to private entrepreneurship can be directly linked to tourism. Often the capital to start a business comes from money earned abroad.

The growing private sector is not the only cause which explains the increasing income differentials between groups of Yugoslav citizens. Within the system of market socialism many have found it possible to earn large 'extra incomes' and to enjoy privileges paid for by the workers. The problems of social differentiation which these differences in wealth create is one which causes concern to the leaders of the LCY.

'Market socialism', in so far as it has been applied, not only increased social and economic inequalities, but also led to demands for the creation of a private capital market. The premier of Slovenia, in 1971, proposed that, in order to utilise the large sums of capital in private hands, it should be possible for investors to hold interest-bearing bonds in industry. He felt that the money would be better used in this way than by being dissipiated in the purchase of foreign luxury cars or in trips to Fiji.

Despite these signs of drift towards the economic and social attitudes of the West, the political framework of Yugoslavia remained that of a one-party state. The League of Communists may no longer exercise direct administrative control, but it still retains the political initiative. It was the LCY which first acted to suppress the Croat unrest of 1971, and the purge of nationalists which followed was also initiated by the League.

The League is far from being united, however, on many fundamental issues of Communist principle. It was always possible for the leadership to produce a public display of unity in times of crisis – as at Brioni in April 1971 and at Karadjordjevo in December, 1971 – but below the surface deep differences of policy remain. During the purge of nationalists in 1972, Latinka Perović declared to the Central Committee of the Serbian League of Communists: 'We know that nationalism had its chance only when it penetrated the League of Communists, but we still lack an explanation of why this penetration was possible'.[4]

Since 1971 there has been a severe curb on the public expression of dissident opinions. At first the attack was strongest against nationalists, but it soon widened to include 'liberals' and in fact anyone who opposed the current policies of the LCY, whether or not the criticism was from a Marxist standpoint. During the fifties and sixties the Yugoslav press enjoyed an increasing measure of free expression, compared with other countries in eastern Europe. At one end of the spectrum there were critical journals of the left, like *Praxis* and *Filosofija*, and a number of lively and irreverent student journals, and at the other were pseudo-pornographic magazines like *Cik*, which projected the values of Western Admass journalism. The 1974 constitution guarantees freedom of the press. Article 176 states, 'Citizens shall have the right to express and publish their opinions through the media of information.' The resolution of the Tenth Congress on this subject suggests, however, that such freedom of expression is not unconditional. It states that 'Newspapermen, and especially communists . . . must, in their professional and social work . . . engage in unmasking technocratic, dogmatic-bureaucratic, nationalistic and pseudo-liberal tendencies . . . that are opposed to the policy of the LCY.' They must also resist 'the penetration of bourgeois and petty-bourgeois world views'.[5]

The League of Communists and its associated political ally, the Socialist Alliance, make their appeal to a limited section of the population. As their influence receded, there was a resurgence of support for the churches. This may be explained partly in terms of a religious revival, but it must be also borne in mind that the religious communities in Yugoslavia are closely identified with specific national groups.

Croat nationalism is strongly identified with the Roman Catholic Church, Serbian and Macedonian nationalism with their respective Orthodox churches, and in Bosnia the Islamic community claims the status of a Moslem ethnic group. The apparent revival of religious belief may be simply a reaffirmation of national identity. Whatever the causes, the growing influence of religious organisations poses problems for the Communists. It is no longer met by bans and discriminations, as in the early post-war years. The dialogue between Christians and Marxists, which was a feature of intellectual life in Slovenia Croatia and Bosnia during the late sixties, was an attempt to find common ground by liberal-minded intellectuals on both sides, rather than a polemical confrontation.

Yugoslav society in the late sixties presented a picture of great diversity. There was no longer one centre of power and influence which operated at all levels; instead, many overlapping centres contended for influence, and there were many openings to the outside world. The tightening of social discipline in the early seventies has not entirely eliminated this picture, although it seems that the LCY is striving to achieve a greater degree of uniformity and to assert its primacy over all other possible centres of influence.

Many facets of Yugoslav life are unique, and may be explained only in terms of its own geographical, historical and human individuality, but there are aspects which may have a bearing on the general problems of developing societies. The sympathetic outsider can only ask questions and hint at possible answers, but he is unwise if he attempts to make dogmatic pronouncements.

The transformation of Yugoslav society during the last thirty years has been brought about by, in the main, the conscious will of a minority of dedicated Communists who have persuaded, cajoled and pressured their fellow citizens into accepting the sacrifices necessary for the rapid industrialisation of the country. In the early years of the revolution the burden of industrialisation was borne mainly by the peasantry, who constituted over two-thirds of the population. The attempt to collectivise the peasantry failed, and gradually the lot of the declining number of peasants began to improve. In the later years the burden of switching from a closed, autarchic system to a more open society, with its economy geared to the 'international division of labour', was borne by the unskilled workers. They were able to escape from its worst consequences by virtue of the opening of the frontiers, which has enabled hundreds of thousands of people to find work in western Europe.

Could Yugoslavia have industrialised in any other way? Were the sacrifices of the earlier years justified by the undoubted rise in living standards and the widening opportunities that are now available to the majority of Yugoslavs? Is the attempt to engage the mass of the people in the decision-making processes through the system of self-management working? Do the workers really participate, or are they in fact manipulated by the technocrats and the bureaucrats? Certainly these tendencies exist, and are recognised by leading Communist spokesmen. Marko Nikezić, the president of the Serbian Central Committee, referred in June 1972 to the dangers of the emergence of a nationally minded technocracy in Serbia:

> In conditions of republican insularity technocratism must become a modernised form of bureaucratic management, and nationalism its social and political expression. Technocratism can be staved off temporarily, but it cannot be defeated if we fight it in individual work organisations, whilst it is relations in the Republic and in society as a whole which maintain the tendency towards concentration of power, both economic and political.[6]

The tendency of concentration of economic power in the hands of large enterprises is not unique to Yugoslavia. It arises partly from the demands of modern industrial technology. Since the reforms of 1965 the Yugoslavs have encouraged mergers among their own firms and have tried to involve international capitalist firms like Krupp, Fiat and Zanussi in various forms of co-operation with Yugoslav enterprises. This has been done in the name of efficiency, and to strengthen Yugoslavia's position in the international division of labour.

Can such policies be carried out without weakening the basis of self-management? Can modern industrial efficiency be combined with workers' self-management?

Socialism is a word with many meanings, but common to most concepts of it is the idea of equality. No one imagines that mathematical equality of incomes is possible, but most expect that a socialist system will reduce income differentials. The slogan 'From each according to his ability; to each according to his work', is not necessarily a recipe for equality. It says nothing about the conditions under which the work is performed. Under market socialism the value of work is assessed by the saleability of the produce of the workers' labour, but the conditions of the market, which determine his reward, are not under the control of the worker. Given unequal conditions of work, the market is bound to produce inequalities in the rewards. Thus, Yugoslavia has been unable to narrow the income differences between regions – or even within regions.[7] Nor has market socialism been able to narrow the income differentials between individuals. All the evidence suggests that differences in wealth are increasing. Are 'market' and 'socialism' terms that are mutually incompatible? This is a question that is now being debated throughout the Soviet and eastern European world, as the communist leaders attempt in the name of efficiency to introduce elements of the market into economies that were previously directed under state-centralised planning systems.

Attempts have been made to suggest that Yugoslavia's experience can provide a model to developing countries. Yugoslavia's position as a leader of the non-aligned group of nations has provided opportunities for the leaders of the developing nations to learn about Yugoslavia's achievements. What are these lessons? That the foundations of industrialisation must be laid during a period of 'dictatorship of the proletariat' within an autarchic economy? (Yugoslavia, phase 1); that the foundations of socialist democracy can be established through workers' self-management? (Yugoslavia, phase 2); that the way forward to equality within the developed nations is through market socialism and a share in the international division of labour? (Yugoslavia, phase 3), or that the inequalities and anomalies from market relations can in some way be controlled by political decisions imposed by the LCY? (Yugoslavia, phase 4).

Finally, when one comes to the crucial question of the men and women in whose name the transformation of society has been carried out, has the new society fundamentally changed the consciousness of the individual? Laski spoke of the main task of revolutionaries being the changing of the everyday thoughts and habits of ordinary people. Besides this task, the overthrow of governments, the achievements of public ownership of the means of production, and the liquidation of capitalist opponents are comparatively easy. Is there in Yugoslavia today a new class of non-acquisitive, socialist-minded men and women, instinctively working for the good of the commonwealth and inspired by the principles of socialist humanism in their everyday relations with their fellow men? Are they to be found among the youth of today, or amongst the ranks of the rising professional classes? If such a class does not yet exist, can its embryonic form be discerned amongst the workers in the factories and fields? Or do such groups exist within the League of Communists and the Socialist Alliance? If they do, can it be said that market socialism encourages them to display their altruism, by diminishing competitiveness and making the path easier for co-operation and mutually harmonious social relations?

The 1974 constitution appears to provide a framework in which the majority of citizens can participate directly in the management of the society. Yet, although large numbers participate, do they really enjoy power? The state and party both stand above the system of self-management at the grass roots, and are able to intervene to impose decisions from outside. Of course, no system is perfect, and it may be argued that it is necessary in order to preserve the system that some residual powers remain to the organs of central power.

It is obvious that Yugoslavia has a long way to travel before it reaches its goal. 'A man's reach must exceed his grasp, or what's a heaven for?' No one can condemn those who fail to achieve their ideals. The question for Yugoslavia is whether the path they have chosen is leading towards the declared objective. Perhaps after another generation of Yugoslav socialism the answer will be clearer.

NOTES

1 1968: industry, 22,059·6 million dinars; agriculture, 7,864·6 million dinars (at 1960 prices). *Statistički Godišnjak* (1970), p. 3351.

2 In 1970 2·6 million of the 4·75 million foreign tourists came from EEC countries.

3 Toša Popovski in February 1971 at a conference in Macedonia which discussed the problems of the Bitola, Resen and Ohrid regions. *Borba* (26 February 1971).

4 Report in *Tanjug* (30 June 1972). Perović was herself forced to resign in 1972.

5 *Socialist Thought and Practice*, p. 196.

6 Nikezić was forced out of office in September 1972.

7 Dr Ksente Bogoev referred in a report to the Macedonian Central Committee to a difference in the ratio of 10:1 in the levels of development within some republics. *Tanjug* (29 June 1972).

Selected bibliography

This bibliography contains a selection of books and articles in English, French and German that are readily available to the western European and American reader, and also a selection of the principal sources in the Yugoslav languages which the author has found useful.

BIBLIOGRAPHICAL WORKS

Carter, F., *A Bibliography on the Geography of Yugoslavia*, Kings College, Cambridge, Department of Geography, Occasional Papers A 1 (1968).

Horečky, P. L. (ed.), *Southeastern Europe: a Guide to Basic Publications* (Chicago 1969).

Pajović, B. and Radević, M. (eds.), *Bibliografija o Ratu i Revoluciji u Jugoslaviji* Works published 1945–65 (Belgrade 1969).

Tadić, J. (ed.), *Ten Years of Yugoslav Historiography, 1945–55* (Belgrade 1965).

Tadić, J. (ed.), *Historiographie Yougoslave, 1955–65* (Belgrade 1965).

Vuchinich, W. S., 'Postwar Yugoslav Historiography', in *Journal of Modern History*, 22 (1950).

GEOGRAPHICAL AND ECONOMIC BACKGROUND

Mardesić, P., and Dugački, Z. (eds.), *Geografski Atlas Jugoslavije* (Zagreb 1961). Contains 37 topographical maps on a scale of 1:500,000, and on the reverse of each 37 distribution maps covering aspects of physical geography, demography, transport, economic geography, and a 100-page index of place names. Also a 95-page geographical survey by Professor R. Petrović and a 53-page survey of political and economic data by P. Mardesić.

Yugoslavia: Official Standard Names Approved by the United States Board on Geographic Names (Washington 1961).

General works

Blanc, A., *Geographie des Balkans* (*Que sais-je?*) (Paris 1965).

Cvijić, J., *La Peninsule Balkanique: geographie humaine* (Paris 1918). A classical work by the father of Serbian geography.

Melik, A., *Yugoslavija-Zemljopisni Pregled* (Zagreb 1952).

Milojević, B., *Yugoslavia: Geographical Survey. Organisation of the Yugoslav State* (Belgrade 1958).

Pounds, N. J. G., *Eastern Europe* (London 1969). Section on Yugoslavia, chapter 12, gives a useful general survey of the geography of Yugoslavia.

Political and economic geography

Avsenek, I., *The Yugoslav Metallurgical Industry* (New York 1955).

Energetski izvori Jugoslavije: Vodne Snage Jugoslavije (Yugoslav National Committee of the World Energy Conference Belgrade 1952).

Fisher, J. C., *Yugoslavia, a Multinational State: Regional Difference and Administrative Response* (San Francisco 1966).

Gehreke, S., 'Die Elektrizitäts Wirtschaft Jugoslaviens', in *Osteuropa Wirtschaft* (1971).

Hamilton, F. E. I., *Yugoslavia: Patterns of Economic Activity* (London 1968).

Hall, D. R., 'The Iron Gates Scheme and its Significance', in *Geography*, 57, part 1 (1972).

Hubeni, M., *Ekonomska Geografija Jugoslavije* (Belgrade 1958).

Lah, A., *Gospodarstvo Jugoslavije: Prispevek k Ekonomski Geografije FNR Jugoslavije* (in Slovene), (Ljubljana 1950).

Melik, A., *Yugoslavia's Natural Resources* (Belgrade 1952).

Frontiers

Cvijić, J., *La Frontière Septentrionale des Yougoslaves* (Paris 1918).

Moodie, A. E., *The Italo–Yugoslav Boundary* (London 1945).

Seidl, F., *La Future Frontière Politique entre la Yougoslavie et L'Italie: Etude geologique et geographique* (Ljubljana 1919).

Miscellaneous

Bičanić, R., 'Effects of War on Rural Yugoslavia', in *Geographical Journal*, no. 103 (1944).

Kiroski, P., 'Geografski Elementi na Ekonomskata Regionalizatija' (in Macedonian with French summary), and 'Ekonomsko Geografski Aspekti na Industrijata vo Makedonija' (in Macedonian with French summary), both in *Proceedings of the VIII Congress of the Yugoslav Geographers* (Skopje 1968).

Melik, A., 'Slovenija: Geografski Opis' (in Slovene), in *Slovenska Matica*, vol. 1, part 1 (1935); vol. 1, part 2 (1936). Part 1: physical geography; part 2: economic geography, demography and settlements.

Roglić, J., 'Geography in Yugoslavia', in *Geographical Journal*, 118, part 2 (1952).

The Skopje Earthquake, 1963 (UNESCO earthquake study mission. Report of UNESCO Technical Assistance Mission, Paris 1968).

Wilkinson, H. R., 'Jugoslav Macedonia in Transition', in *Geographical Journal*, 118, part 4 (1952)

Travel

Brailsford, H. N., *Macedonia* (London 1906). An account of Macedonia during the Balkan Wars and the early twentieth century, based on the author's experiences as a foreign correspondent.

Evans, Sir A., *Illyrian Letters* (London 1878). Based on the early travels of the famous archaeologist.

Jackson, T. G., *Dalmatia, the Quarnero and Istria*, 3 vols (London 1887).

Jelavchich, B., 'The British Traveller in the Balkans: the Abuses of the Ottoman Administration in the Slavonic Provinces', in *Slavonic and East European Review*, 33, no. 81 (1959).

Mackenzie, M. M., and Irby, A. P., *Travels in the Slavonic Provinces of Turkey in Europe* (London 1967, 1877). The journeys of two English ladies in Turkish-occupied Bosnia. Miss Irby stayed on in Sarajevo as a teacher.

West, R., *Black Lamb and Grey Falcon*, 2 vols (London 1942). An account of a journey to Yugoslavia in the 1930s. Much more than a travel book.

HISTORY

General

Babić, V., Grafenauer, B., Perović, D., and Sidak, J. (eds.), *Historija Naroda Jugoslavije* (Zagreb 1953, 1959). Vol. I covers the period before the sixteenth century; vol. II from the sixteenth to the end of the eighteenth century. Vol. III has not yet appeared.

Clissold, S. (ed.), *Cambridge Short History of Yugoslavia from Early Times to 1966* (Cambridge 1968). Based on the historical volume of the *Admiralty Handbooks*, with additional chapters on the wartime period by S. Clissold and on the post-war period to 1966 by P. Auty.

The early history of the Slavs

Dvornik, F., *The Slavs: their Early History and Civilisation* (Boston 1956). Based on a series of lectures given at Harvard in 1951. A standard work on the origin, migration and settlement of the Slavs, and their history to the twelfth century.

Dvornik, F., *The Slavs in European History and Civilisation* (New Brunswick, N. J. 1962).

Vlasto, A. P., *The Entry of the Slavs into Christendom: an Introduction to the Mediaeval History of the Slavs* (Cambridge 1970).

The Byzantine period

Obolensky, D., *The Bogomils – a Study in Balkan Neo-Manichaeism* (Cambridge 1948).

Ostrogorsky, G., *History of Byzantine State* (Oxford 1956). A classic work by a distinguished Yugoslav scholar.

Porphyrogenitus, C., *De Administrando Imperio*, ed. G. Moravcsi̇̃k (Budapest 1949).

The South Slavs under Ottoman rule

Coles, P. H., *The Ottoman Impact on Europe* (London 1968).

Skrivanić, G. A., *Kosovska Bitka* (Cetinje 1956).

Stavrianos, L. S., *The Balkans since 1453* (New York 1958).

Vaughan, D. M., *Europe and the Turk: the Pattern of Alliances, 1300–1700*, 2nd ed. (Liverpool 1960).

The South Slavs under Habsburg rule

Macartney, C. A., *The Habsburg Empire, 1790–1918* (London 1969).

Přibram, A. F., *The Secret Treaties of Austria–Hungary, 1879–1914*, 2 vols (Cambridge, Mass. 1920–1).

Seton-Watson, R. W., *The Southern Slav Question and the Habsburg Monarchy* (London 1911).

Taylor, A. J. P., *The Habsburg Monarchy, 1809–1918* (London 1948). Valuable for its treatment of the relations between the Monarchy and its Slav subjects.

Zwitter, Fran., *Nacionalni Problemi v Habsburski Monarhiji* (in Slovene), (Ljubljana 1962). Revised and enlarged ed. of author's *Les Problemes Nationaux dans la Monarchie des Habsburg* (Belgrade 1960).

The nineteenth century

a) THE RELATIONS OF THE GREAT POWERS TO THE BALKAN STATES

Jelavich, C., *Tsarist Russia and Balkan Nationalism – Russian influence in the Internal Affairs of Bulgaria and Serbia, 1879–1886* (Berkeley, Calif. 1968).

Oakes, Sir A., and Mowat, R. B., *The Great European Treaties of the Nineteenth Century* (Oxford 1918). Texts of treaties and notes on background of diplomatic history. Chapter IX refers to Turkey, Russia and the Balkan States between 1871 and 1914.

Sumner, B. H., *Russia and the Balkans, 1870–1880* (London 1962)

b) BIOGRAPHIES AND MEMOIRS

Djilas, M., *Njegoš – Poet, Prince, Bishop* (New York 1966).

Edwards, L. F. (ed.), *The Memoirs of Proto Matija Nenadović* (Oxford 1969).

McClellan, W. D., *Svetozar Marković and the Origins of Balkan Socialism* (Princeton, N. J. 1964).

Obradović, D., *The Life and Adventures of Dimitrije Obradović*, ed. and trans. G. R. Noyes (Berkeley, Calif. 1953).

Wilson, Sir D., *The Life and Times of Vuk Stefanović Karadžić* (Oxford 1970).

From Sarajevo to Versailles

Baerlein, H., *The Birth of Yugoslavia* (London 1922).

Dedijer, V., *The Road to Sarajevo* (London 1967).

Lederer, I. J., *Yugoslavia at the Paris Peace Conference – A Study in Frontier-making* (New Haven, Conn. 1963).

Remak, J., *Sarajevo* (London 1959).

Smodlaka, J., *Yugoslav Territorial Claims* (Paris 1919). Reprint of speech by Dalmatian member of Yugoslav delegation to the Peace Conference.

South Slav Committee, *South Slav Library:* vol. I, 'The South Slav programme'; vol. II 'The idea of South Slav unity' (Welwyn, Herts. 1915).

Yugoslav Committee, *Southern Slav Bulletin*, no. 38 (15 January 1919). Contains Declaration of Aims of December 1918, made by newly formed Yugoslav government.

The Yugoslav Kingdom, 1918–41

Bogdanov, V., *Historija Političnih Stranaka u Hrvatskoj* (Zagreb 1958).

Durham, M. E., 'Albania and Balkans, 1919–23': MSS and cuttings (Bradford University).

Durham, M. E., Letters and newspaper cuttings, 1922–5 (Bradford University) concerning especially Croat and Serb dissensions (also on Albania and on Serb guilt and the Sarajevo crime).

Hoptner, J. B., *Yugoslavia in Crisis*, 1934–1941 (New York 1962).

Maček, V., *In the Struggle for Freedom* (New York 1957). Memoirs of Radić's successor at head of Croatian Peasant Party.

Peter II, King of Yugoslavia, *A King's Heritage* (London 1955).

Pribičević, S., *Living Space* (London 1940).

Ristić, D. N., *Yugoslavia's Revolution of 1941* (University Park, Penn. 1966).

Slovenia

Kardelj, E. (Sperans), *Razvoj Slovenačkog Nacionalnog Pitanja* (Belgrade 1958).

Croatia

Carter, F., *History of Dubrovnik* (New York 1972).

Črnja, Z., *Kulturna Historija Hrvatske* (Zagreb 1965).

Eterovich, F. H., and Spalatin, C. (eds.), *Croatia: Land, People, Culture*, vol. 1 (Toronto 1964).
Rothenberg, G. E., *The Austrian Military Border in Croatia, 1522–1747* (Urbana, Ill. 1960).
Rothenberg, G. E., *The Military Border in Croatia, 1740–1881: a Study of an Imperial Institution* (Chicago 1966).

Macedonia

Barker, E., *Macedonia – Its Place in Balkan Power Politics* (London 1950).
Čašule, V. (ed.), *From Recognition to Repudiation: Bulgarian Attitudes on the Macedonian Question: Articles, Speeches, Documents* (Skopje 1972).
Državna Arhiva, *Dokumenti za Istorijata na Makedonskiot Narod* (in Macedonian), (Skopje 1963).
Mikhailov, I. (Macedonicus), *Stalin and the Macedonian Question* (St Louis 1948).
Nurigiani, G., *Macedonia Yesterday and Today* (Rome 1967).
Ugrinova, R., *The Macedonian Literary Language* (Belgrade 1958).

Montenegro

Djilas, M., *Montenegro* (New York 1963). An historical novel.
Stevenson, F. S., *History of Montenegro* (London 1914).

Serbia

Jiraček, K., *Istorija Srba*, 2nd rev. ed. (Belgrade 1952).
Jovanović, S., *Vlada Milana Obrenovića, 1868–1899* (Belgrade 1925–7).
Morison, W. A., *The Revolt of the Serbs Against the Turks, 1804–1813* (Cambridge 1942).
Temperley, Sir H., *History of Serbia* (London 1919).
Vuchinich, W. S., *Serbia Between East and West: the Events of 1903–8* (Stanford, Calif. 1954).

Economic history

Dimitrijević, S., *Strani Kapital u Privredi Bivse Jugoslavije* (Belgrade 1958).
Mirković, M., *Ekonomska historija Jugoslavije* (Zagreb 1958).

Sugar, P. E., *Industrialisation of Bosnia–Hercegovina, 1878–1918* (Washington 1963).

Second World War

Clissold, S., *Whirlwind – An Account of Marshal Tito's Rise to Power* (London 1949).

Deakin, F. W., *The Embattled Mountain* (Oxford 1971). An account of the Yugoslav partisan movement and of British–Yugoslav relations in the Second World War by a member of the British mission to the partisans.

Dedijer, V., *With Tito Through the War – Partisan Diary, 1941–44* (London 1951).

Maclean, Sir F., *Eastern Approaches* (London 1949).

Plenča, D., and Donagić, A., *Yugoslavia in the Second World War* (Belgrade 1967). Abbreviated translation of *Jugoslavija u Drugom Svetskom Ratu* (Belgrade 1967).

Rootham, J., *Miss Fire* (London 1946).

The Trial of Dragoljub-Draža Mihailović (Belgrade 1946).

Post-war Yugoslavia

Djilas, M., *The New Class: an Analysis of the Communist System* (London 1957).

Hoffman, G., and Neal, F. W., *Yugoslavia and the New Communism* (New York 1962).

Hondius, Frits W., *The Yugoslav Community of Nations* (The Hague 1968).

Kardelj, E., *On the Principles of the Preliminary Draft of the New Constitution* (Belgrade 1962).

Kardelj, E., *The New Yugoslav Federal Assembly* (Belgrade 1964).

MacVicker, C. P., *Titoism: Patterns for International Communism* (London 1957).

Neal, F. W., *Titoism in Action: the Reforms in Yugoslavia After 1948* (Berkeley, Calif. 1958).

Popović, N. D., *Yugoslavia: the New Class in Crisis* (Syracuse, N.Y. 1968).

'Praxis', *Smisao i Perspektive Socijalizam* (Zagreb 1965). Based on the 1964 Korčula Seminar. Includes articles by leading members of the 'Praxis' group and foreign participants.

Zaninovich, M. G., *Development of Socialist Yugoslavia* (Baltimore, Md 1968).

English texts of constitutions

The Constitution of the SFRY: Constitutional Amendments, Secretariat of Information (Belgrade 1969). Contains the text of the 1963 constitution and amendments I to XIX which came into force between April 1967 and December 1968.

The Constitution of the SFRY, Secretariat of the Federal Assembly Information Service (Belgrade 1974). Contains a 40-page report on the final draft by Mijalko Todorović and the text of the 1974 constitution.

Communist Party

Avakumović, I., *History of the Communist Party of Yugoslavia*, vol. 1 (Aberdeen 1964).

Johnson, A. Ross, *The Transformation of Communist Ideology: The Yugoslav Case 1945–53* (Cambridge, Mass. and London 1972).

Marković, Mihailo, *The Contemporary Marx: Essays on Humanist Communism* (Nottingham 1974).

Morača, P., *The League of Communists of Yugoslavia* (Belgrade 1966).

Morača, P., and Bilandžić, D., *Avangarda, 1919–1969* (Belgrade 1969).

Savez Komunista Yugoslavije (League of Communists of Yugoslavia), *Draft programme of the LCY VII Kongress SKJ* (Belgrade 1968).

Tito, J. B., *Political Report of the Central Committee of the CPY* (Belgrade 1948).

Tito, J. B., *Forty Years of Revolutionary Struggle of the Communist Party of Yugoslavia* (Belgrade 1959).

Yugoslavia, the Cominform and the USSR

Dedijer, V., *Tito Speaks: His Self Portrait and Struggle with Stalin* (London 1953).

Dedijer, V., *Izgubljena Bitka J. V. Stalina* (Sarajevo 1969).

Djilas, M., *Conversations with Stalin* (London 1962).

Halperin, E., *The Triumphant Heretic – Tito's Struggle Against Stalin* (London 1958).

Pijade, M. S., *About the Legend that the Yugoslav Uprising owed its Existence to Soviet Assistance* (London 1950).

Royal Institute of International Affairs, *The Soviet–Yugoslav Dispute: Text of the Published Correspondence* (London 1948).

Ulam, A. B., *Titoism and the Cominform* (Cambridge, Mass. 1952).

Foreign relations

Campbell, J. C., *Tito's Separate Road: America and Yugoslavia in World Politics* (New York 1967).

Holt, S., and Stapleton, K., 'Yugoslavia and the European Community, 1958–1970', in *Journal of Common Market Studies* (September 1971).

Mihailović, I., *Trst Problem Dana* (Zagreb 1951).

Nord, L., *Nonalignment and Socialism* (Uppsala 1974).

Novak, B., *Trieste, 1941–1954 – the Ethnic, Political and Ideological Struggle* (London 1970).

Rubinstein, A. Z., *Yugoslavia and the Non-Aligned World* (Oxford 1970).

ECONOMICS AND SOCIOLOGY

Bakarić, V., *Aktuelni Problemi Izgradnje Našeg Privrednog Sistema* (Zagreb 1963).

Barton, A. H., Denitch, B., and Kadushin, C., *Opinion Making Elites in Yugoslavia* (New York) 1973.

Bičanić, R., 'Economics of Socialism in a Developed Country', in *Foreign Affairs*, no. 44 (1966), pp. 633–50.

Bičanić, R., *Economic Policy in Socialist Yugoslavia* (Cambridge 1973).

Davičo, J., and Bogosavljević, M., *The Economy of Yugoslavia* (Belgrade 1960).

Dimitrijević, D., and Macesich, G., *Money and Finance in Contemporary Yugoslavia* (New York 1973).

Dirlam, J., and Plummer, J., *An Introduction to the Yugoslav Economy* (Columbus, Ohio 1973).

Institute of Economic Affairs, *Communist Economy under Change* (London 1963). Includes L. Sirc, 'State Control and Competition in Yugoslavia'.

Institut za Ekonomiku Investicija, *Problemi i Pravci Razvoja Samoupravnog Privrednog Sistema* (Belgrade 1970). Social self-management in its economic context, with particular reference to problems of public finance and investment.

Kidrić, B., 'Proposals for New Economic Laws', in *Komunist*, 4–5 (1951).

Kraiger, B., 'New Economic Measures', in *Review of International Affairs* (Belgrade) 16 (1965), pp. 16–20.

Livingston, R. C., 'Yugoslavian Unemployment Trends, 1952–1963', in *Monthly Labour Review* (Washington) 87 (1964), pp. 756–62.

Mihailović, K., *Problemi Privrednog Razvoja* (Belgrade 1962).

Obradović, S., 'Employment Trends and Problems in Yugoslavia', in *International Labour Review*, 95 (1967), pp. 553–71.

OECD, *Foreign Investment in Yugoslavia* (Paris 1974).

Pejovski, V., *Yugoslav Investment Policy, 1966–70* (Belgrade 1968).

Petrović, N., *Spoljna Trgovina Jugoslavije* (Belgrade 1947).

Singleton, F. B., 'Yugoslavia's "Market Socialism"', in *Spokesman* (November 1971).

Economic planning

Bičanić, R., *Problems of Planning, East and West* (The Hague 1967).

Macesich, G., *Yugoslavia: the Theory and Practice of Development Planning* (Charlottesville, Va 1964).

Meneghello-Dincic, K., *Les Expériences Yougoslaves d'Industrialisation et Planification* (Paris 1970).

Milenkovitch, B., *Plan and Market in Yugoslav Economic Thought* (New Haven, Conn. 1971).

Pejovich, S., *The Market-Planning Economy of Yugoslavia* (Minneapolis, Minn. 1966).

Samardžija, M., 'The Market and Social Planning in the Yugoslav Economy', in *Quarterly Review of Economics and Business*, 7 (1967), pp. 37–44.

Sirc, L., *Economic Devolution in Eastern Europe* (London 1969).

Sirotković, J., *Planiranje u Sistemu Samoupravljanja* (Zagreb 1966).

Stanovnik, J., 'Planning through the Market: the Yugoslav Experience', in *Foreign Affairs*, 40 (1962), pp. 252–63.

Waterston, A., *Planning in Yugoslavia: Organisation and Implementation* (Washington 1962).

Self-management

Bogosavljević, M., and Pesaković, M., *Workers' Management of a Factory in Yugoslavia* (Belgrade 1959). About the Rade Končar works.

Broekmeyer, M. J. (ed.), *Yugoslav Workers' Self-Management* (Dordrecht 1970).

Central Council of Confederation of Trade Unions, *Congress of Workers' Councils of Yugoslavia* (Belgrade 1957).

Četvrti Kongres Saveza Sindikata Jugoslavije (Belgrade 1959).

First International Conference on Participation and Self-Management, Dubrovnik, 13–17th December, 1972. Reports, vols I, II (Zagreb 1972).

Grozdanić, S., 'Administrative Management of Public Enterprises in Yugoslavia', report presented to 13th International Congress of Administrative Sciences (Paris 1965), in *International Review of Administrative Sciences*, 32, no. 1 (1966), pp. 43–57.

Grozdanić, S., and Radosavljević, M., *Radničko Samoupravljanje u Jugoslaviji* (Belgrade 1970).

Ibrahimagić, O., *Samoupravljanje u Radnoj Organizaciji* (Sarajevo 1968).

Information Service, Belgrade, *Social Government in Yugoslavia* (Belgrade 1957). Includes English text of Basic Law on Self-Management.

International Labour Office, *Workers' Management in Yugoslavia* (Geneva 1962).

Kardelj, E., *Four Factors in the Development of Socialist Social Relations* (Belgrade 1960). Speech at 5th Congress of Socialist Alliance, April 1960.

Kolaja, J. T., *Workers' Councils: the Yugoslav Experience* (London 1965).

Moore, R., *Self-Management in Yugoslavia* (London 1970).

Pesaković, M., *Twenty Years of Self-Management in Yugoslavia* (Belgrade 1970).

Second Congress of Self-Managers of Yugoslavia, *Papers* (Sarajevo, 5–8 May 1971).

Singleton, F. B., and Topham, A. J., *Workers' Control in Yugoslavia* (London 1963).

Singleton, F. B., 'Workers' Self-Management and the Role of Trade Unions in Yugoslavia', in *Trade Union Register* (London 1970).

Tomić, T., *Radni Odnosi u Privredi* (Belgrade 1957).

Trades Union Congress, *Trade Unionism in Yugoslavia* (London 1964).

Vanek, J., *The Economics of Workers' Management: a Yugoslav Case Study* (London 1972).

Workers' Management in Yugoslavia (Belgrade 1970).

Županov, J., *Samoupravljanje i Drustvena Moč: Prilozi za Sociologiju Samoupravne Radne Organizacije* (Zagreb 1969).

Regional economic problems

Čolanović, B., *Yugoslavia's Industrialisation and the Development of the Underdeveloped Regions* (UNIDO 1967).

Dabčević-Kučar, S., 'Regional Planning in Yugoslavia', in *Regional Science Association* (University of Pennsylvania) – Lund Congress (1963); Papers (1964), pp. 239–53.

Hočevar, T., *Slovenia's Role in Yugoslav Economy* (Columbus, Ohio 1964).

Hočevar, T., *The Structure of the Slovenian Economy* (New York 1965).

Hoffman, G., *Regional Development Strategy in Southeast Europe* (New York 1972).

Ivanović, B., 'Classification of Underdeveloped Areas According to the Level of Economic Development', in *Eastern European Economics*, 2, nos 1–2 (1963–4).

Logan, M. I., 'Regional Economic Development in Yugoslavia', in *Tijdschrift Voor Economische en Sociale Geografie*, 59 (1968), pp. 42–52.

Mihailović, K., *Regional Aspects of Economic Development* (New York 1972).

Singleton, F. B., 'Problems of Regional Economic Development: the Case of Yugoslavia', in *Jahrbuch der Wirtschaft Osteuropas*, 2 (1971), pp. 375–95.

Migrant workers

Baučić, I. (ed.), *Porijeklo i Struktura Radnika iz Jugoslavije u S. R. Njemackoj* (Zagreb 1970).

Friganović, M., Morokvašić, M., and Baučić, I., *Migracije Radnika iz Jugoslavije na Rad u Francusku* III (Zagreb 1972).

Agriculture and rural society

Ademović, F., and Bašagić, M., *Agrarian Policy and Agriculture of Yugoslavia* (Belgrade 1968).

Ehrlich, V. S., *Family in Transition: a Study of 300 Yugoslav Villages* (Princeton, N.J. 1966).

Halpern, J., *A Serbian Village – Social and Cultural Change in a Yugoslav Community*, rev. ed. (New York 1967). Condensed version of doctoral dissertation, 'Social and Cultural Change in a Serbian Village' (New York 1956).

Kostić, C., 'Peasant Industrial Workers in Yugoslavia', in *Cahiers Internationaux de Sociologie*, 43 (1967).

The Legal Status of Agricultural Land (Belgrade 1962).

Lodge, O., *Peasant Life in Yugoslavia* (London 1941).

Marković, P., 'Posedovna Struktura Jugoslovensko Poljoprivrede', in *Ekonomist*, vol. I (1960).

OECD, *The Economic Management of State Farms in the Kosmet* (Paris 1966). One of the volumes of the OECD series, 'Problems of Development'.

OECD, *Agricultural Policy in Yugoslavia* (Paris 1973).

Jackson, G. D., *Comintern and Peasant in East Europe, 1919–1930* (New York 1966).

Tomasevich, J., *Peasants, Politics and Economic Change in Yugoslavia* (Stanford, Calif. 1955).

Tomasevich, J., 'Collectivisation of Agriculture in Yugoslavia', chapter 7 in *Collectivisation in Eastern Europe* (Kentucky 1958).

Trouton, R., *Peasant Renaissance in Yugoslavia, 1900–1950: a Study of the Development of Yugoslav Peasant Society as Affected by Education* (London 1952).

Warriner, D., *The Economics of Peasant Farming* (Oxford 1939).

Relations between the nationalities

Jončić, K., *The Relations Between the Nationalities in Yugoslavia* (Belgrade 1967).

Lendvai, P., 'National Tensions in Yugoslavia', in *Conflict Studies*, no. 25 (August 1972).

Palmer, S. E., and King, R. R., *Yugoslav Communism and the Macedonian Question* (London 1971).

Shoup, P., *Communism and the Yugoslav National Question* (New York 1968).

Singleton, F. B., 'The Roots of Discord in Yugoslavia', in *The World Today* (April 1972).

Šuvar, S., *Nacije i Medjunacionalni Odnosi u Socialističkoj Jugoslaviji* (Zagreb 1970).

Demography

Mikolji, B. H., *Current Demographic Trends in Yugoslavia* (New Orleans 1972).

Religion

Falconi, C., *The Silence of Pius XII* (London 1970).
Kečkemet, D., *Židovi u povijesti Splita* (Split 1971).
Mojžes, P., 'Christian–Marxist Encounter', in *Journal of Ecumenical Studies*, 9, no. 1 (1972).
Pattee, R., *The Case of Cardinal Aloysius Stepinac* (London 1953).
Yugoslav Embassy Information Office, *Yugoslavia: the Church and the State* (London 1953).

BIOGRAPHIES

Biographies of Tito

Auty, P., *Tito: A Biography* (London 1970).
Maclean, Sir F., *Disputed Barricade – the Life and Times of Josip Broz-Tito, Marshal of Yugoslavia* (London 1957).
Zilliacus, K., *Tito of Yugoslavia* (London 1952).

Autobiographies of leading Communists

Čolaković, R., *Winning Freedom* (London 1962).
Dedijer, V., *Beloved Land* (London 1961).
Djilas, M., *Land Without Justice: an Autobiography of His Youth* (London 1958).
Vukmanović, S. (Tempo), *Revolucija Koja Teče: Memoari* (Belgrade 1971).

LITERATURE

Literature and the arts

Churchin, M. (ed.), *Ivan Meštrović* (London 1919).
Fiskovic, C., *Juraj Dalmatinac i Njegov Krug* (Zagreb 1967).
Jurčič, J., *George Koziak: a Slovene Janizary* (Montreal 1953).
Levstik, F., *Martin Krpan* (Ljubljana 1960).
Matthews, W. K., and Slodnjak, A., *A Selection of Poems by France Prešeren* (Oxford 1954).
Njegoš, P., *The Mountain Wreath* (London 1930).
Norman, L. R., *The Sculpture of Ivan Meštrović* (Syracuse, N.Y. 1948).

Parry, M., and Lord, A., *Serbo-Croatian Heroic Songs*, vols 1–2 (Cambridge, Mass. and Belgrade 1953–4).
Prličev, G., *The Sirdar* (Skopje 1973). An English Translation by P. and G. Reid.
Rootham, H. (trans.), *Kosovo Polje* (Oxford 1920).
Subotić, D., *Yugoslav Popular Ballads; their Origin and Development* (Cambridge 1932).

Contemporary literature

Andrić, I., *Bosnian Story* (London 1958). One of a series of twelve novels.
Andrić, I., *The Bridge on the Drina* (London 1959).
Davičo, O., *The Poem* (London 1959).
Johnson, B. (ed.), *New Writing in Yugoslavia* (Harmondsworth, Middx 1970).
Krleža, M., *Balade Petrice Kerempuha* (Murska Sobota 1966). Dialect poems about the peasants' revolt of Matija Gubec ,by Croatia's greatest contemporary writer.
Lavrin, J., and Slodnjak, A., *The Parnassus of a Small Nation: an Anthology of Slovene Lyrics*, 2nd ed. (Ljubljana 1965).
Vaupotić, M., *Contemporary Croatian Literature* (Zagreb 1966). Croatian PEN Club. Produced for International PEN.

GENERAL WORKS

Auty, P., *Yugoslavia* (London 1965).
Betts, R. R. (ed.), *Central and South East Europe, 1945–58* (Oxford 1950). Chapter 3 on Yugoslavia by P. Auty gives a concise account of developments between the outbreak of war and the Cominform resolution.
Buchan, J. (ed.), *Yugoslavia* (London 1923).
Burks, R. V., *The Dynamics of Communism in Eastern Europe* (Princeton, N.J. 1961).
Byrnes, R. F. (ed.), *Yugoslavia* (New York 1957).
Cvijić, J., *Les Pays Balkaniques* (Paris 1917).
Enciklopedija Jugoslavije, IV (Zagreb 1960) and V (Zagreb 1962).
Great Britain Admiralty, Naval Intelligence Division, *Jugoslavia* (3 vols), (London 1944).
Heppell, M., and Singleton, F. B., *Yugoslavia* (London 1961).
Kerner, R. (ed.), *Yugoslavia* (Berkeley, Calif. 1949).

Palmer, A. W., *Yugoslavia* (Oxford 1964).
Pavlowitch, S., *Yugoslavia* (London 1971).
Seton-Watson, H., *East European Revolution*, 3rd ed. (London 1956).
Singleton, F. B., *Background to Eastern Europe* (Oxford 1965).
Singleton, F. B., *Yugoslavia: Country and People* (London 1970).
Tornquist, D., *Look East, Look West: the Socialist Adventure in Yugoslavia* (London 1966).
Wolff, R. L., *The Balkans in Our Time* (Cambridge, Mass. 1956).

YUGOSLAV JOURNALS

Daily newspapers

Borba, the official organ of the Socialist Alliance, and *Politika*, which carries the name and a lingering trace of the reputation of the pre-war independent liberal paper, are the two main national dailies. Both are published in Belgrade in Serbian but have Croatian editions. In 1968 *Borba's* circulation was 86,000 copies per day, and *Politika's* 263,000. Both were losing ground in Belgrade to the popular evening paper *Večernje Novosti* (circulation 350,000 in 1968). The principal dailies published outside Belgrade are *Vjesnik* (Zagreb), *Oslobodjenje* (Sarajevo), *Delo* (Ljubljana), *Slobodna Dalmacija* (Split) and *Nova Makedonija* (Skopje). Each of the major non-Slav language groups has its own paper, e.g. *Rilindija* (Albanian) published in Priština, *Magyar Szó* (Magyar) published in Novi Sad, and *La Voce del Popolo* (Italian) in Rijeka.

Joint Translation Service, a useful daily bulletin, summarising in English items from the Yugoslav press, was produced from 1953 to 1972 by the British and US Embassies in Belgrade, and continued since July 1972 as *Translation Service* by Mr V. Jovanović, 42, Generala Ždanova, Belgrade. Collections from 1972 to date are available in Bradford University. English summaries of important articles in Yugoslav journals are also to be found in *ABSEES*, a quarterly published since July 1971 on behalf of the National Association of Soviet and East European Studies by Glasgow University. Also valuable is the *Summary of World Broadcasts*, part 2, Eastern Europe, published daily by the BBC Monitoring Service.

Weeklies

There are a number of serious weekly journals with good coverage of economic, political and cultural activities. The most important are *NIN* (Belgrade), *Ekonomska Politika* (Belgrade), *Privredni Vjesnik* (Zagreb), *Vjesnik u Srijedu* (Zagreb), *Komunist* (Belgrade) and *Student* (Belgrade).

Periodicals

There are a number of lively and controversial periodicals. The best known was *Praxis*, published by the Croatian Philosophical Society (1963–75). An international edition of it contains specially commissioned articles in English, French and German. Other journals of opinion are: *Pogledi* (Skopje), *Gledišta* (Belgrade), *Socijalizam* (Belgrade), *Teorija in Praksa* (Ljubljana), *Pregled* (Sarajevo), *Filosofija* (Belgrade), *Kritika* (Zagreb), (1968–71; suppressed in 1971), *Sociologija Sela* (Institute of Agricultural Economics and Rural Sociology, Zagreb; first issue 1962).

English-language periodicals

Several Yugoslav periodicals are available in English. Although mainly official publications, with a 'public relations' angle to them, they contain useful factual information. They include:

Ekonomist, produced an English edition in 1969 (Zagreb).

Macedonian Review, history, culture, literature and theatre quarterly, first published 1971 (Skopje).

Review of International Affairs, quarterly (Belgrade).

Socialist Thought and Practice, quarterly (Belgrade).

Yugoslav Survey, quarterly, first issue 1960 (Belgrade).

The London-based *emigré* organisation, the Study Centre for Jugoslav Affairs, produces an annual *Review* (first volume 1961), which contains critical articles on current Yugoslav developments written by academics who have left Yugoslavia and are now working in western Europe and the United States.

Statistics

The Federal Institute for Statistics has issued a *Statistical Pocket Book* each year since 1955. It appears in three Yugoslav languages and in English, French, German and Russian.

Savezni Zavod za Statistiku, *Indeks* (Belgrade). Published monthly from January 1952. Monthly survey of economic statistics.

Savezni Zavod za Statistiku, *Jugoslavija 1945–64: statističk pregled* (Belgrade 1965). A survey of statistics covering a 10-year period.

Savezni Zavod za Statistiku, *Statistički Bilten* (Belgrade). Published every year since 1948. Each issue (approximately 20 per year) covers a specific area of economic, demographic, social, cultural or health statistics.

Savezni Zavod za Statistiku, *Statistički Godišnjak* (Belgrade). Statistical yearbooks published by the Federal Institute for Statistics, Belgrade.

Other specialised statistical publications

Jugoslovensko Bankarstvo (Yugoslav banking), Narodna Banka (Belgrade). Monthly since 1971.

SDK Glavna Centrale, *Statistički Bilten Služba Društvenog Knjigovodstva*, Statistical Bulletin of the Service for Social Accounting (Belgrade). Monthly since 1971.

Republican statistics

Central Statistical Office, *Neki pokazatelji razvoja Jugoslavije, socialističkih republika i autonomnih pokrajina, 1950–70* (Belgrade 1971). A comprehensive survey of particular value for students of regional economic development.

There are statistical offices in each of the republics, which issue regular series of statistical information, among them the following.

MACEDONIA

Sokolov, L., *Promene u Strukturi Stanovništva na Teritoriji N. R. Makedonije 1921–53 Godine kao odraz Ekonomskog Razvoja*, Ekonomski Institut na NRM (Skopje 1962).

Statistički Pregled (in Macedonian). Monthly survey of statistics, published by Republički zavod za Statistiku S. R. Makedodonija (Skopje). Monthly since January 1970.

Statistički prikaz na S.R. Makedonija 1959–64 (Skopje 1965).

SLOVENIA

Statistčni Bilten Službe Družbenega Knjigovodstva. Monthly since January 1955 (Ljubljana).

In addition, all six republics issue a monthly statistical review (*Mesečni statistički pregled*) similar to the monthly *Indeks* published by the Federal Institute for Statistics.

Population statistics

Apart from the demographic data given in the Statistical Yearbook (*Statistički Godišnjak*) and the *Statistički Bilten*, demographic statistics are published separately in *Vitalna Statistika* (1950–5) and *Demografska Statistika* (since 1956). Population statistics for former Habsburg territories are contained in the Austrian Census of 1910 and the Hungarian Census of 1910. See also Roglić, J., *Le Recensement de 1910* (Institut Adriatique, Sušak 1946). In pre-war Yugoslavia there were censuses in 1921 and 1931. Figures for the Vojvodina were included in the wartime Hungarian census of 1942.

Since the Second World War there have been censuses in 1948, 1953, 1961 and 1971. Results of the censuses have been published in separate series of volumes, e.g. the 10-volume *Popis Stanovništva 1948*.

Index

Words accented on initial letters č, ć, š, ž are indexed separately after the appropriate c, s or z